D1250000

Philosophical Style

Philosophical Style

An Anthology about the Writing and Reading of Philosophy

Berel Lang, Editor

Nelson-Hall nh Chicago

Library of Congress Cataloging in Publication Data

Main entry under title:

Philosophical style.

Includes index.
1. Methodology—Addresses, essays, lectures.
I. Lang, Berel.
BD241.P44 190 79-20424
ISBN 0-88229-230-7

Manufactured in the United States of America

10 9 8 7 6 5 4 3 2 1

Contents

II. Philosophical Style: The Search for Categories

III. Style and the Reading of Philosophy

Introduction

There may be good reasons as well as bad ones why the topic of philosophical style has been consistently ignored both by literary critics of style and by philosophers themselves. On the one hand, if philosophy is a search for wisdom or more particularly truth (as most philosophers have agreed that it in *some* sense is), the philosopher will understandably concentrate his own efforts and his reader's attention on the object of that search. The most significant issue in an argument for the existence of God, it would then be reasonable to claim, is whether the argument stands up as argument—whether God in fact exists; and little time or interest and perhaps even material would remain, if this first issue could be settled, either for deconstructing or for reconstructing the "style" of that argument as distinguishable from its substance.

The tendency in this direction could only be strengthened, moreover, by the fact that some of the fundamental questions surrounding the general concept of style, let alone the question of how that concept applies to systems of philosophy, have been notably intransigent. Even if we were to put to one side the largest theoretical questions of what style is or what function is served by its discrimination, we find on the more confined, empirical side of the study of style (in such areas as the history of painting or of literature) that the categories deployed in particular instances of judgment raise as many problems conceptually as they resolve critically. In what terms (and on what authority) do we, for example, specify the differences between a baroque and a high renaissance painting? Between the forms of comedy and tragedy? Such questions persist almost as tenaciously as do their subject, and it is evident that whatever logical status the distinctions have, it is not that of simple or brute fact. Both conceptually and in application, the distinctions turn out to be intrinsically problematic, "contestable"—and the would-be critic of philosophical style could hardly be faulted for retreating before these difficulties either into the work of philosophy "proper" or to reflection on the more concrete and accessible appearances of style in the arts.

A second, positive aspect of the systematic analysis of philosophical style, however, shows these methodological difficulties—real as they are—to be quite beside the point. This second aspect embodies the claim that the relevance of style *cannot* be separated from the issue of philosophical substance; that notwithstanding the difficulty of defining stylistic criteria and notwithstanding the sometime inclination of the philosopher to conceive of his work under the ægis of a bare and universal logic of truth or explanation, the process and conclusions of philosophy *in fact* have a form or shape as well as a matter, an outside as well as an inside; that those two features of his work, moreover, demonstrate a characteristic affinity, or at least a characteristic set of correspondences with respect to each other; and finally, that the history of philosophy, that loose and disjointed series of individual works and statements, itself discloses a variety of coherent stylistic patterns. The last of these points is crucial as a starting place for the analysis of philosophical style; in exhibiting the differences which style makes or reflects first as among various philosophers and then, more corporately, as among philosophical "schools" or traditions, it provides all the prima facie evidence which could be either expected or required for the *existence* of philosophical style. The difference between the (or *a*) philosophical dialogue and the (or *a*) philosophical meditation might conceivably *turn out* to be accidental, inessential to what was being asserted—but prima facie, the large differences between a Platonic dialogue and a Cartesian meditation are subsidized by the differences between those forms as well as between Plato and Descartes.

This last claim may seem an item of conventional wisdom, amounting to little more than the assertion that the practice of philosophy, like any other structured or coherent act which originates in a single source—an individual's walk or posture, the choice of colors in clothing in a particular society, the distortion of the human figure in the drawings of children—will be significant for understanding the character both of the activity and of the agent. But this superficially benign thesis, at least as it concerns the work of philosophy, has been explicitly contested. Especially in much recent Anglo-American philosophy do we encounter the premise that if the end of philosophy is the uncovering of certain systematic features of linguistic usage (or even of the world underlying them), the vehicle by which such discovery is made or represented is essentially an irrelevance. The philosopher's purpose, on such accounts, is to arrive at a certain destination; how he travels is held to be incidental to that end. Since style is essentially a matter of technique or ornament, *philosophically* (i.e., substantively) it is without importance.

This contention, finally, is meant to be and is an empirical one, and the largest purpose of this anthology of writings about philosophical style is to provide an empirical response to that challenge—not in the form of another contention or argument, but by showing through examples that the understanding of philosophical texts fairly demands consideration of their modes of presentation and of the way in which that presentation is linked to the meaning of the texts: how the medium both reflects and determines the message. One might go so far as to claim that *especially* in philosophy, for which the self-referential question of what philosophy is is a necessary and constant concern, the manner in which the projects of philosophy are carried on and consequently presented is a consideration of decisive importance. The doing of philosophy, philosophers would in general agree, involves a method; the articulation of that method must find a way among alternative goals, instrumentalities, and criteria—each of them involving philosophical decisions. The selection, furthermore, will in its conclusions be expected to exhibit a consistency or coherence. It can hardly be an accident that nearly all of these terms applied to philosophical structure—method, instrumentalities, consistency—verge precisely on the distinctions that have traditionally given rise to and supported the analysis of style.

The writings collected here, it will be seen, do not

have very much to say about the general concept of philosophical style or rhetoric. It is in fact a significant comment on the recent tendencies of philosophy that slight acknowledgment has been made of the phenomenon of philosophical style as being philosophically important. The scantiness of theoretical discussion in the background to the selections in Section II, titled "Philosophical Style: The Search for Categories," is then quite simply a reflection of a historical phenomenon. On the other hand, even if we agreed on both the fact and the fault of the neglect so represented, we might also agree that the place to begin to remedy it is in practice. And work *has* been done, of which Section III, titled "Style and the Reading of Philosophy," includes a number of telling instances that attempt the stylistic analysis of specific philosophers or texts—although there, too, one might add, only a beginning. Those efforts, by their illumination of individual philosophical works or *oeuvres*, define a presumptive case for the thesis that unless the reader attends to the style or form of philosophical writing, he is unlikely to see very far into whatever he would distinguish from it. The standard interpretations of Mill and Bradley, for example, have undoubtedly displayed important features of the work of those philosophers; but it is a worthy challenge for the reader, I think, that he should attempt to read Alan Donagan's essay on those Victorian authors without having his views of even such technical issues as the status of particulars and universals in Mill or the grounds of moral obligation in Bradley deepened, if not revised.

This is not to say that the authors of the selections in the several sections of this volume would agree on much more than the single principle that the form or manner of a philosophical work or system is one of its significant aspects. The philosophers discussed in the selections in Section III, for example, reveal fundamental differences in philosophical direction and—let us say it—style: what Aristotle hoped to accomplish and the rhetorical means he allowed himself are quite evidently different from what Nietzsche saw as the purpose and related structure of his writing—and of this, Professors Brumbaugh and Shapiro, who discuss those philosophers, are well aware. But there is not even the beginning of a stylistic or rhetorical canon at present available on which a critic hoping to articulate such differences can draw: as the philosophers whose styles are examined differ on many counts of purpose and interest, so one finds a proportionate, even larger variance in the formulation of categories by which those styles are proposed to be understood. Are the categories or criteria of style to be sociological (as Gellner suggests in his discussion of recent analytic philosophy) or psychological (as Scharfstein indicates in analyzing Descartes' dreams)? Will they be intrinsic, evolved from the individual works themselves, rather than extrinsic—as the recent mood in literary studies and poetics (among the structuralists, for example) has argued for fiction and "imaginative literature"? These are, it will be recognized, standard questions in the analysis of style; if there is no ready answer to them with respect to the issues of philosophical style, this can come as no surprise to the reader who has met them before in other, extra-philosophical settings. What may well come as a surprise is that the legitimacy of raising such questions with respect to philosophical writing has itself to be argued in conjunction with the questions.

Both at a theoretical level and in its concrete applications, then, the analysis of form in the writing or reading of philosophy is at an early stage of development, certainly in the United States and England, but even in

France and Germany with the intense interest found there in such writers as Derrida, Foucault, and Gadamer. It is my hope that this volume will suggest what a project with that design can hope to achieve, in providing both a historical understanding of philosophy as it has been practiced and a self-inflective awareness of certain systematic issues which philosophy has neglected to its cost. That philosophers of importance have at least acknowledged the claims in these directions is attested to in the selections taken from the works of such figures as Plato, Aristotle, Hume, and Kierkegaard which serve in Section I as a historical introduction. It is pertinent to note that even those selections are drawn from contexts which are fragmentary and occasional. One could hardly argue, given what they *did* do, that Aristotle or Kant did not do enough—but the magnitude of their accomplishments emphasizes by contrast the questions which they scarcely touched. Perhaps, it might be argued, the self-consciousness implicit in questions concerning philosophical style is psychologically an irrelevance or even a hindrance to the doing of philosophy. But even if this were true for any particular philosopher, it could hardly hold for philosophy in its more corporate appearances. What is finally at stake in such neglect, I should argue, is quite palpable: until amends are made, philosophy will itself have betrayed what it characteristically poses as an ideal for others—self-knowledge.

I

Philosophers on the Writing of Philosophy

1. Plato: Selections from VIIth Letter, *Phaedrus*, and *Phaedo*

Little is accurately known regarding the biography of Plato (428–347 B.C.) despite Whitehead's claim that the whole of Western philosophy has been footnotes to Plato. He is supposed to have come from an aristocratic and politically prominent family. Because of his close association with Socrates, Plato left Athens in 399 B.C. when Socrates was executed. Soon after his return to Athens, he founded a school, the Academy. All of Plato's written work is believed to have survived, in the form of some two dozen philosophical dialogues, which lay fair claim to being the most influential of all philosophical texts. A number of letters attributed to Plato also survive.

VIIth LETTER*

The instruction that I gave to Dionysius was accordingly given with this object in view. I certainly did not

* From *Thirteen Epistles of Plato* translated and edited by

set forth to him all my doctrines, nor did Dionysius ask me to, for he pretended to know many of the most important points already and to be adequately grounded in them by means of the secondhand interpretations he had got from the others.

I hear too that he has since written on the subjects in which I instructed him at that time, as if he were composing a handbook of his own which differed entirely from the instruction he received. Of this I know nothing. I do know, however, that some others have written on these same subjects, but who they are they know not themselves. One statement at any rate I can make in regard to all who have written or who may write with a claim to knowledge of the subjects to which I devote myself—no matter how they pretend to have acquired it, whether from my instruction or from others or by their own discovery. Such writers can in my opinion have no real acquaintance with the subject. I certainly have composed no work in regard to it, nor shall I ever do so in future, for there is no way of putting it in words like other studies. Acquaintance with it must come rather after a long period of attendance on instruction in the subject itself and of close companionship, when, suddenly, like a blaze kindled by a leaping spark, it is generated in the soul and at once becomes self-sustaining.

Besides, this at any rate I know, that if there were to be a treatise or a lecture on this subject, I could do it best. I am also sure for that matter that I should be very sorry to see such a treatise poorly written. If I thought it possible to deal adequately with the subject in a treatise or a lecture for the general public, what finer achievement would there have been in my life than to

---

write a work of great benefit to mankind and to bring the nature of things to light for all men? I do not, however, think the attempt to tell mankind of these matters a good thing, except in the case of some few who are capable of discovering the truth for themselves with a little guidance. In the case of the rest to do so would excite in some an unjustified contempt in a thoroughly offensive fashion, in others certain lofty and vain hopes, as if they had acquired some awesome lore.

It has occurred to me to speak on the subject at greater length, for possibly the matter I am discussing would be clearer if I were to do so. There is a true doctrine, which I have often stated before, that stands in the way of the man who would dare to write even the least thing on such matters, and which it seems I am now called upon to repeat.

For everything that exists there are three classes of objects through which knowledge about it must come; the knowledge itself is a fourth, and we must put as a fifth entity the actual object of knowledge which is the true reality. We have then, first, a name, second, a description, third, an image, and fourth, a knowledge of the object. Take a particular case if you want to understand the meaning of what I have just said; then apply the theory to every object in the same way. There is something for instance called a circle, the name of which is the very word I just now uttered. In the second place there is a description of it which is composed of nouns and verbal expressions. For example the description of that which is named round and circumference and circle would run as follows: the thing which has everywhere equal distances between its extremities and its center. In the third place there is the class of object which is drawn and erased and turned on the lathe and destroyed—processes which do not affect the real circle to which these other circles are all related, because it is different from them. In the fourth place there are knowledge and understanding and correct opinion concerning them, all of which we must set down as one thing more that is found not in sounds nor in shapes of bodies, but in minds, whereby it evidently differs in its nature from the real circle and from the aforementioned three. Of all these four, understanding approaches nearest in affinity and likeness to the fifth entity, while the others are more remote from it.

The same doctrine holds good in regard to shapes and surfaces, both straight and curved, in regard to the good and the beautiful and the just, in regard to all bodies artificial and natural, in regard to fire and water and the like, and in regard to every animal, and in regard to every quality of character, and in respect to all states active and passive. For if in the case of any of these a man does not somehow or other get hold of the first four, he will never gain a complete understanding of the fifth. Furthermore these four [names, descriptions, bodily forms, concepts] do as much to illustrate the particular quality of any object as they do to illustrate its essential reality because of the inadequacy of language. Hence no intelligent man will ever be so bold as to put into language those things which his reason has contemplated, especially not into a form that is unalterable—which must be the case with what is expressed in written symbols.

Again, however, the meaning of what has just been said must be explained. Every circle that is drawn or turned on a lathe in actual operations abounds in the opposite of the fifth entity, for it everywhere touches the straight, while the real circle, I maintain, contains in itself neither much nor little of the opposite character. Names, I maintain, are in no case stable. Nothing prevents the things that are now called round from being called straight and the straight round, and those who have transposed the names and use them in the opposite way will find them no less stable than they are now. The same thing for that matter is true of a description, since it consists of nouns and of verbal expressions, so that in a description there is nowhere any sure ground that is sure enough. One might, however, speak forever about the inaccurate character of each of the four! The important thing is that, as I said a little earlier, there are two things, the essential reality and the particular quality, and when the mind is in quest of knowledge not of the particular but of the essential, each of the four confronts the mind with the unsought particular, whether in verbal or in bodily form. Each of the four makes the reality that is expressed in words or illustrated in objects liable to easy refutation by the evidence of the senses. The result of this is to make practically every man a prey to complete perplexity and uncertainty.

Now in cases where as a result of bad training we are not even accustomed to look for the real essence of anything but are satisfied to accept what confronts us in the phenomenal presentations, we are not rendered ridiculous by each other—the examined by the examiners, who have the ability to handle the four with dexterity and to subject them to examination. In those cases, however, where we demand answers and proofs in regard to the fifth entity, anyone who pleases among those who have skill in confutation gains the victory and makes most of the audience think that the man who was first to speak or write or answer has no acquaintance with the matters of which he attempts to write or speak. Sometimes they are unaware that it is not the mind of the writer or speaker that fails in the test, but rather the character of the four—since that is naturally defective. Consideration of all of the four in turn—moving up and down from one to another—barely begets knowledge of a naturally flawless object in a naturally flawless man. If a man is naturally defective—and this is the natural state of most people's minds with regard to intelligence and to what are called morals—while the objects he inspects are tainted with imperfection, not even Lynceus could make such a one see.

To sum it all up in one word, natural intelligence and a good memory are equally powerless to aid the man who has not an inborn affinity with the subject. Without such endowments there is of course not the slightest possibility. Hence all who have no natural aptitude for and affinity with justice and all the other noble ideals, though in the study of other matters they may be both intelligent and retentive—all those too who have affinity but are stupid and unretentive—such will never any of them attain to an understanding of the most complete truth in regard to moral concepts. The study of virtue and vice must be accompanied by an inquiry into what is false and true of existence in general and must be carried on by constant practice throughout a long period, as I said in the beginning. Hardly after practicing detailed comparisons of names and definitions and visual and other sense perceptions, after scrutinizing them in benevolent disputation by the use of question and answer without jealousy, at last in a flash understanding of each blazes up, and the mind, as it exerts all its powers to the limit of human capacity, is flooded with light.

For this reason no serious man will ever think of writing about serious realities for the general public so as to make them a prey to envy and perplexity. In a word, it is an inevitable conclusion from this that when anyone sees anywhere the written work of anyone, whether that of a lawgiver in his laws or whatever it may be in some other form, the subject treated cannot have been his most serious concern—that is, if he is himself a serious man. His most serious interests have their abode somewhere in the noblest region of the field of his activity. If, however, he really was seriously concerned with these matters and put them in writing, "then surely" not the gods, but mortals "have utterly blasted his wits."

One who has followed my account of the reality and of the deviations from it will be assured of the fact that, whether Dionysius has written anything on the first and highest principles of nature, or anyone else great or small, that man in my opinion has neither received any sound instruction nor profited by it in the subjects of which he wrote. For if he had, he would have felt the same reverence for the subject that I do and would not boldly have cast it out unbecomingly and unfittingly. Neither did he put the doctrine in writing to aid his own memory, for there is no danger of anyone forgetting it, once his mind grasps it, since it is contained in the very briefest statements. If he wrote at all, his motive was an ignoble ambition either to be regarded as the author of the doctrine or as one not destitute of culture—of which he was not worthy if he was enamored of the reputation of having it. Well, if a single interview had the effect of conferring this culture on Dionysius, it may be so, but how it had that effect, God wot, as the Theban says, for on that occasion I described my doctrines to him in the way I have mentioned and once only—after that never again.

PHAEDRUS*

SOCRATES But there remains the question of propriety and impropriety in writing, that is to say the condi-

* From *Phaedrus* by Plato, translated by R. Hackforth (274b–278b). Reprinted by permission of the Cambridge University Press.

tions which make it proper or improper. Isn't that so?

PHAEDRUS Yes.

SOCRATES Now do you know how we may best please God, in practice and in theory, in this matter of words?

PHAEDRUS No indeed. Do you?

SOCRATES I can tell you the tradition that has come down from our forefathers, but they alone know the truth of it. However, if we could discover that for ourselves, should we still be concerned with the fancies of mankind?

PHAEDRUS What a ridiculous question! But tell me the tradition you speak of.

SOCRATES Very well. The story is that in the region of Naucratis in Egypt there dwelt one of the old gods of the country, the god to whom the bird called Ibis is sacred, his own name being Theuth. He it was that invented number and calculation, geometry and astronomy, not to speak of draughts and dice, and above all writing. Now the king of the whole country at that time was Thamus, who dwelt in the great city of Upper Egypt which the Greeks call Egyptian Thebes, while Thamus they call Ammon. To him came Theuth, and revealed his arts, saying that they ought to be passed on to the Egyptians in general. Thamus asked what was the use of them all, and when Theuth explained, he condemned what he thought the bad points and praised what he thought the good. On each art, we are told, Thamus had plenty of views both for and against; it would take too long to give them in detail. But when it came to writing Theuth said, "Here, O king, is a branch of learning that will make the people of Egypt wiser and improve their memories; my discovery provides a recipe for memory and wisdom." But the king answered and said, "O man full of arts, to one it is given to create the things of art, and to another to judge what measure of harm and of profit they have for those that shall employ them. And so it is that you, by reason of your tender regard for the writing that is your offspring, have declared the very opposite of its true effect. If men learn this, it will implant forgetfulness in their souls; they will cease to exercise memory because they rely on that which is written, calling things to remembrance no longer from within themselves, but by means of external marks. What you have discovered is a recipe not for memory, but for reminder. And it is no true wisdom that you offer your disciples, but only its semblance, for by telling them of many things without teaching them you will make them seem to know much, while for the most part they know nothing, and as men filled, not with wisdom, but with the conceit of wisdom, they will be a burden to their fellows."

PHAEDRUS It is easy for you, Socrates, to make up tales from Egypt or anywhere else you fancy.

SOCRATES Oh, but the authorities of the temple of Zeus at Dodona, my friend, said that the first prophetic utterances came from an oak tree. In fact the people of those days, lacking the wisdom of you young people, were content in their simplicity to listen to trees or rocks, provided these told the truth. For you apparently it makes a difference who the speaker is, and what country he comes from; you don't merely ask whether what he says is true or false.

PHAEDRUS I deserve your rebuke, and I agree that the man of Thebes is right in what he said about writing.

SOCRATES Then anyone who leaves behind him a written manual, and likewise anyone who takes it over from him, on the supposition that such writing will provide something reliable and permanent, must be exceedingly simple-minded; he must really be ignorant of Ammon's utterance, if he imagines that written words can do anything more than remind one who knows that which the writing is concerned with.

PHAEDRUS Very true.

SOCRATES You know, Phaedrus, that's the strange thing about writing, which makes it truly analogous to painting. The painter's products stand before us as though they were alive, but if you question them, they maintain a most majestic silence. It is the same with written words; they seem to talk to you as though they were intelligent, but if you ask them anything about what they say, from a desire to be instructed, they go on telling you just the same thing forever. And once a thing is put in writing, the composition, whatever it may be, drifts all over the place, getting into the hands not only of those who understand it, but equally of those who have no business with it; it doesn't know how to address the right people, and not address the wrong. And when it is ill-treated and unfairly abused it always needs its parent to come to its help, being unable to defend or help itself.

PHAEDRUS Once again you are perfectly right.

SOCRATES But now tell me, is there another sort of discourse, that is brother to the written speech, but of unquestioned legitimacy? Can we see how it originates, and how much better and more effective it is than the other?

PHAEDRUS What sort of discourse have you now in mind, and what is its origin?

SOCRATES The sort that goes together with knowledge, and is written in the soul of the learner, that can defend itself, and knows to whom it should speak and to whom it should say nothing.

PHAEDRUS You mean no dead discourse, but the living speech, the original of which the written discourse may fairly be called a kind of image.

SOCRATES Precisely. And now tell me this. If a sensible farmer had some seeds to look after and wanted them to bear fruit, would he with serious intent plant them during the summer in a garden of Adonis, and enjoy watching it producing fine fruit within eight days? If he did so at all, wouldn't it be in a holiday spirit, just by way of pastime? For serious purposes wouldn't he behave like a scientific farmer, sow his seeds in suitable soil, and be well content if they came to maturity within eight months?

PHAEDRUS I think we may distinguish as you say, Socrates, between what the farmer would do seriously and what he would do in a different spirit.

SOCRATES And are we to maintain that he who has knowledge of what is just, honorable, and good has less sense than the farmer in dealing with his seeds?

PHAEDRUS Of course not.

SOCRATES Then it won't be with serious intent that he "writes them in water" or that black fluid we call ink, using his pen to sow words that can't either speak in their own defense or present the truth adequately.

PHAEDRUS It certainly isn't likely.

SOCRATES No, it is not. He will sow his seed in literary gardens, I take it, and write when he does write by way of pastime, collecting a store of refreshment both for his own memory, against the day "when age oblivious comes," and for all such as tread in his footsteps, and he will take pleasure in watching the tender plants grow up. And when other men resort to other pastimes, regaling themselves with drinking parties and suchlike, he will doubtless prefer to indulge in the recreation I refer to.

PHAEDRUS And what an excellent one it is, Socrates! How far superior to the other sort is the recreation that a man finds in words, when he discourses about justice and the other topics you speak of.

SOCRATES Yes indeed, dear Phaedrus. But far more excellent, I think, is the serious treatment of them, which employs the art of dialectic. The dialectician selects a soul of the right type, and in it he plants and sows his words founded on knowledge, words which can defend both themselves and him who planted them, words which instead of remaining barren contain a seed whence new words grow up in new characters, whereby the seed is vouchsafed immortality, and its possessor the fullest measure of blessedness that man can attain unto.

PHAEDRUS Yes, that is a far more excellent way.

SOCRATES Then now that that has been settled, Phaedrus, we can proceed to the other point.

PHAEDRUS What is that?

SOCRATES The point that we wanted to look into before we arrived at our present conclusion. Our intention was to examine the reproach leveled against Lysias on the score of speech writing, and therewith the general question of speech writing and what does and does not make it an art. Now I think we have pretty well cleared up the question of art.

PHAEDRUS Yes, we did think so, but please remind me how we did it.

SOCRATES The conditions to be fulfilled are these. First, you must know the truth about the subject that you speak or write about; that is to say, you must be able to isolate it in definition, and having so defined it you must next understand how to divide it into kinds, until you reach the limit of division; secondly, you must have a corresponding discernment of the nature of the soul, discover the type of speech appropriate to each nature, and order and arrange your discourse accordingly, addressing a variegated soul in a variegated style that ranges over the whole gamut of tones, and a simple soul in a simple style. All this must be done if you are to become competent, within human limits, as a scientific practitioner of speech, whether you propose to expound or to persuade. Such is the clear purport of all our foregoing discussion.

PHAEDRUS Yes, that was undoubtedly how we came to see the matter.

SOCRATES And now to revert to our other question, whether the delivery and composition of speeches is honorable or base, and in what circumstances they may properly become a matter of reproach, our earlier conclusions have, I think, shown . . .

PHAEDRUS Which conclusions?

SOCRATES They have shown that any work, in the past or in the future, whether by Lysias or anyone else, whether composed in a private capacity or in the role of a public man who by proposing a law becomes the author of a political composition, is a matter of reproach to its author—whether or no the reproach is actually voiced—if he regards it as containing important truth of permanent validity. For ignorance of what is a waking vision and what is a mere dream image of justice and injustice, good and evil, cannot truly be acquitted of involving reproach, even if the mass of men extol it.

PHAEDRUS No indeed.

SOCRATES On the other hand, if a man believes that a written discourse on any subject is bound to contain much that is fanciful, that nothing that has ever been written whether in verse or prose merits much serious attention—and for that matter nothing that has ever been spoken in the declamatory fashion which aims at mere persuasion without any questioning or exposition—that in reality such compositions are, at the best, a means of reminding those who know the truth, that lucidity and completeness and serious importance belong only to those lessons on justice and honor and goodness that are expounded and set forth for the sake of instruction, and are veritably written in the soul of the listener, and that such discourses as these ought to be accounted a man's own legitimate children—a title to be applied primarily to such as originate within the man himself, and secondarily to such of their sons and brothers as have grown up aright in the souls of other men—the man, I say, who believes this, and disdains all manner of discourse other than this, is, I would venture to affirm, the man whose example you and I would pray that we might follow.

PHAEDO*

But first there is one danger that we must guard against.

What sort of danger? I asked.

Of becoming misologic, he said, in the sense that people become misanthropic. No greater misfortune could happen to anyone than that of developing a dislike for argument. Misology and misanthropy arise in just the same way. Misanthropy is induced by believing in somebody quite uncritically. You assume that a person is absolutely truthful and sincere and reliable, and a little later you find that he is shoddy and unreliable. Then the same thing happens again. After repeated disappointments at the hands of the very people who might be supposed to be your nearest and most intimate friends, constant irritation ends by making you dislike everybody and suppose that there is no sincerity to be found anywhere. Have you never noticed this happening?

Indeed, I have.

* From *The Last Days of Socrates* (Plato: *Phaedo*, 89d–91e), translated by Hugh Tredennick.

Don't you feel that it is reprehensible? Isn't it obvious that such a person is trying to form human relationships without any critical understanding of human nature? Otherwise he would surely recognize the truth—that there are not many very good or very bad people, but the great majority are something between the two.

How do you make that out? I asked.

On the analogy of very large or small objects, he said. Can you think of anything more unusual than coming across a very large or small man, or dog, or any other creature? Or one which is very swift or slow, ugly or beautiful, white or black? Have you never realized that extreme instances are few and rare, while intermediate ones are many and plentiful?

Certainly.

So you think that if there were a competition in wickedness, very few would distinguish themselves even there?

Probably.

Yes, it is probable, said Socrates. However, you have led me into a digression. The resemblance between arguments and human beings lies not in what I said just now, but in what I said before, that when one believes that an argument is true without reference to the art of logic, and then a little later decides rightly or wrongly that it is false, and the same thing happens again and again—you know how it is, especially with those who spend their time in arguing both sides—they end by believing that they are wiser than anyone else, because they alone have discovered that there is nothing stable or dependable either in facts or in arguments, and that everything fluctuates just like the water in a tidal channel, and never stays at any point for any time.

That is perfectly true, I said.

Well, then, Phaedo, he said, supposing that there is an argument which is true and valid and capable of being discovered, if anyone nevertheless, through his experience of these arguments which seem to the same people to be sometimes true and sometimes false, attached no responsibility to himself and his lack of technical ability, but was finally content, in exasperation, to shift the blame from himself to the arguments, and spend the rest of his life loathing and decrying them, and so missed the chance of knowing the truth about reality—would it not be a deplorable thing?

It would indeed, I said.

Very well, he said, that is the first thing that we must guard against. We must not let it enter our minds that there may be no validity in argument. On the contrary we should recognize that we ourselves are still intellectual invalids, but that we must brace ourselves and do our best to become healthy—you and the others partly with a view to the rest of your lives, but I directly in view of my death, because at the moment I am in danger of regarding it not philosophically but self-assertively. You know how, in an argument, people who have no real education care nothing for the facts of the case, and are only anxious to get their point of view accepted by the audience? Well, I feel that at this present moment I am as bad as they are, only with this difference, that my anxiety will be not to convince my audience, except incidentally, but to produce the strongest possible conviction in myself. This is how I weigh the position, my dear fellow—see how selfish I am! If my theory is really true, it is right to believe it, while, even if death is extinction, at any rate during this time before my death I shall be less likely to distress my companions by giving way to self-pity, and this folly of mine will not live on with me—which would be a calamity—but will shortly come to an end.

That, my dear Simmias and Cebes, is the spirit in which I am prepared to approach the discussion. As for you, if you will take my advice, you will think very little of Socrates, and much more of the truth. If you think that anything I say is true, you must agree with me; if not, oppose it with every argument that you have. You must not allow me, in my enthusiasm, to deceive both myself and you, and leave my sting behind when I fly away.

2. Aristotle: Selections from *Physics*, *Posterior Analytics*, *Nicomachean Ethics*, *Rhetoric*, *On the Heavens*, and *Poetics*

Aristotle's father, a court physician to the King of Macedon, died when Aristotle (384–322 B.C.) was a boy, and Aristotle, not long after, went to Athens, where he entered Plato's Academy (about 367 B.C.). With Plato's death in 347 B.C., Aristotle spent a number of years traveling, and in 342 B.C. he accepted a position as tutor to the thirteen-year-old son of Philip II of Macedon whom history remembers as Alexander the Great. In 335 B.C., Aristotle opened his own school in Athens, the Lyceum. There are few subjects in the intellectual world on which Aristotle did not make a lasting impression, ranging from logic to biology, from psychology to aesthetics.

PHYSICS*

When the objects of an inquiry, in any department, have principles, conditions, or elements, it is through

* Bk. I, Ch. 1, 184a9–184b13.

acquaintance with these that knowledge, that is to say scientific knowledge, is attained. For we do not think that we know a thing until we are acquainted with its primary conditions or first principles, and have carried our analysis as far as its simplest elements. Plainly therefore in the science of Nature, as in other branches of study, our first task will be to try to determine what relates to its principles.

The natural way of doing this is to start from the things which are more knowable and obvious to us and proceed towards those which are clearer and more knowable by nature; for the same things are not "knowable relatively to us" and "knowable" without qualification. So in the present inquiry we must follow this method and advance from what is more obscure by nature, but clearer to us, towards what is more clear and more knowable by nature.

Now what is to us plain and obvious at first is rather confused masses, the elements and principles of which become known to us later by analysis. Thus we must advance from generalities to particulars; for it is a whole that is best known to sense-perception, and a generality is a kind of whole, comprehending many things within it, like parts. Much the same thing happens in the relation of the name to the formula. A name, e.g. "round," means vaguely a sort of whole: its definition analyses this into its particular senses. Similarly a child begins by calling all men "father," and all women "mother," but later on distinguishes each of them.

POSTERIOR ANALYTICS*

We have already said that scientific knowledge through demonstration is impossible unless a man knows the primary immediate premisses. But there are

* Bk. I, Ch. 3, 1094b12–1094a13.

questions which might be raised in respect of the apprehension of these immediate premisses: one might not only ask whether it is of the same kind as the apprehension of the conclusions, but also whether there is or is not scientific knowledge of both; or scientific knowledge of the latter, and of the former a different kind of knowledge; and, further, whether the developed states of knowledge are not innate but come to be in us, or are innate but at first unnoticed. Now it is strange if we possess them from birth; for it means that we possess apprehensions more accurate than demonstration and fail to notice them. If on the other hand we acquire them and do not previously possess them, how could we apprehend and learn without a basis of preexistent knowledge? For that is impossible, as we used to find in the case of demonstration. So it emerges that neither can we possess them from birth, nor can they come to be in us if we are without knowledge of them to the extent of having no such developed state at all. Therefore we must possess a capacity of some sort, but not such as to rank higher in accuracy than these developed states. And this at least is an obvious characteristic of all animals, for they possess a congenital discriminative capacity which is called sense-perception. But though sense-perception is innate in all animals, in some the sense-impression comes to persist, in others it does not. So animals in which this persistence does not come to be have either no knowledge at all outside the act of perceiving, or no knowledge of objects of which no impression persists; animals in which it does come into being have perception and can continue to retain the sense-impression in the soul: and when such persistence is frequently repeated a further distinction at once arises between those which out of the persistence of such sense-impressions develop a power of systematizing them and those which do not. So out of sense-perception comes to be what we call memory, and out of frequently repeated memories of the same thing develops experience; for a number of memories constitute a single experience. From experience again—i.e. from the universal now stabilized in its entirety within the soul, the one beside the many which is a single identity within the all—originate the skill of the craftsman and the knowledge of the man of science, skill in the sphere of coming to be and science in the sphere of being.

We conclude that these states of knowledge are neither innate in a determinate form, nor developed from other higher states of knowledge, but from sense-perception. It is like a rout in battle stopped by first one man making a stand and then another, until the original formation has been restored. The soul is so constituted as to be capable of this process.

NICOMACHEAN ETHICS*

Our discussion will be adequate if it has as much clearness as the subject-matter admits of, for precision is not to be sought for alike in all discussions, any more than in all the products of the crafts. Now fine and just actions, which political science investigates, admit of much variety and fluctuation of opinion, so that they may be thought to exist only by convention, and not by nature. And goods also give rise to a similar fluctuation because they bring harm to many people; for before now men have been undone by reason of their wealth, and others by reason of their courage. We must be content, then, in speaking of such subjects and with such premisses to indicate the truth roughly and in outline, and in speaking about things which are only for the most part true and with premisses of the same

* Bk. III, Ch. 1, 1403b15–20; Bk. III, Ch. 27.

kind to reach conclusions that are no better. In the same spirit, therefore, should each type of statement be *received*; for it is the mark of an educated man to look for precision in each class of things just so far as the nature of the subject admits; it is evidently equally foolish to accept probable reasoning from a mathematician and to demand from a rhetorician scientific proofs.

Now each man judges well the things he knows, and of these he is a good judge. And so the man who has been educated in a subject is a good judge of that subject, and the man who has received an all-round education is a good judge in general. Hence a young man is not a proper hearer of lectures on political science; for he is inexperienced in the actions that occur in life, but its discussions start from these and are about these; and, further, since he tends to follow his passions, his study will be vain and unprofitable, because the end aimed at is not knowledge but action. And it makes no difference whether he is young in years or youthful in character; the defect does not depend on time, but on his living, and pursuing each successive object, as passion directs. For to such persons, as to the incontinent, knowledge brings no profit; but to those who desire and act in accordance with a rational principle, knowledge about such matters will be of great benefit.

These remarks about the student, the sort of treatment to be expected, and the purpose of the inquiry, may be taken as our preface.

RHETORIC*

Our next subject will be the style of expression. For it is not enough to know *what* we ought to say; we must also say it *as* we ought; much help is thus afforded

* Bk. II, Ch. 19, 89b20–100a12.

towards producing the right impression of a speech. The first question to receive attention was naturally the one that comes first naturally—how persuasion can be produced from the facts themselves. The second is how to set these facts out in language. A third would be the proper method of delivery; this is a thing that affects the success of a speech greatly; but hitherto the subject has been neglected. . . .

Now if you have proofs to bring forward, bring them forward, and your moral discourse as well; if you have no Enthymemes, then fall back upon moral discourse: after all, it is more fitting for a good man to display himself as an honest fellow than as a subtle reasoner.

ON THE HEAVENS*

These thinkers seem to push their inquiries some way into the problem, but not so far as they might. It is what we are all inclined to do, to direct our inquiry not by the matter itself, but by the views of our opponents: and even when interrogating oneself one pushes the inquiry only to the point at which one can no longer offer any opposition. Hence a good inquirer will be one who is ready in bringing forward the objections proper to the genus, and that he will be when he has gained an understanding of all the differences. . . .

It is, however, wrong to remove the foundations of a science unless you can replace them with others more convincing. . . .

In fact their explanation of the observations is not consistent with the observations. And the reason is that their ultimate principles are wrongly assumed: they had certain predetermined views, and were resolved to bring everything into line with them. It seems that perceptible things require perceptible principles, eter-

* 294b6–13; 299i52–6, 306a6–16.

nal things eternal principles, corruptible things corruptible principles; and, in general, every subject matter principles homogeneous with itself. But they, owing to their love for their principles, fall into the attitude of men who undertake the defence of a position in argument. In the confidence that the principles are true they are ready to accept any consequence of their application. As though some principles did not require to be judged from their results, and particularly from their final issue!

POETICS*

There is further an art which imitates by language alone, without harmony, in prose or in verse, and if in verse, either in some one or in a plurality of metres. This form of imitation is to this day without a name. We have no common name for a mime of Sophron or Xenarchus and a Socratic Conversation; and we should still be without one even if the imitation in the two instances were in trimeters or elegiacs or some kind of verse—though it is the way with people to tack on "poet" to the name of a metre, and talk of elegiac-poets and epic-poets, thinking that they call them poets not by reason of the imitative nature of their work, but indiscriminately by reason of the metre they write in. Even if a theory of medicine or physical philosophy be put forth in a metrical form, it is usual to describe the writer in this way. . . .

* 1447a26–1447b16.

3. St. Augustine: Selections from *De Magistro*

Augustine (354–430) lived in times of unusual social and intellectual upheaval; he is generally viewed as the single dominant figure in the transition from classical to medieval thought, from paganism to Christianity. Having traveled to Milan from his native Africa, he there made the acquaintance of the Bishop Ambrose, in whose blend of Christianity and Neo-Platonism Augustine found the solution to the moral conflicts he had suffered as a follower of the Manichean doctrines. Baptized a Christian in 386, he began writing the story of his spiritual life, the *Confessions*, in 400. In 395, he returned to Africa and succeeded the Bishop of Hippo.

DE MAGISTRO*

The utmost value I can attribute to words is this. They bid us look for things, but they do not show them

* From *Augustine: Earlier Writings*, Vol. VI, The Library of

to us so that we may know them. He alone teaches me anything who sets before my eyes, or one of my other bodily senses, or my mind, the things which I desire to know. From words we can learn only words. Indeed we can learn only their sound and noise. Even if words, in order to be words really, must also be signs, I do not know that any sound I may hear is a word until I know what it means. Knowledge of words is completed by knowledge of things, and by the hearing of words not even words are learned. We learn nothing new when we know the words already, and when we don't know them we cannot say we have learned anything unless we also learn their meaning. And their meaning we learn not from hearing their sound when they are uttered, but from getting to know the things they signify. It is sound reasoning and truly said that when words are spoken we either know or do not know what they mean. If we know, we do not learn, but are rather reminded of what we know. If we do not know, we are not even reminded, but are perhaps urged to inquire.

But you may say: granted we cannot know those head-coverings, the sound of whose name we remember, unless we see them, and that we cannot fully know the name until we know the thing. But what about those young men of whom we have heard (Dan. 3) how they vanquished King Nebuchadnezzar and his fiery furnace by their faithfulness and religion, how they sang praises to God, and won honours from their enemy? Have we learned about them otherwise than by means of words? I reply, Yes. But we already knew the meaning of all these words. I already knew the meaning of "three youths," "furnace," "fire," "king," "unhurt by fire" and so on. But the names, Ananias,

---

Azarias and Misael, are as unknown to me as *saraballae*, and the names did not help me to know them and could not help me. All that we read of in that story happened at that time and was written down, so that I have to confess I must believe rather than know. And the writers whom we believe were not ignorant of the difference. For the prophet says: "Unless ye believe ye shall not know" (Isa. 7:9:LXX). This he would not have said if he had thought there was no difference. What I know I also believe, but I do not know everything that I believe. All that I understand I know, but I do not know all that I believe. And I know how useful it is to believe many things which I do not know, among them this story about the three youths. I know how useful it is to believe many things of which knowledge is not possible.

Concerning universals of which we can have knowledge, we do not listen to anyone speaking and making sounds outside ourselves. We listen to Truth which presides over our minds within us, though of course we may be bidden to listen by someone using words. Our real Teacher is he who is so listened to, who is said to dwell in the inner man, namely Christ, that is, the unchangeable power and eternal wisdom of God. To this wisdom every rational soul gives heed, but to each is given only so much as he is able to receive, according to his own good or evil will. If anyone is ever deceived it is not the fault of Truth, any more than it is the fault of the common light of day that the bodily eyes are often deceived. Confessedly we must pay heed to the light that it may let us discern visible things so far as we are able.

On the one hand we need light that we may see colours, and the elements of this world and sentient bodies that we may perceive things of sense, and the senses themselves which the mind uses as interpreters in its search for sense-knowledge. On the other hand, to know intelligible things with our reason we pay attention to the interior truth. How, then, can it be shown that words teach us anything besides the sound that strikes the ear? Everything we perceive we perceive either by bodily sense or by the mind. The former we call "sensible things," the latter "intelligible things"; or, to use the terminology of our Christian authors, the former we call "carnal things," the latter "spiritual things." When we are asked about the former we reply if they are present to our senses, for example, if we are looking at the new moon and someone asks what it is or where. If our questioner does not see it he believes our words, or perhaps often does not believe them, but he learns nothing unless he himself sees what he is asking about. When he sees he learns not from words uttered but from the objects seen and his sense of sight. Words would have the same sound whether he saw or not. When the question concerns not things which are present to our senses but which once were, we do not speak of the things themselves, but of images derived from them and imprinted on the memory. I do not know how we can call these things true, since what we have in view are only false images, unless it is because we speak of them not as things we see and feel but as things we have seen and felt. So in the halls of memory we bear the images of things once perceived as memorials which we can contemplate mentally and can speak of with a good conscience and without lying. But these memorials belong to us privately. If anyone hears me speak of them, provided he has seen them himself, he does not learn from my words, but recognizes the truth of what I say by the images which he has in his own memory. But if he has not had these sensations, obviously he believes my words rather than learns from them.

But when we have to do with things which we behold with the mind, that is, with the intelligence and with reason, we speak of things which we look upon directly in the inner light of truth which illumines the inner man and is inwardly enjoyed. There again if my hearer sees these things himself with his inward eye, he comes to know what I say, not as a result of my words but as a result of his own contemplation. Even when I speak what is true and he sees what is true, it is not I who teach him. He is taught not by my words but by the things themselves which inwardly God has made manifest to him. Accordingly, if asked he can make answer regarding these things. What could be more absurd than that he should suppose that by my speaking I have taught him, when, if asked, he could himself have explained these things before I spoke? It often happens that a man, when asked a question, gives a negative answer, but by further questioning can be brought to answer in the affirmative. The reason lies in his own weakness. He is unable to let the light illumine the whole problem. Though he cannot behold the whole all at once, yet when he is questioned about the parts which compose the whole, he is induced to bring them one by one into the light. He is so induced by the words of his questioner, words, mark you, which do not make statements, but merely ask such questions as put him who is questioned in a position to learn inwardly. For example, if I were to ask you the question I am at present discussing: "Can nothing be taught by means of words?" it might at first seem to you to be absurd because you cannot visualize the whole problem. So I must put my question in a way suited to your ability to hear the inward Teacher. Then, when you have admitted that what I said was true, that you are certain of it, and assuredly know it, I should say: "Where did you learn that?" You might reply that I had taught you. Then I should say: "If I were to tell you that I had seen a man flying, would my words render you as certain of their truth as if I had said, 'Wise men are better than fools'?" You would certainly say: "No, I don't believe your first statement, or, if I believe it, I certainly do not *know* that it is true; but your second statement I know most certainly to be true." In this way you would realize that neither in the case of your not knowing what I affirmed, nor in the case of your knowing quite well, had you learned anything from my words, because in answer to each question you were able to answer confidently that you did not know this and that you did know that. When you realize that all the parts which constitute the whole are clear and certain, you will then admit what you had denied. You will agree that a man who has heard what we have said must either not know whether it is true, or know that it is false, or know that it is true. In the first case he must either believe it, or suppose it, or doubt it. In the second case he must oppose it and deny it. In the third case he must testify to its truth. In no case, therefore, will he learn. When my words have been spoken both he who does not know whether my words are true, and he who knows they are false, and he who could have given the same answers when asked are proved to have learned nothing from my words.

Wherefore in matters which are discerned by the mind, whoever cannot discern them from himself listens vainly to the words of him who can, except that it is useful to believe such things so long as ignorance lasts. Whoever can discern them for himself is inwardly a disciple of the truth, and outwardly a judge of the speaker, or rather of what he says. For often enough the hearer knows what is said even when the speaker does not. For example, suppose some believer in the Epicureans, who held that the soul is mortal, should expound the arguments used by wiser men in favour of the soul's immortality in the hearing of one who can behold spiritual things. The latter judges that the former has spoken the truth, though the speaker does not know whether his words are true, and indeed believes them to be utterly false. Are we to think that he can teach what he does not know? Yet he uses the same words as he might use who does know.

Hence words do not even have the function of indicating the mind of the speaker, if it is uncertain whether he knows what he is saying. There are liars too and deceivers, so that you can easily understand that words not only do not reveal the mind, but even serve to conceal it. I do not of course in any way doubt that the words of truthful people are endeavouring to reveal the mind of the speaker and make some claim to do so, and would do so, all would agree, if only liars were not allowed to speak. And yet we have often experienced in ourselves and others that words do not correctly convey thoughts. This can happen in one or other of two ways. A speech committed to memory and frequently conned may be spoken when we are thinking of something else entirely. This often happens when we are singing a hymn. Or by a slip of the tongue some words will get substituted for others against our will, so that those which are heard are not signs of what is in our minds. Liars, too, think of the things they speak about, so that even if we do not know whether they speak the truth, at least we know that they intend what they say, unless either of the two accidents occur which I have mentioned. If anyone contends that this sometimes occurs and can be noticed when it occurs, I make no objection, though it often is hidden and has often escaped my notice when I have been listening.

There is the other kind of accident, very wide-spread and the seed of innumerable dissensions and strifes.

The speaker indeed expresses his thoughts but is understood only by himself and by some others. What he says does not convey the same meaning to those who hear him. For example, someone might say in our hearing that some wild beasts surpass man in virtue. Our impulse would be not to endure it, but to use every effort to refute such a false and pestilential opinion. But possibly he is giving the name of virtue to bodily strength, and has correctly expressed his mind. He is not lying. He is not substantially wrong. He is not uttering words committed to memory while he has something else in mind. He has not spoken the wrong word by a slip of the tongue. He has simply called the thing he has in mind by a different name from the one we are accustomed to use. We should at once agree with him if we could see into his thought, which he had not made clear by the words he used in expressing his opinion. It is said that definition is the remedy for this mistake. If in this question he would define virtue, it would be apparent, they say, that the controversy was not about the substance of his statement but about a word. I should agree that that is so, but how often is a man to be found who is good at definition? Many things, too, are urged against the discipline of definition, but this is not the opportune place to deal with them, and I do not approve of them.

I need not mention the fact that often we do not rightly hear what is said, and enter into lengthy arguments over things we wrongly thought we heard. For example, recently, when I said that a certain Punic word meant mercy, you said that you had heard from those who knew the language better that it meant piety. I objected, insisting that you had quite misunderstood what you had been told, for I thought you said not piety but faith. Now you were sitting quite close to me, and these two words are not so alike in sound as to deceive the ear. For a long time I thought you did not know what had been told you, while all the time I did not know what you had said. If I had heard you aright I should not have thought it absurd that piety and mercy should be expressed by one word in Punic. Such misunderstandings often occur, but, as I said, let us omit them lest I should put upon words the blame that is due to the negligence of listeners, or seem to be troubled by human deafness. My chief troubles are those I have mentioned, where by means of words clearly heard, Latin words when Latin is our mother-tongue, we are yet unable to learn the thoughts of those who speak to us.

Putting aside all these exceptions, I agree that when words are heard by one who knows them, he can also know that the speaker has thought the things which the words signify. Now the question is, does he also learn that the words spoken are true? Do teachers profess that it is their thoughts that are learned and retained, and not the disciplines which they imagine they transmit by their speaking? Who is so foolishly curious as to send his son to school to learn what the teacher thinks? When the teachers have expounded by means of words all the disciplines which they profess to teach, the disciplines also of virtue and wisdom, then their pupils take thought within themselves whether what they have been told is true, looking to the inward truth, that is to say, so far as they are able. In this way they learn. And when they find inwardly that what they have been told is true they praise their teachers, not knowing that they really praise not teachers but learned men, if the teachers really know what they express in words. Men are wrong when they call those teachers who are not. But because very often there is no interval between the moment of speaking and the moment of knowing, and because they inwardly learn immediately after the speaker has given his admonition, they suppose that they have been taught in an external fashion by him who gave the admonition.

At another time, if God permit, we shall inquire into the whole problem of the usefulness of words, for their usefulness properly considered is not slight. Now I have warned you that we must not attribute to them a greater importance than they ought to have, so that now we should not only believe but also begin to understand how truly it is written by divine authority that we are to call no one on earth our teacher, for One is our teacher who is in heaven (cf. Matt. 23:10). What is meant by "in heaven" he will teach us, by whom we are admonished through human agency and by external signs to be inwardly converted to him and so to be instructed. To know and to love him is the blessed life, which all proclaim that they are seeking but few have the joy of really finding. But I should like you to tell me what you think of my whole discourse. If you know that what I have said is true, and if you had been interrogated at every point, you would have answered that you knew it to be true. You see, then, who taught you; certainly not I, for you would of your own accord have given the right answer each time I asked. If, on the other hand, you do not know that what I have said is true, neither I nor the inward teacher has taught you. Not I, because I have never the power to teach anyone; and not he, because you have not yet the power to learn. *Ad.*—I have learned by your warning words, that by means of words a man is simply put on the alert in order that he may learn; also that very little of the thought of a speaker is made evident by his speaking. I have also learned that in order to know the truth of what is spoken, I must be taught by him who dwells within and gives me counsel about words spoken externally in the ear. By his favour I shall love him the more ardently the more I advance in learning. And I am specially grateful that latterly you have spoken without the interruption of questions and answers, because you have taken up and resolved all the difficulties I was prepared to urge against you. You omitted nothing at all that caused me to doubt; and in every case the Secret Oracle of which you have spoken has answered me exactly according to your words.

4. David Hume: Selections from *A Treatise on Human Nature* and *Essays: Moral, Political, and Literary*

Born in Edinburgh of a distinguished family, Hume (1711–1776) was encouraged to enter the law profession. He determined his own course of study, however, which culminated in the publication in 1734 of his *Treatise of Human Nature.* Disappointed at its reception, Hume wrote the two *Enquiries* as elaborations of the empiricist doctrines of which he remains one of the principal philosophical expositors. Much of his life was spent as a public official, and it was in connection with that role that Hume wrote his *History of Great Britain.*

A TREATISE ON HUMAN NATURE*

Here then I find myself absolutely and necessarily determin'd to live, and talk, and act like other people in

* Bk. I, Part IV, Section VII.

the common affairs of life. But notwithstanding that my natural propensity, and the course of my animal spirits and passions reduce me to this indolent belief in the general maxims of the world, I still feel such remains of my former disposition, that I am ready to throw all my books and papers into the fire, and resolve never more to renounce the pleasures of life for the sake of reasoning and philosophy. For those are my sentiments in that splenetic humour, which governs me at present. I may, nay I must yield to the current of nature, in submitting to my senses and understanding; and in this blind submission I shew most perfectly my sceptical disposition and principles. But does it follow, that I must strive against the current of nature, which leads me to indolence and pleasure; that I must seclude myself, in some measure, from the commerce and society of men, which is so agreeable; and that I must torture my brains with subtilities and sophistries, at the very time that I cannot satisfy myself concerning the reasonableness of so painful an application, nor have any tolerable prospect of arriving by its means at truth and certainty. Under what obligation do I lie of making such an abuse of time? And to what end can it serve either for the service of mankind, or for my own private interest? No: If I must be a fool, as all those who reason or believe any thing *certainly* are, my follies shall at least be natural and agreeable. Where I strive against my inclination, I shall have a good reason for my resistance; and will no more be led a wandering into such dreary solitudes, and rough passages, as I have hitherto met with.

These are the sentiments of my spleen and indolence; and indeed I must confess, that philosophy has nothing to oppose to them, and expects a victory more from the returns of a serious good-humour'd disposition, than from the force of reason and conviction. In all the incidents of life we ought still to preserve our scepticism. If we believe, that fire warms, or water refreshes, 'tis only because it costs us too much pains to think otherwise. Nay if we are philosophers, it ought only to be upon sceptical principles, and from an inclination, which we feel to the employing ourselves after that manner. Where reason is lively, and mixes itself with some propensity, it ought to be assented to. Where it does not, it never can have any title to operate upon us.

At the time, therefore, that I am tir'd with amusement and company, and have indulg'd a *reverie* in my chamber, or in a solitary walk by a river-side, I feel my mind all collected within itself, and am naturally *inclin'd* to carry my view into all those subjects, about which I have met with so many disputes in the course of my reading and conversation. I cannot forbear having a curiosity to be acquainted with the principles of moral good and evil, the nature and foundation of government, and the cause of those several passions and inclinations, which actuate and govern me. I am uneasy to think I approve of one object, and disapprove of another; call one thing beautiful, and another deform'd; decide concerning truth and falsehood, reason and folly, without knowing upon what principles I proceed. I am concern'd for the condition of the learned world, which lies under such a deplorable ignorance in all these particulars. I feel an ambition to arise in me of contributing to the instruction of mankind, and of acquiring a name by my inventions and discoveries. These sentiments spring up naturally in my present disposition; and shou'd I endeavour to banish them, by attaching myself to any other business or diversion, I *feel* I shou'd be a loser in point of pleasure; and this is the origin of my philosophy.

But even suppose this curiosity and ambition shou'd

not transport me into speculations without the sphere of common life, it wou'd necessarily happen, that from my very weakness I must be led into such enquiries. 'Tis certain, that superstition is much more bold in its systems and hypotheses than philosophy; and while the latter contents itself with assigning new causes and principles to the phænomena, which appear in the visible world, the former opens a world of its own, and presents us with scenes, and beings, and objects, which are altogether new. Since therefore 'tis almost impossible for the mind of man to rest, like those of beasts, in that narrow circle of objects, which are the subject of daily conversation and action, we ought only to deliberate concerning the choice of our guide, and ought to prefer that which is safest and most agreeable. And in this respect I make bold to recommend philosophy, and shall not scruple to give it the preference to superstition of every kind or denomination. For as superstition arises naturally and easily from the popular opinions of mankind, it seizes more strongly on the mind, and is often able to disturb us in the conduct of our lives and actions. Philosophy on the contrary, if just, can present us only with mild and moderate sentiments; and if false and extravagant, its opinions are merely the objects of a cold and general speculation, and seldom go so far as to interrupt the course of our natural propensities. The CYNICS are an extraordinary instance of philosophers, who from reasoning purely philosophical ran into as great extravagancies of conduct as any *Monk* or *Dervise* that ever was in the world. Generally speaking, the errors in religion are dangerous; those in philosophy only ridiculous.

I am sensible, that these two cases of the strength and weakness of the mind will not comprehend all mankind, and that there are in *England*, in particular, many honest gentlemen, who being always employ'd in their domestic affairs, or amusing themselves in common recreations, have carried their thoughts very little beyond those objects, which are every day expos'd to their senses. And indeed, of such as these I pretend not to make philosophers, nor do I expect them either to be associates in these researches or auditors of these discoveries. They do well to keep themselves in their present situation; and instead of refining them into philosophers, I wish we cou'd communicate to our founders of systems, a share of this gross earthy mixture, as an ingredient, which they commonly stand much in need of, and which wou'd serve to temper those fiery particles, of which they are compos'd. While a warm imagination is allow'd to enter into philosophy, and hypotheses embrac'd merely for being specious and agreeable, we can never have any steady principles, nor any sentiments, which will suit with common practice and experience. But were these hypotheses once remov'd, we might hope to establish a system or set of opinions, which if not true (for that, perhaps, is too much to be hop'd for) might at least be satisfactory to the human mind, and might stand the test of the most critical examination. Nor shou'd we despair of attaining this end, because of the many chimerical systems, which have successively arisen and decay'd away among men, wou'd we consider the shortness of that period, wherein these questions have been the subjects of enquiry and reasoning. Two thousand years with such long interruptions, and under such mighty discouragements are a small space of time to give any tolerable perfection to the sciences; and perhaps we are still in too early an age of the world to discover any principles, which will bear the examination of the latest posterity. For my part, my only hope is, that I may contribute a little to the advancement of knowledge, by giving in some particulars a different turn to the speculations of philosophers, and pointing out to them more distinctly those subjects, where alone they can expect assurance and conviction. Human Nature is the only science of man; and yet has been hitherto the most neglected. 'Twill be sufficient for me, if I can bring it a little more into fashion; and the hope of this serves to compose my temper from that spleen, and invigorate it from that indolence, which sometimes prevail upon me. If the reader finds himself in the same easy disposition, let him follow me in my future speculations. If not, let him follow his inclination, and wait the returns of application and good humour. The conduct of a man, who studies philosophy in this careless manner, is more truly sceptical than that of one, who feeling in himself an inclination to it, is yet so over-whelm'd with doubts and scruples, as totally to reject it. A true sceptic will be diffident of his philosophical doubts, as well as of his philosophical conviction; and will never refuse any innocent satisfaction, which offers itself, upon account of either of them.

Nor is it only proper we shou'd in general indulge our inclination in the most elaborate philosophical researches, notwithstanding our sceptical principles, but also that we shou'd yield to that propensity, which inclines us to be positive and certain in *particular points*, according to the light, in which we survey them in any *particular instant.* 'Tis easier to forbear all examination and enquiry, than to check ourselves in so natural a propensity, and guard against that assurance, which always arises from an exact and full survey of an object. On such an occasion we are apt not only to forget our scepticism, but even our modesty too; and make use of such terms as these, *'tis evident, 'tis certain, 'tis undeniable;* which a due deference to the public ought, perhaps, to prevent. I may have fallen into this fault after the example of others; but I here enter a *caveat* against any objections, which may be offer'd on that head; and declare that such expressions were extorted from me by the present view of the object, and imply no dogmatical spirit, nor conceited idea of my own judgment, which are sentiments that I am sensible can become no body, and a sceptic still less than any other.

OF SIMPLICITY AND REFINEMENT IN WRITING*

Fine writing, according to Mr. ADDISON, consists of sentiments, which are natural, without being obvious. There cannot be a juster, and more concise definition of fine writing.

Sentiments, which are merely natural, affect not the mind with any pleasure, and seem not worthy of our attention. The pleasantries of a waterman, the observations of a peasant, the ribaldry of a porter or hackney coachman, all of these are natural, and disagreeable. What an insipid comedy should we make of the chit-chat of the tea-table, copied faithfully and at full length? Nothing can please persons of taste, but nature drawn with all her graces and ornaments, *la belle nature*; or if we copy low life, the strokes must be strong and remarkable, and must convey a lively image to the mind. The absurd naivety** of *Sancho Pancho* is represented in such inimitable colours by CERVANTES, that it entertains as much as the picture of the most magnanimous hero or softest lover.

* From *Essays: Moral, Political and Literary* by David Hume. Copyright © 1963 Oxford University Press. Reprinted by permission of The Clarendon Press, Oxford.

**[Editions C to K: Naivety, a word which I have borrow'd from the *French*, and which is wanted in our language.]

The case is the same with orators, philosophers, critics, or any author who speaks in his own person, without introducing other speakers or actors. If his language be not elegant, his observations uncommon, his sense strong and masculine, he will in vain boast his nature and simplicity. He may be correct; but he never will be agreeable. It is the unhappiness of such authors, that they are never blamed or censured. The good fortune of a book, and that of a man, are not the same. The secret deceiving path of life, which HORACE talks of, *fallentis semita vitæ*, may be the happiest lot of the one; but is the greatest misfortune, which the other can possibly fall into.

On the other hand, productions, which are merely surprising, without being natural, can never give any lasting entertainment to the mind. To draw chimeras is not, properly speaking, to copy or imitate. The justness of the representation is lost, and the mind is displeased to find a picture, which bears no resemblance to any original. Nor are such excessive refinements more agreeable in the epistolary or philosophic style, than in the epic or tragic. Too much ornament is a fault in every kind of production. Uncommon expressions, strong flashes of wit, pointed similes, and epigrammatic turns, especially when they recur too frequently, are a disfigurement, rather than any embellishment of discourse. As the eye, in surveying a GOTHIC building, is distracted by the multiplicity of ornaments, and loses the whole by its minute attention to the parts; so the mind, in perusing a work overstocked with wit, is fatigued and disgusted with the constant endeavour to shine and surprize. This is the case where a writer overabounds in wit, even though that wit, in itself, should be just and agreeable. But it commonly happens to such writers, that they seek for their favourite ornaments, even where the subject does not afford them;

and by that means, have twenty insipid conceits for one thought which is really beautiful.

There is no subject in critical learning more copious, than this of the just mixture of simplicity and refinement in writing; and therefore, not to wander in too large a field, I shall confine myself to a few general observations on that head.

First, I observe, *That though excesses of both kinds are to be avoided, and though a proper medium ought to be studied in all productions; yet this medium lies not in a point, but admits of a considerable latitude.* Consider the wide distance, in this respect, between Mr. POPE and LUCRETIUS. These seem to lie in the two greatest extremes of refinement and simplicity, in which a poet can indulge himself, without being guilty of any blameable excess. All this interval may be filled with poets, who may differ from each other, but may be equally admirable, each in his peculiar stile and manner. CORNEILLE and CONGREVE, who carry their wit and refinement somewhat farther than Mr. POPE (if poets of so different a kind can be compared together), and SOPHOCLES and TERENCE, who are more simple than LUCRETIUS, seem to have gone out of that medium, in which the most perfect productions are found, and to be guilty of some excess in these opposite characters. Of all the great poets, VIRGIL and RACINE, in my opinion, lie nearest the center, and are the farthest removed from both the extremities.

My *second* observation on this head is, *That it is very difficult, if not impossible, to explain by words, where the just medium lies between the excesses of simplicity and refinement, or to give any rule by which we can know precisely the bounds between the fault and the beauty.* A critic may not only discourse very judiciously on this head, without instructing his readers, but even without understanding the matter perfectly himself. There is not a finer piece of criticism than *the dissertation on pastorals* by FONTENELLE; in which, by a number of reflections and philosophical reasonings, he endeavours to fix the just medium, which is suitable to that species of writing. But let any one read the pastorals of that author, and he will be convinced, that this judicious critic, notwithstanding his fine reasonings, had a false taste, and fixed the point of perfection much nearer the extreme of refinement than pastoral poetry will admit of. The sentiments of his shepherds are better suited to the toilettes of PARIS, than to the forests of ARCADIA. But this it is impossible to discover from his critical reasonings. He blames all excessive painting and ornament as much as VIRGIL could have done, had that great poet writ a dissertation on this species of poetry. However different the tastes of men, their general discourse on these subjects is commonly the same. No criticism can be instructive, which descends not to particulars, and is not full of examples and illustrations. It is allowed on all hands, that beauty, as well as virtue, always lies in a medium; but where this medium is placed, is the great question, and can never be sufficiently explained by general reasonings.

I shall deliver it as a *third* observation on this subject, *That we ought to be more on our guard against the excess of refinement than that of simplicity; and that because the former excess is both less* beautiful, *and more* dangerous *than the latter.*

It is a certain rule, that wit and passion are entirely incompatible. When the affections are moved, there is no place for the imagination. The mind of man being naturally limited, it is impossible that all its faculties can operate at once: And the more any one predominates, the less room is there for the others to exert their vigour. For this reason, a greater degree of simplicity is required in all compositions, where men, and actions, and passions are painted, than in such as consist of reflections and observations. And as the former species of writing is the more engaging and beautiful, one may safely, upon this account, give the preference to the extreme of simplicity above that of refinement.

We may also observe, that those compositions, which we read the oftenest, and which every man of taste has got by heart, have the recommendation of simplicity, and have nothing surprising in the thought, when divested of that elegance of expression, and harmony of numbers, with which it is cloathed. If the merit of the composition lie in a point of wit; it may strike at first; but the mind anticipates the thought in the second perusal, and is not longer affected by it. When I read an epigram of MARTIAL, the first line recalls the whole; and I have no pleasure in repeating to myself what I know already. But each line, each word in CATULLUS, has its merit; and I am never tired with the perusal of him. It is sufficient to run over COWLEY once: But PARNEL, after the fiftieth reading, is as fresh as at the first. Besides, it is with books as with women, where a certain plainness of manner and of dress is more engaging than that glare of paint and airs and apparel, which may dazzle the eye, but reaches not the affections. TERENCE is a modest and bashful beauty, to whom we grant everything, because he assumes nothing, and whose purity and nature make a durable, though not a violent impression on us.

But refinement, as it is the less *beautiful*, so is it the more *dangerous* extreme, and what we are the aptest to fall into. Simplicity passes for dulness, when it is not accompanied with great elegance and propriety. On the contrary, there is something surprizing in a blaze of wit and conceit. Ordinary readers are mightily struck with it, and falsely imagine it to be the most difficult, as well as most excellent way of writing. SENECA abounds with agreeable faults, says QUINTILIAN, *abundat dulcibus vitiis;* and for that reason is the more dangerous, and the more apt to pervert the taste of the young and inconsiderate.

I shall add, that the excess of refinement is now more to be guarded against than ever; because it is the extreme, which men are the most apt to fall into, after learning has made some progress, and after eminent writers have appeared in every species of composition. The endeavour to please by novelty leads men wide of simplicity and nature, and fills their writings with affectation and conceit. It was thus the ASIATIC eloquence degenerated so much from the ATTIC: It was thus the age of CLAUDIUS and NERO became so much inferior to that of AUGUSTUS in taste and genius: And perhaps there are, at present, some symptoms of a like degeneracy of taste, in FRANCE as well as in ENGLAND.

5. Immanuel Kant: Selections from *Critique of Pure Reason* and *Philosophical Correspondence* *(1759–1799)*

Kant (1724–1804) was born in and virtually never left Königsberg (in Prussia); it was there that he was educated and appointed as a professor in 1770. For the decade following that he worked in silence and, in 1781, published the *Critique of Pure Reason.* This was followed, among other works, by *Prolegomena to Every Future Metaphysics* (1783), the *Critique of Practical Reason,* and the *Critique of Judgement* in 1790. Kant's conception of a "critical idealism" was forseen by him as a "Copernican Revolution" in philosophy. Few modern philosophical movements are comprehensible without reference to Kant's revision of the empiricist and rationalist traditions.

CRITIQUE OF PURE REASON*

While I am saying this I can fancy that I detect in the face of the reader an expression of indignation, min-

* From *Critique of Pure Reason,* translated by N. K. Smith.

gled with contempt, at pretensions seemingly so arrogant and vain-glorious. Yet they are incomparably more moderate than the claims of all those writers who on the lines of the usual programme profess to prove the simple nature of the soul or the necessity of a first beginning of the world. For while such writers pledge themselves to extend human knowledge beyond all limits of possible experience, I humbly confess that this is entirely beyond my power. I have to deal with nothing save reason itself and its pure thinking; and to obtain complete knowledge of these, there is no need to go far afield, since I come upon them in my own self. Common logic itself supplies an example, how all the simple acts of reason can be enumerated completely and systematically. The subject of the present enquiry is the [kindred] question, how much we can hope to achieve by reason, when all the material and assistance of experience are taken away.

So much as regards *completeness* in our determination of each question, and *exhaustiveness* in our determination of all the questions with which we have to deal. These questions are not arbitrarily selected; they are prescribed to us, by the very nature of knowledge itself, as being the subject-matter of our critical enquiry.

As regards the *form* of our enquiry, *certainty* and *clearness* are two essential requirements, rightly to be exacted from anyone who ventures upon so delicate an undertaking.

As to *certainty*, I have prescribed to myself the maxim, that in this kind of investigation it is in no wise permissible to hold *opinions*. Everything, therefore, which bears any manner of resemblance to an hy-

---

pothesis is to be treated as contraband; it is not to be put up for sale even at the lowest price, but forthwith confiscated, immediately upon detection. Any knowledge that professes to hold *a priori* lays claim to be regarded as absolutely necessary. This applies still more to any *determination* of all pure *a priori* knowledge, since such determination has to serve as the measure, and therefore as the [supreme] example, of all apodeictic (philosophical) certainty. Whether I have succeeded in what I have undertaken must be left altogether to the reader's judgment; the author's task is solely to adduce grounds, not to speak as to the effect which they should have upon those who are sitting in judgment. But the author, in order that he may not himself, innocently, be the cause of any weakening of his arguments, may be permitted to draw attention to certain passages, which, although merely incidental, may yet occasion some mistrust. Such timely intervention may serve to counteract the influence which even quite undefined doubts as to these minor matters might otherwise exercise upon the reader's attitude in regard to the main issue.

I know no enquiries which are more important for exploring the faculty which we entitle understanding, and for determining the rules and limits of its employment, than those which I have instituted in the second chapter of the Transcendental Analytic under the title *Deduction of the Pure Concepts of Understanding.* They are also those which have cost me the greatest labour—labour, as I hope, not unrewarded. This enquiry, which is somewhat deeply grounded, has-two sides. The one refers to the objects of pure understanding, and is intended to expound and render intelligible the objective validity of its *a priori* concepts. It is therefore essential to my purposes. The other seeks to investigate the pure understanding itself, its possibility and the cognitive faculties upon which it rests; and so deals with it in its subjective aspect. Although this latter exposition is of great importance for my chief purpose, it does not form an essential part of it. For the chief question is always simply this:—what and how much can the understanding and reason know apart from all experience? not:—how is the faculty of thought itself possible? The latter is, as it were, the search for the cause of a given effect, and to that extent is somewhat hypothetical in character (though, as I shall show elsewhere, it is not really so); and I would appear to be taking the liberty simply of expressing an *opinion*, in which case the reader would be free to express a different *opinion*. For this reason I must forestall the reader's criticism by pointing out that the objective deduction with which I am here chiefly concerned retains its full force even if my subjective deduction should fail to produce that complete conviction for which I hope. . . .

As regards *clearness*, the reader has a right to demand, in the first place, a *discursive* (logical) clearness, through *concepts*, and secondly, an *intuitive* (aesthetic) clearness, through *intuitions*, that is, through examples and other concrete illustrations. For the first I have sufficiently provided. That was essential to my purpose; but it has also been the incidental cause of my not being in a position to do justice to the second demand, which, if not so pressing, is yet still quite reasonable. I have been almost continuously at a loss, during the progress of my work, how I should proceed in this matter. Examples and illustrations seemed always to be necessary, and so took their place, as required, in my first draft. But I very soon became aware of the magnitude of my task and of the multiplicity of matters with which I should have to deal; and as I perceived that even if treated in dry, purely *scholastic* fashion, the outcome would by itself be already quite sufficiently large in bulk, I found it inadvisable to enlarge it yet further through examples and illustrations. These are necessary only from a *popular* point of view; and this work can never be made suitable for popular consumption. Such assistance is not required by genuine students of the science, and, though always pleasing, might very well in this case have been self-defeating in its effects. Abbot Terrasson has remarked that if the size of a volume be measured not by the number of its pages but by the time required for mastering it, it can be said of many a book, *that it would be much shorter if it were not so short*. On the other hand, if we have in view the comprehensibility of a whole of speculative knowledge, which, though wide-ranging, has the coherence that follows from unity of principle, we can say with equal justice *that many a book would have been much clearer if it had not made such an effort to be clear.* For the aids to clearness, though they may be of assistance in regard to details, often interfere with our grasp of the whole. The reader is not allowed to arrive sufficiently quickly at a conspectus of the whole; the bright colouring of the illustrative material intervenes to cover over and conceal the articulation and organisation of the system, which, if we are to be able to judge of its unity and solidity, are what chiefly concern us.

The reader, I should judge, will feel it to be no small inducement to yield his willing co-operation, when the author is thus endeavouring, according to the plan here proposed, to carry through a large and important work in a complete and lasting manner. Metaphysics, on the view which we are adopting, is the only one of all the sciences which dare promise that through a small but concentrated effort it will attain, and this in a short time, such completion as will leave no task to our successors save that of adapting it in a *didactic* manner according to their own preferences, without their being able to add anything whatsoever to its content. For it is nothing but the *inventory* of all our possessions through *pure* reason, systematically arranged. In this field nothing can escape us. What reason produces entirely out of itself cannot be concealed, but is brought to light by reason itself immediately the common principle has been discovered. The complete unity of this kind of knowledge, and the fact that it is derived solely from pure concepts, entirely uninfluenced by any experience or by *special* intuition, such as might lead to any determinate experience that would enlarge and increase it, make this unconditioned completeness not only practicable but also necessary. . . .

Such a system of pure (speculative) reason I hope myself to produce under the title *Metaphysics of Nature*. It will be not half as large, yet incomparably richer in content than this present *Critique*, which has as its first task to discover the sources and conditions of the possibility of such criticism, clearing, as it were, and levelling what has hitherto been waste-ground. In this present enterprise I look to my reader for the patience and impartiality of a *judge*; whereas in the other I shall look for the benevolent assistance of a *fellow-worker*. For however completely all the *principles* of the system are presented in this *Critique*, the completeness of the system itself likewise requires that none of the *derivative* concepts be lacking. These cannot be enumerated by any *a priori* computation, but must be discovered gradually. Whereas, therefore, in this *Critique* the entire *synthesis* of the concepts has been exhausted, there will still remain the further work of making their *analysis* similarly complete, a task which is rather an amusement than a labour. . . .

THE ARCHITECTONIC OF PURE REASON*

No one attempts to establish a science unless he has an idea upon which to base it. But in the working out of the science the schema, nay even the definition which, at the start, he first gave of the science, is very seldom adequate to his idea. For this idea lies hidden in reason, like a germ in which the parts are still undeveloped and barely recognisable even under microscopic observation. Consequently, since sciences are devised from the point of view of a certain universal interest, we must not explain and determine them according to the description which their founder gives of them, but in conformity with the idea which, out of the natural unity of the parts that we have assembled, we find to be grounded in reason itself. For we shall then find that its founder, and often even his latest successors, are groping for an idea which they have never succeeded in making clear to themselves, and that consequently they have not been in a position to determine the proper content, the articulation (systematic unity), and limits of the science.

It is unfortunate that only after we have spent much time in the collection of materials in somewhat random fashion at the suggestion of an idea lying hidden in our minds, and after we have, indeed, over a long period assembled the materials in a merely technical manner, does it first become possible for us to discern the idea in a clearer light, and to devise a whole architectoni-

* From *Critique of Pure Reason,* translated by N. K. Smith. Reprinted by permission of St. Martin's Press, Inc., Macmillan & Co., Ltd.

cally in accordance with the ends of reason. Systems seem to be formed in the manner of lowly organisms, through a *generatio aequivoca* from the mere confluence of assembled concepts, at first imperfect, and only gradually attaining to completeness, although they one and all have had their schema, as the original germ, in the sheer self-development of reason. Hence, not only is each system articulated in accordance with an idea, but they are one and all organically united in a system of human knowledge, as members of one whole, and so as admitting of an architectonic of all human knowledge, which, at the present time, in view of the great amount of material that has been collected, or which can be obtained from the ruins of ancient systems, is not only possible, but would not indeed be difficult. We shall content ourselves here with the completion of our task, namely, merely to outline the *architectonic* of all knowledge arising from *pure reason*; and in doing so we shall begin from the point at which the common root of our faculty of knowledge divides and throws out two stems, one of which is *reason*. By reason I here understand the whole higher faculty of knowledge, and am therefore contrasting the rational with the empirical.

If I abstract from all the content of knowledge, objectively regarded, then all knowledge, subjectively regarded, is either historical or rational. Historical knowledge is *cognitio ex datis*; rational knowledge is *cognitio ex principiis*. However a mode of knowledge may originally be given, it is still, in relation to the individual who possesses it, simply historical, if he knows only so much of it as has been given to him from outside (and this in the form in which it has been given to him), whether through immediate experience or narration, or (as in the case of general knowledge) through instruction. Anyone, therefore, who has *learnt* (in the strict sense of that term) a system of philosophy, such as that of Wolff, although he may have all its principles, explanations, and proofs, together with the formal divisions of the whole body of doctrine, in his head, and, so to speak, at his fingers' ends, has no more than a complete *historical* knowledge of the Wolffian philosophy. He knows and judges only what has been given him. If we dispute a definition, he does not know whence to obtain another. He has formed his mind on another's, and the imitative faculty is not itself productive. In other words, his knowledge has not in him arisen *out* of reason, and although, objectively considered, it is indeed knowledge due to reason, it is yet, in its subjective character, merely historical. He has grasped and kept; that is, he has learnt well, and is merely a plaster-cast of a living man. Modes of rational knowledge which are rational objectively (that is, which can have their first origin solely in human reason) can be so entitled subjectively also, only when they have been derived from universal sources of reason, that is, from principles—the sources from which there can also arise criticism, nay, even the rejection of what has been learnt.

All knowledge arising out of reason is derived either from concepts or from the construction of concepts. The former is called philosophical, the latter mathematical. I have already treated of the fundamental difference between these two modes of knowledge in the first chapter [of this Transcendental Doctrine of Method]. Knowledge [as we have just noted] can be objectively philosophical, and yet subjectively historical, as is the case with most novices, and with all those who have never looked beyond their School, and who remain novices all their lives. But it is noteworthy that mathematical knowledge, in its subjective character, and precisely as it has been learned, can also be regarded as knowledge arising out of reason, and that there is therefore in regard to mathematical knowledge no such distinction as we have drawn in the case of philosophical knowledge. This is due to the fact that the sources of knowledge, from which alone the teacher can derive his knowledge, lie nowhere but in the essential and genuine principles of reason, and consequently cannot be acquired by the novice from any other source, and cannot be disputed; and this, in turn, is owing to the fact that the employment of reason is here *in concreto* only, although likewise *a priori*, namely, in intuition which is pure, and which precisely on that account is infallible, excluding all illusion and error. Mathematics, therefore, alone of all the sciences (*a priori*) arising from reason, can be learned; philosophy can never be learned, save only in historical fashion; as regards what concerns reason, we can at most learn to *philosophise*.

Philosophy is the system of all philosophical knowledge. If we are to understand by it the archetype for the estimation of all attempts at philosophising, and if this archetype is to serve for the estimation of each subjective philosophy, the structure of which is often so diverse and liable to alteration, it must be taken objectively. Thus regarded, philosophy is a mere idea of a possible science which nowhere exists *in concreto*, but to which, by many different paths, we endeavour to approximate, until the one true path, overgrown by the products of sensibility, has at last been discovered, and the image, hitherto so abortive, has achieved likeness to the archetype, so far as this is granted to [mortal] man. Till then we cannot learn philosophy; for where is it, who is in possession of it, and how shall we recognise it? We can only learn to philosophise, that is, to exercise the talent of reason, in accordance with its universal principles, on certain actually existing attempts at philosophy, always, however, reserving the right of reason to investigate, to confirm, or to reject these principles in their very sources.

Hitherto the concept of philosophy has been a merely scholastic concept—a concept of a system of knowledge which is sought solely in its character as a science, and which has therefore in view only the systematic unity appropriate to science, and consequently no more than the *logical* perfection of knowledge. But there is likewise another concept of philosophy, a *conceptus cosmicus*, which has always formed the real basis of the term "philosophy," especially when it has been as it were personified and its archetype represented in the ideal *philosopher*. On this view, philosophy is the science of the relation of all knowledge to the essential ends of human reason (*teleologia rationis humanae*), and the philosopher is not an artificer in the field of reason, but himself the lawgiver of human reason. In this sense of the term it would be very vainglorious to entitle oneself a philosopher, and to pretend to have equalled the pattern which exists in the idea alone.

The mathematician, the natural philosopher, and the logician, however successful the two former may have been in their advances in the field of rational knowledge, and the two latter more especially in philosophical knowledge, are yet only artificers in the field of reason. There is a teacher, [conceived] in the ideal, who sets them their tasks, and employs them as instruments, to further the essential ends of human reason. Him alone we must call philosopher; but as he nowhere exists, while the idea of his legislation is to be found in that reason with which every human being is endowed, we shall keep entirely to the latter, determining more precisely what philosophy prescribes as regards systematic unity, in accordance with this cosmical concept,* from the standpoint of its essential ends.

Essential ends are not as such the highest ends; in view of the demand of reason for complete systematic unity, only one of them can be so described. Essential ends are therefore either the ultimate end or subordinate ends which are necessarily connected with the former as means. The former is no other than the whole vocation of man, and the philosophy which deals with it is entitled moral philosophy. On account of this superiority which moral philosophy has over all other occupations of reason, the ancients in their use of the term 'philosopher' always meant, more especially, the *moralist*; and even at the present day we are led by a certain analogy to entitle anyone a philosopher who appears to exhibit self-control under the guidance of reason, however limited his knowledge may be. . . .

LETTER TO MOSES MENDELSSOHN, AUGUST 16, 1783**

[Kant discusses a man whom Mendelssohn had recommended. He goes on to deny the rumor that he is planning a trip. He subscribes to the medical principle, "Every man has his own particular way of preserving his health, which he must not alter if he values his safety. . . . One lives longest if one does not strain or worry about lengthening one's life but also refrains

* By "cosmical concept" [*Weltbegriff*] is here meant the concept which relates to that in which everyone necessarily has an interest; and accordingly if a science is to be regarded merely as one of the disciplines designed in view of certain optionally chosen ends, I must determine it in conformity with *scholastic concepts*.

**From Kant: *Philosophical Correspondence* (1759–1799) translated by A Zweig.

from shortening it by disturbing the benevolent nature in us."]

. . . That you feel yourself dead to metaphysics does not offend me, since virtually the entire learned world seems to be dead to her, and of course, there is the matter of your nervous indisposition (of which, by the way, there is not the slightest sign in your book, *Jerusalem*). I do regret that your penetrating mind, alienated from metaphysics, cannot be drawn to the *Critique*, which is concerned with investigating the foundations of that structure. However, though I regret this, and regret that the *Critique* repels you, I am not offended by this. For although the book is the product of nearly twelve years of reflection, I completed it hastily, in perhaps four or five months, with the greatest attentiveness to its content but less care about its style and ease of comprehension. Even now I think my decision was correct, for otherwise, if I had delayed further in order to make the book more popular, it would probably have remained unfinished. As it is, the weaknesses can be remedied little by little, once the work is there in rough form. For I am now too old to devote uninterrupted effort both to completing a work and also to the rounding, smoothing, and lubricating of each of its parts. I certainly would have been able to clarify every difficult point; but I was constantly worried that a more detailed presentation would detract both from the clarity and continuity of the work. Therefore I abstained, intending to take care of this in a later discussion, after my statements, as I hoped, would gradually have become understood. For an author who has projected himself into a system and become comfortable with its concepts cannot always guess what might be obscure or indefinite or inadequately demonstrated to the reader. Few men are so fortunate as to be able to think for themselves and at the same time be able to put themselves into someone else's position and adjust their style exactly to his requirements. There is only one Mendelssohn. . . .

But I wish I could persuade you, dear sir (granted that you do not want to bother yourself further with the book you have laid aside), to use your position and influence in whatever way you think best to encourage an examination of my theses, considering them in the following order: One would first inquire whether the distinction between analytic and synthetic judgments is correct; whether the difficulties concerning the possibility of synthetic judgments, when these are supposed to be made a priori, are as I describe them; and whether the completing of a deduction of synthetic a priori cognitions, without which all metaphysics is impossible, is as necessary as I maintain it to be. Second, one would investigate whether it is true, as I asserted, that we are incapable of making synthetic a priori judgments concerning anything but the formal condition of a possible (outer or inner) experience in general, that is, in regard to sensuous intuition and the concepts of the understanding, both of which are presupposed by experience and are what first of all make it possible. Third, one would inquire whether the conclusion I draw is also correct: that the a priori knowledge of which we are capable extends no farther than to objects of a possible experience, with the proviso that this field of possible experience does not encompass all things in themselves; consequently, there are other objects in addition to objects of possible experience—indeed, they are necessarily presupposed, though it is impossible for us to know the slightest thing about them. If we were to get this far in our investigations, the solution to the difficulties in which reason entangles itself when it strives to transcend entirely the bounds of possible experience would make itself clear, as would the even more important solution to the question why it is that reason is driven to transcend its proper sphere of activity. In short, the dialectic of pure reason would create few difficulties any more. From there on, the critical philosophy would gain acceptability and become a promenade through a labyrinth, but with a reliable guidebook to help us find our way out as often as we get lost. I would gladly help these investigations in whatever way I can, for I am certain that something substantial would emerge, if only the trial is made by competent minds. But I am not optimistic about this. Mendelssohn, Garve, and Tetens have apparently declined to occupy themselves with work of this sort, and where else can anyone of sufficient talent and good will be found? I must therefore content myself with the thought that a work like this is, as Swift says, a plant that only flowers when its stem is put into the soil. Meanwhile, I still hope to work out, eventually, a textbook for metaphysics, according to the critical principles I mentioned; it will have all the brevity of a handbook and be useful for academic lectures. I hope to finish it sometime, perhaps in the distant future. This winter I shall have the first part of my [book on] moral [philosophy] substantially completed.* This work is more adapted to popular tastes, though it seems to me far less of a stimulus to broadening people's minds than my other work is, since the latter tries to define the limits and the total content of the whole of human reason. But moral philosophy, especially when it tries to complete itself by stepping over into religion without adequate preparation and definition of the critical sort, entangles itself unavoidably either in objections and misgivings or in folly and fanaticism. . . .

* Possibly the *Foundations of the Metaphysics of Morals*, which appeared in April, 1785.

6. Søren Kierkegaard: Selections from *Either/Or*, *The Point of View for My Work as an Author*, and *The Concept of Dread*

The epitaph of Kierkegaard (1813–1855) states simply: "That Individual"—a phrase which characterizes the individuality of both his life and his philosophical work. His study of Hegel at the University of Copenhagen initiated a lifelong protest against systematic, orthodox metaphysics and church dogmatics. In order to underscore the individualistic and unsystematic character of his work, many of Kierkegaard's most important writings, such as *Either/Or* and *Concluding Unscientific Postscripts*, were published pseudonymously. Kierkegaard is commonly linked with the origins of twentieth-century existentialism.

EITHER/OR*

Tested Advice for Authors: Set down your reflections carelessly, and let them be printed; in correcting the

* From *Either/Or*, Vol. I, translated by D. F. Swenson (New York: Doubleday Anchor Books, 1959) pp. 20, 31.

proof sheets a number of good ideas will gradually suggest themselves. Therefore, take courage, all you who have not yet dared to publish anything; even misprints are not to be despised, and an author who becomes witty by the aid of misprints, must be regarded as having become witty in a perfectly lawful manner. . . .

It happened that a fire broke out backstage in a theater. The clown came out to inform the public. They thought it was a jest and applauded. He repeated his warning, they shouted even louder. So I think the world will come to an end amid general applause from all the wits, who believe that it is a joke. . . .

What the philosophers say about Reality is often as disappointing as a sign you see in a shop window, which reads: Pressing Done Here. If you brought your clothes to be pressed, you would be fooled; for the sign is only for sale.

THE AESTHETIC WORKS*

Why the beginning of the work was aesthetic, or what this signifies, understood in relation to the whole.**

§ 1

That "Christendom" is a prodigious illusion.

Every one with some capacity for observation, who seriously considers what is called Christendom, or the conditions in a so-called Christian country, must surely be assailed by profound misgivings. What does it mean that all these thousands and thousands call themselves Christians as a matter of course? These

*From Søren Kierkegaard, *The Point of View for My Work as an Author: A Report to History*, trans. Walter Lowrie (New York: Harper & Row, 1962) pp. 22–41.

**Once and for all I must earnestly beg the kind reader always to bear *in mente* that the thought behind the whole work is: what it means to become a Christian.

many, many men, of whom the greater part, so far as one can judge, live in categories quite foreign to Christianity! Any one can convince himself of it by the simplest observation. People who perhaps never once enter a church, never think about God, never mention His name except in oaths! People upon whom it has never dawned that they might have any obligation to God, people who either regard it as a maximum to be guiltless of transgressing the criminal law, or do not count even this quite necessary! Yet all these people, even those who assert that no God exists, are all of them Christians, call themselves Christians, are recognized as Christians by the State, are buried as Christians by the Church, are certified as Christians for eternity!

That at the bottom of this there must be a tremendous confusion, a frightful illusion, there surely can be no doubt. But to stir up such a question! Yes, I know the objections well. For there are those who understand what I mean, but would say with a good-natured slap on the back, "My dear fellow, you are still rather young to want to embark on such an undertaking, an undertaking which, if it is to have any success at all, will require at least half a score of well-trained missionaries; an undertaking which means neither more nor less than proposing to reintroduce Christianity . . . into Christendom. No, my dear fellow, let us be men; such an undertaking is beyond your powers and mine. It is just as madly ambitious as wanting to reform the 'crowd,' with which no sensible person wants to mix. To start such a thing is certain ruin." Perhaps; but though ruin were certain, it is certain also that no one has learnt this objection from Christianity; for when Christianity came into the world it was still more definitely "certain ruin" to start such a thing—and yet it was started. And it is certain, too, that no one learnt this objection from Socrates; for he mixed with the "crowd" and wanted to reform it.

This is roughly how the case stands. Once in a while a parson causes a little hubbub from the pulpit, about there being something wrong somewhere with all these numerous Christians—but all those *to* whom he is speaking are Christians, and those he speaks *about*, are not present. This is most appropriately described as a feigned emotion. Once in a while there appears a religious enthusiast: he storms against Christendom, he vociferates and makes a loud noise, denouncing almost all as not being Christians—and accomplishes nothing. He takes no heed of the fact that an illusion is not an easy thing to dispel. Supposing now it is a fact that most people, when they call themselves Christians, are under an illusion—how do they defend themselves against an enthusiast? First and foremost, they do not bother about him at all, they do not so much as look at his book, they immediately lay it aside, *ad acta*; or, if he employs the living word, they go round by another street and do not hear him. As the next step, they spirit him out of the way by carefully defining the whole concept, and settle themselves securely in their illusion: they make him a fanatic, his Christianity an exaggeration—in the end he remains the only one, or one of the few, who is not seriously a Christian (for exaggeration is surely a lack of seriousness), whereas the others are all serious Christians.

No, an illusion can never be destroyed directly, and only by indirect means can it be radically removed. If it is an illusion that all are Christians—and if there is anything to be done about it, it must be done indirectly, not by one who vociferously proclaims himself an extraordinary Christian, but by one who, better instructed, is ready to declare that he is not a Christian at all.* That is, one must approach from behind the person who is under an illusion. Instead of wishing to have the advantage of being oneself that rare thing, a Christian, one must let the prospective captive enjoy the advantage of being the Christian, and for one's own part have resignation enough to be the one who is far behind him—otherwise one will certainly not get the man out of his illusion, a thing which is difficult enough in any case.

If then, according to our assumption, the greater number of people in Christendom only imagine themselves to be Christians, in what categories do they live? They live in aesthetic, or, at the most, in aesthetic-ethical categories.

Supposing then that a religious writer has become profoundly attentive to this illusion, Christendom, and has resolved to attack it with all the might at his disposal (with God's aid, be it noted)—what then is he to do? First and foremost, no impatience. If he becomes impatient, he will rush headlong against it and accomplish nothing. A direct attack only strengthens a person in his illusion, and at the same time embitters him. There is nothing that requires such gentle handling as an illusion, if one wishes to dispel it. If anything prompts the prospective captive to set his will in opposition, all is lost. And this is what a direct attack achieves, and it implies moreover the presumption of requiring a man to make to another person, or in his presence, an admission which he can make most profitably to himself privately. This is what is achieved by the indirect method, which, loving and serving the truth, arranges

* One may recall the *Concluding Unscientific Postscript*, the author of which, Johannes Climacus, declares expressly that he himself is not a Christian.

everything dialectically for the prospective captive, and then shyly withdraws (for love is always shy), so as not to witness the admission which he makes to himself alone before God—that he has lived hitherto in an illusion.

The religious writer must, therefore, first get into touch with men. That is, he must begin with aesthetic achievement. This is earnest-money. The more brilliant the achievement, the better for him. Moreover he must be sure of himself, or (and this is the one and only security) he must relate himself to God in fear and trembling, lest the event most opposite to his intentions should come to pass, and instead of setting the others in motion, the others acquire power over him, so that he ends by being bogged in the aesthetic. Therefore, he must have everything in readiness, though without impatience, with a view to bringing forward the religious promptly, as soon as he perceives that he has his readers with him, so that with the momentum gained by devotion to the aesthetic they rush headlong into contact with the religious.

It is important that religion should not be introduced either too soon or too late. If too long a time elapses, the illusion gains ground that the aesthetic writer has become older and hence religious. If it comes too soon, the effect is not violent enough.

Assuming that there is a prodigious illusion in the case of these many men who call themselves Christians and are regarded as Christians, the way of encountering it which is here suggested involves no condemnation or denunciation. It is a truly Christian invention, which cannot be employed without fear and trembling, or without real self-denial. The one who is disposed to help bears all the responsibility and makes all the effort. But for that reason such a line of action possesses intrinsic value. Generally speaking, a method has value only in relation to the result attained. Some one condemns and denounces, vociferates and makes a great noise—all this has no intrinsic value, though one counts upon accomplishing much by it. It is otherwise with the line of action here contemplated. Suppose that a man had dedicated himself to the use of it, suppose that he used it his whole life long—and suppose that he accomplished nothing: he has nevertheless by no means lived in vain, for his life was true self-denial.

§ *2*

That if real success is to attend the effort to bring a man to a definite position, one must first of all take pains to find HIM *where he is and begin there.*

This is the secret of the art of helping others. Any one who has not mastered this is himself deluded when he proposes to help others. In order to help another effectively I must understand more than he—yet first of all surely I must understand what he understands. If I do not know that, my greater understanding will be of no help to him. If, however, I am disposed to plume myself on my greater understanding, it is because I am vain or proud, so that at bottom, instead of benefiting him, I want to be admired. But all true effort to help begins with self-humiliation: the helper must first humble himself under him he would help, and therewith must understand that to help does not mean to be a sovereign but to be a servant, that to help does not mean to be ambitious but to be patient, that to help means to endure for the time being the imputation that one is in the wrong and does not understand what the other understands.

Take the case of a man who is passionately angry, and let us assume that he is really in the wrong. Unless you can begin with him by making it seem as if it were he that had to instruct you, and unless you can do it in such a way that the angry man, who was too impatient to listen to a word of yours, is glad to discover in you a complaisant and attentive listener—if you cannot do that, you cannot help him at all. Or take the case of a lover who has been unhappy in love, and suppose that the way he yields to his passion is really unreasonable, impious, unchristian. In case you cannot begin with him in such a way that he finds genuine relief in talking to you about his suffering and is able to enrich his mind with the poetical interpretations you suggest for it, notwithstanding you have no share in this passion and want to free him from it—if you cannot do that, then you cannot help him at all; he shuts himself away from you, he retires within himself . . . and then you only prate to hin. Perhaps by the power of your personality you may be able to coerce him to acknowledge that he is at fault. Ah! my dear, the next moment he steals away by a hidden path for a rendezvous with his hidden passion, for which he longs all the more ardently, and is almost fearful lest it might have lost something of its seductive warmth; for now by your behaviour you have helped him to fall in love all over again, in love now with his unhappy passion itself . . . and you only prate to him!

So it is with respect to what it means to become a Christian—assuming that the many who call themselves Christians are under an illusion. Denounce the magical charm of aesthetics—well, there have indeed been times when you might have succeeded in coercing people. But with what result? With the result that privately, with secret passion, they love that magic. No, let it come out. And remember, serious and stern as you are, that if you cannot humble yourself, you are not genuinely serious. Be the amazed listener who sits and hears what the other finds the more delight in telling you because you listen with amazement. But above all do not forget one thing, the purpose you have in mind, the fact that it is the religious you must bring forward. If you are capable of it, present the aesthetic with all its fascinating magic, enthral if possible the other man, present it with the sort of passion which exactly suits him, merrily for the merry, in a minor key for the melancholy, wittily for the witty, &c. But above all do not forget one thing, the purpose you have to bring forward...the religious. By all means do this, and fear not to do it; for truly it cannot be done without fear and trembling.

If you can do that, if you can find exactly the place where the other is and begin there, you may perhaps have the luck to lead him to the place where you are.

For to be a teacher does not mean simply to affirm that such a thing is so, or to deliver a lecture, &c. No, to be a teacher in the right sense is to be a learner. Instruction begins when you, the teacher, learn from the learner, put yourself in his place so that you may understand what he understands and in the way he understands it, in case you have not understood it before. Or if you have understood it before, you allow him to subject you to an examination so that he may be sure you know your part. This is the introduction. Then the beginning can be made in another sense.

An objection I have constantly raised in my own mind against a class of the orthodox here at home is that they shut themselves up in little groups and confirm one another in the belief that they are the only Christians—and therefore know of nothing else to do about Christendom as a whole but to vociferate that the others are not Christians. If it is true that there really are so very few Christians in Christendom, these orthodox people are *eo ipso* under obligation to be missionaries, although a missionary in Christendom will always look rather different from a missionary to the heathen. It will easily be perceived that this objection of mine attacks our orthodox in correct fashion, from behind; for it proceeds upon the admission, or the assumption, that they really are true Christians, the only true Christians in Christendom.

So then the religious writer, whose all-absorbing thought is how one is to become a Christian, starts off rightly in Christendom as an aesthetic writer. For a moment let it remain undetermined whether Christendom is a monstrous illusion, whether it is a vain conceit for the many to call themselves Christians; let the opposite rather be assumed. Well then, this beginning is a superfluity, counting upon a situation which does not exist—yet it does no harm. The harm is much greater, or rather the only harm is, when one who is not a Christian pretends to be one. On the other hand, when one who is a Christian gives the impression that he is not, the harm is not great. Assuming that all are Christians, this deception can at the most confirm them more and more in being such.

§ 3

The illusion that religion and Christianity are something one first has recourse to when one grows older.

The aesthetical always overrates youth and this brief instant of eternity. It cannot reconcile itself to the seriousness of age, let alone the seriousness of eternity. Hence the aesthete is always suspicious of the religious person, supposing either that he never had any feeling for aesthetics, or else that essentially he would have preferred to remain in the enjoyment of it, but that time exercised its debilitating influence, and he became older and took refuge in religion. Life is divided into two parts: the period of youth belongs to the aesthetical; the later age to religion—but, speaking honestly, we all would prefer to remain young.

How *may* this illusion be dispelled? I say "may," for whether the effort actually succeeds is another question; but it may be dispelled by the simultaneous achievement of aesthetic and religious production. In this case no room is left for doubt, for the aesthetic production attests the fact of youth—and so the simultaneous achievement in the religious sphere cannot be explained upon any accidental ground.

Assuming that Christendom is a prodigious illusion, that it is a vain conceit for the many to call themselves Christians, there seems to be every probability that the illusion we are now talking about is exceedingly common. But this illusion is still farther aggravated by the conceit that one is a Christian. One lives in aesthetic categories, and if once in a while thoughts about Christianity occur, the question is deferred till one becomes older. "For," one says to oneself, "in fact I am essentially a Christian." It certainly cannot be denied that in Christendom there are those who live just as sensually as ever any heathen did; yes, even more sensually, because they have this disastrous sense of security that essentially they are Christians. But the decision to become a Christian one shirks as long as possible; indeed one encounters an additional hindrance in the fact that one takes pride in being young as long as possible (and only when one grows old does one have recourse to Christianity and religiousness). Then one will be compelled to make the admission that one has become old—but only when one becomes old will one have recourse to Christianity and religiousness.

If one could always remain young, one would not have the least need either of Christianity or religion.

This is an error most pernicious to all true religiousness. It is rooted in the fact that people confuse the notion of growing older in the sense of time with that of growing older in the sense of eternity. It cannot indeed be denied that one not infrequently sees the unedifying spectacle of a youth who was the hot and passionate spokesman of aesthetics transformed into a type of religiousness which has all the faults of old age, in one sense feeble, in another too highly strung. It cannot be denied that many who represent the religious do so too sternly and too crabbedly, for fear of not being serious enough. This and much else may contribute to make the illusion more general and to establish it more firmly. But what help is there for it? The only help is what will help to dispel this illusion.

So if a religious author wishes to deal with this illusion, he must be at the same time an aesthetic and a religious author. But one thing above all he must not forget, the intention of the whole undertaking, that what must come decisively to the fore is the religious. The aesthetic works remain only a means of communication; and for those who possibly may need it (and on the assumption that Christendom is a prodigious illusion these must be many) it serves as a proof that it is impossible to explain the religious production by the notion that the author has become older; for it is in fact simultaneous, and surely one has not grown older simultaneously.

Perhaps success may not attend such an effort—perhaps, but at all events no great harm is done. The harm is, at the most, that some will not believe in the religiousness of such a communicator. All right then! A communicator of the religious may very often be over-anxious on his own behalf to be regarded as religious. If such be the case, it shows clearly that he is not truly a religious character. It is like the case of a teacher who is too much concerned about the judgement his pupils may pass upon his instruction, his knowledge,

&c. Such a teacher when he tries to teach is unable to move hand or foot. Suppose, for example, he thought it best for his pupils' sake to say of something he understood quite well that he did not understand it. Good gracious! This he could not venture to do, for fear the pupils might really believe that he did not understand it. That is to say, he is not fit to be a teacher—though he calls himself a teacher, he is so far from being such a thing that he actually aspires to be cited for commendation . . . by his pupils. Or as in the case of a preacher of repentance who, when he wants to chastise the vices of the age, is much concerned about what the age thinks of him. He is so far from being a preacher of repentance that he resembles rather a New Year's visitor who comes with congratulations. He merely makes himself a bit interesting in a costume which is rather queer for a New Year's visitor. And so it is with the religious character who, if worse come to worst, cannot endure to be regarded as the only person who is not religious. For to be able to endure this is, in the sphere of reflection, the most accurate definition of essential religiousness.

§ 4

That even if a man will not follow where one endeavours to lead him, one thing it is still possible to do for him—compel him to take notice.

One man may have the good fortune to do much for another, he may have the good fortune to lead him whither he wishes, and (to stick to the subject which here is our constant and essential interest) he may have the good fortune to help him to become a Christian. But this result is not in my power; it depends upon so many things, and above all it depends upon whether he will or no. In all eternity it is impossible for me to compel a person to accept an opinion, a conviction, a belief. But one thing I can do: I can compel him to take notice. In one sense this is the first thing; for it is the condition antecedent to the next thing, i.e. the acceptance of an opinion, a conviction, a belief. In another sense it is the last—if, that is, he will not take the next step.

That this is a charitable act there can be no dispute, but it also must not be forgotten that it is a rash act. By obliging a man to take notice I achieve the aim of obliging him to judge. Now he is about to judge—but how he judges is not under my control. Perhaps he judges in the very opposite sense to that which I desire. Moreover, the fact that he was compelled to judge may perhaps have embittered him, furiously embittered him, against the cause and against me. And perhaps I am the victim of my rash act. Compelling people to take notice and to judge is the characteristic of genuine martyrdom. A genuine martyr never used his might but strove by the aid of impotence. He compelled people to take notice. God knows, they took notice—they put him to death. But with that he was well content. He did not count that his death put a stop to his work; he understood that his death was a part of it, indeed that his work first gained headway by means of his death. For verily those who put him to death took notice in their turn; they were compelled to consider the cause again, and to an entirely different effect. What the living man was unable to do, the dead man could—he won for his cause those who had taken notice.

There is an objection I have raised again and again in my own mind against the preachers we ordinarily find preaching Christianity in Christendom. Surrounded as they are by too much illusion and rendered secure by it, they have not the courage to make men take notice. That is to say, they are not sufficiently self-denying in view of their cause. They are glad to win adherents, but they want to win them for the sake of strengthening their cause, and so they do not inquire any too carefully whether they truly are adherents. Again, this means that in a deeper sense they have no cause. Their cause is one to which they are selfishly attached. Hence they do not venture to go out among men in a real sense, or to let go of the illusion for the sake of imparting an impression of the pure idea. They have an obscure apprehension that it is a dangerous thing to compel people in truth to take notice. In untruth to make people take notice—that is, to bow and scrape before them, to flatter them, to implore their attention and their indulgent judgement, to refer (the truth!) to the ballot—this indeed is not attended by any danger, at least not here on earth, where on the contrary it is attended with advantages of every sort. And yet perhaps it is also attended with the danger that some day, in eternity, one may be "plucked."

And now with reference to the assumption that it is a vain conceit on the part of the many who call themselves Christians. If a man lives in this conceit, lives, that is to say, in categories entirely foreign to Christianity, in purely aesthetic categories, and if some one is capable of winning and captivating him with aesthetic works, and then knows how to introduce the religious so promptly that with the momentum of his abandonment to the aesthetic the man rushes straight into the most decisive definitions of the religious—what then? Why, then, he must take notice. What follows after this, however, no one can tell beforehand. But at least he is compelled to take notice. Possibly he may come to his senses and realize what is implied in calling himself a Christian. Possibly he may be furious with the person who has taken this liberty with him; but at least he has begun to take notice, he is on the point of expressing a judgement. Possibly, in order to protect his retreat, he may express the judgement that the other is a hypocrite, a deceiver, a dunce—but there is no help for it, he must judge, he has begun to take notice.

Normally one reverses the relationship; and it was indeed reversed when Christianity dealt with paganism. But the fact that the situation was entirely altered by the notion of Christendom, which transposes everything into the sphere of reflection, is completely overlooked. In Christendom, the man who endeavours to lead people to become Christians normally gives every sort of assurance that he himself is a Christian. He protests and protests. But he fails to observe that from the very beginning there has been a terrible confusion at this point; for in fact the people he addresses are already Christians. But if it is Christians he is addressing, what can be the sense of getting them to become Christians? If, on the contrary, they are not Christians, in his opinion, although they call themselves such, the very fact that they call themselves Christians shows that here we have to do with a situation which demands reflection, and with that the tactics must be entirely reversed.

Here I cannot develop further the pressing need Christendom has of an entirely new military science permeated through and through by reflection. In several of my books I have furnished suggestions about the principal factors of such a science. The gist of it all can be expressed in *one* word: the method must be indirect. But the development of this method may require the labour of years, alert attention every hour of the day, daily practice of the scales, or patient finger-exercise in the dialectical, not to speak of a never-slumbering fear and trembling. In the communication of Christianity, where the situation is qualified by Christendom, there is no direct or straightforward relationship, inasmuch as a vain conceit has first to be disposed of. All the old military science, all the apologetic and whatever goes with it, serves rather—candidly speaking—to betray the cause of Christianity. At every instant and at every point the tactics must be adapted to a fight which is waged against a conceit, an illusion.

So then when a religious author in Christendom whose all-absorbing thought is the task of becoming a Christian would do all that he possibly can to make people take notice (for whether he succeeds or not is another question), he must begin as an aesthetic writer and up to a definite point he must maintain this role. But there is necessarily a limit; for the aim of it is to make people take notice. And one thing the author must not forget, namely, his purpose, the distinction between this and that, between the religious as the decisive thing and the aesthetic incognito—lest the criss-cross of dialectics end in twaddle.

§ 5

That the whole of the aesthetic work, viewed in relation to the work as a whole, is a deception—understanding this word, however, in a special sense.

Any one who considers the aesthetic work as the whole and then considers the religious part from this point of view, could only consider it as a falling away, a falling off. I have shown in the foregoing that the assumption upon which this point of view is based is not tenable. There it was established that from the very beginning, and simultaneously with the pseudonymous work, certain signals, displaying my name, gave telegraphic notice of the religious.

But from the point of view of my whole activity as an

author, integrally conceived, the aesthetic work is a deception, and herein is to be found the deeper significance of the use of pseudonyms. A deception, however, is a rather ugly thing. To this I would make answer: One must not let oneself be deceived by the word "deception." One can deceive a person for the truth's sake, and (to recall old Socrates) one can deceive a person into the truth. Indeed, it is only by this means, i.e. by deceiving him, that it is possible to bring into the truth one who is in an illusion. Whoever rejects this opinion betrays the fact that he is not overwell versed in dialectics, and that is precisely what is especially needed when operating in this field. For there is an immense difference, a dialectical difference, between these two cases: the case of a man who is ignorant and is to have a piece of knowledge imparted to him, so that he is like an empty vessel which is to be filled or a blank sheet of paper upon which something is to be written; and the case of a man who is under an illusion and must first be delivered from that. Likewise there is a difference between writing on a blank sheet of paper and bringing to light by the application of a caustic fluid a text which is hidden under another text. Assuming then that a person is the victim of an illusion, and that in order to communicate the truth to him the first task, rightly understood, is to remove the illusion—if I do not begin by deceiving him, I must begin with direct communication. But direct communication presupposes that the receiver's ability to receive is undisturbed. But here such is not the case; an illusion stands in the way. That is to say, one must first of all use the caustic fluid. But this caustic means is negativity, and negativity understood in relation to the communication of the truth is precisely the same as deception.

What then does it mean, "to deceive"? It means that

one does not begin *directly* with the matter one wants to communicate, but begins by accepting the other man's illusion as good money. So (to stick to the theme with which this work especially deals) one does not begin thus: I am a Christian; you are not a Christian. Nor does one begin thus: It is Christianity I am proclaiming; and you are living in purely aesthetic categories. No, one begins thus: Let us talk about aesthetics. The deception consists in the fact that one talks thus merely to get to the religious theme. But, on our assumption, the other man is under the illusion that the aesthetic is Christianity; for, he thinks, I am a Christian, and yet he lives in aesthetic categories.

Although ever so many parsons were to consider this method unjustifiable, and just as many were unable to get it into their heads (in spite of the fact that they all of them, according to their own assertion, are accustomed to use the Socratic method), I for my part tranquilly adhere to Socrates. It is true, he was not a Christian; that I know, and yet I am thoroughly convinced that he has become one. But he was a dialectician, he conceived everything in terms of reflection. And the question which concerns us here is a purely dialectical one, it is the question of the use of reflection in Christendom. We are reckoning here with two qualitatively different magnitudes, but in a formal sense I can very well call Socrates my teacher—whereas I have only believed, and only believe, in One, the Lord Jesus Christ.

THE CONCEPT OF DREAD*

In what sense the subject of this deliberation is a theme of interest to psychology, and in what sense, after having interested psychology, it points precisely to dogmatics.

* From Soren Kierkegaard, *The Concept of Dread,* trans-

The notion that every scientific problem within the great field embraced by science has its definite place, its measure and its bounds, and precisely thereby has its resonance in the whole, its legitimate consonance in what the whole expresses—this notion, I say, is not merely a *pium desiderium* which ennobles the man of science by the visionary enthusiasm or melancholy which it begets, is not merely a sacred duty which employs him in the service of the whole, bidding him renounce lawlessness and the romantic lust to lose sight of land, but it is also in the interest of every more highly specialized deliberation, which by forgetting where its home properly is, forgets at the same time itself, a thought which the very language I use with its striking ambiguity expresses; it becomes another thing, and attains a dubious perfectibility by being able to become anything at all. By thus failing to let the scientific call to order be heard, by not being vigilant to forbid the individual problems to hurry by one another as though it were a question of arriving first at the masquerade, one may indeed attain sometimes an appearance of brilliancy, may give sometimes the impression of having already comprehended, when in fact one is far from it, may sometimes by the use of vague words strike up an agreement between things that differ. This gain, however, avenges itself subsequently, like all unlawful acquisitions, which neither in civic life nor in the field of science can really be owned.

Thus when a person entitles the last section of his Logic "Reality," he thereby gains the advantage of appearing to have already reached by logic the highest thing, or, if one prefers to say so, the lowest. The loss is

---

lated by Walter Lowrie (Copyright 1944 © 1957 by Princeton University Press; Princeton Paperback, 1967) footnotes omitted, pp. 9–13. Reprinted by permission of Princeton University Press.

obvious nevertheless, for this is not to the advantage either of logic or of reality. Not to that of reality, for the contingent, which is an integral part of reality, cannot be permitted to slip into logic. It is not to the advantage of logic, for if logic has conceived the thought of reality it has taken into its system something it cannot assimilate, it has anticipated what it ought merely to predispose. The punishment is clear: that every deliberation about what reality is must by this be made difficult, yea, perhaps for a long time impossible, because this word "reality" will, as it were, require some time to recall to mind what it is, must have time to forget the mistake.

Thus when in dogmatics a person says that *faith* is the *immediate,* without more precise definition, he gains the advantage of convincing everyone of the necessity of not stopping at faith, yea, he compels even the orthodox man to make this concession, because this man perhaps does not at once penetrate the misunderstanding and perceive that it is not due to a subsequent flaw in the argument but to this *πρῶτον ψεῦδος.* The loss is indubitable, for thereby faith loses by being deprived of what legitimately belongs to it: its historical presupposition. Dogmatics loses for the fact that it has to begin, not where it properly has its beginning, within the compass of an earlier beginning. Instead of presupposing an earlier beginning, it ignores this and begins straightway as if it were logic; for logic in fact begins with the most volatile essence produced by the finest abstraction: the immediate. What then logically is correct, namely, that the immediate is *eo ipso* annulled, becomes twaddle in dogmatics; for to no one could it occur to want to stop with the immediate (not further defined), seeing that in fact it is annulled the instant it is mentioned, just as a sleepwalker awakes the instant his name is called.

Thus when sometimes in the course of investigations which are hardly more than propaedeutic one finds the word "reconciliation" used to designate speculative knowledge, or the identity of the knowing subject and the thing known, the subjective-objective, etc., then one easily sees that the author is brilliant and that by the aid of his *esprit* he has explained all riddles, especially for those who do not even scientifically take the precaution, which yet one takes in everyday life, to listen carefully to the words of the riddle before guessing it. Otherwise one acquires the incomparable merit of having by one's explanation propounded a new riddle, namely, how it could occur to any man that this might be the explanation. That thought possesses reality was the assumption of all ancient philosophy as well as of the philosophy of the Middle Ages. With Kant this assumption became doubtful. Suppose now that the Hegelian school had really *thought through* Kant's scepticism (however, this ought always to remain a big question, in spite of all Hegel and his school have done, by the help of the catchwords "Method and Manifestation," to hide what Schelling recognized more openly by the cue "intellectual intuition and construction," the fact, namely, that this was a new point of departure) and then reconstructed the earlier view in a higher form, in such wise that thought does not possess reality by virtue of a presupposition—is then this consciously produced reality of thought a reconciliation? In fact philosophy is merely brought back to the point where in old days one began, in the old days when precisely the word "reconciliation" had immense significance. We have an old and respectable philosophical terminology: thesis, antithesis, synthesis. They invent a newer one in which mediation occupies the third place. Is this to be considered such an extraordinary step in advance? Mediation is equivocal, for it designates at once the relation between the two terms and the result, that in which they stand related to one another as having been brought into relationship; it designates movement, but at the same time rest. Whether this is a perfection, only a far deeper dialectical test will decide; but for that unfortunately we are still waiting. They do away with synthesis and say "mediation." All right. But *esprit* requires more—so they say "reconciliation." What is the consequence? It is of no advantage to their propaedeutic investigations, for of course they gain as little as truth thereby gains in clarity, or as a man's soul increases in blessedness by acquiring a title. On the contrary, they have fundamentally confounded two sciences, ethics, and dogmatics—especially in view of the fact that, having got the word "reconciliation" introduced, they now hint that logic is properly the doctrine about the λόγος. Ethics and dogmatics contend in a fateful *confinium* about reconciliation. Repentance and guilt torture out reconciliation ethically, whereas dogmatics in its receptivity for the proffered reconciliation has the historically concrete immediateness with which it begins its discourse in the great conversation of science. What then will be the consequence? That language will presumably have to celebrate a great sabbatical year, in order to be able to begin with the beginning.

In logic they use *the negative* as the motive power which brings movement into everything. And movement in logic they must have, any way they can get it, by fair means or foul. The negative helps them, and if the negative cannot, then quibbles and phrases can, just as the negative itself has become a play on words.*

* *Exempli gratia:* Wesen ist was ist gewesen; ist gewesen is the preterite tense of "to be," *ergo* Wesen is das aufgehoben being "the being which has been." This is a logical movement! If in the Hegelian logic (such as it is in itself and

In logic no movement can *come about*, for logic *is*, and everything logical simply is,* and this impotence of logic is the transition to the sphere of being where existence and reality appear. So when logic is absorbed in the concretion of the categories it is constantly the same that it was from the beginning. In logic every movement (if for an instant one would use this expression) is an immanent movement, which in a deeper sense is no movement, as one will easily convince oneself if one reflects that the very concept of movement is a transcendence which can find no place in logic. The negative then is the immanence of movement, it is the vanishing factor, the thing that is annulled (*aufgehoben*). If everything comes to pass in that way, then nothing comes to pass, and the negative becomes a phantom. But precisely for the sake of getting something to come to pass in logic, the negative

---

through the contributions of the School) one were to take the trouble to pick out and make a collection of all the fabulous hobgoblins and kobolds which like busy swains help the logical movement along, a later age would perhaps be astonished to discover that witticisms which then will appear superannuated once played a great role in logic, not as incidental explanations and brilliant observations, but as masters of movement which made Hegel's logic a miracle and gave the logical thoughts feet to walk on, without anybody noticing it, since the long cloak of admiration concealed the performer who trained the animals, just as Lulu [in a play] comes running without anybody seeing the machinery. Movement in logic is the meritorious service of Hegel, in comparison with which it is hardly worth the trouble of mentioning the never-to-be-forgotten merits which Hegel has, and has disdained in order to run after the uncertain—I mean the merit of having in manifold ways enriched the categorical definitions and their arrangement.

*The eternal expression of logic is that which the Eleatic School transferred by mistake to existence: Nothing comes into existence, everything is.

becomes something more, it becomes the producer of the opposition, and not a negation but a counterposition. The negative then is not the muteness of the immanent movement, it is the "necessary other," which doubtless must be very necessary to logic in order to set things going, but the negative it is not. Leaving logic to go on to ethics, one encounters here again the negative, which is indefatigably active in the whole Hegelian philosophy. Here too a man discovers to his amazement that the negative is the evil. Now the confusion is in full swing; there is no bound to brilliancy, and what Mme. de Staël-Holstein said of Schelling's philosophy, that it gave a man *esprit* for his whole life, applies in every respect to the Hegelian philosophy. One sees how illogical movements must be in logic since the negative is the evil, and how unethical they must be in ethics since the evil is the negative. In logic this is too much, in ethics too little; it fits nowhere if it has to fit both places. If ethics has no other transcendence, it is essentially logic; if logic is to have so much transcendence as after all has been left in ethics out of a sense of shame, then it is no longer logic.

What I have expounded is perhaps rather prolix for the place where it stands (in relation to the subject with which it deals it is far from being too long), but it is by no means superfluous, since the particular observations are selected with reference to the subject of this work. The examples are taken from the greater world, but what occurs in the great may be repeated in the lesser, and the misunderstanding remains the same, even if the injurious consequences are less. He who gives himself the airs of writing the System has the great responsibility, but he who writes a monograph can be and ought to be faithful over a little.

7. C. S. Peirce: Selections from *Collected Papers*

Peirce (1839–1914) graduated from Harvard (1859) and continued his studies at Lawrence Scientific School where he took a degree in chemistry. As an astronomer at Harvard, he did landmark work in photometrics, and he later worked as a physicist for the U.S. Coast and Geodetic Survey. His publications in philosophy date from 1866. In 1879 he was appointed lecturer in logic at the Johns Hopkins University. His later years were spent in isolation and relative obscurity in Milford, Pennsylvania, and it is only fairly recently that Peirce has been recognized as one of the most original and powerful philosophers the United States has produced.

PHILOSOPHICAL NOMENCLATURE*

Concerning the matter of philosophical nomenclature, there are a few plain considerations, which the

* Reprinted by permission of the publishers from *Col-*

writer has for many years longed to submit to the deliberate judgment of those few fellow-students of philosophy, who deplore the present state of that study, and who are intent upon rescuing it therefrom and bringing it to a condition like that of the natural sciences, where investigators, instead of contemning each the work of most of the others as misdirected from beginning to end, coöperate, stand upon one another's shoulders, and multiply incontestible results; where every observation is repeated, and isolated observations go for little; where every hypothesis that merits attention is subjected to severe but fair examination, and only after the predictions to which it leads have been remarkably borne out by experience is trusted at all, and even then only provisionally; where a radically false step is rarely taken, even the most faulty of those theories which gain wide credence being true in their main experiential predictions. To those students, it is submitted that no study can become scientific in the sense described, until it provides itself with a suitable technical nomenclature, whose every term has a single definite meaning universally accepted among students of the subject, and whose vocables have no such sweetness or charms as might tempt loose writers to abuse them—which is a virtue of scientific nomenclature too little appreciated. It is submitted that the experience of those sciences which have conquered the greatest difficulties of terminology, which are unquestionably the taxonomic sciences, chemistry, mineralogy, botany, zoölogy, has conclusively shown that the one only way in which the requisite unanimity and requisite ruptures with individual habits and prefer-

---

ences can be brought about is so to shape the canons of terminology that they shall gain the support of *moral principle* and of every man's sense of decency; and that, in particular (under defined restrictions), the general feeling shall be that he who introduces a new conception into philosophy is under an obligation to invent acceptable terms to express it, and that when he has done so, the duty of his fellow-students is to accept those terms, and to resent any wresting of them from their original meanings, as not only a gross discourtesy to him to whom philosophy was indebted for each conception, but also as an injury to philosophy itself; and furthermore, that once a conception has been supplied with suitable and sufficient words for its expression, no other *technical* terms denoting the same things, considered in the same relations, should be countenanced. Should this suggestion find favor, it might be deemed needful that the philosophians in congress assembled should adopt, after due deliberation, convenient canons to limit the application of the principle. Thus, just as is done in chemistry, it might be wise to assign fixed meanings to certain prefixes and suffixes. For example, it might be agreed, perhaps, that the prefix *prope-* should mark a broad and rather indefinite extension of the meaning of the term to which it was prefixed; the name of a doctrine would naturally end in *-ism*, while *-icism* might mark a more strictly defined acception of that doctrine, etc. Then again, just as in biology no account is taken of terms antedating Linnaeus, so in philosophy it might be found best not to go back of the scholastic terminology. To illustrate another sort of limitation, it has probably never happened that any philosopher has attempted to give a general name to his own doctrine without that name's soon acquiring in common philosophical usage, a signification much broader than was originally intended.

Thus, special systems go by the names Kantianism, Benthamism, Comteanism, Spencerianism, etc., while transcendentalism, utilitarianism, positivism, evolutionism, synthetic philosophy, etc., have irrevocably and very conveniently been elevated to broader governments.

8. R. G. Collingwood: Selections from *An Essay on Philosophical Method*

Collingwood's life (1889–1943) and writings demonstrated an unusual diversity of interest and accomplishment. Active early in the field of British–Roman archaeology, he contributed a number of important works of archaeological method and interpretation. He became Waynflete Professor at Oxford in 1934 and held that position until his retirement in 1941. His philosophical writings include *The Idea of History* (1946), *Principles of Art* (1938), and *An Essay on Philosophical Method* (1933), from which the present selection is taken.

PHILOSOPHY AS A BRANCH OF LITERATURE*

§ *1*

1. Philosophy is a name that belongs not only to a certain realm of thought, but also to the literature in

* From *An Essay on Philosophical Method* by R. G. Col-

which that thought finds or seeks expression. It belongs to the subject of this essay, therefore, if only by way of appendix, to ask whether philosophical literature has any peculiarities corresponding to those of the thought which it tries to express.

Literature as a genus is divided into the species poetry and prose. Prose is marked by a distinction between matter and form: what we say and how we say it. The formal elements are those which we call literary quality, style, writing, and so forth; the material elements are what we generally call the 'contents' of the work. Each part has its own scale of values. On its formal side, prose should be clear, expressive, and in the most general sense of that word beautiful; on its material side, it should be well thought out, intelligent, and in a general sense true. To satisfy the first claim the prose writer must be an artist; to satisfy the second, he must be a thinker.

2. These parts are distinct, but they cannot be separated. As elements in prose, neither can exist without the other. If it were possible for a book to be well thought out but ill written, it would not be literature at all; if it could be well written but ill thought out, it would at any rate not be prose. But the two do not exist in equilibrium. The formal part is the servant of the material. We speak well, in prose, only in order to say what we mean: the matter is prior to the form. This priority, no doubt, is rather logical than temporal. The matter does not exist as a naked but fully formed thought in our minds before we fit it with a garment of words. It is only in some dark and half-conscious way that we know our thoughts before we come to express them. Yet in that obscure fashion they are already

---

lingwood, published by Oxford University Press (1933) pp. 119–220. Reprinted by permission of the publisher.

within us; and, rising into full consciousness as we find the words to utter them, it is they that determine the words, not vice versa.

3. In poetry, this distinction between matter and form does not exist. Instead of two linked problems, finding out what he wants to say and finding out how to say it, the poet has only one problem. Instead of having to satisfy two standards of value, beauty and truth, the poet recognizes only one. The sole business of a poem is to be beautiful; its sole merits are formal or literary merits. In the sense in which the prose writer is trying to say something, there is nothing that the poet is trying to say; he is trying simply to speak.

4. Prose and poetry are philosophically distinct species of a genus; consequently they overlap. Literary excellence, which is the means to an end in prose and the sole end or essence of poetry, is the same thing in both cases. Judged by a purely literary or artistic standard, the merits of even the best prose are inferior to those of even commonplace poetry; for these qualities are of necessity degraded in becoming means instead of ends; yet the prose writer does inhabit the mountain of poetry, though he lives only on its lower slopes, and drinks of its waters not fresh from their spring but muddy with the silt of their stream-beds.

5. This distinction must not be confused with the distinction between prose and verse, which is an empirical division between two ways of writing, either of which may be poetical or prosaic in character. There is no doubt a tendency for poetry to take the outward shape of verse; that is because verse, in its patterns of rhythm and rhyme, expresses a native tendency on the part of language to organize itself according to intrinsic formal characters whenever it is liberated from the task of expressing thought. Similar formal patterns are always emerging in the structure of prose, only to be lost

again; they emerge because without them language would be wholly non-poetical and would therefore cease to be language; they are lost again because form is here subordinate to matter, and the poetry inherent in language is therefore shattered into an infinity of inchoate poems.

§ 2

6. Philosophy as a kind of literature belongs to the realm of prose. But within that realm it has certain characteristics of its own, which can best be seen by comparing it with the literatures of science and of history.

Scientific literature contains, as a noteworthy element in its vocabulary, a number of technical terms. If the scientist were refused permission to use these terms, he could not express his strictly scientific thoughts at all; by using them more and more freely, he comes to express himself with greater and greater ease and sureness. In philosophical literature, technical terms are regarded with some suspicion. They are slightingly described as jargon, and philosophers who use them much are derided as pedants or criticized for evading the duty of explaining themselves and the even more urgent duty of understanding themselves.

This impression of a difference between the ideals of a scientific vocabulary and a philosophical is only deepened by observing that many of the greatest philosophers, especially those who by common consent have written well in addition to thinking well, have used nothing that can be called a technical vocabulary. Berkeley has none; Plato none, if consistency of usage is a test; Descartes none, except when he uses a technical term to point a reference to the thoughts of others; and where a great philosopher like Kant seems to revel in them, it is by no means agreed that his thought gains proportionately in precision and intelligibility, or that the stylist in him is equal to the philosopher.

A general review of the history of philosophy compared with the equally long history of mathematics, would show that whereas exact science has from the first been at pains to build up a technical vocabulary in which every term should have a rigid and constant meaning, philosophy has always taken a different road: its terms have shifted their meaning from one writer to another, and in successive phases of the same writer's work, in a way which is the exact opposite of what we find in science, and would justify the assertion that, in the strict sense of the word technical, philosophy has never had anything that deserved the name of a technical vocabulary.

Before concluding that this is a state of things calling for amendment, it may be well to ask what technical terms are, and why they are needed in the expression of scientific thought.

7. Technical terms are terms not used in ordinary speech, but invented *ad hoc* for a special purpose, or else they are borrowed from ordinary speech but used *ad hoc* in a special sense. They are needed because it is desired to express a thought for whose expression ordinary speech does not provide. Hence, because they are essentially innovations in vocabulary, and artificial or arbitrary innovations, they cannot be understood and therefore must not be used unless they are defined: and definition, here, means "verbal" as distinct from "real" definition.

It has sometimes been maintained that all language consists of sounds taken at pleasure to serve as marks for certain thoughts or things: which would amount to saying that it consists of technical terms. But since a technical term implies a definition, it is impossible that all words should be technical terms, for if they were we could never understand their definitions. The business of language is to express or explain; if language cannot explain itself, nothing else can explain it; and a technical term, in so far as it calls for explanation, is to that extent not language but something else which resembles language in being significant, but differs from it in not being expressive or self-explanatory. Perhaps I may point the distinction by saying that it is properly not a word but a symbol, using this term as when we speak of mathematical symbols. The technical vocabulary of science is thus neither a language nor a special part of language, but a symbolism like that of mathematics. It presupposes language, for the terms of which it consists are intelligible only when defined, and they must be defined in ordinary or non-technical language, that is, in language proper. But language proper does not presuppose technical terms, for in poetry, where language is most perfectly and purely itself, no technical terms are either used or presupposed, any more than in the primitive speech of childhood or the ordinary speech of conversation.

Thus the technical element in scientific language is an element foreign to the essence of language as such. So far as scientific literature allows itself to be guided by its natural tendency to rely on technical terms, scientific prose falls apart into two things: expressions, as a mathematician speaks of expressions, made up of technical terms, which signify scientific thought but are not language, and the verbal definitions of these terms, which are language but do not signify scientific thought.

8. Philosophical literature shows no such tendency. Even when, owing to the mistaken idea that whatever is good in science will prove good in philosophy, it has tried to imitate science in this respect, the imitation has

been slight and superficial, and the further it has gone the less good it has done. This is because the peculiar necessity for a technical vocabulary in science has no counterpart in philosophy.

Technical terms are needed in science because in the course of scientific thought we encounter concepts which are wholly new to us, and for which therefore we must have wholly new names. Such words as chiliagon and pterodactyl are additions to our vocabulary because the things for which they stand are additions to our experience. This is possible because the concepts of science are divided into mutually exclusive species, and consequently there can be specifications of a familiar genus which are altogether new to us.

In philosophy, where the species of a genus are not mutually exclusive, no concept can ever come to us as an absolute novelty; we can only come to know better what to some extent we knew already. We therefore never need an absolutely new word for an absolutely new thing. But we do constantly need relatively new words for relatively new things: words with which to indicate the new aspects, new distinctions, new connexions which thought brings to light in a familiar subject-matter; and even these are not so much new to us as hitherto imperfectly apprehended.

This demand cannot be satisfied by technical terms. On the contrary, technical terms, owing to their rigidity and artificiality, are a positive impediment to its satisfaction. In order to satisfy it, a vocabulary needs two things: groups of words nearly but not quite synonymous, differentiated by shades of meaning which for some purposes can be ignored and for others become important; and single words which, without being definitely equivocal, have various senses distinguished according to the ways in which they are used.

9. These two characteristics are precisely those which ordinary language, as distinct from a technical vocabulary, possesses. It is easy to verify this statement by comparing the scientific definition of such a word as circle with the account given for example in the *Oxford English Dictionary* of what the same word means or may mean in ordinary usage. If it is argued, according to the method followed elsewhere in this essay, that since technical terms are used in science something corresponding to them, *mutatis mutandis*, will be found in philosophy, the modifications necessary to change the concept of a technical term from the shape appropriate to science into the shape appropriate to philosophy will deprive it exactly of what makes it a technical term and convert it into ordinary speech.

The language of philosophy is therefore, as every careful reader of the great philosophers already knows, a literary language and not a technical. Wherever a philosopher uses a term requiring formal definition, as distinct from the kind of exposition described in the fourth chapter, the intrusion of a non-literary element into his language corresponds with the intrusion of a non-philosophical element into his thought: a fragment of science, a piece of inchoate philosophizing, or a philosophical error; three things not, in such a case, easily to be distinguished.

The duty of the philosopher as a writer is therefore to avoid the technical vocabulary proper to science, and to choose his words according to the rules of literature. His terminology must have that expressiveness, that flexibility, that dependence upon context, which are the hall-marks of a literary use of words as opposed to a technical use of symbols.

A corresponding duty rests with the reader of philosophical literature, who must remember that he is reading a language and not a symbolism. He must neither think that his author is offering a verbal definition when he is making some statement about the essence of a concept—a fertile source of sophistical criticisms—nor complain when nothing resembling such a definition is given; he must expect philosophical terms to express their own meaning by the way in which they are used, like the words of ordinary speech. He must not expect one word always to mean one thing in the sense that its meaning undergoes no kind of change; he must expect philosophical terminology, like all language, to be always in process of development, and he must recollect that this, so far from making it harder to understand, is what makes it able to express its own meaning instead of being incomprehensible apart from definitions, like a collection of rigid and therefore artificial technical terms.

§ *3*

10. In using words as words, that is, in writing literary or artistic prose, the philosopher resembles the historian. But here again there are differences. Expounding a concept and narrating a sequence of events both demand artistic writing; but the difference in subject-matter entails a corresponding difference in style.

Historical writing is an attempt to communicate to the reader something which the writer selects for communication out of his store of knowledge. He never tries to write down all he knows about his subject, but only a part of it. Indeed, this is all he can do. Events in time fall outside one another; but they are connected by chains of consequence; and therefore, since those we know are linked in this way with others which we do not know, there is always a certain element of incomprehensibility even in those we know best. Therefore our knowledge of any given fact is incomplete; because it is incomplete, we cannot say how incomplete it is; and all we can be sure of is some central nucleus of knowledge, beyond which there extends in every direction a penumbra of uncertainty. In historical writing, what we aim at doing is to express this nucleus of knowledge, ignoring the uncertainties that lie outside it. We try to steer clear of doubts and problems, and stick to what is certain. This division of what we know into what we know for certain and what we know in a doubtful or problematic way, the first being narrated and the second suppressed, gives every historical writer an air of knowing more than he says, and addressing himself to a reader who knows less than he. All historical writing is thus primarily addressed to a reader, and a relatively uninformed reader; it is therefore instructive or didactic in style. The reader is kept at arm's length, and is never admitted into the intimacy of the writer's mind; the writer, however conscientiously he cites authorities, never lays bare the processes of thought which have led him to his conclusions, because that would defer the completion of his narrative to the Greek calends, while he discussed his own states of consciousness, in which the reader is not interested.

11. Philosophy is in this respect the opposite of history. Every piece of philosophical writing is primarily addressed by the author to himself. Its purpose is not to select from among his thoughts those of which he is certain and to express those, but the very opposite: to fasten upon the difficulties and obscurities in which he finds himself involved, and try, if not to solve or remove them, at least to understand them better. The philosopher is forced to work in this way by the inextricable unity of the object which he studies; it is not dispersed over space, as in physics, or over time, as in history; it is not a genus cut up into mutually exclusive

species, or a whole whose parts can be understood separately; in thinking of it, therefore, he must always be probing into the darkest parts, as a guide trying to keep his party together must always be hastening the hindmost. The philosopher therefore, in the course of his business, must always be confessing his difficulties, whereas the historian is always to some extent concealing them. Consequently the difference between the writer's position and the reader's, which is so clear in historical literature, and is the cause of its didactic manner, does not exist in the literature of philosophy. The philosophers who have had the deepest instinct for style have repeatedly shrunk from adopting the form of a lecture or instructive address, and chosen instead that of a dialogue in which the work of self-criticism is parcelled out among the dramatis personae, or a meditation in which the mind communes with itself, or a dialectical process where the initial position is modified again and again as difficulties in it come to light.

Common to all these literary forms is the notion of philosophical writing as essentially a confession, a search by the mind for its own failings and an attempt to remedy them by recognizing them. Historians may be pardoned, even praised, for a slightly dogmatic and hectoring tone, a style calculated to deepen the sense of division between themselves and their readers, an attempt to impress and convince. Philosophers are debarred from these methods. Their only excuse for writing is that they mean to make a clean breast, first to themselves, and then to their readers, if they have any. Their style must be the plain and modest style proper to confession, a style not devoid of feeling, yet devoid of the element of bombast which sits not ungracefully upon the historian. They must sedulously avoid the temptation to impress their readers with a sense of inferiority in learning or ingenuity to their authors. They must never instruct or admonish; or at least, they must never instruct or admonish their readers, but only themselves.

12. There is accordingly a difference in attitude towards what he reads between the reader of historical literature and the reader of philosophical. In reading the historians, we "consult" them. We apply to the store of learning in their minds for a grant of knowledge to make good the lack in our own. We do not seek to follow the processes of thought by which they came to know these things; we can only do that by becoming equally accomplished historians ourselves, and this we cannot do by reading their books, but only by working as they have worked at the original sources. In reading the philosophers, we "follow" them: that is, we understand what they think, and reconstruct in ourselves, so far as we can, the processes by which they have come to think it. There is an intimacy in the latter relation which can never exist in the former. What we demand of the historian is a product of his thought; what we demand of the philosopher is his thought itself. The reader of a philosophical work is committing himself to the enterprise of living through the same experience that his author lived through; if for lack of sympathy, patience, or any other quality he cannot do this, his reading is worthless.

§ 4

13. In this respect philosophy resembles poetry; for in poetry also the writer confesses himself to the reader, and admits him to the extremest intimacy. Hence the two things are sometimes confused, especially by persons who look upon each with suspicion as an outrage on the privacy of the individual mind; and because the resemblance becomes increasingly

evident as philosophy becomes increasingly philosophical, this hostility singles out the greatest philosophers for peculiar obloquy, and finds in their writing a mere expression of emotion, or poem.

Even granting the justice of that description, it is incomplete. A philosophical work, if it must be called a poem, is not a mere poem, but a poem of the intellect. What is expressed in it is not emotions, desires, feelings, as such, but those which a thinking mind experiences in its search for knowledge; and it expresses these only because the experinece of them is an integral part of the search, and that search is thought itself. When this qualification is added, it becomes plain that philosophical literature is in fact prose; it is poetry only in the sense in which all prose is poetry—poetry modified by the presence of a content, something which the writer is trying to say.

14. What explains the confusion is that philosophy represents the point at which prose comes nearest to being poetry. Owing to the unique intimacy of the relation between the philosophical writer among prose writers and his reader, a relation which elsewhere exists only in fine art or in the wide sense of that word poetry, there is a constant tendency for philosophy as a literary *genre* to overlap with poetry along their common frontier. Many of the greatest philosophers, and notably those among them who have been the best writers and therefore ought to know in what style to write philosophy, have adopted an imaginative and somewhat poetic style which would have been perverse in science and ridiculous in history but in philosophy is often highly successful. The dialogue form of Plato, where philosophies come to life as dramatic characters, the classical elegance of Descartes, the lapidary phrases of Spinoza, the tortured metaphor-ridden periods of Hegel, are neither defects in

philosophical expression nor signs of defects in philosophical thought; they are signal instances of a tendency that is universal in philosophical literature, and to which it yields in proportion as its thought is more profound and its expression more adequate.

15. This provides a clue to the main principle which must be followed in learning to write philosophy, as distinct from learning to think it. Quite otherwise than the scientist, and far more than the historian, the philosopher must go to school with the poets in order to learn the use of language, and must use it in their way: as a means of exploring one's own mind, and bringing to light what is obscure and doubtful in it. This, as the poets know, implies skill in metaphor and simile, readiness to find new meanings in old words, ability in case of need to invent new words and phrases which shall be understood as soon as they are heard, and briefly a disposition to improvise and create, to treat language as something not fixed and rigid but infinitely flexible and full of life.

The principles on which the philosopher uses language are those of poetry; but what he writes is not poetry but prose. From the point of view of literary form, this means that whereas the poet yields himself to every suggestion that his language makes, and so produces word-patterns whose beauty is a sufficient reason for their existence, the philosopher's word-patterns are constructed only to reveal the thought which they express, and are valuable not in themselves but as means to that end. The prose-writer's art is an art that must conceal itself, and produce not a jewel that is looked at for its own beauty but a crystal in whose depths the thought can be seen without distortion or confusion; and the philosophical writer in especial follows the trade not of a jeweller but of a lens-grinder. He must never use metaphors or imagery in such a way that they attract to themselves the attention due to his thought; if he does that he is writing not prose, but, whether well or ill, poetry; but he must avoid this not by rejecting all use of metaphors and imagery, but by using them, poetic things themselves, in the domestication of prose: using them just so far as to reveal thought, and no farther.

§ 5

16. The reader, on his side, must approach his philosophical author precisely as if he were a poet, in the sense that he must seek in his work the expression of an individual experience, something which the writer has actually lived through, and something which the reader must live through in his turn by entering into the writer's mind with his own. To this basic and ultimate task of following or understanding his author, coming to see what he means by sharing his experience, the task of criticizing his doctrine, or determining how far it is true and how far false, is altogether secondary. A good reader, like a good listener, must be quiet in order to be attentive; able to refrain from obtruding his own thoughts, the better to apprehend those of the writer; not passive, but using his activity to follow where he is led, not to find a path of his own. A writer who does not deserve this silent, uninterrupting attention does not deserve to be read at all.

17. In reading poetry this is all we have to do; but in reading philosophy there is something else. Since the philosopher's experience consisted in, or at least arose out of, the search for truth, we must ourselves be engaged in that search if we are to share the experience; and therefore, although our attitude to philosophy and poetry, simply as expressions, is the same, our attitude towards them differs in that philosophy expresses

thought, and in order to share that experience we must ourselves think.

It is not enough that we should in a general way be thoughtful or intelligent; not enough even that we should be interested and skilled in philosophy. We must be equipped, not for any and every philosophical enterprise, but for the one which we are undertaking. What we can get by reading any book is conditioned by what we bring to it; and in philosophy no one can get much good by reading the works of a writer whose problems have not already arisen spontaneously in the reader's mind. Admitted to the intimacy of such a man's thought, he cannot follow it in its movement, and soon loses sight of it altogether and may fall to condemning it as illogical or unintelligible, when the fault lies neither in the writer's thought nor in his expression, nor even in the reader's capacities, but only in the reader's preparation. If he lays down the book, and comes back to it ripened by several years of philosophical labour, he may find it both intelligible and convincing.

These are the two conditions on which alone a reader can follow or understand a philosophical writer: one relating to the reader's aesthetic or literary education or his fitness to read books in general, the other to his philosophical education as fitting him to read this particular book. But in addition to understanding his author, the reader must criticize him.

18. Comprehension and criticism, or understanding what the writer means and asking whether it is true, are distinct attitudes, but not separable. The attempt to comprehend without criticizing is in the last resort a refusal to share in one essential particular the experience of the writer; for he has written no single sentence, if he is worth reading, without asking himself "is that true?", and this critical attitude to his own

work is an essential element in the experience which we as his readers are trying to share. If we refuse to criticize, therefore, we are making it impossible for ourselves to comprehend. That conversely it is impossible to criticize without comprehending is a principle which needs no defence.

Though the two cannot be separated, however, one is prior to the other: the question whether a man's views are true or false does not arise until we have found out what they are. Hence the reader's thought must always move from comprehension to criticism: he must begin by postponing criticism, although he knows it will come, and devote himself entirely to the task of comprehending; just as the writer, however ready and able to criticize himself, must begin by framing to himself some statement of what he thinks, or he will have nothing on which to exercise his self-criticism.

There is accordingly no contradiction between saying that comprehension is inseparable from criticism, and saying that a good reader must keep quiet and refrain from obtruding his own thoughts when trying to understand his author. Comprehension is inseparable from criticism in the sense that the one necessarily leads to the other, and reaches its own completion only in that process; but in this development, as in all others, we must begin at the beginning; and the first phase of the process is a phase in which criticism is latent. In this phase the reader must refrain from obtruding his own thoughts, not because he ought to have none of his own, but because at this stage his author's are more important: criticism is not forbidden, it is only postponed.

19. Granted, then, that the preliminary question what the author means is answered, and the reader is qualified to begin criticizing, how should he proceed? Not by seeking for points of disagreement, however well

founded. If criticism must go with comprehension, and if comprehension means sharing the author's experience, criticism cannot be content with mere disagreement; and in fact, whenever we find a critic systematically contradicting everything his author says, we are sure that he has failed to understand him. There are no doubt occasions on which a reader may say of a book, "for my part, I do not propose to spend time on it; it seems to me a mere tissue of errors and confusions." But this is not criticism. Criticism does not begin until the reader has overcome this attitude, and has submitted to the discipline of following the author's thought and reconstructing in himself the point of view from which it proceeds. When this has been done, any rejection is of necessity qualified by certain concessions, a certain degree of sympathy and even of assent.

This implies that criticism has two sides, a positive and a negative, neither of which can be altogether absent if it is to be genuine or intelligent. The critic is a reader raising the question whether what he reads is true. In order to answer this question he must disentangle the true elements in the work he is criticizing from the false. If he thinks it contains no true elements, or that it contains no false, that is as much as to say he finds in it no work for a critic to do. The critic is a reader who agrees with his author's views up to a certain point, and on that limited agreement builds his case for refusing a completer agreement.

The critic must therefore work from within. His negative position is based on his positive: his primary work is to supplement his author's partial account of some matter by adding certain aspects which the author has overlooked; but, since the parts of a philosophical theory never stand to one another in a relation of mere juxtaposition, the omission of one part will upset the balance of the whole and distort the remaining parts; so his additions will entail some correction even of those elements which he accepts as substantially true.

20. Criticism, when these two aspects of it are considered together, may be regarded as a single operation: the bringing to completeness of a theory which its author has left incomplete. So understood, the function of the critic is to develop and continue the thought of the writer criticized. Theoretically, the relation between the philosophy criticized and the philosophy that criticizes it is the relation between two adjacent terms in a scale of forms, the forms of a single philosophy in its historical development; and in practice, it is well known that a man's best critics are his pupils, and his best pupils the most critical.

9. Maurice Merleau-Ponty: Selections from *Signs* and *Sense and Non-Sense*

Educated at the Ecole Normale Superieure in Paris, Merleau-Ponty (1908–1961) taught in a number of lycees until World War II intervened. In 1945 he returned to teaching, at Lyons and then at the Sorbonne; in 1952, he was named to the chair of philosophy at the Collège de France. During the early post-war period, he founded with Sartre the influential journal *Le Temps Moderne*. His first and probably his most significant books are *The Structure of Behavior* (1942) and *Phenomenology of Perception* (1945).

THE PHILOSOPHER AND HIS SHADOW*

Establishing a tradition means forgetting its origins, the aging Husserl used to say. Precisely because we

* From *Signs* by Maurice Merleau-Ponty, translated by R. C. McCleary (Evanston, Ill.: Northwestern University Press, 1964) pp. 159–160. Reprinted by permission.

owe so much to tradition, we are in no position to see just what belongs to it. With regard to a philosopher whose venture has awakened so many echoes, and at such an apparent distance from the point where he himself stood, any commemoration is also a betrayal —whether we do him the highly superfluous homage of our thoughts, as if we sought to gain them a wholly unmerited warrant, or whether on the contrary, with a respect which is not lacking in distance, we reduce him too strictly to what he himself desired and said. But Husserl was well aware of these difficulties—which are problems of communication between "egos"—and he does not leave us to confront them without resources. I borrow myself from others; I create others from my own thoughts. This is no failure to perceive others; it is the perception of others. We would not overwhelm them with our importunate comments, we would not stingily reduce them to what is objectively certified of them, if they were not there for us to begin with. Not to be sure with the frontal evidence of a thing, but installed athwart our thought and, like different selves of our own, occupying a region which belongs to no one else but them. Between an "objective" history of philosophy (which would rob the great philosophers of what they have given others to think about) and a meditation disguised as a dialogue (in which we would ask the questions and give the answers) there must be a middle-ground on which the philosopher we are speaking about and the philosopher who is speaking are present together, although it is not possible even in principle to decide at any given moment just what belongs to each.

The reason why we think that interpretation is restricted to either inevitable distortion or literal reproduction is that we want the meaning of a man's works to be wholly positive and by rights susceptible to an inventory which sets forth what is and is not in those works. But this is to be deceived about works and thought. "When we are considering a man's thought," Heidegger says in effect, "the greater the work accomplished (and greatness is in no way equivalent to the extent and number of writings) the richer the unthought-of-element in that work. That is, the richer is that which, through this work and through it alone, comes toward us as never yet thought of."* At the end of Husserl's life there is an unthought-of element in his works which is wholly his and yet opens out on something else. To think is not to possess the objects of thought; it is to use them to mark out a realm to think about which we therefore are not yet thinking about. Just as the perceived world endures only through the reflections, shadows, levels, and horizons between things (which are not things and are not nothing, but on the contrary mark out by themselves the fields of possible variation in the same thing and the same world), so the works and thought of a philosopher are also made of certain articulations between things said. There is no dilemma of objective interpretation or arbitrariness with respect to these articulations, since they are not *objects* of thought, since (like shadow and reflection) they would be destroyed by being subjected to analytic observation or taken out of context, and since we can be faithful to and find them only by thinking again.

We should like to try to evoke this unthought-of element in Husserl's thought in the margin of some old

* "Je grösser das Denkwerk eines Denkers ist, das sich keineswegs mit dem Umfang und der Anzahl seiner Schriften deckt, um so reicher ist das in diesem Denkwerk Ungedachte, d.h. jenes, was erst und allein durch dieses Denkwerk als das Noch-nicht-Gedachte heraufkommt." *Der Satz vom Grund*, pp. 123–24.

pages. This will seem foolhardy on the part of someone who has known neither Husserl's daily conversation nor his teaching. Yet this essay may have its place alongside other approaches. Because for those who have known the visible Husserl the difficulties of communicating with an author are added on to those of communicating with his works. For these men, certain memories helpfully supply an incident or a short-circuit in conversation. But other memories would tend to hide the "transcendental" Husserl, the one who is at present being solemnly installed in the history of philosophy—not because he is a fiction, but because he is Husserl disencumbered of his life, delivered up to conversation with his peers and to his omnitemporal audacity. Like all those near to us, Husserl present in person (and in addition with the genius' power to fascinate and to deceive) could not, I imagine, leave those surrounding him in peace. Their whole philosophical life must have lain for a time in that extraordinary and inhuman occupation of being present at the continuing birth of a way of thinking, and of helping it become objective or even exist as communicable thought. Afterwards, when Husserl's death and their own growth had committed them to adult solitude, how could they easily recover the full meaning of their earlier meditations, which they certainly pursued freely whether they agreed or disagreed with Husserl, but in any case pursued on the basis of his thought? They rejoin him across their past. Is this way always shorter than the way through a man's works? As a result of having put the whole of philosophy in phenomenology to begin with, do they not now risk being too hard on it at the same time they are too hard on their youth? Do they not risk reducing given phenomenological motifs to what they were in their original contingency and their empirical humility, whereas for the outside observer, these motifs retain their full relief?

METAPHYSICS AND THE NOVEL*

"What surprises me is that you are touched in such a concrete way by a metaphysical situation."

"But the situation is concrete," said Françoise, "the whole meaning of my life is at stake."

"I'm not saying it isn't," Pierre said. "Just the same, this ability of yours to put body and soul into living an idea is exceptional."

S. de Beauvoir, *L'Invitée*

The work of a great novelist always rests on two or three philosophical ideas. For Stendhal, these are the notions of the Ego and Liberty; for Balzac, the mystery of history as the appearance of a meaning in chance events; for Proust, the way the past is involved in the present and the presence of times gone by. The function of the novelist is not to state these ideas thematically but to make them exist for us in the way that things exist. Stendhal's role is not to hold forth on subjectivity; it is enough that he make it present.**

It is nonetheless surprising that, when writers do take a deliberate interest in philosophy, they have such

* From *Sense and Non-Sense* by Maurice Merleau-Ponty, translated by H. L. Dreyfus and P. A. Dreyfus (Evanston, Ill.: Northwestern University Press, 1964) pp. 26–28. Reprinted by permission.

** As he does in *Le Rouge et le noir*: "Only I know what I might have done . . . , for others I am at most a 'perhaps.'" "If they had notified me of the execution this morning, at the moment when death seemed ugliest to me, the public eye would have spurred me on to glory. . . . A few perceptive people, if there are any among these provincials, could have guessed my weakness. . . . But nobody would have seen it."

difficulty in recognizing their affinities. Stendhal praises ideologists to the skies; Balzac compromises his views on the expressive relations of body and soul, economics and civilization, by couching them in the language of spiritualism. Proust sometimes translates his intuition about time into a relativistic and skeptical philosophy and at other times into hopes of immortality which distort it just as much. Valéry repudiated the philosophers who wanted at least to annex the *Introduction à la méthode de Léonard de Vinci.* For a long time it looked as if philosophy and literature not only had different ways of saying things but had different objects as well.

Since the end of the 19th century, however, the ties between them have been getting closer and closer. The first sign of this reconciliation was the appearance of hybrid modes of expression having elements of the intimate diary, the philosophical treatise, and the dialogue. Péguy's work is a good example. Why should a writer from then on need to use simultaneous references to philosophy, politics, and literature in order to express himself? Because a new dimension of investigation was opened up. "Everyone has a metaphysics—explicit or implicit—or he does not exist."* Intellectual works had always been concerned with establishing a certain attitude toward the world, of which literature and philosophy, like politics, are just different expressions; but only now had this concern become explicit. One did not wait for the introduction of existential philosophy in France to define all life as latent metaphysics and all metaphysics as an "explicitation" of human life.

That in itself bears witness to the historical necessity and importance of this philosophy. It is the coming to

* Charles Péguy, *Notre Jeunesse.*

consciousness of a movement older than itself whose meaning it reveals and whose rhythm it accelerates. Classical metaphysics could pass for a speciality with which literature had nothing to do because metaphysics operated on the basis of uncontested rationalism, convinced it could make the world and human life understood by an arrangement of concepts. It was less a matter of explicitating than of explaining life, or of reflecting upon it. What Plato said about "same" and "other" doubtless applies to the relations between oneself and other people; what Descartes said about God's being the identity of essence and existence pertains in a certain way to man and, in any event, pertains to that locus of subjectivity where it is impossible to distinguish the recognition of God from thought's recognition of itself. What Kant said about Consciousness concerns us even more directly. But after all, it is of "same" and "other" that Plato is speaking; it is God that Descartes is talking about in the end; it is Consciousness of which Kant speaks—not that other which exists opposite from me or that self which I am. Despite the most daring beginnings (for example: in Descartes), philosophers always ended by describing their own existence—either in a transcendental setting, or as a moment of a dialectic, or again in concepts, the way primitive peoples represent it and project it in myths. Metaphysics was superimposed in man upon a robust human nature which was governed by tested formulas and which was never questioned in the purely abstract dramas of reflection.

Everything changes when a phenomenological or existential philosophy assigns itself the task, not of explaining the world or of discovering its "conditions of possibility," but rather of formulating an experience of the world, a contact with the world which precedes all thought *about* the world. After this, whatever is metaphysical in man cannot be credited to something outside his empirical being—to God, to Consciousness. Man is metaphysical in his very being, in his loves, in his hates, in his individual and collective history. And metaphysics is no longer the occupation of a few hours per month, as Descartes said; it is present, as Pascal thought, in the heart's slightest movement.

From now on the tasks of literature and philosophy can no longer be separated. When one is concerned with giving voice to the experience of the world and showing how consciousness escapes into the world, one can no longer credit oneself with attaining a perfect transparence of expression. Philosophical expression assumes the same ambiguities as literary expression, if the world is such that it cannot be expressed except in "stories" and, as it were, pointed at. One will not only witness the appearance of hybrid modes of expression, but the novel and the theater will become thoroughly metaphysical, even if not a single word is used from the vocabulary of philosophy. Furthermore, a metaphysical literature will necessarily be amoral, in a certain sense, for there is no longer any human nature on which to rely. In every one of man's actions the invasion of metaphysics causes what was only an "old habit" to explode.

II

Philosophical Style: The Search for Categories

10. Brand Blanshard: Selections from *On Philosophical Style*

Blanshard (b. 1892) received his Ph.D. from Harvard, and taught philosophy at Michigan and Swarthmore before going to Yale where he presently holds the title of Professor Emeritus. His principal works are *The Nature of Thought* (1939), and the books which came out of the Carus Lectures (1959) and the Gifford Lectures (1952-3): *Reason and Analysis, Reason and Goodness, Reason and Belief.*

ON PHILOSOPHICAL STYLE*

Lord Macaulay once recorded in his diary a memorable attempt—his first and apparently also his last—to read Kant's *Critique:* "I received today a translation of Kant. . . . I tried to read it, but found it utterly unintel-

* From *On Philosophical Style,* by Brand Blanshard (Manchester: Manchester University Press, 1954), pp. 1–37. Reprinted by permission.

ligible, just as if it had been written in Sanscrit. Not one word of it gave me anything like an idea except a Latin quotation from Persius. It seems to me that it ought to be possible to explain a true theory of metaphysics in words that I can understand. I can understand Locke, and Berkeley, and Hume, and Reid, and Stewart. I can understand Cicero's Academics, and most of Plato; and it seems odd that in a book on the elements of metaphysics . . . I should not be able to comprehend a word."

What sort of writing was it that Macaulay was called upon to read? I quote a single fairly typical sentence: "Because a certain form of sensuous intuition exists in the mind *a priori* which rests on the receptivity of the representative faculty (sensibility), the understanding, as a spontaneity, is able to determine the internal sense by means of the diversity of given representations, conformably to the synthetical unity of apperception, and thus to cogitate the synthetical unity of the apperception of the manifold of sensuous intuition *a priori*, as the condition to which must necessarily be submitted all objects of human intuition."

In a recent book Hans Reichenbach records a similar adventure with his illustrious fellow-countryman, Hegel. He picked up Hegel's *Philosophy of History* and, before getting past the introduction, read the following: "Reason is substance, as well as infinite power, its own infinite material underlying all the natural and spiritual life; as also the infinite form which sets the material in motion. Reason is the substance from which all things derive their being." Now, says Reichenbach, "the term 'reason,' as generally used, means an abstract capacity of human beings, manifesting itself in their behaviour, or to be modest in parts of their behaviour. Does the philosopher quoted wish to say that our bodies are made of an abstract capacity of themselves?

Even a philosopher cannot mean such an absurdity. What then does he mean?" Reichenbach discusses it for two pages, but gives it up as hopeless.

I venture to give another example. One of the most eminent philosophers of this century conceived logic as the theory of inquiry, and it was therefore important for him to define inquiry in the clearest possible terms. He thought much about it, and finally offered this as the considered result: "Inquiry is the controlled or directed transformation of an indeterminate situation into one that is so determinate in its constituent distinctions and relations as to convert the elements of the original situation into a unified whole." Bertrand Russell, having to comment on this definition, points out that, far from distinguishing clearly one intellectual process from others, it could be taken with at least equal propriety as describing a sergeant drilling a group of recruits, or a bricklayer laying bricks.

Here are three philosophers of the highest standing writing on subjects of which they were masters. And here are three readers of the highest intelligence who have to confess that to them the philosophers seem to be talking gibberish. How is this failure in communication to be explained?

There are various ways of explaining it. One way, not unpopular to-day, is to say that philosophy *is* gibberish, and that if readers generally had the courage and intelligence of these three, they too would call a spade a spade. This theory has its points, and under other circumstances I should like to pause over it. Unfortunately the people who hold it commonly go on to defend it by philosophizing about it, and very lucidly too, which shows, unless I am mistaken, that one can philosophize without gibberish, and that their theory needs amendment. Then there is the explanation that philosophy, like mathematics and theoretical physics, is a very difficult business, that nothing can render abstract and sustained thought easy, and that it is really absurd to demand of the philosopher that he should be intelligible to men whose intelligence—to use a phrase of Principal Caird's—must be supplemented by a surgical operation. All this seems to be true. Philosophy *is* hard, in ways that we must consider in a moment. But again the defence overlooks too much, this time including history. Hard as philosophy is, there have been writers who have actually succeeded in making it intelligible and even exciting, not to the exceptionally gifted alone, but to a wide public. Socrates talked it, and Plato wrote it, in a way that some millions of readers have not been willing to forget. Bergson, without once descending to vulgarity, made it for a time one of the excitements of Paris. The British tradition in philosophy has been exceptionally fertile in writers with the gift of making crooked things straight. So if a philosophical writer cannot be followed, the difficulty of his subject can be pleaded only in mitigation of his offence, not in condonation of it. There are too many expert witnesses on the other side.

Nevertheless, in this matter of style philosophy is in a difficult position. The trouble is that it belongs to the literature of knowledge, but that people demand of it all the virtues of the literature of power. Philosophizing proper is a purely intellectual enterprise. Its business is to analyse fundamental concepts, such as self, matter, mind, good, truth; to examine fundamental assumptions, such as that all events have causes; and to fit the conclusions together into a coherent view of nature and man's place in it. Now this is an austerely intellectual business. To be sure, philosophy must take account of values, and in the appropriate fields it has much to say of beauty and deformity, of good and evil, and of the issues of religious belief. But it is pledged to discuss these issues with scientific detachment and dispassionateness.

Yet in trying to do so the philosopher feels a tension that the scientist seldom has occasion to feel. There are three reasons for this. In the first place, his problems—at least the greatest of them—engage very deeply men's hopes and fears. No one opens a book on algebra with anxiety as to whether the author is going to treat the binomial theorem roughly, or a book of physics with the feeling that hope will be blighted if Ohm's law comes out badly. But people do feel that it is of importance whether their religious belief is honeycombed, or their hope of survival blasted, or even whether pleasure is made out to be the only good.

Secondly, because they feel these issues to be so important practically and emotionally, they are not contented unless the philosopher shows some sense of this too. No one would expect that as the proof of the binomial theorem comes in sight, the mathematician should go off into a little purple patch of triumph and relief, or that the physicist should give us Ohm's law in a burst of exultation. These things were exciting to their discoverers; perhaps they are to their expositors; but for all that most of us care, both formulae could be abandoned to-morrow, and to write about them as if men's hopes and fears were visibly hanging on them would be absurd. But on the great issues of philosophy many of men's hopes and fears do hang, and plain men feel that their philosopher should be alive to this and show it. It is not that they want him to give up his intellectual rigour and scrupulousness—at least they do not think that it is; it is rather that when men with hearts as well as heads are dealing with themes of human importance they should not deal with them as if nothing but their heads, and somewhat desiccated heads at that, were involved.

Thirdly, because these problems are humanly so important, plain men make a further demand on the philosopher. They want him to speak about them in such a way that they can overhear and, so far as practicable, understand. Academic tradition makes no requirement of this kind; indeed, in some quarters there seems to be a presumption that anyone who writes in such a way as to be understood of the many is debasing the coinage of scholarship. But plain men do not see why this should be true, and, being one of them, neither do I. Indeed I think it an inversion of the truth. *Noblesse oblige,* in scholarship as elsewhere. In other fields, when a man amasses much that others do not have but want and need, this is supposed to place some obligation on him to consider those wants and needs. Why should this not hold also in the realm of the mind? No doubt if there is such an obligation, it holds with different force in different regions. I do not know why a biologist, presenting a paper on a technical point to colleagues, should not write in a way as unintelligible as he pleases to those outside the circle, provided it is no obstacle to those inside. But suppose that his subject is one of general interest, that the session is open to the public and that he knows many of his audience will be drawn from that public. Should he then travel the same high and unheeding road? No murmur may come from these visitors if he does. They have been told that he is a man of very great knowledge, presenting a subject that is deep, dark, and difficult; and when he reaches his impressively incomprehensible close they may tiptoe respectfully out, reflecting a little sadly that in spite of their interest and effort, these matters are quite beyond them. And so, of course, they may be. So far as they are, the situation will not concern us here. But they are not always so. Sometimes, to anyone who really knows what is going on, it is obvious that in the arts of presentation the learned speaker is almost illiterate, sometimes that, though not illiterate, he thinks that only substance matters and form can take care of itself, sometimes again that he is merely exhibiting bad manners in a region where he does not suspect there are any manners. He would not whisper a fascinating titbit of information to one friend while another who is equally interested is present, but he feels no hesitation in talking to an audience in a language lost on half of them. The French, who have earned a right to speak on these matters, have a saying in point: *La clarté est la politesse.* In philosophical speaking and writing, one's manners are connected very intimately with one's manner.

Unhappily, an awareness of this only increases the tension within the philosopher between thinker and writer. This tension grows from the double fact that feeling is the life of style, and yet that in philosophy it is generally an impertinence and a danger. Suppose that as a person concerned to lift one's prose a notch above M. Jourdain's, one asks oneself who are the writers that have managed to make their ideas most uniformly interesting. I cannot imagine one's mentioning Kant or Hegel; it is extremely improbable that anyone would mention even such masters of lucidity as Bentham or Sidgwick. For my own part I should think at once of some of the great English stylists—of Macaulay, of Froude, of Carlyle, of Hazlitt, of Lamb, of Ruskin (for special reasons I omit novelists and contemporaries). These men wrote in different ways and on different subjects—not always easy subjects by any means. But there is one trait they all have in common: they are unfailingly interesting. That makes one suspect that they have at least one other trait in common, and with a little reflection one finds it: what they wrote is saturated with feeling. The emotions of these men, to be sure, are most various; but though their feeling varies, there is no question of its presence or its strength; far from keeping themselves out of what they write, they throw themselves into it headlong; they love and hate publicly, eloquently, and with all their hearts. Now we know that all the world loves a lover, and Dr. Johnson knew that, like himself, it loves a good hater. Readers want their writers to make them feel alive and when they can sit with their authors and jeer and laugh and scold and rejoice and admire with them, they feel intensely alive.

Not one of the writers we have named could be called exact or cautious in the handling of ideas. Yet should any of us wish that these writers had indeed kept themselves out of their work? Surely not. What makes their style so attractive to us is precisely that with them style is so individually and revealingly the man. Carlyle without his mournfulness, his cackling derision, his pity for men generally and contempt for them in particular, and all the odd devices by which he smouldered and exploded into speech, would not only cease to be "the Rembrandt of English prose," he would cease to be Carlyle.

But consider how impossible all this is in philosophic writing. Philosophy is not an attempt to excite or entertain; it is not an airing of one's prejudices; it is not an attempt to tell a story, or paint a picture, or to get anyone to do anything, or to make anyone like this and dislike that. It is , as James said, "a peculiarly stubborn effort to think clearly," to find out by thinking what is true. Any person who has made this attempt with the seriousness which alone justifies writing about it knows what an austere business it is. He knows that his hopes and fears and likes and dislikes are to be rated philosophically at zero or worse, that they not only make no difference to the truth, but get in the way of his seeing it. Of course he has such feelings; he may well have become a philosopher precisely because he felt so strongly about these issues. But he realizes more clearly than most men that "things are what they are, and will be what they will be," whether he tears a passion to tatters about them or not. He knows from inner experience how often and how easily the needle of the compass is deflected away from truth by the presence in its neighbourhood of egotism, impatience, or the desire to score off somebody; and he would feel like a charlatan if he used on others methods he would resist in his own thinking. If he catches others in the attempt to use them on himself, his opinion of them plummets.

I must confess that often, when I have tried to read the most popularly effective of German philosophical writers, Nietzsche, I have felt like throwing the book across the room. He is a boiling pot of enthusiasms and animosities, which he pours out volubly, skilfully, and eloquently. If he were content to label these outpourings "Prejudices," as Mr. Mencken so truly and candidly labels his own, one could accept them in the spirit in which they were offered; there is no more interesting reading than the aired prejudices of a brilliant writer. But he obviously takes them for something more and something better; he takes them as philosophy instead of what they largely are, pseudo-Isaian prophesyings, incoherent and unreasoned Sibylline oracles.

Does it follow from all this that philosophers and their readers are doomed to roam a stylistic desert, and munch cactus as the sole article of their diet? Happily the situation is not so desperate as that. It is true that the philosopher must live in a drier climate than most men would find habitable, and be content with what Bacon called the *lumen siccum* or dry light as distinct from the *lumen humidum*, or light drenched in the affections. But that is not necessarily fatal to the life of feeling; even a rigorous austerity does not require that one's heart stop beating altogether. Of course if it did stop, one's thought would stop too. "Pure intellection," as Dr. Schiller used to say, "is not a fact in nature"; our actual thinking is always moved by feeling and desire; and unless these were felt by the writer, and somehow awakened and sustained in the reader, we should have nothing to-day to talk about. No philosopher is or can be a disembodied cerebrum; what he is called on to exclude is not all emotions but only irrelevant emotions. That does exclude most applicants, including all the gaudier and more exciting ones, but it is not, after all, a clean sweep.

What is left him? For one thing, the gusto he will feel in the business of thinking if he is really in love with his calling. Many philosophers have felt this, but found that it grows quickly cold when they put pen to paper. When it does come radiating through, it helps to keep the reader gratefully warm. Again, if a philosopher is a good human being, he knows that many of the beliefs he is attacking are intertwined inextricably with the hopes and feelings of those who hold them, and his controversial manner will take note of these involvements. Even if he thinks that religion and morals are the political progeny that flattery begets upon pride, he will know that this is hardly the most persuasive way of putting his case. The first examples that spring to my mind of this sympathy-rooted tact are not philosophers at all but theologians, in whom natural courtesy was perhaps vivified by Christian charity; Dean Church and Cardinal Newman were fine exemplars of it, though Newman at times suddenly bared a tiger's claw. Among philosophers, one would surely nominate William James, "that adorable philosopher," as

Whitehead calls him, who could write a letter of vigorous expostulation in the most winning of terms. James suggests another respect in which philosophic writing may and should give evidence of feeling. The philosopher who discusses religion, as James did in the "Varieties," can hardly bring before his readers the thing he is talking about unless he has entered at first hand into an experience of deep feeling and can convey some idea of what this is like. James could do this because he had the needed resources of heart and speech. But how often writers on religion, morals, or art leave one with the bleak impression that they have never come within miles of what these experiences are like to the people who have them!

There is another kind of feeling, already touched on in passing, that I personally like in philosophic writing, though I admit the danger of it. It is not so much any single feeling as the range of feelings that answer to the degrees of elevation in the subject. Solemnity and the grand style in talking about the syllogism would deserve a laugh, and no doubt get it. But we have seen already that philosophy takes us at times into regions where feelings of a certain high kind are all but irrepressible. Kant, you will remember, confessed that he felt them when he thought of the moral law or the starry heavens; and when Pascal looked at those same heavens, he too broke out in the same way: "Le silence éternel de ces espaces infinis m'effraie."

If these little outbursts of great and rigorous thinkers stick in our minds, as they do, there is a reason for it. They are not excrescences or lapses; they live in our memories because on the contrary, they are so natural, human, and just. Sir Thomas Browne said that he liked to pursue his reason to an *O Altitudo.* I follow him far enough to own that I like, in my philosophers, some responsiveness of mood to matter. With Mr. Garrod, I deplore the passing from among us of what he calls "magnificence of mind." It is the sort of presence you feel unmistakably in Plato, and I am not at all sure that it clouded those clear eyes. You feel it strongly in Spinoza, especially as his thought mounts towards its close and has to guard itself against breaking out with wings. Such feeling does not have to beg questions. The thinker who sees plainly, as Goethe did, that "existence divided by human reason leaves a remainder," and a remainder of unimaginable dimensions, will not feel flip and jaunty as he faces it. In common-sense English writers this high semimystical seriousness is perhaps less natural than elsewhere, though it does break through at times. It is clearly present in Bradley's remark that for him metaphysics was a way of experiencing Deity, and that perhaps no one who did not feel this way had ever cared much for metaphysics. It is present again in that curious ground-swell of feeling that runs through the formal periods of T. H. Green, and still again in the organ notes of Mansel, that powerful but forgotten writer who was praised even by Pater for his "repression, with economy, of a fine rhetorical gift."

The mention of Dean Mansel reminds us that three of the greatest orators of modern times were teachers and writers of philosophy—Bossuet, Chalmers, and John Caird. They were all deeply religous men whose philosophy was an articulation of their faith, and as they were tremendous masters of the spoken word, they were irresistible when they could plead their case in person. Indeed if one wants an example of how far the oratorical manner can go, even when unsupported by matter, I should suggest that one look into Chalmers' *Astronomical Discourses*. He knew little enough about astronomy, but, convinced that the other planets were hovered over by angelic intelligences and were probably inhabited by souls more or less like ourselves, he prepared a discourse in whose very title we catch some echoes of his rolling periods: "On the Sympathy that is Felt for Man in the Distant Places of Creation." No doubt he swept his audience off their feet, and not improbably out of their senses. Here we have gone far over the line. Feeling and imagination, discontented with being servants and ministers to thought, have got quite out of hand and are leading it about by the nose.

The fact is that there is only one feeling that is always safe in thinking and writing about philosophy, and that is the one A. E. Housman has described as "the faintest of human passions," the love of truth. This takes two forms, both of which are brought out in a sentence of Pater's, who was an attentive student of both philosophy and style. "In the highest as in the lowliest literature, then," he writes, "the one indispensable beauty is, after all, truth:—truth to bare fact in the latter, as to some personal sense of fact, diverted somewhat from men's ordinary sense of it, in the former; truth there as accuracy, truth here as expression, that finest and most intimate form of truth, the *vraie vérité*." The love of truth in the first of these forms, the wanting to see the facts as they are, to follow the argument where it leads, even if it leads to the painful flouting of one's other wants, the readiness to consider all evidence, to give full weight to objections, to believe and admit that one has been wrong, this transparent honesty and objectivity of mind is rarer, I fear, even among philosophers, than pre-Freudians at least would have thought. It is a virtue more marked, perhaps, among empiricists than among rationalists. The philosophers who have displayed it in highest measure have not been the most consistent thinkers; but even through palpable inconsistencies they have, by their disinterestedness and candour, kept a hold on their readers which the builders of more impressive systems might well envy. If a man is less concerned to see what is the case than to make out a case, if, whatever evidence is offered against him, his system absorbs it without a tremor, and goes on trumpeting its triumph, readers begin to suspect, even without definite evidence, that this is quite too good to be true.

It would be invidious to indict by name, where the evidence could only be equivocal, but it is not at all hard to name names on the other side. Of philosophers of high rank who have written in English two of the most inconsistent are John Locke and John Stuart Mill. It is easy to criticize either of them, and many a wayside sharpshooter has put his little air gun in rest and scored palpable hits on them. But Locke and Mill, if I am not mistaken, are still with us, and still read with a will, while most of the sharpshooters are forgotten. This is not wholly because Locke and Mill stood on such a philosophic eminence. Surely it is partly because of the spirit in whch they thought and wrote. Each had the enviable faculty of making people say: "If he is not right, at least he deserves to be; he puts all his cards on the table; he keeps nothing back; he fights, thinks, and writes fairly, even to the point of writing clearly enough to be found out."

But it is with the love of truth in its other meaning that we are primarily concerned to-day, not so much the adjustment of thought to facts as the adjustment of expression to thought. The two are different and seem at times to fall apart. For example, John Dewey showed much of the former while deficient in the latter; Cardinal Newman, I think, was rather deficient in the former while so exquisite a master in the latter that he gained credit for the former, too. However that may be, this love for the perfect accommodation of speech to thought is a rare thing, rarer, though less important, than the love of knowledge itself. It is the special feeling of the artist, the delight in creating a picture, a melody, a pattern of words, that will embody precisely and adequately, without loss or excess, what is in the maker's mind. An artist who lacked this interest would be a contradiction in terms; but there have been plenty of scientists and not a few philosophers who have lacked it almost wholly.

We must admit, therefore, that a philosopher can do without it; and since we are saying so much about style to-day, let me underline this remark by way of keeping our sense of proportion. "It is by style we are saved," said Henry James. That is simply not true in philosophy, at any rate at the top. There have been many powerful and athletic minds who would have regarded fastidiousness in style as effeminacy if not narcissism, and were far too engrossed with what they were saying to give much thought to how they were saying it. If there is anyone who reads Aristotle or Kant or Hegel or Whitehead for the joy of perfect expression, I have still to hear of him. These men did not need style to save them, for they had something more important. I would go further and say that a preoccupation with style may sterilize a philosopher or even an artist. When an artist becomes so "abstract," so lost in pure form, that he has nothing left to express, he finds himself in a vacuum, and the step is not a long one from inanity to insanity. A philosopher who is precious, mannered, and self-conscious is a bore, either in person or on paper. But that style, though not all-important, is important nevertheless is plain enough if we pair some eminent names that naturally occur together. If you were to cover a stretch of a hundred pages in either Plato or Aristotle, which would you find more inviting? If you knew that the same theory had been set out by Bradley and by Bosanquet, to which would you turn the more willingly? The fact is that we want of our philosophers, as of our artists, both forms of the love of truth. "Subject without style," said Professor Collingwood, "is barbarism; style without subject is dilettantism. Art is the two together."

When we turn to look more closely at this craft of philosophic expression, we find to our relief that it is less exacting than the art of the true man of letters. What the philosopher must manage to embody in words is not the whole of him, nor the impulsive and imaginative part of him, but his intellectual part, his ideas and their connections. And his prime object must be to convey these to his readers at the cost of a minimum of effort on their part. He must get them to follow a process of distinguishing, abstracting, and inferring—in short, of thinking. That implies thinking on their part as well as his; and thinking is hard work.

Now the way to save work for the reader is simply to write clearly. How easy it is to say that! "Simply to write clearly"—if that were not one of the hardest things in the world! It is hard even to say what clearness means, let alone exemplify it in speech and writing. Indeed, there is no such thing if taken by itself; it lies in the relation between a giver-out and a taker-in. If there is trouble, it is sometimes wholly with the taker-in. Many a schoolboy has thought Euclid abominably obscure, and so he was—to the schoolboy. We have all known students who sat helpless before philosophers who were classics of clarity. On the other hand there are some purveyors of philosophy who pass all understanding, no matter whose. A master expositor, W. K. Clifford, said of an acquaintance: "He is writing a book on metaphysics, and is really cut out for it; the clearness with which he thinks he understands things and his total inability to express what little he knows will make his fortune as a philosopher." Unhappily, the gibe has point. There are philosophers, or pseudo-philosophers, to understand whom would be a reflection on the reader's own wit. But suppose, to revert to our opening illustrations, that the reader happens to be Macaulay reading Kant, or Reichenbach reading Hegel, or Russell reading the logician whom we quoted. If there is failure to understand in cases like this, it is not normally because the writer has nothing to say, and certainly not because the hearer is witless. The writer has simply failed to cross the bridge. Why?

There are many reasons for such failure. One of the commonest is excessive generality in statement. Look at the statement by the eminent logician whom Russell had trouble with. One's thought has to travel so great a distance from the point where this generalization leaves it to the thing it is supposed to describe that it might lose itself in a hundred different directions before hitting on the right one. It is unjust, I grant, to tear a passage from its context in this way, and the context would undoubtedly help; but if the context is of the same sort, that too will be obscure.

Listen to this from a great philosopher. I leave out only the first word and ask you to form the best conjecture you can of what he is talking about: "X is the self-restoration of matter in its formlessness, its liquidity; the triumph of its abstract homogeneity over specific definiteness; its abstract, purely self-existing continuity as negation of negation is here set as activity." You might guess the writer of this—it is Hegel—but I would almost wager the national debt that you do not have the faintest suggestion of what he is actually talking about. Well, it happens to be heat—the good familiar heat that one feels in the sunshine or around fireplaces. I strongly suspect that this farrago is nonsense, but that is not my point. My point is that even if it is not nonsense, even if a reader, knowing that heat was being talked about, could make out, by dint of a dozen rereadings and much knitting of eyebrows, some application for the words, no one has a right to ask this sort of struggle of his reader.

Barrett Wendell, in his admirable book on writing, points out that clearness and vividness often turn on mere specificity. To say that Major André was hanged is clear and definite; to say that he was killed is less definite because you do not know in what way he was killed; to say that he died is still more indefinite because you do not even know whether his death was due to violence or to natural causes. If we were to use this statement as a varying symbol by which to rank writers for clearness, we might, I think, get something like the following: Swift, Macaulay, and Shaw would say that André was hanged. Bradley would say that he was killed. Bosanquet would say that he died. Kant would say that his mortal existence achieved its termination. Hegel would say that a finite determination of infinity had been further determined by its own negation.

Some philosophers would surely do better here if they bore in mind what great writers seem to know by instinct, that a generalization which we can make without trouble if we are allowed to start from the bottom may be quite beyond us if we have to start from the top. Most of us are incapable of moving freely in the world of pure universals or "as suches"; we are like Antaeus, and must touch ground again pretty often to renew our strength and courage. To be sure, there is some risk in such returns, for concrete things are complex, and if you are offered one as an example, you may pick out the wrong point in it. Kant was so convinced that this would happen that, for the most part, he deliberately abstained from illustrations. With all due respect, this seems to me rather silly. Most men's minds are so constituted that they have to think by means of examples; if you do not supply these, they will supply them for themselves, and if you leave it wholly to them, they will do it badly. On the other hand, if you start from familiar things, they are very quick to make the necessary generalizations. In a sense they are making such generalizations constantly; whenever they recognize the thing before them as a chair or a lamp-post, they are leaping from the particular to the general by a process of implicit classification.

How wrong Kant was is shown by the fact that even he finds it necessary at times to lapse into illustration, and that when he does, the going becomes strangely easier. Is the causal sequence temporal or not? Put that question to the man who is at home in philosophy, and he will no doubt find it specific enough. Put it to the ordinary reader, and the chances are that you will draw a blank. Causality? Temporality? Nothing burgeons for him out of those dry sticks. Then try the tack that Kant, by a happy inspiration, did try. Instead of leaving the reader in midair to float down to the right case if he can find it, start him out with a particular case, a crucial one if possible, and let him see the general problem, and perhaps its solution, by himself. A lead ball is resting on a cushion. The pressure of the ball is causing a dent in the cushion. Is that situation clear? Yes. Very well, does the dent come after the pressure that causes it or not? That is the same problem as before. But what a difference in clearness and interest!

I said that in respect to clearness, empiricists come out on the whole better than rationalists. We can see now that this is no accident. Empiricists think that the meaning and test of thought lie in sensible experience, and hence they hover about this hearthstone much more closely than the far-ranging rationalists. Locke, Berkeley, and Hume are much more intelligible to most readers than their rationalist contemporaries, Spinoza,

Leibniz, and Kant. Some philosophers of an empirical turn have speculated helpfully on what their advantage consists in. Charles Sanders Peirce, for example, wrote an essay on "How to Make Our Ideas Clear," which has had a very wide reading. Peirce links clarity and concreteness so intimately that he virtually reduces the one to the other; he holds that unless there are particular things or events in experience at which one can ideally point and say "that is what I meant," one really means nothing at all. What does the theologian mean when he talks about God? A being, he may say, that eye has not seen, nor ear heard, neither has it entered into the heart of man to conceive him. Exactly, Peirce would point out; if you cannot see or hear or otherwise perceive him, you cannot conceive him either. What, if anything, then, does the word mean? It means solely, Peirce would say, the differences that would be made in experience if God did exist; "Our idea of anything," he says, "*is* our idea of its sensible effects"; "our conception of these effects is the whole of our conception of the object." Now this, as stated, does not, I think, make sense. If our thought of a thing is really exhausted in our thought of its sensible effects, to talk about the "it" that causes these effects must be meaningless. But what Peirce was trying to say has now been said rather more coherently by the positivists. Outside mathematics, they would say, to think and write clearly is to give every statement a reference to one distinct fact of sense perception; a statement means the experience that would serve to verify it, and if there is no such experience, we are not really thinking about anything.

This doctrine seems to me at once deplorable philosophy and admirable literary advice. It is deplorable as philosophy because there are too many things that I can obviously think of which never have been or will be part of my own or anyone else's sense experience, such as your ideas as you listen to this, or the physicist's wavicles, or the relation of implication. But it is a useful admonition nevertheless, because if we cannot convert our generalizations on call into statements about particular instances, that does show in nine cases out of ten that we are not yet clear as to what precisely we are trying to say. If we are going to deal in paper money, let us at least be sure it is convertible into coin. The habitual practice of such conversion is one of the surest devices for responsible thinking and clear writing. On the logical side it serves to bring to light the instances that might shake or destroy our principle; and, as T. H. Huxley said, there is nothing like a sordid fact to slay a beautiful theory. On the expository side, it supplies a liberal chest of tools with which to sharpen and drive home our point. On this matter there are philosophers who might contemplate with profit the lively figure of Bernard Shaw. The "dismal science" of economics, with its complicated laws of price fixation and its still more complicated theory of international exchange, had long been a forbiddingly technical affair to the man who must do such reading in his slippers if at all. Shaw, in his *Intelligent Woman's Guide*, discussed these formidable problems in terms of a housewife shopping for frocks, and, to the pleased astonishment of thousands of readers, they became for the first time clear.

11. Berel Lang: "Space, Time, and Philosophical Style"

Lang (b. 1933) received degrees from Yale and Columbia, and is presently professor of philosophy at the University of Colorado. He edited (with Forrest Williams) *Marxism and Art* (1972), *The Concept of Style* (1979), and he is the author of *Art and Inquiry* (1975).

SPACE, TIME, AND PHILOSOPHICAL STYLE*

The light dove, cleaving the air in her free flight, and feeling its resistance, might imagine that its flight would be still easier in empty space.

Kant, Introduction to *Critique of Pure Reason*

My work consists of two parts: the one presented here plus all that I have *not written*.

Wittgenstein, letter to von Ficker, referring to the *Tractatus*.

* Originally published in *Critical Inquiry*, Volume 2, Number 2.

It is a continuing irony that in an age of philosophical self-consciousness philosophers have been largely indifferent to questions about their own means of expression. It is as though they had tacitly established a distinction between form and matter, and had also asserted an order of priority between them: the "matter" was what they would deal with—the form of its expression being an accidental feature of the acts of conception and communication. To be sure, there is a method, or at least a dogma, behind this inclination. If one assumed that philosophical discourse cloaks the outline of a natural propositional logic, then the mode of discourse would indeed be arbitrarily related to its substance; at most, the medium of discourse would reflect an aesthetic decision—where "aesthetic" is meant to suggest a matter of taste, and "taste" in turn, a non-cognitive ground. However one first put the utterance, it could be translated into a proposition of standard form which was either true or false.

But this presumption at once concedes too much to the grasp of logical structure and too little to the contingencies of philosophical truth. At all events it is a dogma, and if not the first or largest in the line of such "scandals to philosophy," it yet warrants attention, specifically to the question of how the kernel of truth from which (like most dogmas) it grew turned against itself. The issue thus raised need not be pre-judged by us either: everything said here will be directed to the question of whether there is a connection between the form and the substance of philosophical expression; or again, later, of what in the same source has acted in so many accounts to render the connection invisible. I shall be suggesting, from small beginnings, that the link between the form and the content of philosophical writing is more fundamental even conceptually than the distinction between them; and that from the recognition of this bond may follow a larger program for the analysis of philosophical style—a program which bears directly on the practice or "doing" of philosophy itself.

1. In its recent work, literary theory has fruitfully employed the concept of the author's "point-of-view."[1] That concept refers to the way in which the author of the literary work or, more precisely, his persona in the work affects the pattern of literary action. The possible variety of these appearances, once the principle is indicated, is evident. The author may, for example, act openly as a "teller," explicitly directing the reader's attention, asking questions, passing judgment on the events of the literary process as or after or before they occur. He may otherwise, under a superficial cover, establish his presence through one of the characters of the work, by means of the authorial "I" or by such emphasis or autobiographical fidelity that the identification becomes unmistakable. Again, he may act less overtly, as the concealed narrator who reports a sequence of events under the semblance of a bystander's neutrality. Here, too, variations occur. The more fully the author is informed on private events—feelings, thoughts—in the lives of his characters, the more the author, however concealed, asserts himself as omnipotent controller and thus principal of the narration: to know all, where the knower is also creator, is to be accountable for everything. At the other extreme, the fullest attempt at self-effacement will occur as the very notion of a sequence of narrated events is placed in doubt—where, as in the "New Novel" of Saurraute and Robbe-Grillet, the figure of the author is submerged in an express reluctance even to impose continuity on the events of the narration. (It is important to note the limits to this extreme: the author will be with us in *some* form unless, *per impossibile,* the events described and also their descriptions are fully random.)

Analysis of these variations on the author's point-of-view affords a useful means of stylistic discrimination: its categories have served to make intelligible the procedural differences among such authors as Sterne, Dickens, and James—and also among the works of a single author (for example, those of Conrad[2]). These concrete stylistic differences also subtend more abstract features like the generic status of the individual works. The lyric poem, for example, involves a distinctive appearance of the author's persona: the "I" usually figures as both "subject" and "substance" (to cite Dewey's distinction) of the poem—related in both those aspects to a single and personal moment of experience. A ready contrast to this generic feature marks the epic poem where the author's persona is transpersonal or intersubjective—to the extent that Lukacs in *The Theory of the Novel* argues that the point-of-view which shapes the epic is that not of the individual author, but of the author's society as a whole.

These distinctions are crucial for a grasp of the significance of individual works, of their kinds, and finally of the medium of the literary art as such: the questions of what the import is of individual literary structures, of genres, and of literature in general, what ends they realize and what the conditions are which enable them to do this, would be problematic even as questions without these and related distinctions, even if the distinctions by themselves do not fully answer those questions. What we accomplish by such conceptual clarification may be only a ground from which speculation sets out—but that ground also, it seems, comprises a *sine qua non*.

I shall be suggesting that a similar method of analysis will be fruitful in uncovering the structural intentions and finally the meaning of philosophical texts. *Prima facie*, of course, substantial differences separate philosophical discourse and the forms of writing conventionally labeled literature—fiction, drama, poetry; the pertinence of similar analytic techniques thus remains to be established. But at least one item in the cluster of superficial differences between the two forms suggests that the issue of the author's point-of-view will be still more decisive in its bearing on the philosophical work than it is with respect to poetry or to fictional prose. The question "What is literature?" is not a necessary concern, even tacitly, of the literary author; the point-of-view which he asserts as author imputes no general character to literature. "What is literature?" in other words is not itself a literary question. The philosopher's position differs markedly from this. "Philosophy," Simmel writes, "is the first of its own problems"; and one could hardly be accused of hyperbole in finding that for the history of philosophical writing this has been its *only* problem. The point-of-view embodied in philosophical writing represents a claim about the character of philosophy as a project if only because there is no way of dissociating the point-of-view from that project. Few philosophers have conceived of their writings as belonging to one of several possible media or genres; and although I shall suggest that in fact there may be good reason for speaking of philosophical genres, this traditional reticence is not of itself a symptom of parochialism. More basically, it reflects the end towards which the philosopher moves and specifically in some sense of that term, the truth which he hopes to uncover. Whatever tolerance he may plead for variety in the modes of truth or knowledge, the statement of that variety remains a single statement or schema; we should not be surprised to discover a corresponding singleness of purpose in the point-of-view embodied in his work and concurrently reflected in his choice of a method.

2. In the following discussion, then, I attempt to derive or "deduce" a typology of philosophical writing from the category of the author's point-of-view. Because of its intended breadth, the typology will be rough both in definition and in the applications to be cited. Yet the distinctions marked even in this approximation are, I should argue, real enough; they can or at least ought to make a difference in the reading—and perhaps, at some remote end, in the writing—of philosophy. The prospect of that difference, in any event, provides for the account a criterion of confirmation.

The main distinction proposed here delineates three modes of philosophical writing: the "Expository," the "Performative," and the "Reflexive" Modes. The differences among these modes, again, are centered in the role asserted in the work by the author or his persona. That role is a function of the author's conception of the audience whom he addresses; the boundaries of the subject matter of which the point-of-view is a view; and the purpose which that view is meant to accomplish. The author, I shall be arguing, speaks tacitly of each of these through the medium of the point-of-view; the three modes differ from each other in one or more of these respects.

The Expository Mode reflects the literal force of the term "exposition" as we understand it to suggest a putting or laying out. The preeminent feature of this Mode is the static and independent character of each of its foci: the author, his audience, the subject of his exposition, and the exposition itself. The relations among these and thus finally the act of communication in which they are actualized are accidental; the process makes little difference to any of them. The author may be named in the body of the work, designated by an editorial "we" or the less formal "I"; but he need not introduce himself at all, and the difference between the works in which he does and those in which he does not is irrelevant to the Mode. The philosopher conceives the subject of his writing as an intelligible "given" whose status is independent of anything he says about it and *a fortiori* of the fact that he, or anybody else, addresses it. In other words, he *exposes* a subject-matter for philosophical analysis; his writing is an attempt to mirror or to represent that subject-matter. He may hope that this representation will be original insofar as it makes identifications which previously had not been or had been insufficiently remarked—but even if he succeeds in this, his act is one of discovery rather than of invention; he articulates what had otherwise been indistinct.

In this manner of address, the Expository Mode also assigns a character to the author himself. Specifically, it supposes that as his subject-matter is fully formed and open to analysis, he, the philosopher, is also complete, at least in the sense that what it is he is examining and the results to which that examination may lead neither affect nor are affected by him significantly. He appears as a detached observer who possesses a power of comprehension corresponding in elements of its process to elements in the object to which the process is directed. The object, as it happens, is intelligible—and he, also as it happens, has the capacity for penetrating that intelligibility.

Related features distinguish the audience addressed in the Expository Mode. These differ from the elements of the answer to the merely psychological question of *why* the philosopher writes—a question which could evoke a multiplicity of reasons including the possible one that finally he writes only for his own pleasure, indifferent as to whether anyone will ever read, let alone agree with, what he says. Even in such an extreme case, he will have built into his work a conception of what the reader *would* be who *did* read his work—and it follows reasonably, if not inevitably that the image of the conjectured reader closely approximates the same ideal of detachment assumed by the writer himself: independent of the subject-matter being examined and also of the author's representation of it, yet capable—like the author—of grasping that representation and of recognizing its relation to the subject-matter from which it has been abstracted. The reader is thus held to be essentially identical with the writer; the accidental fact that he is not the writer is in effect amended when the reader has understood what the writer has written. He then has in his head what the author had had in his—and this, it seems, represents success on both sides of the venture.

So far, the portrait is an abstraction, and like any portrait, references to the sitter in the flesh may not by themselves demonstrate its aptness. But consider, for example, the opening lines of Hume's *Treatise*, that paradigm of analytic method which "falling still-born from the press," still continues to beget descendants in the philosophical literature:

> All the perceptions of the human mind resolve themselves into two distinct kinds, which I shall call *impressions* and *ideas*. The difference betwixt these consists in the degree of force and liveliness, with which they strike upon the mind, and make their way into our thought or consciousness. . . . I believe it will not be very necessary to employ many words in explaining this distinction.

The essayist in these lines injects himself into his prose, and one may find in this fact the intimation of a less impersonal manner of philosophical writing than that referred above to the Expository Mode. But counter-evidence appears even in the brief passage cited, and that counter-evidence is dominant in the

Treatise as a whole. In his reference to the "human mind," it seems clear, Hume also includes the Humean mind: he looks on himself no less than on others as an object of experience (the difficulties he has in *finding* such objects, in himself or any other self, do not detract from the intention); his own self, he asks his reader's warrant, is a typical or characteristic self—most certainly, if the work as a whole is to make an impression, also the reader's self. The latter, too, will recognize the division of quality which separates impressions from ideas; he, too, will acknowledge that all perceptions are subsumable under one or the other category; and he, too, will come to see, as the *Treatise* expands its range of analysis to include such topics as substance, abstract ideas, space and time, causality, that they are indeed aspects of perception reducible in accordance with the principle asserted in Hume's opening lines.

A portrait is thus defined by the point-of-view shaping the *Treatise* of an author who is addressing what James later named a "block universe"—a conglomerate "given" which is all the philosopher or any observer can start from and conclude with. If impressions and ideas do not constitute a world identical to that of which the more traditional realist would speak, it is only because the realist's world is for Hume quite beyond either speech or comprehension. Impressions and ideas comprise all the world to which we have access, and there is nothing problematic either about it or about the way its inhabitants inhabit it. This is a model of knowing, if we seek parallels, to which science and the scientist, since the seventeenth century at least, have been committed. There exists, on the one hand, a public or at least a common subject-matter; on the other hand, addressing it, an investigator. The assertions of the latter are open to inspection by an audience which stands in the same position before their source as does the philosopher. It is not to the immediate point, although it is very much to another point, that in the example cited the image projected by the author's point-of-view is quite at odds with the conception both of the self and its relations which the author *purports* to be bringing into view. The former is a feature *of* the writing which in this case, it seems, differs from what emerges *in* the writing. How such discrepancy is to be interpreted is a separate issue, however, from the fact that the author's point-of-view on his subject-matter, on his own work, and finally, on his audience is firmly lodged in his written words even if those words say nothing explicitly about any of them. It will be evident, furthermore, how traditionally philosophical in character the implied assertions thus ascribed to the Expository style are; they include claims about both human nature and the reality of which that nature is part—claims which if they were expressed more overtly would certainly not go without saying and which may, in the event, not go even with the saying.

Consider next two other familiar passages from the philosophical literature, one written in the seventeenth century, the other in the twentieth. These are instances of what I shall be calling, in John Austin's term,[3] the Performative Mode. The first of these selections appears in Part IV of Descartes' *Discourse on Method:*

> Thus, on the grounds that our senses sometimes deceive us, I was prepared to suppose that no existing thing is such as the senses make us image it to be; and because in respect even of the very simplest geometric questions some men err in reasoning and commit paralogisms, I therefore rejected as false (recognizing myself to be no less fallible than others) all the reasoning I had previously accepted as demonstrations; and finally when I considered that all the thoughts we have when awake can come to us in sleep (none of the latter being then true), I resolved to feign that all the things which had

> entered my mind were no more true that the illusions of my dreams. But I immediately became aware that while I was then disposed to think that all was false, it was absolutely necessary that I who thus thought should be somewhat; and noting that this truth I think, therefore I am, was so steadfast and so assumed that the suppositions of the sceptics, to whatever extreme they might all be carried, could not avail to shake it, I concluded that I might without scruple accept it as being the first principle of the philosophy I was seeking.[4]

The second appears in G. E. Moore's essay "Proof of an External World":

> It seems to me that, so far from its being true, as Kant declares to be his opinion, that there is only one possible proof of the existence of things outside of us . . . I can now give a large number of different proofs, each of which is a perfectly rigorous proof; and that at many other times I have been in a position to give many others. I can prove now, for instance, that two human hands exist. How? By holding up my two hands, and saying, as I make a certain gesture with the right hand, "Here is one hand," and adding, as I make a certain gesture with the left, "and here is another." And if, by doing this, I have proved *ipso facto* the existence of external things, you will all see that I can also do it in a number of other ways: there is no need to multiply examples.[5]

It has been argued by Hintikka[6] that Descartes's statement of the Cogito satisfies (and gains its force from this fact) the criteria laid down by Austin for performative utterance. I prefer in the present context not to argue this point or to examine those criteria in their original formulation, but only to suggest that certain features of the statements by Descartes and Moore define a characteristic—performative—mode of expression recognizably different from that identified in the passage from Hume.

The first of these features concerns the way in which

the authorial "I" literally *shapes* the philosophical structure. In their statements, Descartes and Moore (in contrast to Hume) are referring not to a general or common self, but specifically to the individual who is making the statement and performing whatever other actions than the saying itself accompany it. Descartes himself wrote in Part I of the *Discourse* that ". . . My present design is not to teach a method which every one ought to follow for the right conduct of his reason, but only to show in what manner I have endeavoured to conduct my own." And even if we hear in these words a nuance of ritual modesty, the longer quotation cited from Descartes testifies to the presence of other elements as well. Both Descartes and Moore present themselves as selves engaged in an action; they are not speaking of independent facts or a world they never made. To be sure, what they uncover in their discourse has a life of its own and independent of the work of philosophy: Moore's hands (if his account is correct) *are* there, and were there quite apart from his proof (this is in the main what he claims to have proven). Descartes's self (if his argument stands) demonstrably exists. But the view from which Descartes and Moore as philosophers write of this is a view—if we take them at their words—of contingency, of a state of affairs which might or might not obtain, not because contingency is itself in question, but because the identities of philosophy and the philosopher themselves are initially regarded as contingent. The shift here has moved from a detached view of the philosopher's "I" as an object both like the objects of its scrutiny and causally independent of them to an assertion of the "I" as a subject affecting and being affected by that assertion.

The same point might be put in terms of a current distinction: the "I" of the author is not only "mentioned" in the passages quoted, it is also "used." The author's persona is in balance in the work itself and thus dependent on its conclusions, not in the hypothetical sense that we would all of us be different if the force of gravity on the earth's surface were ten times greater than it is, but insofar as what he says or does at certain junctures in his work makes a difference at once in him as philosopher and in the philosophical work, if not quite in the subject-matter of his analysis. The process of philosophical discourse unfolds not as an image or reflection of a given state of affairs but as a construction or performance of both the state of affairs and the philosopher himself; one hears something of this simply in the rhetorical emphasis on the authorial "I." An intelligible or "given" reality is perhaps being asserted by the two statements—but that status as given philosophically remains a function of the involvement of the authors in the statements.

The requirement which such presentation imposes on the reader is correspondingly different from that encountered in the Expository Mode where the attention of the reader—like that of the writer—is directed to an external reality for which his own presence is a matter of indifference. Here, too, he is invited to duplicate the writer, but not in the sense that if he simply opens his eyes, or his mind's eye, and reads, a faculty of his will be joined by affinity to an object—and that even if he does not, the object will be essentially unchanged. Rather, *if* the reader chooses to re-enact what the author has done, if he follows the procedure indicated by the latter, he may establish for himself what the writer has established; it is that personal and individual construction, a constitution of the philosophical self, which is the prospect offered by the writer. The reader *need* not accept; neither the procedure nor the question to which it is directed is a "fact." The author thus *wills* the shape of the assertion—and perhaps, as that will persists, the shape of his reader as well.

The claim is admittedly vague that the writer in the Performative Mode takes the concept of a person more seriously than is the case in the Expository Mode; but it is no accidental appreciation of their work that Descartes is so often linked to the beginnings of "modern" thought with its divergent emphasis from that in the medieval tradition on the status of the individual thinker; or that Moore appeared to his Bloomsbury followers to have struck a blow for individual as well as for philosophical freedom from the cumbersome apparatus of Idealism. The figure of the writer appears in this mode, then, not simply as a rhetorical image (although it is also that), but because the writer finds it conceptually impossible to take the self and its objects—even his own self and *its* objects—for granted. The contrast here with the Expository Mode is not meant to imply that experiment or the process of verification is irrelevant to the latter—but that the questions on which such procedures bear are posterior in the Expository Mode to the philosophical starting point. The Performative Mode, on the other hand, attempts to start with the reader at the beginning of philosophy as well as at the beginning of the individual problems admitted by philosophy; and whether or not it successfully reaches back to that first self-conscious point, this suggests a different sense of purpose from the one we have previously seen in the Expository Mode according to which the writer, the reader, and the world of which they are part are all confortably settled before the Owl of Minerva takes wing. It is some further evidence of this emphasis on the origin and person of the philosopher that in Descartes the problem of "other minds"—of how the individual knowing himself can know anybody else—

enters philosophy; and that in Moore and the tradition that follows him, this same question and one parallel to it, concerning the possibility of a private language, appear so vividly. Persons pose a problem here, given the beginning of reflection from an inside, which they could not for Hume who had rejected, to begin with, the formal distinction between insides and outsides. Moore's statement in his autobiography that he would probably never have been engaged by philosophical problems were it not for the foolish things which other people had said about them speaks more concisely to the same point: starting with the self, occupied with it, one first discovers the possibility of philosophical discourse not by the contemplation of some variation on Hume's matters-of-fact, but by the personification of those matters-of-fact in language.

The Reflexive Mode appears as a mediating point between the other two modes. We have noted thus far the author in his role as an external observer or agent, acting to represent a given subject-matter; and we have seen, on the other hand, the author setting out from his starting place as author, internal to the questions of philosophy, governing their resolution only insofar as he establishes his own place with respect to them. In the Reflexive Mode, the point-of-view of the author attempts to transcend the exclusivity of these two points-of-view by affecting a characteristic and deliberate ambivalence in the form of presentation. This ambivalence or shifting between an external and internal center is the most striking stylistic feature, for example, of Plato's Dialogues and of Kierkegaard's pseudonymous writings. The reader can never be free, in his encounter with these works, of the search for the author's persona. What, we continually (and finally) ask ourselves, is *Plato* asserting—about the soul, about knowledge, about the philosophical life? The same opacity persists in subtler form when, even as we close in on what we take to be the doctrine of the author (and surely we do this, whatever the obstructions, for both Plato and Kierkegaard), the reader finds himself moved not by a redirection of perception to an object which the author has seen, or by an invitation to perform an action first completed by the author—but by a lure which would involve the reader, *together with the author,* in a process which promises only that it will continue to take them as seriously (and long) as they take it, perhaps, finally, to a common point of realization.

Consider as an example of this mode the short Platonic dialogue *Euthyphro* in which the course of action follows a regular and consistent pattern. Euthyphro has brought criminal charges against his father for the killing of a slave; Socrates encounters him in court before the trial, and after the two have agreed that such charges raise the issue of filial piety, Socrates asks Euthyphro to explain to him the standard of holiness which justifies his suit. Euthyphro first begs the question by replying that what he is doing is holy; pressed by Socrates, he offers a definition of the holy as that which is pleasing to the Gods. But Socrates, after pointing out that the Gods often disagree among themselves, raises the subtler question of whether what is holy pleases the Gods. Euthyphro takes this question seriously (or as seriously as he can) only to find that however he answers it, he is still begging the initial question: either one of the alternatives presupposes a general conception of holiness. Socrates tries again by inquiring after the relation between holiness and other virtues such as justice; holiness, according to Euthyphro is a part of justice, the other part having to do with the service performed by mankind. By such services, it turns out, Euthyphro also means holiness—that is, a commerce between man and the Gods which gives the Gods what they desire. But how can man give the Gods anything which they lack? or how can the Gods lack anything? "And so we must go back again," Socrates concludes, "and start from the beginning to find out what the holy is." Euthyphro, however discovers that he is in a hurry: "Another time, then, Socrates . . . ."

Socrates' own impending trial serves as a background to the developing confusion in which this dialogue ends. The conclusion suggests that Euthyphro knows no more what he is about in bringing his own father to trial than do his friends who have brought the charges against Socrates. But the Dialogue is more than a period piece. It raises even for the reader ignorant of the historical context an abstract question about the nature of virtue; but for him, as for Euthyphro, it provides a series of apparently false starts in place of an answer. Where, the reader asks, is Plato the writer in this? To be so adroit in uncovering what virtue is not *seems* to presuppose a grasp of what it is—and yet the reader is apparently to be allowed no share of this. It might be held, of course, that the Dialogue is the historical record of an actual conversation; in this case the question of the author's point-of-view would be hermeneutically if not historically an irrelevance. But if we accept the external and internal evidence that this is not the case for *any* of Plato's dialogues, the original questions remain: what can we make of the author's persona? Does he have one? And if so, what relation is meant to be asserted between the persona and his audience?

The evidence that there *are* answers to these questions is compelling: Plato's Socrates may be neither the historical Socrates nor the historical Plato, but he is, nonetheless, the dominant figure in this Dialogue as in nearly all of the others. The questions raised in the

Dialogue remain unanswered; but the force of the questions and of the method by which they are addressed is only intelligible in terms of an object to be realized—an object which, however, makes no obvious appearance in the Dialogue. Enough has been said about the substantive role of the dialogue form in Plato's writing to suggest how fundamental that role is; I deal here only and rather sketchily with the topic of the author's point-of-view that we have been following. The articulation of that point-of-view in the Euthyphro is, it seems, two-fold—emerging both within the Dialogue (insofar as Socrates is evidently the dominant figure) and from outside the Dialogue, in the sense that the sequence of discussion comprising the work, however inconclusive, nonetheless defines a pattern for the whole which is separable from the statements of even the dominant figure.[7] The discourse internal to the Dialogue, in other words, is aimed at a goal which stands beyond it; as this is the case, both the participants in the Dialogue and the reader who follows them are also intended to reach beyond it. This does not mean that the *process* initiated in the Dialogue is ultimate—that Plato is intimating, as has sometimes been supposed, that philosophy is no more than a method. For the method disclosed in the structure of the Dialogue is only intelligible as it is understood to reach towards a substantive end: the question of what virtue is, and the elements which compose that question, are real enough. There is then for philosophy a subject-matter—but one for which the process by which it will be comprehended is intrinsic to the comprehension and inseparable from the persons of both the reader and the writer. The point at which the reader enters the dialectic will vary according to the place he is in to begin with; the author himself is at one such point. Like the author acting both within the work and in his control of the structure as a whole, the reader is incomplete—to be realized, as a first step, through the process of the work. Like the author who has shaped the dialogue, the reader who commits himself to the process *commits* himself also to the presumption of completion or fulfillment: the drive of *eros,* Plato suggests in the *Symposium*, is itself sufficient evidence of an object.

The presumption of the existence of an object for philosophy constrains both the object and the role of the reader. The object is for Plato quite real—but it is not a "given" which the reader can expect to fit into a prefabricated framework. Both the individual dialogues and philosophy as a project are intended to uncover the ground on which such frameworks are constructed—and this, too, we understand from the indirection of the dialogue form. There is no "thing" to be communicated or transferred from writer to reader. The end for philosophical discourse is in the comprehension of that point from which the specific questions of the Dialogues devolve—knowledge which requires a merging or identification between the object and the knower (whether he be writer or reader). Euthyphro, hurrying away from the conversation to continue his suit, may obliterate in his own mind the seed of doubt planted by Socrates's refutations; the reader who observes that doubt planted has less excuse for ignoring it himself. So far as he admits the doubt, he will, like Socrates, continue to search for its resolution, or finally attempt *to become* its resolution.

3. The conceptual possibility of the typology outlined or of any other like it would exist, it seems, only insofar as questions directed to style as an aspect of the philosophical surface were imbedded in the deeper structure of philosophical matter—if, that is, in asking after the author's point-of-view, we acknowledged a

bond between that apparently rhetorical appearance and the philosophically systematic assertions whose appearance it is. The anatomy of that bond so far has been gross; the possibilities of refining the anatomy are implicit, however, and return us, after some indirection, to the title of this paper.

The stylistic concept of point-of-view is a visual metaphor, and even within the limits of the metaphor cites a single item in a complex transaction. But the elements of the metaphor, the perspectival field of space and time which composes a point-of-view are not merely symbolic. As philosophers have written about the fundamental character of space and time, so, *in* their writings we may locate those same categories or parameters. They serve at that level as something more than either a manner-of-speaking or merely theoretical answer to a traditional problem of metaphysics; they articulate the philosopher's world, more precisely, the world of his work. The persona of the philosopher appears as a moment or unit of force on that space-time grid—and the question left over by every philosophical work is whether and to what extent the analogous framework from within which the reader reads, which defines *his* point-of-view, can be linked to that other framework. The distinctions among the alternate modes cited above thus appear as variations in the action and place of a unit traced internally by means of the categories of space and time.

In the Expository Mode, the interior space and time of the written work define a structure of stable dimensions; by his motion across them, the author serves as a pointer, focusing the attention of the reader on objects located in the matrix. Contingency is excluded from the movement of the effective unit of force, if only because it is excluded from the dimensions themselves; at most, the movement may bring to light unpredicted but not unpredictable occurrence. The grid as a whole underwrites a neutrality of impulse and a governing disinterest to which any activity taking place subordinates itself: the interior time and space of the written work permit no alternative. There is thus nothing originative—with respect either to itself or to the objects it encounters—in the motion of the unit of force. That unit may assume various guises, but whether it assumes the role of a bundle of impressions and ideas or of mind contemplating a particular event under the aegis of Spinoza's third level of knowledge, its formal identity is constant: the activity, its viewer is made to understand, is for the sake of circumscribing an object and quite indifferent to the results of that discrimination. The system may in some sense be self-reflective; according to information returned in its process, the process as a whole may become more or less active—or free, as Spinoza would designate this possibility. But even this variation will make no essential difference to the discursive structure as structure or to the movement that takes place within it. The image presented is finally that of a Newtonian universe in which space and time are autonomous elements and for which the only intelligible motion is that of physical bodies themselves defined in terms of those elements. The formal work of philosophy on this model, as it is seen clearly and to its end, converges on the work of physics.

In the Performative Mode, the interior space and time of the work are not laid out *for* the activity which takes place; they may only be laid out *by* it. This contingency which turns on the unit of force, the sense of intimacy which established between the latter and the structure which finally emerges, involves the viewer as well. The contingency of interior space and time is shared; those features and the structure which depends on them emerge only in the act of constitution. There are alternate proceudres which that act may follow; it is as if the resulting structure has *chosen* its form, conveying the sense of individuality which such choice ever marks out. Such apparent inconclusiveness does not deny the activity of the unit of force—but that unit now represents a process which creates the conditions of its own coming to be, a network of space and time the sanction for which is finally a sanction for the structure itself. It may seem odd that the figures named in connection with this mode—Descartes and Moore—should be identified with a manner of formulation which, in its more systematic appearances, seems the characteristic pattern of traditional Idealism. But there is an historical point here: that Idealism, however it ends (as in Hegel) by the subordination of the individual to logical form, at least thinks to have derived that subordination from the character of the individual himself. And there is a systematic point here as well: that the persona which speaks from within the philosophical work may (like the rest of us) sometimes speak more or less than it has in mind to speak and even, at times, against it. Here, too, intentions are revealed not only by what is said about them, but, more largely, by what is done with or through them.

The interior space and time of writing in the Reflexive Mode appear on both sides of the pair of frameworks distinguishable as Appearance and Reality; the purpose of the author in bridging those frameworks (and he has similar designs on the future of the reader) is to move from the former of them to the latter. Kierkegaard's aesthetic man takes himself as seriously as he feels anyone ought to: for him, the ethical and religious lives are aberrations, exaggerations which fail to heed evident boundaries. But these limits of space and time which define a framework for the unit of force representing Kierkegaard's pseudonymous aesthetes, are otherwise shown to the reader to be arbitrary, as illusory in their restrictions as the "moving image of eternity," by which phrase Plato labels the time of the apparent world. The problem for the agent in the Reflexive Mode is ultimately how to span the two frameworks, how to lead both himself and the viewer from the structure of appearance to that of reality. In humility before the problem—since it is *his* problem no less than the reader's, the problem which set him to writing in the first place—the agent conceals himself in his work and in his intimation of an object beyond it; which he engenders, if anything at all, can overcome the bifurcation. Even to explain the *fact* of that bifurcation requires concealment: thus Plato finds refuge in the "likely story" of the *Timaeus*, and thus Kierkegaard's dialectic consists always of leaps forward, never (as we might anticipate or at least wish to comprehend) backwards.

This triadic schematism of the written work is, it seems, orthodoxly philosophical in character, both in its assumptions and in its consequences; and this would be the case, I should argue for any such schematism, quite irrespective of its specific merits or faults. It finds in the work, on behalf of the author, a presentation of self together with a conception of the process of philosophical discourse; few philosophical writers can be named who, if they have not examined their own manner of expression for such themes, have not spoken about those same themes, in the abstract, as items of philosophical importance. It may be a version of humility that philosophers have commonly refrained from seeing in their own figures or manners of expression a rendering of the character of philosophy; it is more likely, I suggest, that this failure reflects a lack of self-consciousness where such consciousness is at least professed by the writer's profession.

If the interior forms described are not equivalent, in their implied discourse, to the author's written words, they nonetheless project assertive images of the persona of the philosophical author. We do not know—we for whom a mass of images have become concrete elements of the self—how that incorporation takes place; and this is due in part to the variety of selves. But the child in man of whom Plato speaks in the *Phaedo* and Aristotle in the *Poetics,* who never quite escapes his original impulses, begins life, Plato and Aristotle attest, as an imitator; as this is so, in greater or lesser measure, we may expect the interior life of the philosophical work to produce echoes in the interior of those who encounter it. The medium of expression, if it is not all of the message, is nothing apart from it either; also the form of philosophy has a philosophical texture.

The implication of these distinctions, in contrast to the distinctions themselves, is not, then, primarily formal. Even the question of consistency between the author's point-of-view and his explicit assertions soon leads, I have claimed, to issues of philosophical substance. The distinctions drawn thus comprise a background to the philosophical text as a whole, and this is no less the case for the reader who turns first to more specific elements in the philosophical thesis being argued. Within the overarching question of "What is philosophy?" other, limited questions occur; it would be foolhardy to insist that the broader question be settled or even that it be addressed before the others are taken up. And yet, of course, the larger question is never far away. "What is justice?" (as an example) remains a constant and urgent concern, one which if the philosopher ignores it is not likely to be acknowledged by anyone else. But it depends for sense as a question as much on the philosophically systematic context in which it holds a place as on the political or moral conflict which first suggested that it should have a place. The philosopher who addresses the limited question will thus also and at the same time be speaking about the nature both of that question and of philosophical questions (and answers) in general—of what he expects to gain from them and of what he or anyone else can contribute to them. Such literally peripheral stipulations often remain unspoken, but this does not mean that they do not affect what is explicitly stated; the question addressed can hardly avoid being asked and answered from some point-of-view. Nietzsche lays about him with a broad brush when he castigates the "ascetic ideal" of traditional philosophy, that standard of scholarly detachment or disinterest which the philosopher thought to honor by rising out of or above himself. But the moral of the attack in *The Genealogy of Morals* on that ideal is one which the philosopher, finally, *cannot* escape: that it is *he* who is asserting what is asserted—and that his writing will involuntarily if not by design reveal its own biography. The Expository Mode as described above purports to escape the force of this claim or at least to defy it. But that attitude (or point-of-view) is itself subject to the weight of Nietzsche's criticism—a critique which is also formulated, more gently but to the same effect, in the epigraph from Kant cited at the beginning of this essay: the author, try as he may, cannot leave himself out. As an expressionless face is still to be interpreted as having an expression, so the most covert or self-denying style will remain a style.

4. A number of summary comments may be attached to (in some ways, against) the foregoing account. For

one, it has been indicated that the modes of expression through which an author speaks may be mixed—the author shifting his vantage point within a single work, and still more probably among his several works. The conflicts reflected in such shifts provide data as well as problems for interpretation. Why, we will be concerned to find out, do the changes occur? Again, the typology outlined seems only to mark the beginning of a process whose applications remain to be determined. Can we derive from it, as has been done at the same point for literary works, a pattern of philosophical genres? The lyric poem and the novel, the comic and the tragic modes, accomplish various ends in expression. It is unlikely that the same generic distinctions will hold for philosophical writing; but the differences to which the typology outlined extends, as between, for example, the presentation of self in Augustine's *Confessions* and the universal reason which writes (and underwrites) Leibniz' *Monadology*, between Spinoza's geometry and the Hegelian dialectic suggest that analogous distinctions are there to be made. The encompassing question also remains, of what, given such formal distinctions as are described here, *accounts* for the linkage between them and the substantive assertions of philosophical discourse? The suspicion, even the fact of that connection does not of itself reveal its source.

The need is thus indicated for a "poetics" of philosophical composition—a need, it turns out, if much turns out at all, which affects the philosopher as philosopher, and not simply as stylist or rhetorician. I have not claimed for the schematism outlined here priority over alternative analyses of philosophical style, still less that it could be useful only with their exclusion. My emphasis has been quite openly formal; even within the limits of this approach, other possibilities extend beyond or around the elements of the author's point-of-view. I have not alluded, for example, to the analysis of philosophical language; and it seems probable that such analysis, of the choice of philosophical metaphor and still more basically, of the syntactic composition of individual sentences—the ontological status of subjects and predicates, after all, is a long-standing fundamental philosophical problem—would further illuminate the individual philosophical project.

It will be evident, moreover, that these same issues are also open to consideration which is less strictly formal. The appearances of philosophical writing, for example, will unavoidably figure as social devices or instruments. Whether the social reality be defined as class struggle or harmonious individualism, there is no reason for locating the work of philosophy outside of that definition; we should thus expect to find that style as a social mechanism, reflecting and opposing specific values and interests, operates also in the philosophical text. An analogous point might be made with respect to the influence of psychological forces acting on an author as he builds a systematic structure the shape of which reflects characteristic dominances and modulations, distinctions and conjunctions. Simply to mention these possibilities is at once, it seems evident, to suggest the past indifference to them of writers on the history of philosophy and the benefits in comprehension which their study would afford.

These prospective questions make clear, once again, that the present discussion has been an overture rather than a program. But at least one of its features seems to me to constitute a necessary theoretical ground for any analysis of philosophical style. A long tradition in the study of style, and not only in the lack of philosophical self-consciousness with respect to that topic, has viewed style as an adverbial concept which represents the *how* of an action—an action which could, by implication, have been effected as readily by some other means. Style, on this account, is at most a symptom—the outside of an internal process where it is the internal process which finally is at issue. Nothing I have said, I believe, would preclude this manner of speaking about the concept of style—but everything I have said, I would hope, contributes to the more fundamental thesis that symptoms, finally, are integral to the phenomenon itself. The outside of the written work, in other words, is no more—because it *can't* be more—than the inside looking out. This is, I suppose, but another recital of Buffon's line that "Style is the man himself"—even when the man is a philosopher and even if the style and the man and finally his philosophy are nothing much to write home about. The happy fortune which enabled Buffon to invent a cliche, should not, I have been suggesting, be looked askance; but if we have found a clue to the immortality of his words, we have yet to see where they lead.

NOTES

[1] Cf., e.g., Percy Lubbock, *The Craft of Fiction* (New York: Viking, 1957); Wayne C. Beoth, *The Rhetoric of Fiction* (Chicago: University of Chicago Press, 1961); David Goldknopf, *The Life of the Novel* (Chicago: University of Chicago Press, 1972).

[2] Cf. Van Meter Ames, *Aesthetics of the Novel* (Chicago: University of Chicago Press, 1928), pp. 177–93.

[3] As, e.g., in "Performative Utterances" in J. L. Austin, *Philosophical Papers* (Oxford: Oxford University Press, 1961).

[4] Descartes, *Discourse on Method* in *Descartes' Philosophical Writing*, trans. N. K. Smith (New York: St. Martin's Press, 1952).

[5] G. E. Moore, *Philosophical Papers* (London: G. Allen and Unwin, 1959), p. 144.

[6] J. Hintikka, "Cogito, Ergo Sum: Inference or Performance?" *Philosophical Review* (1962): 3–32.

[7] Note the difference in this respect between the Platonic dialogues and, *e.g.*, Berkeley's *Dialogues between Hylas and Philonous*. The point at issue, then, bears not on the dialogue "form"—but precisely on the representation of the author's point-of-view. In Berkeley's *Dialogues*, the external and internal author are one and the same; the dialogue form itself is thus accidental to the primarily Expository Mode of his writing.

12. Leo Strauss: Selections from *Persecution and the Art of Writing*

Born in Germany, Strauss (1899–1973) received his Ph.D. from Hamburg, served in the German army in World War I and came to America in 1938. He taught at the New School for Social Research until 1949, when he went to the University of Chicago. There he taught generations of political scientists and students of classical and Jewish philosophy. His books include studies or editions of Machiavelli, Plato, Hobbes, Spinoza, Maimonides, Socrates, and Aristophanes.

PERSECUTION AND THE ART OF WRITING*

> That vice has often proved an emancipator of the mind, is one of the most humiliating, but, at the same time, one of the most unquestionable, facts in history."
>
> —W.E.H. Lecky

I

In a considerable number of countries which, for about a hundred years, have enjoyed a practially complete freedom of public discussion, that freedom is now suppressed and replaced by a compulsion to coordinate speech with such views as the government believes to be expedient, or holds in all seriousness. It may be worth our while to consider briefly the effect of that compulsion, or persecution, on thoughts as well as actions.[1]

A large section of the people, probably the great majority of the younger generation,[2] accepts the government-sponsored views as true, if not at once at least after a time. How have they been convinced? And where does the time factor enter? They have not been convinced by compulsion, for compulsion does not produce conviction. It merely paves the way for conviction by silencing contradiction. What is called freedom of thought in a large number of cases amounts to—and even for all practical purposes consists of—the ability to choose between two or more different views presented by the small minority of people who are public speakers or writers.[3] If this choice is prevented, the only kind of intellectual independence of which many people are capable is destroyed, and that is the only freedom of thought which is of political importance. Persecution is therefore the indispensable condition for the highest efficiency of what may be called *logica equina*. According to the horse-drawn Parmenides, or to Gulliver's Houyhnhnms, one cannot say, or one cannot reasonably say "the thing which is not": that is, lies are inconceivable. This logic is not peculiar to horses or horse-drawn philosophers, but determines, if in a somewhat modified manner, the thought of many ordinary human beings as well. They would admit, as a matter of course, that man can lie and does lie. But they would add that lies are short-lived and cannot stand the test of repetition—let alone of constant repetition—and that therefore a statement which is constantly repeated and never contradicted must be true. Another line of argument maintains that a statement made by an ordinary fellow may be a lie, but the truth of a statement made by a responsible and respected man, and therefore particularly by a man in a highly responsible or exalted position, is morally certain. These two enthymemes lead to the conclusion that the truth of a statement which is constantly repeated by the head of the government and never contradicted is absolutely certain.

This implies that in the countries concerned all those whose thinking does not follow the rules of *logica equina*, in other words, all those capable of truly independent thinking, cannot be brought to accept the government-sponsored views. Persecution, then, cannot prevent independent thinking. It cannot prevent even the expression of independent thought. For it is as true today as it was more than two thousand years ago that it is a safe venture to tell the truth one knows to benevolent and trustworthy acquaintances, or more precisely, to reasonable friends.[4] Persecution cannot prevent even public expression of the heterodox truth, for a man of independent thought can utter his views in public and remain unharmed, provided he moves with circumspection. He can even utter them in print without incurring any danger, provided he is capable of writing between the lines.

The expression "writing between the lines" indicates the subject of this article. For the influence of persecution on literature is precisely that it compels all writers who hold heterodox views to develop a peculiar technique of writing, the technique which we have in mind when speaking of writing between the lines. This expression is clearly metaphoric. Any attempt to express its meaning in unmetaphoric language would lead to the discovery of a terra incognita, a field whose very dimensions are as yet unexplored and which offers ample scope for highly intriguing and even important investigations. One may say without fear of being presently convicted of grave exaggeration that almost the only preparatory work to guide the explorer in this field is buried in the writings of the rhetoricians of antiquity.

To return to our present subject, let us look at a simple example which, I have reason to believe, is not so remote from reality as it might first seem. We can easily imagine that a historian living in a totalitarian country, a generally respected and unsuspected member of the only party in existence, might be led by his investigations to doubt the soundness of the government-sponsored interpretation of the history of religion. Nobody would prevent him from publishing a passionate attack on what he would call the liberal view. He would of course have to state the liberal view before attacking it; he would make the statement in the quiet, unspectacular and somewhat boring manner which would seem to be but natural; he would use many technical terms, give many quotations and attach undue importance to insignificant details; he would seem to forget the holy war of mankind in the petty squabbles of pedants. Only when he reached the core of the argument would he write three or four sentences in that terse and lively style which is apt to arrest the attention of young men who love to think. That central passage would state the case of the adversaries more clearly, compellingly and mercilessly than it had ever been stated in the heyday of liberalism, for he would silently drop all the foolish excrescences of the liberal creed which were allowed to grow up during the time when liberalism had succeeded and therefore was approaching dormancy. His reasonable young reader would for the first time catch a glimpse of the forbidden fruit. The attack, the bulk of the work, would consist of virulent expansions of the most virulent utterances in the holy book or books of the ruling party. The intelligent young man who, being young, had until then been somehow attracted by those immoderate utterances, would now be merely disgusted and, after having tasted the forbidden fruit, even bored by them. Reading the book for the second and third time, he would detect in the very arrangement of the quotations from the authoritative books significant additions to those few terse statements which occur in the center of the rather short first part.

Persecution, then, gives rise to a peculiar technique of writing, and therewith to a peculiar type of literature, in which the truth about all crucial things is presented exclusively between the lines. That literature is addressed, not to all readers, but to trustworthy and intelligent readers only. It has all the advantages of private communication without having its greatest disadvantage—that it reaches only the writer's acquaintances. It has all the advantages of public communication without having its greatest disadvantage—capital punishment for the author. But how can a man perform the miracle of speaking in a publication to a minority, while being silent to the majority of his readers? The fact which makes this literature possible can be expressed in the axiom that thoughtless men are careless readers, and only thoughtful men are careful readers. Therefore an author who wishes to address only thoughtful men has but to write in such a way that only a very careful reader can detect the meaning of his book. But, it will be objected, there may be clever men, careful readers, who are not trustworthy, and who, after having found the author out, would denounce him to the authorities. As a matter of fact, this literature would be impossible if the Socratic dictum that virtue is knowledge, and therefore that thoughtful men as such are trustworthy and not cruel, were wrong.

Another axiom, but one which is meaningful only so long as persecution remains within the bounds of legal procedure, is that a careful writer of normal intelligence is more intelligent than the most intelligent censor, as such. For the burden of proof rests with the censor. It is he, or the public prosecutor, who must prove that the author holds or has uttered heterodox views. In order to do so he must show that certain literary deficiencies of the work are not due to chance, but that the author used a given ambiguous expression deliberately, or that he constructed a certain sentence badly on purpose. That is to say, the censor must prove not only that the author is intelligent and a good writer in general, for a man who intentionally blunders in writing must possess the art of writing, but above all that he was on the usual level of his abilities when writing the incriminating words. But how can that be proved, if even Homer nods from time to time?

II

Suppression of independent thought has occurred fairly frequently in the past. It is reasonable to assume that earlier ages produced proportionately as many men capable of independent thought as we find today, and that at least some of these men combined understanding with caution. Thus, one may wonder whether some of the greatest writers of the past have not adapted their literary technique to the requirements of persecution, by presenting their views on all the then crucial questions exclusively between the lines.

We are prevented from considering this possibility, and still more from considering the questions connected with it, by some habits produced by, or related to, a comparatively recent progress in historical research. This progress was due, at first glance, to the general acceptance and occasional application of the following principles. Each period of the past, it was demanded, must be understood by itself, and must not be judged by standards alien to it. Each author must, as far as possible, be interpreted by himself; no term of any consequence must be used in the interpretation of an author which cannot be literally translated into his language, and which was not used by him or was not in fairly common use in his time. The only presentations of an author's views which can be accepted as true are those ultimately borne out by his own explicit statements. The last of these principles is decisive: it seems to exclude a priori from the sphere of human knowledge such views of earlier writers as are indicated exclusively between the lines. For if an author does not tire of asserting explicitly on every page of his book that *a* is *b*, but indicates between the lines that *a* is not *b*, the modern historian will still demand explicit evidence showing that the author believed *a* not to be *b*. Such evidence cannot possibly be forthcoming, and the modern historian wins his argument: he can dismiss any reading between the lines as arbitrary guess-work, or, if he is lazy, he will accept it as intuitive knowledge.

The application of these principles has had important consequences. Up to a time within the memory of men still living, many people, bearing in mind famous statements of Bodin, Hobbes, Burke, Condorcet and others, believed that there is a difference in fundamental conceptions between modern political thought and the political thought of the Middle Ages and of antiquity. The present generation of scholars has been taught by one of the most famous historians of our time that "at least from the lawyers of the second century to the theorists of the French Revolution, the history of political thought is continuous, changing in form, modified in content, but still the same in its fundamental conceptions."[5] Until the middle of the nineteenth century, Averroes was thought to have been hostile to all religion. After Renan's successful attack on what is now called a medieval legend, present-day scholars consider Averroes a loyal, and even a believing, Muslim.[6] Previous writers had believed that "the abrogation of religious and magical thought" was characteristic of the attitude of the Greek physicians. A more recent writer asserts that "the Hippocratic physicians . . . as scientists embraced a supernatural dogma."[7] Lessing, who was one of the most profound humanists of all times, with an exceedingly rare combination of scholarship, taste and philosophy, and who was convinced that there are truths which should not or cannot be pronounced, believed that "all ancient philosophers" had distinguished between their exoteric and their esoteric teaching. After the great theologian Schleiermacher asserted, with an unusually able argument, the view that there is only one Platonic teaching, the question of the esotericism of the ancient philosophers was narrowed down, for all practical purposes, to the meaning of Aristotle's "exoteric speeches": and in this regard one of the greatest humanists of the present day asserts that the attribution of a secret teaching to Aristotle is "obviously a late invention originating in the spirit of Neo-Pythagoreanism."[8] According to Gibbon, Eusebius "indirectly confesses that he has related whatever might redound to the glory, and that he has suppressed all that could tend to the disgrace of religion." According to a present-day historian, "the judgment of Gibbon, that the *Ecclesiastical History* was grossly unfair, is itself a prejudiced verdict."[9] Up to the end of the nineteenth century many philosophers and theologians believed that Hobbes was an atheist. At present many historians tacitly or explicitly reject that view; a contemporary thinker, while feeling that Hobbes was not exactly a religious man, has descried in his writings the outlines of a neo-Kantian philosophy of religion.[10] Montesquieu himself, as well as some of his contemporaries, believed that *De l' esprit des lois* had a good and even a wonderful plan; Laboulaye still believed that the apparent obscurity of its plan as well as its other apparent literary deficiencies were due to censorship or persecution. One of the most outstanding present day historians of political thought, however, asserts that "there is not in truth much concatenation of subject-matter, and the amount of irrelevance is extraordinary," and that "it cannot be said that Montesquieu's *Spirit of the Laws* has any arrangement."[11]

This selection of examples, which is not wholly arbitrary, shows that the typical difference between older views and more recent views is due not entirely to progress in historical exactness, but also to a more basic change in the intellectual climate. During the last few decades the rationalist tradition, which was the common denominator of the older views, and which was still rather influential in nineteenth-century positivism, has been either still further transformed or altogether rejected by an ever-increasing number of people. Whether and to what extent this change is to be considered a progress or a decline is a question which only the philosopher can answer.

A more modest duty is imposed on the historian. He will merely, and rightly, demand that in spite of all changes which have occurred or which will occur in the intellectual climate, the tradition of historical exactness shall be continued. Accordingly, he will not accept an arbitrary standard of exactness which might exclude a priori the most important facts of the past from human knowledge, but will adapt the rules of certainty which guide his research to the nature of his subject. He will then follow such rules as these: Reading between the lines is strictly prohibited in all cases where it would be less exact than not doing so. Only such reading between the lines as starts from an exact consideration of the explicit statements of the author is legitimate. The context in which a statement occurs, and the literary character of the whole work as well as its plan, must be perfectly understood before an interpretation of the statement can reasonably claim to be adequate or even correct. One is not entitled to delete a passage, nor to emend its text, before one has fully considered all reasonable possibilities of understanding the passage as it stands—one of these possibilities being that the passage may be ironic. If a master of the art of writing commits such blunders as would shame an intelligent high school boy, it is reasonable to assume that they are intentional, especially if the author discusses, however incidentally, the possibility of intentional blunders in writing. The views of the author of a drama or dialogue must not, without previous proof, be identified with the views expressed by one or more of his characters, or with those agreed upon by all his characters or by his attractive characters. The real opinion of an author is not necessarily identical with that which he expresses in the largest number of passages. In short, exactness is not to be confused with refusal, or inability, to see the wood for the trees. The truly exact historian will reconcile himself to the fact that there is a difference between winning an argument, or proving to practically everyone that he is right, and understanding the thought of the great writers of the past.

It must, then, be considered possible that reading between the lines will not lead to complete agreement among all scholars. If this is an objection to reading between the lines as such, there is the counter-objection that neither have the methods generally used at present led to universal or even wide agreement in regard to very important points. Scholars of the last century were inclined to solve literary problems by having recourse to the genesis of the author's work, or even of his thought. Contradictions or divergences within one book, or between two books by the same author, were supposed to prove that his thought had changed. If the contradictions exceeded a certain limit it was sometimes decided without any external evidence that one of the works must be spurious. That procedure has lately come into some disrepute, and at present many scholars are inclined to be rather more conservative about the literary tradition, and less impressed by merely internal evidence. The conflict between the traditionalists and the higher critics is, however, far from being settled. The traditionalists could show in important cases that the higher critics have not proved their hypotheses at all; but even if all the answers suggested by the higher critics should ultimately prove to be wrong, the questions which led them away from the tradition and tempted them to try a new approach often show an awareness of difficulties which do not disturb the slumber of the typical traditionalist. An adequate answer to the most serious of these questions requires methodical reflection on the literary technique of the great writers of earlier ages, because of the typical character of the literary problems involved—obscurity of the plan, contradictions within one work or between two or more works of the same author, omission of important links of the argument, and so on. Such reflection necessarily transcends the boundaries of modern aesthetics and even of traditional poetics, and will, I believe, compel students sooner or later to take into account the phenomenon of persecution. To mention something which is hardly more than another aspect of the same fact, we sometimes observe a conflict between a traditional, superficial and doxographic interpretation of some great writer of the past, and a more intelligent, deeper and monographic interpretation. They are equally exact, so far as both are borne out by explicit statements of the writer concerned. Only a few people at present, however, consider the possibility that the traditional interpretation may reflect the exoteric teaching of the author, whereas the monographic interpretation stops halfway between the exoteric and esoteric teaching of the author.

Modern historical research, which emerged at a time when persecution was a matter of feeble recollection rather than of forceful experience, has counteracted or even destroyed an earlier tendency to read between the lines of the great writers, or to attach more weight to their fundamental design than to those views which they have repeated most often. Any attempt to restore the earlier approach in this age of historicism is confronted by the problem of criteria for distinguishing between legitimate and illegitimate reading between the lines. If it is true that there is a necessary correlation between persecution and writing between the lines, then there is a necessary negative criterion: that the book in question must have been composed in an era of persecution, that is, at a time when some political or other orthodoxy was enforced by law or custom.

One positive criterion is this: if an able writer who has a clear mind and a perfect knowledge of the orthodox view and all its ramifications, contradicts surreptitiously and as it were in passing one of its necessary presuppositions or consequences which he explicitly recognizes and maintains everywhere else, we can reasonably suspect that he was opposed to the orthodox system as such and—we must study his whole book all over again, with much greater care and much less naīveté than ever before. In some cases, we possess even explicit evidence proving that the author has indicated his views on the most important subjects only between the lines. Such statements, however, do not usually occur in the preface or other very conspicuous place. Some of them cannot even be noticed, let alone understood, so long as we confine ourselves to the view of persecution and the attitude toward freedom of speech and candor which have become prevalent during the last three hundred years.

III

The term persecution covers a variety of phenomena, ranging from the most cruel type, as exemplified by the Spanish Inquisition, to the mildest, which is social ostracism. Between these extremes are the types which are most important from the point of view of literary or intellectual history. Examples of these are found in the Athens of the fifth and fourth centuries B.C., in some Muslim countries of the early Middle Ages, in seventeenth-century Holland and England, and in eighteenth-century France and Germany—all of them comparatively liberal periods. But a glance at the biographies of Anaxagoras, Protagoras, Socrates, Plato, Xenophon, Aristotle, Avicenna, Averroes, Maimonides, Grotius, Descartes, Hobbes, Spinoza, Locke, Bayle, Wolff, Montesquieu, Voltaire, Rousseau,

Lessing and Kant,[12] and in some cases even a glance at the title pages of their books, is sufficient to show that they witnessed or suffered, during at least part of their lifetimes, a kind of persecution which was more tangible than social ostracism. Nor should we overlook the fact, not sufficiently stressed by all authorities, that religious persecution and persecution of free inquiry are not identical. There were times and countries in which all kinds, or at least a great variety of kinds, of worship were permitted, but free inquiry was not.[13]

What attitude people adopt toward freedom of public discussion, depends decisively on what they think about popular education and its limits. Generally speaking, premodern philosophers were more timid in this respect than modern philosophers. After about the middle of the seventeenth century an ever-increasing number of heterodox philosophers who had suffered from persecution published their books not only to communicate their thoughts but also because they desired to contribute to the abolition of persecution as such. They believed that suppression of free inquiry and of publication of the results of free inquiry, was accidental, an outcome of the faulty construction of the body politic, and that the kingdom of general darkness could be replaced by the republic of universal light. They looked forward to a time when as a result of the progress of popular education, practically complete freedom of speech would be possible, or—to exaggerate for purposes of clarification—to a time when no one would suffer any harm from hearing any truth.[14] They concealed their views only far enough to protect themselves as well as possible from persecution; had they been more subtle than that they would have defeated their puspose, which was to enlighten an ever-increasing number of people who were not potential philosophers. It is therefore comparatively easy to read between the lines of their books.[15] The attitude of an earlier type of writers was fundamentally different. They believed that the gulf separating "the wise" and "the vulgar" was a basic fact of human nature which could not be influenced by any progress of popular education: philosophy, or science, was essentially a privilege of "the few." They were convinced that philosophy as such was suspect to, and hated by, the majority of men.[16] Even if they had had nothing to fear from any particular political quarter, those who started from the assumption would have been driven to the conclusion that public communication of the philosophic or scientific truth was impossible or undesirable, not only for the time being but for all times. They must conceal their opinions from all but philosophers, either by limiting themselves to oral instruction of a carefully selected group of pupils, or by writing about the most important subject of means of "brief indication."[17]

Writings are naturally accessible to all who can read. Therefore a philosopher who chose the second way could expound only such opinions as were suitable for the nonphilosophic majority: all of his writings would have to be, strictly speaking, exoteric. These opinions would not be in all respects consonant with truth. Being a philosopher, that is, hating "the lie in the soul" more than anything else, he would not deceive himself about the fact that such opinions are merely "likely tales," or "noble lies," or "probable opinions," and would leave it to his philosophic readers to disentangle the truth from its poetic or dialectic presentation. But he would defeat his purpose if he indicated clearly which of his statements expressed a noble lie, and which the still more noble truth. For philosophic readers he would do almost more than enough by drawing their attention to the fact that he did not object to telling lies which were noble, or tales which were merely similar to truth. From the point of view of the literary historian at least, there is no more noteworthy difference between the typical premodern philosopher (who is hard to distinguish from the premodern poet) and the typical modern philosopher than that of their attitudes toward "noble (or just) lies," "pious frauds," the "ductus obliquus"[18] or "economy of the truth." Every decent modern reader is bound to be shocked by the mere suggestion that a great man might have deliberately deceived the large majority of his readers.[19] And yet, as a liberal theologian once remarked, these imitators of the resourceful Odysseus were perhaps merely more sincere than we when they called "lying nobly" what we would call "considering one's social responsibilities."

An exoteric book contains then two teachings: a popular teaching of an edifying character, which is in the foreground; and a philosophic teaching concerning the most important subject, which is indicated only between the lines. This is not to deny that some great writers might have stated certain important truths quite openly by using as mouthpiece some disreputable character: they would thus show how much they disapproved of pronouncing the truths in question. There would then be good reason for our finding in the greatest literature of the past so many interesting devils, madmen, beggars, sophists, drunkards, epicureans and buffoons. Those to whom such books are truly addressed are, however, neither the unphilosophic majority nor the perfect philosopher as such, but the young men who might become philosophers: the potential philosophers are to be led step by step from the popular views which are indispensable for all practical and political purposes to the truth which is merely and purely theoretical, guided by certain obtrusively enigmatic features in the presentation of the popular teaching—obscurity of the plan, contradictions, pseudonyms, inexact repetitions of earlier statements, strange expressions, etc. Such features do not disturb the slumber of those who cannot see the wood for the trees, but act as awakening stumbling blocks for those who can. All books of that kind owe their existence to the love of the mature philosopher for the puppies[20] of his race, by whom he wants to be loved in turn: all exoteric books are "written speeches caused by love."

Exoteric literature presupposes that there are basic truths which would not be pronounced in public by any decent man, because they would do harm to many people who, having been hurt, would naturally be inclined to hurt in turn him who pronounces the unpleasant truths. It presupposes, in other words, that freedom of inquiry and of publication of all results of inquiry, is not guaranteed as a basic right. This literature is then essentially related to a society which is not liberal. Thus one may very well raise the question of what use it could be in a truly liberal society. The answer is simple. In Plato's *Banquet*, Alcibiades—that outspoken son of outspoken Athens—compares Socrates and his speeches to certain sculptures which are very ugly from the outside, but within have most beautiful images of things divine. The works of the great writers of the past are very beautiful even from without. And yet their visible beauty is sheer ugliness, compared with the beauty of those hidden treasures which disclose themselves only after very long, never easy, but always pleasant work. This always difficult but always pleasant work is, I believe, what the philosophers had in mind when they recommended education. Education, they felt, is the only answer to the always pressing question, to the political question par excellence of how to reconcile order which is not oppression with freedom which is not license.

NOTES

[1] *Scribere est agere.* See Sir William Blackstone, *Commentaries,* Book IV, chap. 6. Compare Machiavelli, *Discorsi,* III, 6 (*I Classici del Giglio,* pp. 424–26) and Descartes, *Discours de la méthode,* VI, beginning.

[2] *Socrates:* Do you know by what means they might be persuaded to accept this story? *Glaucon:* By no means, as far as they themselves are concerned, but I know how it could be done as regards their sons and their descendants and the people of a later age generally speaking. *Socrates:* . . . I understand, more or less, what you mean." Plato, *Republic,* 415 c6-d5.

[3] "Reason is but choosing" is the central thesis of Milton's *Areopagitica.*

[4] Plato, *Republic,* 450 d3-e1.

[5] A. J. Carlyle, *A History of Mediaeval Political Theory in the West,* I (and ed., London, 1927), 2.

[6] Ernest Renan, *Averroes et l'Averroïsme* (3rd ed., Paris, 1866). 292 ff. Leon Gauthier, *La théorie d'Ibn Roche (Averroès) sur les rapports de la religion et de la philosophie* (Paris, 1909), 126 ff. and 177 ff. Compare the same author's "Scolastique musulmane et scolastique chrétienne," *Revue d'Histoire de la Philosophie,* II (1928). 221 ff. and 333 ff.

[7] Ludwig Edelstein, "Greek Medicine in its Relation to Religion and Magic," *Bulletin of the Institute of the History of Medicine,* V (1937), 201 and 211.

[8] Lessing, *Ernst und Falk,* 2nd dialogue; and "Leibniz von den ewigen Strafen," Werke (Petersen and v. Olshausen edition), XXI, 147. Friedrich Schleiermacher, *Platons Werke* (Berlin, 1804), vol. I, 1, pp. 12–20. Werner Jaeger, *Aristotle* (Oxford, 1934), 33. See also Sir Alexander Grant, *The Ethics of Aristotle* (London, 1874) I, 398 ff. and Eduard Zeller, *Aristotle and the Earlier Peripatetics* (London, 1897), I, 120 ff.

[9] James T. Shotwell, *The History of History,* I (New York, 1939), 356 ff.

[10] Ferdinand Tönnies, *Thomas Hobbes* (3rd ed., Stuttgart, 1925), 148. George E. G. Catlin, *Thomas Hobbes* (Oxford, 1922), 25. Richard Hönigswald, *Hobbes und die Staatsphilosophie* (Munich, 1924), 176 ff. Leo Strauss, *Die*

Religionskritik Spinozas (Berlin, 1930), 80. Z. Lubienski, *Die Grundlagen des ethisch-politischen Systems von Hobbes* (Munich, 1932), 213 ff.

[11] George H. Sabine, *A History of Political Theory* (New York, 1937), 556 and 551. Friedrich Meinecke, *Die Entstehung des Historismus* (Munich, 1936), 139 ff. and 151, footnote 1. Édouard Laboulaye, "Introduction à l'Esprit des Lois," *Oeuvres complètes de Montesquieu* (Paris, 1876) vol. 3, pp. xviii ff. Laboulaye quotes in that context an important passage from d'Alembert's "Éloge de Montesquieu." See also Bertolini's "Analyse raisonnée de l'Esprit des Lois," *ibid.*, pp. 6, 14, 23 ff., 34 and 60 ff. The remarks of d'Alembert, Bertolini and Laboulaye are merely explanations of what Montesquieu himself indicates for example when he says in the preface: "Si l'on veut chercher le dessein de l'auteur, on ne le peut bien découvrir que dans le dessein de l'ouvrage." (See also the end of the eleventh book and two letters from Helvétius, *ibid.*, vol. 6, pp. 314, 320). D'Alembert says: "Nous disons de l'*obscurité* que l'on peut se permettre dans un tel ouvrage, la même chose que du *défaut d'ordre*. Ce qui seroit obscur pour les lecteurs vulgaires, ne l'est pas pour ceux que l'auteur a eus en vue; d'ailleurs l'obscurité volontaire n'en est pas une. M. de Montesquieu avant à présenter quelquefois des vérités importantes, dont l'énoncé absolu et direct auroit pu blesser sans fruit, a eu la prudence de les envelopper; et, par cet innocent artifice, les a voilées à ceux à qui elles seroient nuisibles, sans qu'elles fussent perdues pour les sages." Similarly, certain contemporaries of the "rhetor" Xenophon believed that "what is beautifully and methodically written, is not beautifully and methodically written" (*Cynegeticus*, 13.6).

[12] In regard to Kant, whose case is in a class by itself, even a historian so little given to suspicion or any other sort of skepticism as C. E. Vaughan remarks: "We are almost led to suspect Kant of having trifled with his readers, and of nursing an esoteric sympathy with Revolution." (*Studies in the History of Political Philosophy*, Manchester, 1939, II, 83.)

[13] See the "fragment" by H. S. Reimarus, "Von Duldung der Deisten," in Lessing's *Werke* (Petersen and v. Olshausen edition) XXII, 38 ff.

[14] The question whether that extreme goal is attainable in any but the most halcyon conditions has been raised in our time by Archibald MacLeish in "Post-War Writers and Pre-

War Readers," *Journal of Adult Education*, vol. 12 (June, 1940) in the following terms: "Perhaps the luxury of the complete confession, the uttermost despair, the farthest doubt should be denied themselves by writers living in any but the most orderly and settled times. I do not know."

[15] I am thinking of Hobbes in particular, whose significance for the development outlined above can hardly be overestimated. This was clearly recognized by Tönnies, who emphasized especially these two sayings of his hero: "Paulatim eruditur vulgus" and "Philosophia ut crescat libera esse debet nec metu nec pudore coercenda." (Tönnies, *op. cit.*, pp. iv, 195.) Hobbes also says: "Suppression of doctrines does but unite and exasperate, that is, increase both the malice and power of them that have already believed them." (*English Works*, Molesworth edition, VI, 242.) In his *Of Liberty and Necessity* (London 1654, 35 ff.) he writes to the Marquess of Newcastle: "I must confess, if we consider the greatest part of Mankinde, not as they should be, but as they are . . . I must, I say, confess that the dispute of this question will rather hurt than help their piety, and therefore if his Lordship [Bishop Bramhall] had not desired this answer, I should not have written it, nor do I write it but in hopes your Lordship and his, will keep it private."

[16] Cicero, *Tusculanae Disputationes*, II, 4. Plato, *Phaedo*, 64 b; *Republic*, 520 b2-3 and 494 a4-10.

[17] Plato, *Timaeus*, 28 c3-5, and *Seventh Letter*, 332 d6-7, 341 c4-e3, and 344 d4-e2. That the view mentioned above is reconcilable with the democratic creed is shown most clearly by Spinoza, who was a champion not only of liberalism but also of democracy (*Tractatus politicus*, XI, 2, Bruder edition). See his *Tractatus de intellectus emendatione*, 14 and 17, as well as *Tractatus theologico-politicus*, V 35-39, XIV 20 and XV end.

[18] Sir Thomas More, *Utopia*, latter part of first book.

[19] A rather extensive discussion of the "magna quaestio, latebrosa tractatio, disputatio inter doctos alternans," as Augustinus called it, is to be found in Crotius' *De Jure Belli ac Pacis*, III, chap. I, §7 ff., and in particular §17, 3. See also *inter alia* Pascal's ninth and tenth *Provinciales* and Jeremy Taylor, *Ductor Dubitantium*, Book III, chap. 2, rule 5.

[20] Compare Plato, *Republic*, 539 a5-d1, with *Apology of Socrates*, 23 c2-8.

13. Stephen Pepper: "Root Metaphors"

Born in New Jersey, Pepper (1891–1972) was educated at Harvard, finishing his Ph.D. in 1916. From 1919–58, he was Professor of Intellectual and Moral Philosophy at the University of California, Berkeley. He was the author of numerous essays and books, principally in the areas of philosophical method, aesthetics, and ethics.

ROOT METAPHORS*

. . . Here I shall offer a hypothesis concerning the origin of world theories—a hypothesis which, if true, shows the connection of these theories with common sense, illumines the nature of these theories, renders

* From "Root Metaphors" in *World Hypotheses: A Study in Evidence* by Stephen C. Pepper. Originally published by the University of California Press, 1942, 1970. Reprinted by permission of the Regents of the University of California.

them distinguishable from one another, and acts as an instrument of criticism for determining their relative adequacy.

Logically, this chapter should follow our study of such theories; for it purports to be no more than a summary of conclusions gained by studying them and the men who made them. But to serve the purposes of exposition the theory comes better first and the evidence afterward. I call it the "root-metaphor theory." Such a theory of world theories seems to me much less important than the clarification it introduces into the field of cognition it covers. Our interest is not so much in the truth of a certain theory about world theories as in the cognitive value of the world theories themselves.

Strangely enough, if this root-metaphor theory is correct, its truth could be established by the adequacy of the theories which constitute its evidence. For this theory is itself a structural hypothesis—at least, it would be such in its ultimate corroboration—and, as we have seen, a structural hypothesis only attains full confirmation in a world theory. Hence, if this theory is true, an adequate world theory will support it. This theory would then, so to speak, become absorbed in its own evidence, that is, become an item in the very theory which it is a theory about. If this sounds like a dark saying, we reply that a world theory that cannot adequately explain it is not an adequate world theory.

But it is not a dark saying, though it does constitute a curious puzzle like that of the bottle carrying a label of the picture of that bottle, which picture of that bottle is pictured with a label which pictures the picture of that bottle, and so on—*if* so on. A bottle with a label like that is a fact of some sort in the world—a dubitandum, at least—and so is a world theory, and a theory about a world theory. And we know that the critical refinement of, at any rate, the second and third of the facts just presented lies in the direction of danda and world theories. There is nothing but dogmatism that can stop such criticism. To say, therefore, that a theory about world theories is something the cognitive value of which will depend ultimately on the value ascribed to it by an adequate world theory is merely to say that this theory, like any other criticizable cognitive item, is as valuable as the relevant evidence that corroborates it. And I stress this point at once to make it clear that our interest is not in a particular theory but in the nature and value of cognition itself.

This . . . root-metaphor theory, the purpose of which is to link dubitanda and data to danda, and indirectly to link different sorts of danda together, would therefore drop completely out of sight so far as it were true. Ideally, we should pass directly from dubitanda and data to fully adequate danda which would exhibit all things cognitively in their proper order. Unfortunately, danda are not at present nearly adequate. We are therefore prompted to ask ourselves why. The result of the inquiry is this root-metaphor theory, which in its content is in the nature of a rough dandum. This theory, therefore, definitely does not legislate over world theories except so far as these voluntarily accept it and thereby refine it. On the contrary, an adequate world theory by virtue of its refinement legislates over this theory or any like it. There is no reliable cognitive appeal beyond an adequate world theory. But when world theories show themselves to be inadequate we accept what makeshifts we can find. This root-metaphor theory is such a makeshift. Its purpose is to squeeze out all the cognitive values that can be found in the world theories we have and to supply a receptacle in which their juices may be collected, so that they will not dry up from dogmatism, or be wasted over the ground through the indiscriminate peeking of marauding birds.

§2. *Can logical postulates make world theories?*—How could world theories be generated? Barring the refined account from world theories themselves, and sticking to the levels of common sense and data, two suggestions emerge. One of these is typical of common sense, the other of data. The first suggestion is analogy; the second, permutations of logical postulates. The root-metaphor theory is an elaboration of the first suggestion. It has the advantage of being practically a common-sense theory and therefore inviting refinement and self-development along the lines of structural corroboration, so that each refined interpretation of the root-metaphor theory by a relatively adequate world theory appears as simply the natural and fully detailed exposition of precisely what a root metaphor is. Just as common-sense fact always calls for refinement, so a common-sense theory of world theories will call for refinement, and that refinement by the very nature of the material itself is bound to culminate in a world theory or in a number of alternative world theories.

But the suggestion that comes from the field of data would also seem worth considering. Coming as it does from a field of cognition already refined, it might seem more promising than the common-sense suggestion. So it has seemed to many men. And yet, that such is its source may be why it has proved less successful.

At the break of the century, when the potentialities of the new symbolic logic were dawning upon men, there were some who expected that mathematical logical systems would yield all that traditional metaphysical systems had, and more too, and would therefore in time completely supplant the traditional modes of metaphysical thought. These hopes have waned. But the possibility still remains of using the apparatus of symbolic logic as a means of generating world theories.

The idea is to conceive a world theory in the form of a deductive system with theorems derived from postulates. Once obtain such a system, and new world theories might then be generated like new geometries by simply adding or dropping or changing a postulate and noting the result in the self-consistency of the system and in the application of the theorems to *all* the observed facts of the world.

The idea is particularly attractive to the positivist. Suppose we conceive such a system as a summary of the facts of the world, that is, as a conventionalistic hypothesis. Something like this is being done with a degree of success in physical cosmology, both microscopic and macroscopic. Just conceive such mathematical speculation of physicists and astronomers expanded to cover all facts, and then we have a conventionalistic world hypothesis. By manipulating the postulates, hypotheses might be spawned by the dozens, and many of them might be adequate world hypotheses according to the conventionalistic standard of adequacy, namely, intellectual convenience.

Here we seem to avoid the difficulties of dictatorial positivism. . . . Danda are not denied. They are not denominated false, nor even ignored, for by definition a conventionalistic hypothesis affirms nothing. It merely organizes the facts observed in such a manner as to be most conveniently used and perused. If no dictatorial claims are made, and these conventionalistic hypotheses are merely presented as alternative world theories to be considered along with the analogically generated world theories, what objections can there be?

None, if the proponents of this method do really maintain an undictatorial attitude. But it is to be noticed that no conventionalistic world hypothesis has ever been generated by the postulational method. The method, therefore, is quite speculative so far as it applies to world theories. It does not, therefore, actually exist as an alternative to the analogical method, which we shall develop. It is only a *possible* alternative. This fact in itself is noteworthy.

Can any reasons be given for this failure? We suspect that there is a good reason; which is, that the postulational method itself is not quite free from structural presuppositions. For this method is an application of multiplicative corroboration in terms of logical data. And all types of multiplicative corroboration seem to take for granted the fact of exact repetition or exact similarity. The corroboration of man by man seems to take it for granted that each man agrees with the others that their observations are the same.

But, from the standpoint of structural criticism, the unquestioning acceptance of the principle of multiplicative corroboration and its apparent assumption of exact repetitions of observation is rather naïve. The fact of repetition itself is something that needs refinement, and by the nature of the case multiplicative corroboration cannot give it; only structural corroboration can. From the standpoint of structural corroboration, a datum is barely more than a dubitandum—something very curious and problematic just because in its extremes of pointer readings it is so reliable.

Now, among the relatively adequate structural world theories which we shall study there is only one that accepts exact repetition of observations at its face value, that is, accepts a refined datum as a refined dandum. The other world theories, of course, accept the evidence of the reliability of data; but they account for this reliability not in terms of exact repetition, but in quite different terms. We therefore reach the curious result that so far as the postulational method is accepted at its face value (even as purely conventionalistic) the cognitive values it offers fall within only one of several alternative structural world hypotheses. In other words, the idea of a conventionalistic world hypothesis (even barring the consideration of chapter iii) is not so innocent as it sounds. It presupposes the danda of a certain structural world theory, namely, formism.

Hence it does not seem likely that adequate world theories will be generated in the postulational way. Subsidiary theories of limited scope can be generated in this way; but probably not world theories, for the cogent reason that an uncritical acceptance of data at their face value already commits a man to *one* structural world theory, and all the permutations of postulates he can make will never get him out of that theory. If he accepts the interpretation of data in terms of some other structural world theory the same condition will hold there.

The postulational method might accordingly be suggestive of alternative ways of presenting the categories of a single structural hypothesis already generated in the analogical way, or it might do other subordinate services, but it is unlikely to prove a fertile method of generating new sets of categories or new world theories.

§3. *The root-metaphor method.*—So we return to the traditional analogical method of generating world theories. The method in principle seems to be this: A man desiring to understand the world looks about for a clue to its comprehension. He pitches upon some area of common-sense fact and tries if he cannot understand other areas in terms of this one. This original area becomes then his basic analogy or root metaphor. He describes as best he can the characteristics of this area, or, if you will, discriminates its structure. A list of its structural characteristics becomes his basic concepts of explanation and description. We call them a set of categories. In terms of these categories he proceeds to study all other areas of fact whether uncriticized or previously criticized. He undertakes to interpret all facts in terms of these categories. As a result of the impact of these other facts upon his categories, he may qualify and readjust the categories, so that a set of categories commonly changes and develops. Since the basic analogy or root metaphor normally (and probably at least in part necessarily) arises out of common sense, a great deal of development and refinement of a set of categories is required if they are to prove adequate for a hypothesis of unlimited scope. Some root metaphors prove more fertile than others, have greater powers of expansion and of adjustment. These survive in comparison with the others and generate the relatively adequate world theories.

As a simple illustration of the growth of a root metaphor let us consider and imaginatively reconstruct the probable development of the Milesian theory, which was the first self-conscious world theory in European thought. Thales, wondering about the world, and dissatisfied with the explanations of mythology, suggested, "All things are water." He picked out a range of common-sense fact, water, which impressed him, a citizen of a seaport town, as likely to possess the secret of all things. Water stretches far and wide. It evaporates, generating fogs, and mists, and clouds, and these in turn condense in dampness and rain. Life springs out of its slime and mud, and the absence of water is death.

Anaximander followed Thales and thought the selection of common water rather crude. The substance of all things, metaphysical water, was not after all just common water. It was common water plus all its phases and acquired qualities. He accordingly emphasized the extensive category of infinity and a category of qualitative change which he called "shaking out." He gave the substance of all things the name *apeiron* or "infinite." In the "infinite" lay the "mixture" of all qualities: hardnesses, softnesses, shapes, colors, tastes, and odors. For any particular object in the world, such as a ship, a leaf, a pebble, or a fire, some of these qualities were "shaken out" of the "infinite mixture" as perhaps rain is shaken out of heavy clouds. These segregated qualities then congregated in the familiar forms we perceive.

After Anaximander came Anaximenes, who felt that Anaximander was very near to substituting an abstraction for the concrete substance of things, but apparently agreed that water did not connote the infinity which a world substance should have. He accordingly suggested air, denoting by this something more akin to what we should now call mist, which was, after all, one of the phases of Thales' "water." Anaximenes also added the clear discrimination of a category of quantitative change, namely, rarefaction-condensation, which seems to have been assumed by Thales and perhaps by Anaximander, but was not defined. It amounts to a category of the phases of matter: solid, liquid, and gas.

The root metaphor of this theory thus ultimately turns out to be the characteristics of a basic material out of which all the facts of the universe can be generated by certain processes of change. The set of categories may be listed as (1) a generating substance (or maybe several), (2) principles of change like "shaking out," and rarefaction-condensation, and (3) generated substances produced by (1) through (2). We might call this the "generating-substance theory."

It is not a very adequate theory, though its shadow falls upon the works of many men who developed much more adequate theories. It is periodically revived in practically pure form, but always by men of relatively small caliber. It was revived by Bernadino Telesio in the sixteenth century and by Büchner, Haeckel, and Herbert Spencer in the nineteenth. The trouble with the theory is that it lacks scope. There are too many facts that cannot be satisfactorily described in terms of these categories. We shall examine in detail one instance of this sort of inadequacy in this sort of theory when we study types of inadequacy in the next chapter.

When attempts are made to develop these categories further so as to render them more adequate and give them the scope required of a world theory, we discover either that they break down or that they break out into various types of cognitive fallacy, or that new sets of categories are in the making and men are seeking inspiration from new groups of common-sense facts, seeking new root metaphors.

So, after Anaximenes came Empedocles, who proposed in his perplexity over the inadequacies of water, *apeiron*, and air a plurality of generating substances and some new principles of change; and, in the same perplexity, but following another path, Anaxagoras; and also Parmenides and Zeno, who boldly but not so wisely proposed to solve the difficulties by believing only in elemental substance, denying generating change; and Heracleitus, who equally boldly and unwisely proposed believing only in generating change and apparently denying permanent substance. So we see how a world theory beginning promisingly with a root metaphor fresh from vital common sense grows for a while, meets obstacles in fact, is incapable of overcoming these obstacles, desperately juggles its categories, forgets the facts in the juggling of the categories, till these presently become so empty that some men can cast half of them overboard, devoutly believe the other half, substitute concepts for the facts, and deem it unnecessary to look back upon the forgotten facts. When an inadequate theory reaches such a state of intellectual chaos, there is stimulus for criticism and for new insight. Both came at once in Greece. The Sophists offered plenty of criticism, and two of the most adequate world theories came to birth: mechanism, through Leucippus and Democritus; and formism, through Socrates, Plato, and Aristotle. These theories were not sudden births, as the generating-substance theory seems to have been. There were germs of them in the disintegrating stages of the generating-substance theory itself, as if this disintegration of a promising theory turned men's eyes back toward common sense to find new sources of cognitive inspiration, that is to say, new root metaphors.

This brief account of the Milesian theory is a good parable for all of us who are interested in structural hypotheses and world theories. Never again do we see so simply and clearly the full course of a world theory—its promise, its bloom, its difficulties, its struggles, its collapse—and the type of men for every stage of it, exhibited almost in caricature. The genius Thales, who intuited the root metaphor and left only vague hints and a central saying, "All things are water"; the systematizers Anaximenes and Empedocles, who in different ways brought the theory to a high point of reasonableness by their careful reflection and extensive observation; Parmenides and Zeno, confident, brilliant, and clever jugglers of concepts, confounding to their opponents, uncompromising in their logic, who preserved some of the categories of the theory only by rejecting the others, and emptying all of them of the facts which generated them; Anaxagoras, observant again, but confused, reminiscent of Anaximander, full of promise, and yet disappointing to the young Socrates, for Anaxagoras was an eclectic bridging the way from a theory he could not make work to a theory which as yet, from lack of a clear intuition of its root metaphor, he did not comprehend. The counterparts of all these men reappear over and over again in the later history of thought, and it is a good thing to mark their type here where they are so simply seen, and judge their reliability and worth.

On the slim basis of this illustrative sketch of one root metaphor and its world theory let us make some critical generalizations. These will find their full justification, of course, only later. Once more, in the interest of clarity of exposition, we are led to state first what in the order of evidence should come last. Let us put these generalizations in the form of maxims:

§4. *Maxim I: A world hypothesis is determined by its root metaphor.*—When we speak of different world hypotheses, we mean the several developments of different root metaphors. The theories of Thales, Anaximenes, Empedocles, Telesio, and Spencer are all one world theory, because they are derived from one root metaphor. The statements of the theory may differ in the degree of refinement of the categories, in terminology, in emphasis on certain details, in omission of some details, and even in omission of some basic categories. Still, all these statements will be reckoned as statements of one world theory in that they are all generated from and related to a single root metaphor.

Moreover, it is implied that there is some statement or number of statements which represent the world theory, its categories, and root metaphor, at the height of its development. So we suggested that Anaximenes and Empedocles represented the generating-substance theory at the height of its Greek development. It is always possible that a theory may develop farther than the best statement we have of it. In a sense, Herbert Spencer's statement was a development beyond the Greek. It was a development, however, chiefly in respect to the vast accumulation of factual detail over what the Greeks had, and hardly a development at all in respect to the refinement of the categories. It is the latter sort of development we chiefly have in mind when we speak of the development of a world hypothesis. For its adequacy depends on its potentialities of description and explanation rather than upon the accumulation of actual descriptions, though its power of description is never fully known short of actual performance.

This fact brings out that the unlimited scope essential to a world hypothesis is more a matter of intent and accepted responsibility than a matter of actual test. Obviously, all the facts in the world can never be described literally by any hypothesis. The testing of a world hypothesis consists in presenting to it for description types of fact or specimens from diverse fields of facts, and if it can adequately describe these we assume that it can describe the rest. Experience has made philosophers pretty well aware of what are likely to be the hardest facts for a world theory to handle, and these are at once respectfully presented for solution to any young hypothesis that ventures to claim world-wide scope. If the description of these facts tolerably well passes criticism, critics scour the universe for some other evidence which will break the theory down. The world-wide scope of a theory, therefore, is actually a challenge rather than an accomplishment.

Our best world hypotheses, however, seem to have this scope. They seem to handle fairly adequately any fact that is presented to them. Their inadequacies arise not so much from lack of scope as from internal inconsistencies, so that the minimum requirement nowadays for a world hypothesis is unlimited scope. We therefore speak only of the relative inadequacies of world theories, their world-wide scope being taken for granted.

§5. *Maxim II: Each world hypothesis is autonomous.*—This follows from our observation in the previous paragraph. If two or more world hypotheses handle their facts with the same degree of adequacy (so far as can be judged), and there is no world hypothesis of greater adequacy available, then there is no appeal beyond these hypotheses and each must be held to be as reliable as the other. The reason, of course, is that structural refinement reaches its culmination in world hypotheses, so that there is no cognitive appeal beyond the most adequate world hypotheses we have. Several important corollaries may be stated:

i) *It is illegitimate to disparage the factual interpretations of one world hypothesis in terms of the categories of another—if both hypotheses are equally adequate.* This disparagement is an almost universal procedure, very plausible and entirely fallacious. We believe that at the present time there are four world hypotheses of about equal adequacy. We shall call them formism, mechanism, contextualism, and organicism. Now, the very statement that these are relatively adequate hypotheses means that they are capable of presenting credible interpretations of any facts whatever in terms of their several sets of categories. Indeed, these interpretations are so convincing that a man who has not had an opportunity to compare them with the parallel interpretations of a rival hypothesis will inevitably accept them as self-evident or indubitable. The basic danda, that is, the refined evidence, of every one of these rather reliable world hypotheses has traditionally been presented and accepted as indubitable by the believers in these hypotheses, so obviously pure fact do the refined danda of any good world hypothesis appear through the lenses of its categories. Remember the danda of Price and Dewey. It is the apparent transparency of danda for cognition that makes dogmatism so easy to accept and so hard to dispel. The exponents of the theories which we are about to study have in the past, almost to a man, been dogmatists. They have believed their theories implicitly, accepted their danda as indubitable, and their categories generally as self-evident.

One reason they have been so sure of themselves is that whichever of these hypotheses they have espoused, they have been able to give relatively adequate interpretations *in their own terms* of the danda and categories of the other hypotheses. "You see," they say, "we are able to explain what these other mistaken philosophers have thought to be facts, and to show where the errors of their observations lay, how they rationalized their prejudices, accepting interpretations for facts and missing the real facts. Our hypothesis includes theirs and is accordingly the true account of the nature of things."

This would be a good argument if the other hypotheses were not equally well able to make the same argument. Among the facts in the world that a relatively adequate world theory must adequately interpret are, of course, other world theories, and a world theory that cannot reasonably interpret the errors of other world theories is automatically inadequate. By that much it lacks the requisite scope. The four world theories which we shall consider have no difficulty in explaining each other's errors.

It follows that what are pure facts for one theory are highly interpreted evidence for another. This does not imply that there are no pure facts in the universe, but only that we do not know where they are. The danda of the best world hypotheses, however, are our best bet. It is the cognitive obligation of a world theory to interpret the danda and categories of other world theories in terms of its own categories. Within the mode of interpretation of any world theory, the categories of that theory legislate without appeal. But this privilege belongs to any other equally adequate theory. One set of categories, therefore, cannot legislate over another set of categories unless the latter fails to reciprocate or in any other way indicates a lesser degree of adequacy.

ii) *It is illegitimate to assume that the claims of a given world hypothesis are established by the exhibition of the shortcomings of other world hypotheses.* This may be called the fallacy of clearing the ground. It assumes that if a theory is not perfect it is no good, and that if all other suggested theories are no good, then the ground is clear for whatever one's own theory can produce. This holds, of course, only if the suggested theory is more adequate than those rejected.

This is so obvious a fallacy that it is remarkable it should be so frequently used and to such persuasive effect. Yet a great proportion of philosophical—and not only philosophical—books give a large part of their space to polemic, finding the faults in rival theories with an idea that this helps to establish the theory proposed. The cognitive value of a hypothesis is not one jot increased by the cognitive errors of other hypotheses. Most polemic is a waste of time, or an actual obfuscation of the evidence. It is generally motivated by a proselytizing spirit supported on dogmatic illusions. If a theory is any good it can stand on its own evidence. The only reason for referring to other theories in constructive cognitive endeavor is to find out what other evidence they may suggest, or other matters of positive cognitive value. We need all world hypotheses, so far as they are adequate, for mutual comparison and correction of interpretative bias.

iii) *It is illegitimate to subject the results of structural refinement (world hypotheses) to the cognitive standards (or limitations) of multiplicative refinement.* Data cannot legislate over danda. Data must be accepted as evidence to be accounted for in a world hypothesis, but a world hypothesis does not have to accept data at their face value, or to exclude acceptance of any other sort of evidence than data. This point was discussed in detail earlier, in our examination of the positivistic proposals.

iv) *It is illegitimate to subject the results of structural refinement to the assumptions of common sense.* Dubitanda must be accepted as evidence to be accounted for, but, as we have seen, hardly ever at their face value. And this is without disparagement to the ultimate cognitive security of common sense.

v) *It is convenient to employ common-sense concepts as bases for comparison for parallel fields of evidence among world theories.* Dubitanda definitions of a group of facts are the best *test* definitions for the comparison of parallel danda definitions in different world theories. For instance, suppose we wanted to compare the interpretations of "red tomato" in the four relatively adequate world theories we are to study. From the brief earlier quotations from Price and Dewey on such a subject, it is pretty obvious that the field of fact covered by "red tomato" would, for Dewey and Price, not exactly correspond. Some items of evidence which for Price would be rather or quite irrelevant in determining what "red tomato" is, would for Dewey be vitally relevant. For Dewey, "red tomato" spreads over, so to speak, a different area of fact from what it does for Price. Yet the descriptions these two men give of "red tomato" are as nearly descriptions of the "same" fact as can be found from their respective points of view. If we want to compare the views of the two men, we can do no better than compare their different interpretations of what may be called the "same" fact. Yet the fact is never literally the same, because, if it were, the description or interpretation would be just the same, which never happens if the categories are really different.

If, let us imagine, there were an omniscient mind who looked upon the world with the "true" categories, which in such a case would, of course, be the actual structural order of nature and not interpretative conceptions at all, he could correct the interpretations of Dewey and Price, showing just where one perhaps took in too much fact here, and the other too little there. For such a mind Dewey's and Price's descriptions would be definitely two different facts of interpretation different from a third fact, which is the real red tomato truly intuited by this omniscient mind. (Any dogmatist of a theory other than Dewey's or Price's would also say just that, believing his *interpretation* of the red tomato to be the real red tomato.) But since we do not have (we find reason to believe) the fully adequate view of the world which definitely would tell us the difference in fact between the "same" red tomato interpreted by Price and by Dewey, how can we compare the two interpretations? Why, of course, as we have been comparing them—by noting the interpretation which each gives of the *same* common-sense fact.

We take a common-sense dubitandum, red tomato, and we note the structural refinement of that fact which culminates in Dewey's dandum, and also the refinement which culminates in Price's dandum. We then say that Dewey's dandum is the "same" fact in his world view that Price's dandum is in his. Though in any specific instance there is some risk in such ascriptions of equivalence, in the end (that is, in the comparison of all the ascriptions made by both theories) there is no risk; for within world hypotheses having unlimited scope, the *totality* of interpretations in any two world hypotheses must be literally equivalent since they both take in all the facts there are.

As a maxim of method, then, we find that there is no better way of entering upon the study of a field of fact than through common sense. Let the subject be perception, physical body, personal freedom, the law of gravitation, legal right, aesthetic beauty, myself, identity, space, yellow, saltiness, anger, air, action, truth—whatever you will, the essay or the book will most profitably begin with the common-sense meanings of these terms and then proceed to refinements of interpretation which can be compared with one another on the basis of their mutual points of origin.

§6. *Maxim III: Eclecticism is confusing.*—This maxim follows from the second. If world hypotheses are autonomous, they are mutually exclusive. A mixture of them, therefore, can only be confusing. We are speaking now as having cognition in mind, not practice, which often entails other than purely cognitive considerations.

When we say that world theories are mutually exclusive, we do not mean that they stand apart from one another like so many isolated posts. Each theory is well aware of the others, criticizes and interprets them and entirely includes them within its scope. It is only from the perspective of common sense, in the recollection of the different theories' diverse courses of critical refinement that we are aware of their mutual exclusiveness.

More perspicuously, it is only through our study of their factual conflicts, their diverse categories, their consequent differences of factual corroboration, and —in a word—their distinct root metaphors that we become aware of their mutual exclusiveness.

It is not to be denied (especially after our perception that root metaphors become themselves refined in consort with the refinement of the very theories they generate) that the root metaphor of one theory may merge with that of another, and eventually all may come harmoniously together. But this idea itself is a principle derived from *one* world theory, and cannot be affirmed until, or if, that theory (organicism) should turn out to be completely adequate. For, contrariwise, it is barely possible that the world has no determinate structure, but that the past is being continually revised by the future and that the present is consequently utterly indeterminate and likely to change its nature without notice at any time, so that an indefinite number of structural hypotheses are all equally pertinent and equally impertinent. Though this latter proposal skims perilously close to the dogma of utter skepticism, something very like it is defended by some pragmatists and therefore receives some support from the categories of contextualism.

The point is, once more, that there is no way of obtaining better cognitive judgments than in terms of the best cognitive criticism we have. At present this criticism seems to be concentrated in four diverse modes of cognition or world hypotheses. While all sorts of things might happen to these diverse theories so far as abstract possibility is concerned, as a fact (in the best sense of fact we know) these four theories are just now irreconcilable. Any creditable attempt to reconcile them turns out to be the judgment of one of the theories on the nature of the others—as just now we saw was the case with the organic idea. This is a good idea, one of the best. But it would be dogmatic to accept it, when other equally adequate hypotheses have other ideas on the subject.

Yet it is a tempting notion, that perhaps a world theory more adequate than any of the world theories mentioned above (those bound to their metaphors) might be developed through the selection of *what is best* in each of them and organizing the results with a synthetic set of categories. This seems to be the deliberate principle of method used by Whitehead in his *Process and Reality*. It is the eclectic method. Our contention is that this method is mistaken in principle in that it adds no factual content and confuses the structures of fact which are clearly spread out in the pure root-metaphor theories; in two words, that it is almost inevitably sterile and confusing.

The literature of philosophy is, of course, full of eclectic writings. Moreover, it is probably true that all (or nearly all) the great philosophers were in various degrees eclectic. There are various reasons for this. One is undue faith in self-evidence and indubitability of fact, another the desire to give credit to all good intuitions with the idea that these all have to be put inside of *one* theory. But the best reason is that many of the great philosophers were not so much systematizers as seekers of fact, men who were working their way into new root metaphors and had not yet worked their way out of old ones. The eclecticism of these writers is, therefore, cognitively accidental and not deliberate, though psychologically unavoidable.

There are, then, two sorts of eclecticism: the static, deliberate sort; and the dynamic, accidental sort. Whitehead is mainly an example of the first, Peirce or James of the second. Both sorts are confusing and (I believe) can be clarified only by unraveling their eclectic tangles in terms of the different root metaphors that got mixed up. The dynamic sort, however, is obviously not sterile. This eclecticism contains the best creative work in philosophy. But its cognitive value comes not from the eclectic factor (which is entirely obstructive), but from the creative factor. The dynamic eclectic tries to divest himself of his eclectic encumbrances, and the drama of his struggle often produces great literature as well as great philosophy. But the greatness of his philosophy is not so much intrinsic as prospective. Peirce and James intuited the pragmatic, or contextualistic, root metaphor. But their intuitions were primitive, and they were in need of a technical vocabulary, and were constantly enmeshed in formistic categories. As pragmatists their cognitive achievements were probably inferior to those of Dewey and Mead, though as creative thinkers they were probably superior. Dynamic eclecticism is, therefore, the sort of exception that proves the rule. We honor its exponents above all other cognizers because of their keen scent for new facts. But it is not for their eclecticism that we honor them, for that is still only a source of confusion.

Static and deliberate eclecticism, however, cannot claim the discovery of new fact or insight, but only the merit of a method different from that of the root-metaphor method. The two methods are not in any way in contradiction with each other. The issue between the two is consequently not fatally serious. Nevertheless, it would greatly simplify the critical problem of estimating the value of world theories if we had reason to believe that eclectic theories were in principle less reliable than pure root-metaphor theories. The question is this: Does a deliberate eclectic theory add anything that is not better found in the alternative root-metaphor theories from which an eclectic theory must obtain its materials? If not, we can safely limit our attention to pure root-metaphor theories.

There are theoretically two ways of deliberately constructing an eclectic world theory. One is to combine all the adequate world theories we have into one synthetic whole. The merit of this way is supposed to be greater comprehensiveness. But clearly nothing could be more comprehensive than the complete comprehensiveness of a theory of world-wide scope. Every relatively adequate world theory is completely comprehensive. The reason that there are several root-metaphor theories is precisely that they are all fully comprehensive and their categories refuse to merge and their danda refuse to harmonize. So that way is impossible. The other alternative is to make selections, generally said to be of "the best," from the several theories, and then out of the combined selections to elicit a new synthetic set of categories. The merit of this way is supposed to be greater adequacy.

But the trouble with this second way is how to determine a reliable ground of selection. What shall determine "the best" in the various theories? If anyone can suggest any other mode of cognitive refinement (that is, mode of finding "the best" in cognition) than multiplicative or structural refinement, he is certainly to be listened to attentively. But if not, how can the selection be made? As we have seen, multiplicative refinement will not help us. As to structural refinement, there are as many "bests" as there are world theories on an equal footing of adequacy. What, then, or who determines the "best" that is better than the "best" guaranteed by the relative adequacy of each world theory? Apparently only the personal preferences of the eclectic selector.

But is it not true that some world hypotheses seem to be especially strong in some cognitive fields, others in others? And would not an eclectic theory which combined these strong fields be more adequate than any pure root-metaphor theory? For instance, is it not true that the mechanistic theory seems to be particularly effective in the field of the physical sciences and rather shallow in the field of values, and is not the organistic theory rather strained in the field of the physical sciences and strong in the field of values? Would not an eclectic theory which accepted the mechanistic interpretations of physical facts and the organistic interpretations of facts of value be a more adequate world theory than either pure mechanism or pure organicism?

But would it? We must not forget that the main strength of a world hypothesis comes from structural corroboration. That means that the greater the spread of corroborative fact, the greater the cognitive reliability of the interpretations of each separate fact and field of facts. Now, the cognitive strength of both mechanism and organicism lies in their relative adequacy of unlimited scope. If their scope were limited, their interpretations would lack full corroboration. We find them credible precisely because their scope is unlimited. But the eclectic suggestion amounts to a limitation in the scope of both interpretations. In the eclectic theory the interpretations of physical facts would not be corroborated by the interpretations of value facts, and vice versa. The eclectic theory would actually lack universal scope and would not literally be a world theory at all.

More than that, can we afford to sacrifice the mechanistic interpretations of value or the organistic interpretations of physical facts? These interpretations are convincing to many men, and they do have structural corroboration. There is refined cognitive evidence for them. On what cognitive grounds can we discard them?

There are indeed some grounds. It may be pointed out that the mechanistic root metaphor springs out of the common-sense field of uncriticized physical fact, so that there would be no analogical stretch, so to speak, in the mechanistic interpretations of this field, while the stretch might be considerable in the mechanistic interpretation of the common-sense field of value; and somewhat the same, in reverse order, with respect to organistic interpretations. Moreover, mechanism has for several generations been particularly congenial to scientists, and organicism to artists and to persons of religious bent. Also, the internal difficulties which appear from a critical study of the mechanistic theory seem to be particularly acute in the neighborhood of values, and contrariwise the internal difficulties with organicism seem to be particularly acute in the neighborhood of physical fact.

These are cognitive grounds, and they all converge on the suspicion that mechanistic interpretations are perhaps more trustworthy for physical fact, while organistic interpretations are more trustworthy for values. But can more be legitimately said than that? And is not this suspicion based on the universal structural adequacy of *both* theories? Is it not precisely because both of these theories generate unlimited factual corroboration, and because their relative adequacy is about the same, because, in short, they are cognitively of equal weight and reliability, that we are somewhat justified in considering these external grounds of criticism? We, as practical human beings having to make practical choices in a pressing world, may well take these suspicions into account when we make our choices—rely more confidently on the judgment of a mechanist, perhaps, if we are building a bridge, more on the judgment of an organicist if we are building a society. But can we do more than that with these grounds of suspicion?

For these grounds of suspicion cannot legislate over

world theories, over the most highly refined cognitive criticism we have. The mechanistic interpretation of value has, after all, the powerful corroboration of the remarkably satisfactory mechanistic interpretations of physical fact. And the mechanistic interpretations of value are by no means unsatisfactory. Many men have been satisfied to be dogmatic about them. Those corroborative grounds are cognitively stronger than our grounds of suspicion in the previous paragraph. For in status these latter are little better than common-sense hunches—cognitive grounds all right, but dubitanda grounds, chiefly valuable in irritating us into the search for still better world theories.

But our proposed eclectic theory has by definition no root metaphor, and does not, so far as we can see, carry cognition forward at all. If such a combination of mechanism and organicism were proposed as a substitute for the two pure theories, the cognitive loss would be obvious. If it is proposed simply as another alternative, there is not so much objection. But why do it? As a flight of fancy it may be amusing, as men have fancied fauns, centaurs, angels, and dragons. But it can hardly be a genuinely creative cognitive achievement. If a man is to be creative in the construction of a new world theory, he must dig among the crevices of common sense. There he may find the pupa of a new moth or butterfly. This will be alive, and grow, and propagate. But no synthetic combination of the legs of one specimen and the wings of another will ever move except as their fabricator pushes them about with his tweezers. Moreover, what happens at the joints? What happens under the skin between the centaur's neck and body? How do the wings of angels fit into their shoulders? Either the eclectic glosses these difficulties over, or we perceive confusion.

How far such criticisms apply to Whitehead's *Pro-*

cess and Reality, it is for each man to decide. There are many genuinely creative touches in the book, where Whitehead pushes forward now one mode of interpretation, now another, especially many insignts into the implications of contextualism. But all agree that it is a hard book. The question is whether it is not an intrinsically confused book. When Whitehead writes in the Preface, "The history of philosophy discloses two cosmologies. . . . In attempting an enterprise of the same kind, it is wise to follow the clue that perhaps the true solution consists in a fusion of the two previous schemes, with modifications demanded by self-consistency and the advance of knowledge,"* the question is whether he is not proposing to himself something impossible. He has, I think, underestimated the number of cosmologies that he is about to "fuse." But to "fuse" even two and to have the fusion "self-consistent" is, on the evidence of our root-metaphor theory, impossible. All that can result is confusion, and I suggest that that is just what did result.

§7. *Maxim IV: Concepts which have lost contact with their root metaphors are empty abstractions.*—This fault is one stage worse than eclecticism, and is very likely to grow out of it. When a world theory grows old and stiff (as periodically it does and then has to be rejuvenated), men begin to take its categories and subcategories for granted and presently forget where in fact these come from, and assume that these have some intrinsic and ultimate cosmic value in themselves. The concepts are often pretty thin by that time, little more than names with a cosmic glow about them. Such has been the fate of many good terms and some not so good—substance, matter, mind, spirit, God, ego, con-

* Whitehead, *Process and Reality* (New York: Macmillan, 1930), p. ix.

sciousness, essence, identity, phlogiston, ether, force, energy, magnetism. As a fallacy this cognitive propensity is sometimes called hypostatization.

The fallacy is somewhat tricky, however. Every world theory considers the danda and categories of other world theories as hypostatizations. Terms are only genuinely hypostatized, clearly, if some cognitive weight is given to their very emptiness, if the absence of evidence they have attained is actually used as evidence—word magic, in short. A term or concept is no better than the corroborative evidence it stands for. When it begins to demand respect in its own right, it is beginning to be hypostatized. The fallacy is often hard to detect because the process of hypostatization is gradual and rarely complete. It is for this reason all the more disturbing to cognition, for its detection depends upon a careful weighing of the cognitive evidence for a concept against its cognitive claims. The detection is easier, however, once the dogmatic claims of infallibility, self-evidence, and indubitability have been recognized as fallacious. All that remains to be done, then, is to find the concept's actual significance in terms of multiplicative or structural corroboration—or, for our immediate purposes, to trace it back to its root metaphor.

We must not forget, however, that there are many root metaphors. A concept or category derived from even an inadequate root metaphor is not a hypostatization. It is simply a concept of an inadequate hypothesis. That is, there is no cognitive trouble with the term, which is functioning as well as it can. The trouble is with the hypothesis which generates the term. Nevertheless, there is a strong tendency to hypostatize the terms of a weak hypothesis. For where cognitive claims cannot be legitimately produced they tend to be illegitimately sought.

14. Maurice Natanson: "Rhetoric and Philosophical Argumentation"

Natanson received his Ph.D. from the University of Nebraska. Before his appointment in 1976 as Professor of Philosophy at Yale University, he had taught at the University of North Carolina and at the University of California, Santa Cruz. He is the author of *Literature, Philosophy, and the Social Sciences* (1962), *The Journeying Self* (1970), and *Edmund Husserl* (1973), among other works.

RHETORIC AND PHILOSOPHICAL ARGUMENTATION*

The species "philosophical argumentation" stands to the genus "argumentation" in a rather special rela-

* Originally published in the *Quarterly Journal of Speech*, vol. 48, no. 1; February 1962, pp. 24–30. Reprinted by permission of the author and the Speech Communication Association.

tionship, for included within the former is the rationale of the latter. The logic of argumentation is the theme of philosophical argumentation. Clearly, then, by philosophical argumentation is meant a subsidiary discipline of tremendous depth and with great implications. It is not the arguments philosophers employ which constitute the subject matter of philosophical argumentation but rather the nature of argumentation as such within philosophical discourse. However, it is through the study of philosophical arguments that we come to appreciate the problems of philosophical argumentation. A first approach to the nature of what is distinctive about philosophical argumentation may then be made by considering briefly the features of philosophical arguments. Some preliminary distinctions may prove to be valuable.

First, philosophical arguments are essentially *a priori* in character; i.e., they are not about matters of fact. They differ from mathematical and purely formal arguments to the extent that they have experiential or phenomenological bearing. Isaiah Berlin once put the matter this way: If you have a factual question you go to a scientist for the answer; if you have a formal question you go to a mathematician for the answer; but if your question is neither factual nor formal, you go to a philosopher for help. An equivalent expression of the same position is made by George Santayana in his Preface to *Scepticism and Animal Faith.* "Here is one more system of philosophy," Santayana writes. "If the reader is tempted to smile, I can assure him that I smile with him, and that my system . . . differs widely in spirit and pretensions from what usually goes by that name. . . . I am merely attempting to express for the reader the principles to which he appeals when he smiles."[1]

Second, philosophical arguments are never synonymous with their techniques of articulation; modes of argument are not the same as philosophical arguments. Thus, one may show that a certain form of argument is invalid—traditional syllogistic fallacies, for example—without concluding that what is being argued is philosophically unacceptable. Philosophic content appears to transcend its formal vestment.

Third, the relationship between speaker (or writer) and audience is different in philosophy from other fields; accordingly, a rather special problem arises in trying to understand philosophical arguments in relation to their authors and the audiences they are intended to address. Here we enter a still wider region in which rhetorical considerations become relevant, indeed central. I prefer to approach this set of problems in the context of a recent and admirable book, *Philosophy and Argument* by Henry W. Johnstone, Jr. In a section on "Persuasion and Validity in Philosophy" Johnstone discusses the relationship between author and audience. He contrasts in particular the differences between the speaker as rhetorician and the speaker as philosopher. A summary statement of some of the differences he finds may prove helpful at this point:

1. The aim of the rhetorician is to persuade his audience; the aim of the philosopher is to explain his position.

2. The persuasive speaker must necessarily hide his rhetorical technique if he is to succeed as a persuader of men; the philosopher fails if he knowingly or designedly conceals his techniques.

3. The rhetorician argues unilaterally toward his audience; the philosopher proceeds bilaterally toward his colleagues.[2]

The method of the philosopher, then, according to Johnstone, is necessarily and essentially bilateral: "The philosopher is obligated not only not to conceal from his audience any of the techniques he uses in arguing, but also to make available to it all the techniques that he does use."[3] It would appear on this account that rhetoric and philosophy are disparate activities. To the extent that the philosopher deliberately chooses rhetorical devices to make his position more attractive, he fails in his professional role.[4]

Through Johnstone's argument we have now come to one view of what characterizes, in decisive fashion, a philosophical argument and differentiates it from other modes of argumentation, especially those employed by the rhetorician. The philosopher is professionally committed to a "nothing may be concealed" mode of expression. If he fails it must be because of his inability or inexactitude, not because of a choice to hide something. The philosopher, on this account, turns out to be an open man. His methodology must remain as much available for inspection as his conclusions and supporting reasons. The total philosophical machinery is involved, then, in philosophical argumentation. Rhetoric, on the contrary, is grounded in the principle of disguise. Even if the rhetorician's motives are noble and his conclusions sound, his devices are chosen from a different base, one that bears a secretive nature. The machinery of his method is never open for inspection while the engine of his argument is in operation. But a further question arises to complicate the present discussion. If the speaker as rhetorician and the speaker as philosopher are qualitatively different, what about their respective audiences? Are there distinctive differences in audiences as well? The differences to be noted here are not between audiences as such but rather between different relationships to audiences speakers stand in. The relationship of the rhetorician to his audience is not that of the philosopher to his audience. As Johnstone points out, persuasive argumentation hinges upon the fact that the rhetorical speaker must have an initial disagreement with his audience which he struggles to overcome by making use of attitudes, beliefs, and prejudices held by that audience. In philosophical argumentation, however, the philosopher does not have the right to take advantage of either his audience's disagreements or its fundamental assumption, as Johnstone notes:

> In the rhetorical situation, disagreement exists only to be overcome through the exploitation of an initial agreement, and the desire of an audience to reach its own conclusions must be circumvented. In philosophical discussions, on the other hand, whether there is an initial agreement or not, it cannot be exploited to overcome disagreement, since the latter is radical, permitting no compromise. What must be exploited is just the desire of each participant to reach his own conclusions. A conclusion has no philosophical use if it is not reached freely. To be philosophically useful, it must represent the unconstrained attempt on the part of its advocate to fulfill his obligation to defend and clarify his position. Thus philosophical discussion is, in effect, a collaborative effort to maintain the conditions under which disagreement is possible.[5]

But before proceeding further with the analysis of our problem, it is necessary to admit a rather central point into the discussion of audiences: the rhetorician's audience may be specified; the philosopher's audience is specifiable with great difficulty. To whom is the philosopher really addressing his arguments? Obviously, all sorts of answers are possible: to other professional philosophers, to graduate students in his field, to philosophically trained laymen or specialists in other related fields. But to answer in this way is to admit of essential ambiguities. Clearly, the question here is not, Who is professionally qualified to understand what the philosopher has written? Is the philosopher interested in addressing any individual capable of comprehending his arguments? What about the more nearly human factors of time and place? Surely, a philosopher answering another philosopher in a journal article is primarily interested in an immediate response, discussion of his views, etc., and not in what future philosophers will think of his arguments two or three thousand years hence. But psychological considerations must be kept to one side, and practical considerations as well. We are interested, in the immediate context, in what is professionally germane to the philosopher's activity *qua* philosopher. And here it is possible to say, candidly, that the philosopher's audience is at best a problematic concept. At one extreme the philosopher is addressing his fellow philosophers active on the professional scene. At another extreme it can be argued, as Perelman and Olbrechts-Tyteca do in *Rhétorique et philosophie*,[6] that philosophical arguments are addressed to mankind, a universal audience. Accordingly, the proper audience of the philosopher is an ideal-type, a model, or universal construct, having only an ideal existence. At this point I propose to part company with Johnstone's analysis and to turn to certain problems it raises for rhetoric and philosophy. What follows now is a forward-looking summary of my argument.

Whatever the philosopher *believes* himself to be doing, there is immanent within his professional activity something antecedent to either a unilateral or a bilateral mode of procedure: there is a mono-lateral or proto-lateral activity. To translate simply: the philosopher is trying to uncover something about himself. Philosophical activity is self-discovery. Philosophical reports, spoken or written, are self-reports first, arguments later. "First" here is intended in a logical, not a chronological sense. Even if the argument is chronologically first, its probing is a matter of uncovering its original intent in relationship to the self that intended it. The self that seeks an alter ego, the philosopher who looks for an interlocutor, the teacher in quest of his student—all are involved in a primary situation in which rhetoric and philosophy are integral, although the problem of rhetorical technique gives way to the underlying question of philosophical communication. The philosophical form closest, in this sense, to the original fusion of rhetoric and philosophy is dialogic philosophy in the Socratic tradition. The mode of argument that is generated out of this tradition is at once distinctively and truly philosophical as well as rhetorical. Persuasion, however, will be treated as dialectical transformation of the self through indirect argumentation. The category of "indirection" is the operative one here; Socrates, Montaigne, and Kierkegaard may serve as triple moments in the exploration of indirect argumentation. It may be well to note that I have chosen a very special aspect of philosophical argumentation as a basis for going beyond Johnstone's position. This is at once the weakness and the strength of what follows. I am not concerned with classical rhetoric. I am not concerned with the full range of all philosophical argumentation. But neither am I concerned to present a compromise of any order, for I believe that my special case generates decisively important features of both philosophy and rhetoric. Here, then, is a philosophical approach to rhetoric through the mode of indirect argumentation.

The image of Socrates is prominent in the writings of both Montaigne and Kierkegaard; the humanity of Socrates invites the pleasure of the later thinkers. "Socrates' purpose was not vague and fanciful," Montaigne writes, "his aim was to furnish us with things and precepts that are really and more directly serviceable to life."[7] And Kierkegaard celebrates the same common touch. But far from simple utility being at issue, it is a fundamental method of procedure that is in question here. Montaigne is not suggesting that Socrates is a good philosopher because his activity was pragmatically helpful. Far from being helpful, it was severely hurtful. The point of Montaigne's consideration of Socrates lies in a different direction, then. To understand Montaigne on Socrates it is necessary to turn to Montaigne on Montaigne, his central subject. Self-knowledge is the clue to as much of our comprehension of the world as man can gain. For Montaigne, we can be certain of very little indeed: but we can achieve apodictic knowledge of ourselves. The proper course of knowing can consist only in determining the limits of the self, and for Montaigne those limits are not to be found in exalted places but rather in comnonplace circumstances. The world of daily life carries within it the secret of our being. Socrates more than any other philosopher was first of all simply himself; that was his art and his genius. "He was besides," Montaigne writes, "always one and the same, and raised himself not by fits and starts, but by his natural temperament, to the highest pitch of vigour. Or to speak more correctly, he raised nothing, but rather brought down, reduced and subjected vigour to his natural and original pitch, as well as all asperities and difficulties."[8] Self-knowledge, then, presupposes an epistemic condition: knowledge is within the person, and teaching must be restricted to a process of dialectical occasioning. To learn is to confront another and thereby come to confront oneself. Here is the first lesson in philosophical indirection.

Kierkegaard carries on Montaigne's theme:

> From the standpoint of the Socratic thought every point of departure in time is *eo ipso* accidental, an

> occasion, a vanishing moment. The teacher himself is no more than this; and if he offers himself and his instruction on any other basis, he does not give but takes away, and is not even the other's friend, much less his teacher. Herein lies the profundity of the Socratic thought, and the noble humanity he so thoroughly expressed, which refused to enter into a false and vain fellowship with clever heads, but felt an equal kinship with a tanner; whence he soon "came to the conclusion that the study of Physics was not man's proper business, and therefore began to philosophize about moral matters in the workshops and in the market-place" . . . but philosophized with equal absoluteness everywhere.[9]

Here is the second lesson in philosophical indirection.

And now by indirection we arrive at a new way of differentiating philosophical argumentation from all other modes of argumentation. What is at issue in the philosopher's argumentation is himself. There is no ideal observer in philosophy any more than there is an agreed upon and necessary starting point. Each philosopher must be a beginner because philosophy is a science of beginnings. One contemporary philosopher, Edmund Husserl, would have preferred to call philosophy "archeology" had that term not already been taken for a separate discipline. Philosophy is a science of origins, of roots, of foundations or beginnings.[10] As a foundation digger, then, the philosopher is confronted first of all with himself; he is his own primary datum. How is he to describe himself, talk about himself, converse with himself? Is the philosopher an ideal observer of his own being? And can the philosopher's reports stand as evidence for other philosophers? The notion of philosophical indirection is an effort to explore some of these interrelated questions. In the Socratic-Kierkegaardian tradition we have discussed, the following style of answer arises.

There can be no substitution in philosophy proper,

i.e., I cannot stand in relationship to your findings as you do or should. My task is to uncover my own truth, or more properly, my own relationship to truth. To say with Kierkegaard that "truth is subjectivity" is to locate the domain of the true in vital nexus with the inquiring agent—not the ideal or artificial observer but the unique and but once given ego. It is not truth that interests Kierkegaard, but himself in relationship to truth. Philosophical argument is not rendered impossible; instead it can operate existentially only by means of indirect communication, by what we have called indirection. I am now suggesting that this procedure has a logic of its own which can tell us much about philosophical argumentation and rhetoric as well. But some cautions must be taken. Once again, I repeat that my analysis by no means is intended to handle the total range of philosophical thought. There are major arguments in the history of philosophy in the fields of logic, epistemology, and metaphysics which are untouched by what I have to say here. Nor will the implications of my argument for rhetoric pertain to the full range of that discipline. I content myself with small conclusions in the hope that meaningful questions of a larger scope may be articulated. This itself is an instance of indirect procedure, and what follows now is a third lesson in philosophical indirection.

What one thinker finds in another transcends the former's arguments and relates instead to his mode of argumentation. The latter has an overt and a covert form. The overt mode of philosophical argumentation in Hume's analysis of causation or in Kant's transcendental deduction presents itself directly for examination. What is hidden is not intended to be hidden; rather Hume and Kant failed to make themselves clear to the extent that their methodological procedures remain obscure. Here we agree with Johnstone's analysis of bilateral argumentation. The philosopher's prime responsibility is to make his argumentation as clear as his arguments. But this pertains to overt argumentation alone. There is also what I have termed the covert mode of philosophical argumentation. It is here that indirection enters, and it is here that rhetoric enters, for it is here that the essential being of the philosopher, his subjectivity, is at issue. Prior to arguments there is argumentation, and argumentation involves the style of the philosopher's existence. What kinds of questions does he take as significant? What order of problem presents itself to him as having primary force? What is it he is essentially striving to do in his philosophizing? We look to men for answers to these questions as much as we look to their works. Or to express it differently, we look to works as indirect clues to their authors. The result of our inquiry is not an esoteric domain of personality that presents itself; rather, it is a proto-argumentative level of suasion that is encountered here. I prefer to think of it as an aspect of rhetoric.

At the level of covert argumentation, the philosopher *does* make a choice about his mode of procedure, the style of his presentation, the ultimate technique he is going to employ. One such radical choice is to proceed by means of philosophical indirection, and that choice precludes the philosopher's making his dialectical technique, his mode or argumentation, available in his argument. At least in one important instance, then, Johnstone's criterion for what sets apart philosophy and rhetoric breaks down. Indeed, his differentiating point is precisely what unites philosophy and rhetoric at this juncture. To be sure, the instance is a limited one—all philosophers do not fall in the camp of Socrates, Montaigne, and Kierkegaard. Yet there is an importance to a connection once seen that ought not to be dropped or abandoned. Expanded beyond its formulation here, the notion of a proto-argumentative procedure involving the subjectivity of the philosopher would lead to what might be termed the rhetoric of commitment not merely to his work but to the overriding importance of his problems. One can sense such commitment in philosophers as different as Husserl and Wittgenstein. The problem is not a psychological one. I am not talking about the "personalities" of philosophers.

The specific arguments philosophers use are not synonymous with the underlying structure of philosophical argumentation. Concrete arguments are rooted in a more primordial ground, the fundamental intent of the philosopher. When that intent is shared and sympathetically taken up, philosophers seem to attract and even educate each other; dialogue is possible. When that intent is clearly unshared, only arguments are possible. The analysis of arguments is the proper business of theory of argumentation, but the consideration of fundamental intent is generated out of philosophical indirection alone. The resonance a philosopher feels with a point of view or a thesis involves a rhetorical presupposition. Rhetoric in this sense is concerned with proto-argumentation and a primordial choice of styles of philosophizing. Its ultimate subject matter is the unique person committed in his uniqueness to a way of seeing and having a world. Perhaps another name for what I have in mind here is *ethos*. If this suggestion is warranted, then it might be fairly said that I have interpreted the philosophical self in rhetorical terms. Philosophical indirection, however, is less concerned with rhetoric as persuasion than it is with rhetoric as involvement. The alter ego is to be freed, not overcome. The philosopher achieves his own freedom in helping the other to free himself. This is the final lesson in philosophical indirection.

NOTES

[1] George Santayana, *Scepticism and Animal Faith*, p. v.

[2] Johnstone, p. 142.

[3] Ibid.

[4] Cf. Johnstone, pp. 139–141.

[5] Ibid., p. 146.

[6] Ch. Perelman and L. Olbrechts-Tyteca, *Rhétorique et philosophie: pour une théorie de l'argumentation en philosophie*. See p. 20 ff., esp. p. 22. Cf. Johnstone, p. 147 and see Ch. Perelman, "Reply to Henry W. Johnstone, Jr." . . .

[7] "Of Physiognomy," *The Essays of Montaigne*, translated by E. J. Trechmann, II, p. 509.

[8] Ibid., pp. 509–510.

[9] Søren Kierkegaard, *Philosophical Fragments*, pp. 6–7.

[10] See Herbert Spiegelberg, *The Phenomenological Movement*, I, p. 82.

15. Lewis White Beck: "Philosophy as Literature"

Presently Burbank Professor of Intellectual and Moral Philosophy at the University of Rochester, Beck (b. 1913) has also held the post of president of the American Philosophical Association. He is the author of *Early German Philosophy* and a *Commentary on Kant's Critique of Practical Reason*, among other works.

PHILOSOPHY AS LITERATURE*

My choice of the topic, "Philosophy as Literature," is a result of experiences which I do not believe are unique to me, yet which have been largely ignored by both philosophers and students of polite letters.[1] The experiences are those of aesthetic satisfaction upon reading many a fine work of philosophy, a gratification

* Used by permission of the author. This essay is published here for the first time.

comparable in kind, and sometimes in degree, to that which I have upon reading a good novel, play, or poem. For me, philosophy is, among other things, a genre of literature.

Yet if it is literature, it is literature neglected by critics and ignored by most people who love literature. The student of English literature of the eighteenth century is told that Locke's influence upon it is pervasive, and that he cannot understand *Tom Jones* and *Tristram Shandy* unless he knows the *Essay Concerning the Human Understanding.* So he dutifully learns about the *Essay*. He may even read it, but never, I think, with any other motive than to understand the "real" literature. He does not think the *Essay* is itself literature, a work to be approached with the canons of literary criticism or with the joyous anticipation he feels when he comes to the works of Swift, Addison, and Johnson.

My choice of Locke is perhaps not entirely fair to the student of letters, for there are a few authors whom he reads as literature and whom the philosopher reads as philosophy. Notable examples are Plato and Nietzsche. What the philosopher finds and admires most in them is rather different from what the student of literature and the educated general reader most admire. The philosopher prefers *The Will to Power*, the litterateur *Zarathustra*. The philosopher prefers the *Sophist, Theaetetus*, and *Parmenides*, while the man of letters prefers the *Phaedrus, Phaedo*, and *Symposium*. But they are at one in their devotion to one book of Plato's: the *Republic*, paradoxically the one book in which Plato is most hostile to the poet, the hero of the student of letters. At the end of the *Republic*, Plato recounts the "ancient quarrel between philosophy and poetry" and banishes the poet from the ideal city because the poet may mislead the citizen by the sweetness of his song. The poet makes illusion attractive, and takes the mind away from truth, the realm of the philosopher. But the existence of the *Republic* is itself an argument against banishing the poets. It is itself a work of art, and had Plato succeeded in establishing an earthly city according to its pattern, it would have been a tribute to his writing literature of power, not literature of knowledge. I cited Plato as a counter-example to my statement that men of letters have neglected philosophical writings; but I did so with the assurance that Plato is the best example I can cite for my thesis that works of philosophy *can* be works of literature too.

Other counter-examples are not as clear as that of Plato. I refer to some closer to home, namely Emerson and Carlyle. Consider Emerson. I will be told, correctly, that students of American literature have a far deeper love and better understanding of Emerson than professional philosophers do. Precisely. What professional ever thought of Emerson as one of theirs? American literature is welcome to him. This attitude may be unjust to Emerson, and it may be question-begging in a dispute over whether literary scholars study real philosophers. So I must make clear how, at least at the beginning of this essay, I am going to use the words "philosophy" and "literature."

The source books assigned by professors of English and other languages constitute Literature with a capital L. The source books in the syllabi of professors of philosophy constitute Philosophy with a capital P. There is little overlap between the two sets of books. My thesis is that this is not due to any inherent lack of literary quality in all the works called Philosophy, or of philosophical merit in all the works called Literature.

This is an offer, and a plea. It offers to the student of literature an almost virgin field for his critical exploration. And it is a plea to the sensitive student of literature to furnish the rest of us with imaginative insights into the literature of philosophy, to teach philosophers the crafts of criticism and techniques for the articulation of literary taste in philosophy, and to make the literary experience of philosophy more understandable.

But before I expatiate on philosophy as literature, there are two other topics I must touch upon. They are: philosophy *of* Literature, and philosophy *in* Literature.

II. PHILOSOPHY OF LITERATURE[2]

I have given a rough-and-ready description of what I mean by Literature. But in a serious philosophical discourse I must try to explain why professors of literature choose just the books they do for their students to study. Why, I am asking, are *David Copperfield*, *Hamlet*, *Paradise Lost*, *The Antiquities and Natural History of Selborne*, and *Holy Living and Holy Dying* chosen as Literature with a capital L, while Locke's *Essay*, Hobbes' *Leviathan* and Mill's *Utilitarianism* are not chosen? I will now try to answer that question.

Literature, like any art, is jealous of the attention we pay to other things. It holds attention to itself, and it rewards the single-minded attention we give it, delighting us if we take it exactly as it is. It concentrates into a single vision what we may see piece-meal on scattered occasions; and it may embody what we would never see had we not been helped to see it by the artist's vivid presentation of it.

Literature, however, is unlike any other art in its most important feature, which I shall try to make salient by comparing it with music and painting. Music is not normally *about* anything. It is tone and rhythm and pattern to be enjoyed for themselves; its ideas, if there are any, are musical ideas. Only rarely, and then not very successfully, does it tell a story, present a philosophy, or imitate anything that is not music. Painting is sometimes like music in that tone and rhythm and pattern of light and color hold our attention, but usually it is also like literature in that it is a painting *of* something.

Literature, however, is *always* about something. The surface-values of the physical text are not like beautiful tones and colors, and if the spoken text has beauty of rhythm, consonance, and tone this is always parasitic upon its meaning. Euphonious nonsense syllables do not make poetry.

Here lies the paradox of the art of literature. Like any art, it is jealous of the attention we pay to other things, yet the personalities depicted, the events narrated, the emotions aroused or recollected in tranquillity, and the ideas conveyed by literature do get our attention. How, then, can we give literature the undivided focal attention which any art-work demands, and yet experience facts and values which are not visible on the surface of the text?

The paradox arises from an ambiguity in the word "about." Literature is about something that does not take our attention away from the text. Compare *The Origin of Species*, which is about the life of plants and animals, with *Ulysses*, which is about a day in the life of Leopold Bloom. The two "abouts" function very differently. One is a "reportorial about," and the other a "fictive about."[3] The *Origin of Species* is about plants and animals; Darwin studied them, his writing refers to them, and the worth of his writing is the precise degree to which he told the truth about them. Darwin had no other relevant purpose than to reveal and explain these antecedent facts. His success is not that he wrote a book one loves to read, or whose style one admires, but that he wrote a book that instructs us about plants and animals. The meaning of *The Origin of Species*, what it is reportorially about, is meaning in the mode of *semantic transparency*. The rich ambiguity, the over-determination, and the invitation to diverse levels of interpretation which rivet our attention to a literary text would be faults in a scientific treatise.

Briefly, his point is as follows. "Dr. Johnson was a lexicographer" is about Johnson, and *about* is a semantic two-place predicate, (. . .) *is about* (. . .), the blanks to be filled by an existing sentence and the name of an existing man. "Dr. Grantly was an archdeacon" is about Grantly; but here *about* is a syntactic one-place predicate, (. . .) *is about Grantly*, where the blank is to be filled by a sentence Trollope wrote, and the predicate "is about Grantly" tells us what kind of sentence it is; Goodman calls it a "Grantly-about" sentence, and it is to be distinguished from another sentence which Trollope wrote which is a "Harding-about" sentence. Ordinary syntax does not differentiate between these one-place and two-place predicates, but once this is done the difference between the reportorial and the fictive about is evident.

We do not ordinarily give devoted and single-minded attention to the medium of Darwin's message—we *see through it* to the biological facts and theories he is talking about. The semantic transparency of the reportorial about puts a constraint on freedom of interpretation of *The Origin of Species*. To the extent that Darwin was successful, there is one right way of reading his book.[1]

None of this is true of literature. Transparency to antecedent fact is here not controlling. The literary "fictive about" is not transparent to antecedent fact; there may indeed be no antecedent fact. The author of a work of literature may create what it is about by creating that which seems to be about it. There was no Barchester until Trollope created it. Even if there is an antecedent fact, the transparent truth about it is not what is important, as it was for Darwin: "what is said" may be more interesting than whatever it is "about which it is said." Boswell attempted to report the truth about Dr. Johnson, whom he knew but did not create. But Boswell created the Johnson whom we know. Boswell's *Life of Samuel Johnson* as a work of literature is not depreciated by a more accurate biography; in fact, a more accurate one may make us more aware than we were of Boswell's literary power. The *Life of Johnson* would cease to be biography, but would remain literature, even if it should turn out, *mirabile dictu*, that Dr. Johnson never existed.

All this is summarized when I say that the fictive about is a mode of semantic arrest,[5] in contrast to the semantic transparency of the nonliterary text with its reportorial about. But there are different degrees of semantic arrest. It may be almost total, as in *Finnegan's Wake*; almost absent, as in *The Natural History of Selborne*. In Trollope, the semantic arrest is much greater than in Boswell, for there never was an Archdeacon Grantly about whom Trollope wrote. Yet we do not miss him! The medium has become the message; in Denys de Rougement's metaphor, it is "a trap for attention." The Archdeacon is literally a creation of Trollope's, while at most we can say not quite literally that Johnson was Boswell's creation.

Trollope gives his created world whatever power or reality it has by arresting our attention at the medium in which he created it. We do not, like early readers of *Utopia*, look for it on a map. We love the book, *Barchester Towers*, which exists, not the city, which does not exist. Our attention is arrested by those qualities which pervade the medium through which (better: in which) we seem to see what Trollope seems to be talking *about*. But there is, literally, nothing, no existing thing, he is reporting the truth about.

Yet even in what is officially called fiction, there is

no creation *ex nihilo.* Had Trollope created the book and the town of Barchester *out of nothing,* we could understand it. Trollope lived, along with us, in a world he never made; he transformed parts of it into a world he did make. The constraint on Trollope's creation was not antecedent facts *about* Barchester which he had to report truly, but antecedent facts about life, *to* which he wanted to be true.

In a work of literary art, *truth to* must be distinguished from *truth about,*[6] especially since, as I have been arguing, much literature is not the truth *about* anything. *Truth about* is the achievement of the reportorial about; but *truth to* does not perfectly correspond to the fictive about, though the fictive about depends upon *truth* to. "Trollope is true to life" does not mean that his sentences are the truth about real life in real Barchester, because there is no real Barchester. It means, rather, that what he says fictively about Barchester coheres with the truth about life which he knew as the background of his creation and which we know as the apperceptive mass enabling us to understand his creation. The life *to* which he was true is not the life which he is talking *about*, for he is talking about Barchester which, unlike the cathedral towns he and you and I know, never existed. But it is only because we know something about real cathedral towns that we can easily move back and forth between those to which he was true and the one which he created.

The interpretation of life and that of literature differ in one important respect, however much they overlap in other respects. Even if the life discovered in literature is brutely factual, tediously repetitious, and is dispersively disorganized, it can be and by successful literature is changed, made lucid and redeemed. None of the tedium and fortuitousness and chaos of real life is changed, made lucid, or redeemed by fine talk in real life. Literature, while still true to what we know about this life, can effect this organization, elucidation, and redemption by creating an image of another life.

III. PHILOSOPHY IN LITERATURE

The literary artist creates, but he does not create out of nothing. What he knows of human nature and history and of what people have felt and thought are the materials he uses in building another world. Only because of this can that new world delineate and illuminate the features of the old world. "We can learn from texts," writes Peter Jones, "by using them for the construction of propositions applicable to the world we live in."[7] It is for this reason that Aristotle said tragedy is more philosophical than history.

Perhaps the most important facts about the world which are transmuted into literature are human beliefs. High literature contains ideas and beliefs and doubts which have traditionally been the subject matter of philosophy: fate and freedom, nature and convention, truth and illusion, man and God, the one and the many, what is and what ought to be, vice and virtue, happiness and misery. High literature almost always deals with such ideas, and where it does not do so explicitly, it nevertheless shows that it has been shaped by them. Students of literature are ignorant of philosophy at their own peril, even when not dealing with what they themselves call "philosophical literature."

There is a spectrum of philosophical literature, stretching from what I shall call "philosophical quotation" to "philosophical exhibition." These are pure types, but most philosophical literature lies somewhere in between.

By philosophical quotation I mean the explicit and didactic use of philosophical ideas, the author's own or more often those he has learned from others. The two best known examples of this occur in *De rerum natura* and *The Essay on Man*. Lucretius is disarmingly frank about the quotations in his poem. The ideas come from Epicurus, and he compares his verse to the honey which Roman mothers would rub on the lip of a vessel from which the child was to drink a noxious-tasting medicine:

> ". . . by such method haply I might hold
> The mind of thee upon these lines of ours."[8]

Were this a just description of his poem, it would not be great poetry but metrical philosophy, and the metre would be meretricious decoration. The genius of Lucretius consists in the way he rendered into genuine poetry a system of philosophy to which the sensuous charm of verse would seem to be most impervious.

Pope's *Essay on Man* came under close philosophical scrutiny in 1751 when the Berlin Academy offered a prize for the best essay on "Pope's System, comprised in the sentence, 'Whatever is, is right'."[9] Lessing and Mendelssohn did not compete for the prize, but wrote a polemic against both Pope and the Academy under the title *Pope a Metaphysician*. They attacked the academicians' thought that Pope had a system or, as a poet, could have one.

> The philosopher who climbs Parnassus and the poet who descends to the plain and gives out quiet wisdom meet each other half way; they meet, exchange costume, and return to where they started. Each brings the other's appearance with him, but nothing more. The poet has become a philosophical poet, and the philosopher a poetical philosopher. But the philosophical poet isn't for that reason a philosopher, and a poetical philosopher isn't a poet.[10]

The reason why the poet cannot be a philosopher and the philosopher a poet lies in the style and function of philosophy and poetry. A philosopher has to prove, and each of the twenty-one steps in his proof is equally important, no matter how tedious it may be. The poet, a light and winged creature, will not get entangled in proofs. So what does he do with what he has learned from the philosopher? He quotes, approximately. He quotes Epicurus in favor of pleasure and Epictetus in praise of virtue, but he cannot make a system out of these antithetical quotations—only a poem. Lessing and Mendelssohn make sport looking for these inconsistent quotations which Pope had strung together from Leibniz, Plato, Shaftesbury, Spinoza, and King's *De origine mali*.

It was to such "philosophical poetry," I think, that George Boas was referring when he said, "The ideas of poetry are usually stale and often false, and no one older than sixteen would find it worth his while to read poetry merely for what it says."[11]

But what about the great philosophical poets who did not just quote—Dante, Milton, Goethe, Wordsworth, Hardy? Their mode of poetically philosophising is not quoting, but exhibiting.[12] They embody philosophical stances in situations and character so that the reader can *see* philosophical models instead of having to think about abstract philosophical concepts. Theirs is a logic of images, not of concepts. The eighteenth century is full of such philosophical exhibition: I mention only *Candide* and *Rameau's Nephew*. In *The Magic Mountain* there is the conflict between Settembrini and Naphta, who incarnate opposing philosophies; the reader *sees* the price that must be paid for embracing either. In *Middlemarch*, in Peter Jones' interpretation,[13] we see a conflict between two forms of egoism which are consequences of different functionings of the imagination, each with its history in philosophy, but each here embodied in single characters in opposition to others. One of the most abstruse philosophical problems is that of personal identity. Locke, Hume, and Kant tried to solve it conceptually, but Conrad takes the problem out of the study and exhibits alternative trials at its solution in Lord Jim's attempts to come to terms with his fatal mistake.[14]

My favorite philosophical exhibition is the scene in *Huckleberry Finn* where Huck decides not to turn Jim in. He believes he is sinning, and that he will be damned, yet at the same time he knows he is doing the right thing. The philosophical ideas here are the same as in Plato's *Euthyphro*, yet Mark Twain exhibits the conflict in a man we admire whereas Plato recounts it in an explicit conceptual argument between Socrates and a prig. The same ideas are presented once in the mode of what De Quincy called the literature of power, and once in the mode of the literature of knowledge.

IV. PHILOSOPHY AS LITERATURE

In saying that literature exists in the mode of semantic arrest, I may have rendered it impossible to regard philosophy as literature. At least it appears to degrade the claim that philosophy is literature to two trivialities. These are: (a) that there are, in many philosophical writings, passages that merit the approbative adjective "literary"; (b) that there are a few whole books of philosophy that can be read with literary delight. I shall comment upon each.

(a) Just as there are philosophical quotations in literature, there are literary interludes in philosophical works. These interludes may occur in the most unexpected places; there are several even in that book aptly called "a literary wasteland," the *Critique of Pure Reason*.[15] There are one or two in Spinoza, many in Descartes, Berkeley, and Hume, one even in Hegel. In general, however, modern philosophy has characteristically eschewed literary decoration in favor of "the plain, historical method" and imitated the language which Thomas Sprat, in his *History of the Royal Society*, recommended as the language of science: "a close, naked, natural way of speaking." Contenting himself with being "an humble underlabourer" in the garden cultivated "by the incomparable Mr. Newton," Locke, who was a fellow of the Royal Society, was unlikely to affect a style which was passing out in science though still prevalent in philosophy (e.g., in Shaftesbury). He tried to put an end to the time when "Philosophy, which is nothing but the true Knowledge of Things, was thought unfit, or uncapable to be brought into well-bred Company, and polite Conversation."[16] With him, English philosophy set its course firmly in the direction of the literature of knowledge and away from the literature of power which, in De Quincy's words, "move[s] . . . through affections and pleasure and sympathy."

After an exuberant emancipation from scholastic restraint and the full exploitation of the stylistic elegance of the humanists, philosophy returned to a style close to that of scholasticism. (We should not allow difference in typography to hide resemblance of style.) It is a style of definition, analysis, and proof, a style which makes no apologies for being unedifying and often boring. The model for modern philosophy has been Locke and Hobbes, not Shaftesbury and Pascal. A few passages of poetry, a few of the more sensuous rhetorical tropes, may occasionally lighten the burden of heavy and dry impersonal philosophical work; but they do not convert philosophy into literature.

(b) Yet the stylistic splendours of literature are sometimes evident in philosophical writings about ideas. There have been philosophers like Nietzsche writing philosophy as if they were writing literature of power to charm or coerce the reader into agreement. (Everyone remembers the quip about Henry and William James.) Everyone can take delight in Schopenhauer's misery and agony with as purely a literary attitude as one brings to *The Sorrows of Young Werther.* The eighteenth century had great philosophical stylists who can be, and have been, poorly imitated since then: in Germany, Mendelssohn; in France, Diderot; in England, Berkeley and Hume. Russell at his best, which is not in his purplest passages, reminds us of these Enlightenment philosophers with his clarity, economy, and wit. Bergson and Santayana, on the other hand, are warnings to other philosophers not to write *too* well. Their lush style is as evocative as Swinburne, and the richness of their imagery exhibits philosophical ideas when the reader has a right to demand analysis and proof, an argument and not an aphorism.

Of course, there is nothing wrong with a philosopher's writing attractively and well; Brand Blanshard has written a book, *On Philosophical Style,* urging him to do so. But in exhibition which gives philosophy the power of literature lies a threat to philosophy which wants to be more than a commentary on and guide to life. Philosophy can pretend to be a guide to life only because it professes to tell the *truth about* the most pervasive features of reality and our knowledge of it. Therefore no philosopher wants his book to be read under the conditions of semantic arrest. He may want his message to be persuasive and use his skill to make it so; but to the extent that he depends upon his rhetorical skill at persuasion, his persuasiveness will distract from the philosophical work of testing what he says. Kant complained about Rousseau for this very thing; he said he must read Rousseau "until the beauty of his expression no longer distracts me at all, and only then can I survey him with reason."[17] A too obvious artistry produces semantic arrest in a book which the author wanted to be semantically transparent; when this happens, the philosophical reader will dismiss it contemptuously as "mere literature."

But I think we know enough about philosophy, and enough about "about," not to believe that philosophy is about all time and all existence in the same way that *The Origin of Species* is about all plants and animals. Semantic arrest exists also in philosophy, though it is not usually engendered by the charm of the medium. There is a deeper reason why philosophy is not simply reportorial. Modern philosophy begins with Descartes' *cogito, ergo sum*. Descartes erected a system of truths about the world which derived their inferential certainty from the intuitive certainty he had of himself as thinker. The primary task of reporting on the world, without constant reminder that our knowledge of it depends as much on ourselves as on the world, has been taken over by the scientist little troubled by epistemological scruples. Almost all modern philosophy is predicated on the Cartesian thesis of the priority of the cognitive consciousness.

This much Cartesianism underlies Kant's Copernican Revolution in philosophy. Kant taught that the world which can be known is constituted by laws whose original legislation lay not with God or nature but with the knower. The world, even the world of science and mathematics as well as that of history and ethics, is a human world. It may not be a part of, or even a reflection of, things as they are. It is created by constructive operations of the mind. For Kant, the human world is necessarily as it appears to be—Euclidean and Newtonian—because that is the only way the mind can "spell appearances in order that they may be read as experience" of objects.[18] The transcendental imagination constructs the world, but the Kantian transcendental imagination is rigorously controlled by the rules of understanding.

But the imagination did not long remain in this subordinate position, and Kant's construction of a unique universal human world was pluralized by the romanticists, led by Herder and Coleridge. This pluralization was later made more radical by Nietzsche, Dilthey, and Cassirer. More recently, Pepper and Turbayne[19] have explored the ways in which the choice of metaphors within a single language gives shape to entire systems of philosophy. But Kant based his metaphor of spelling and reading on the eighteenth-century theory of universal grammar. When this doctrine was rejected by his disciple von Humboldt, who saw irreducible differences in the tongues of men and saw each language as in part reflecting and in part determining a form of life, these philosophers interpreted the variety of readings that philosophers had made of the world as the product of creative acts of the imagination determined by the varieties of temperament, language, and culture. They saw the thinking and speaking of the philosopher as one act of creativity comparable to that of artists. Nietzsche says: "Gradually it has become clear to me what every great philosophy has been: namely, the personal confession of its author, and a kind of involuntary and unconscious memoir."[20]

One effect of this has been the increasing attention that philosophers have given to communication and expression. How could philosophy fail to be exceedingly "linguistic" in our century? Why indeed should it try not to be, when the understanding of the linguistic process is as central a concern to our century as discovering the laws of motion was to the seventeenth?

Philosophy, says Whitehead, is an attitude of mind towards doctrines ignorantly entertained, a critique of the abstractions current in one's culture.[21] Language is the abstraction dominant in our culture today. Language and communication theory have supplied models and metaphors which are pervasive in almost all modern thought from genetics to theology. Linguistic philosophy is an effort to become self-conscious and critical about them. Linguistic philosophy is reflexive meta-philosophy, and philosophy and its expression have become problematic.

"The limits of my language," says Wittgenstein,[22] "are [*bedeuten*] the limits of my world." But notice: this is parallel to what I have been saying about literature, that its meaning and value are not located in antecedent and independent fact about which it reports, but that it hedges its value and meaning in itself through semantic arrest. The limits of the world of Barchester are the limits of Trollope's language. Philosophy is as much a "language-game" as a mathematical system, a crossword puzzle, a novel or poem is. Whitehead said, "In the real world it is more important that a proposition be interesting than that it be true,"[23] and Archibald MacLeish wrote:

> "A poem should be equal to:
> Not true
> . . .
> A poem should not mean
> But be"[24]

To see philosophy in this light is offensive to those who adhere to the ideal of perennial philosophy, to those who believe that philosophical truth is like scientific truth and not at all like the values of literature. Most philosophers can bring themselves to see philosophies they think are wrong in this way, but not their own. Philosophy may be *read* as literature; but it is not written that way.

Not only philosophy is seen to be human-all-too-human; even the truth of science has lost some of its inhuman luster. We see science not as a photographic report on nature, but as an image refracted through human temperament standardized by human institutions. The paradigms and metaphors of science[25] are not exclusively reportorial about nature, but are imaginative models the construction of which is comparable to the act of the writer who converts a mere chronicle into a history or vague feelings into a lyric. In both science and philosophy we discern operations of the mind which have previously been regarded as operative only in the creation of art and literature.

***

My time is almost up, and I cannot go into detail about what follows from regarding philosophy as literature, e.g., about the canons for judging philosophy as literature. I will speak of only one problem, namely that of genre. What are the proper relations of substance to form in philosophical writing? I once jotted down fifty-three generic names of kinds of philosophical writings. They ranged from aphorisms and apologies at the beginning of the alphabet, through meditations and quodlibetal questions, to term papers and treatises at the end. Of each it may be asked: what relations obtain, or ought to obtain, between the content of a philosophy and its literary expression? Rather than discuss this vast question *in abstracto*, let me raise two specific questions which may be more easily answered and which may throw some light on the more general question.

(1) Why is Nietzsche's style aphoristic instead of systematic? It is not that Nietzsche could not sustain a long philosophical argument. It is, rather, that his perspectivism in epistemology makes him think that reality can be grasped better by a quick glance (in an apercu) than with the use of a deductive apparatus. The will to systematic thought, he wrote, is a symptom of lack of integrity.[26] And why did Hegel not write aphorisms? Because in the structure of his world all things are related essentially to all others, and truth is the whole.

(2) Second, why did Plato write dialogues? Did he have the same reasons that Boethius, Hume, and Fontenelle did? Why did Leibniz call his commentary on Locke *New Essays*, yet write them in dialogue form? Why did Berkeley write almost exactly the same philosophy twice, once in the *Treatise* and once in the *Three Dialogues*? Why is the philosophical outcome of Hume's *Dialogues* so obscure?

I cannot answer all these questions.[27] I shall conclude, however, with an attempt to answer the question about Plato. Was the dialogue form just a literary decoration, or was it inherently related to the world-view of which it was the vehicle? External reasons—the infamous litigiousness of the Athenian character, Plato's desire to celebrate Socrates—have been given; but these answers are superficial. There is a deeper philosophical reason which *required* the dialogue genre. Both Plato and Socrates believed that genuine knowledge is knowledge of the universal, of the form common to many things and the idea common to many minds. Dialogue is the method of eliminating the accidents and transiencies of private experiences of particular things. Dialogue leaves in the mind a common denominator of the diverse experiences of each participant. It is the outward dramatic form of dialectic, which Socrates defined as the discourse of the soul with itself.

In his old age there was a marked change in Plato's style. Though the *Timaeus* and the *Critias* are called dialogues, that seems hardly the right name. Timaeus speaks uninterruptedly for 64 pages, and Critias is still going strong when, after 13 pages without interruption, the fragment breaks off. One thinks Plato might have done better to give up the conventional dialogue form present in the first few pages of each work. Do we still have the perfect matching of style and content, of expression and method, which was perfected in the dialogues of the early and middle periods?

Obviously not, if we take dialogue to be only the outward form of dialectic. But dialogue has other functions too. It can create an artificial voice for which the author does not have to take full public responsibility. A character in a dialogue (even when he talks without interruption for 64 pages) can say things which the author, or the protagonist with whom he is identified, does not dare say *in propria persona.* Though the philosophical substance of the *Timaeus* is not itself presented in dialogue, it is in a dialogic frame. In the short and graceful natural dialogue at the beginning, a stage is set for an "entertainment" (*Tim.* 17) in which legends, travelers' tales, and a man's recollection of his grandfather's stories are to be narrated. The speakers bid for forbearance and indulgence from the hearers; Critias appeals for help from the muse of memory (*Crit.* 108), as well he might. When Timaeus' main speech begins, he reminds the others that "I who am the speaker, and you who are the hearers, are only mortal men, and we ought to accept a tale (or myth) which is likely and enquire no further" (*Tim.* 29D). For Socrates, who had been skeptical of cosmology since reading Anaxagoras, the proper vehicle for cosmology is tale, fable, and myth. The dialogic medium under the rubric of "entertainment" provides insulation against his dialectical questioning, his trusted instrument in the search for truth which is above and beyond likelihood and "noble fiction."[28]

NOTES

[1] While there is a small amount of writing which deals with the topic, the only formal and explicit full treatment I know is William Charlton, "Is Philosophy a Form of Literature?", *British Journal of Aethetics* 14 (1974) 3–16. His answer is affirmative, but is reached by quite a different route from the one I follow here. Since writing this essay I have found several articles dealing explicitly with the topic have come to my attention: Berel Lang, "Space, Time, and Philosophical Style", *Critical Inquiry* II, 263–80; and see footnote 27.)

[2] In this section, I have to deal briefly with the classical problem of 'truth' in the arts, a problem which is once again in the center of interest of critics and aestheticians. I hope the brevity of my treatment will not be mistaken for dogmatism.

[3] The ambiguities in "about" and the paradoxes arising from them are well known to philosophers. Very generally, I am here following a suggestion by Nelson Goodman ("About," *Mind* 70 (1961), pp. 1–24 at p. 18) in his discussion of "rhetorically about" (like my "fictive about").

[4] This seems *prima facie* to be true, or at least far more nearly true of *The Origin of Species* than it is of, say, *The Wasteland*. Later I shall indicate at least some modifications that may need to be made.

[5] I formulated this concept first in "Judgments of Meaning in Art," *Journal of Philosophy* 41 (1944), pp. 169–178. A similar concept under the title "intransitive attention" was subsequently developed by Eliseo Vivas in *Problems of Aesthetics*, pp. 406–411.

[6] See John Hospers, *Meaning and Truth in the Arts* (University of North Carolina Press, 1947), p. 163.

[7] *Philosophy in the Novel* (Oxford, 1975), p. 194.

[8] Lucretius I lines 960–61.

[9] The Academy misquoted: "Whatever is, is good."

[10] *Lessings Werke* (Petersen u.v. Olshausen, eds.), vol. 24, p. 100.

[11] *Philosophy and Poetry* (Norton, Mass., 1932), p. 9

[12] Corresponding to Wittgenstein's distinction between saying and showing, *Tractatus* 4.022; and to Eliot's ideas "as matter for argument" and "as matter for inspection" (*The Sacred Wood* [1928], p. 162). But the distinction is an older one. Philip Sidney wrote, "Whatsoever the Philosopher sayth shoulde be doone, hee [the poet] giveth a perfect picture of it in someone, by whom he supposeth it was doone" (*Apologie*).

[13] Op. cit., ch. i.

[14] See Bruce Johnson, *Conrad's Metaphors of the Mind* (Minneapolis, 1971), pp. 6, 91.

[15] David Tarbet, "The Fabric of Metaphor in the *Critique of Pure Reason*," *Journal of the History of Philosophy* 6 (1968), pp. 357–70.

[16] *Essay Concerning the Human Understanding*, "Epistle to the Reader."

[17] *Fragmente aus dem Nachlasse* (Hartenstein ed.) p. 315.

[18] *Critique of Pure Reason*, B 371

[19] *World Hypotheses* (University of California Press, 1942) *The Myth of Metaphor* (Yale University Press, 1962).

[20] *Beyond Good and Evil*, §6.

[21] *Modes of Thought* (New York, 1938), p. 233.

[22] *Tractatus* 5.6.

[23] *Process and Reality*, pp. 395–6

[24] "Ars Poetica," in MacLeish's *Poems, 1924–1933* (Houghton-Mifflin, 1933), pp. 122–123.

[25] See Thomas Kuhn, *The Structure of Scientific Revolutions* (Chicago, 1962) and C. M. Turbayne, *op. cit.* Earlier, in discussing *The Origin of Species* I intentionally ignored this aspect of scientific theory-construction and writing, for I wished to use a common-sense foil to bring out the peculiar strength of the artistic imagination. I cannot here explore this feature.

[26] *Twilight of the Idols*, §26.

[27] But most of them have been answered by Albert William Levi in an article published since the completion of this paper: "Philosophy as Literature: The Dialogue," *Philosophy and Rhetoric* 9 (1976) 1–20. On Hume see John Bricke, "On the Interpretation of Hume's *Dialogues*," *Religious Studies* II, pp. 1–18.

[28] I am indebted to Professor Colin M. Turbayne and Professor Russell Peck for advice especially on this last paragraph.

III

Style and the Reading of Philosophy

16. José Ortega y Gasset: "The Attitude of Parmenides and Heraclitus"

One of the most accomplished stylists in all of contemporary philosophy and certainly one of its most ardent contributors, Ortega (1883–1955) was a key figure in the development of twentieth-century Spanish thought. Graduating from the University of Madrid in 1910, he went to Germany for five years. He taught for many years following this at the University of Madrid, but went into exile in Argentina as a consequence of the Spanish Civil War, not returning to Spain until 1948. Often identified with existentialism, his works include: *Dehumanization of Art, Revolt of the Masses, What is Philosophy*, and *Man and People*.

THE ATTITUDE OF PARMENIDES AND HERACLITUS*

Parmenides and Heraclitus were probably born around the year 520 B.C.[1] Thus their thought dates to

* Reprinted from *The Origin of Philosophy* by José Ortega

around the year 500. What was the nature of the mental *soil* in which they were implanted? What intellectual trends, what general modes of thought attracted their youthful minds? What then-contemporary trends delineated for them the *adversary*?

No mention of a proper noun appears in Parmenides' work to serve as a guide. He "cites" neither friend nor foe. And that is not accidental. Parmenides poured his ideas into the mold of a solemn poem,[2] which is in keeping with the most characteristic literary genre of the period—the theological-cosmogenic poem of the Orphic mystics. The genre is mystical and tragic in tone, and the language imposed upon it is aloof and mythical. Although it is composed in the first person, this person is abstract: a youth—*κοῦρος*—who for some reason is protected by young goddesses, vague feminine divinities who are perhaps the Muses or the Hours, for they are called "daughters of the Sun." This vagueness in the lines, this shadowy spectral quality of the mythological setting evident in Parmenides, clearly and unquestionably reveals that Parmenides obliquely, coldly, and calculatingly adopted an "archaic genre" and used it for his pronouncements. Or to put it another way: Parmenides used the mythological-mystical poem without any longer believing in it, as a mere instrument of expression—in short, as a vocabulary. The defunct beliefs lasted for a long time transformed into mere words.[3] Mythology, once it is dead, has an awesome tenacity. While a belief that is not ours remains alive in others, we take it seriously and grapple with it, and at the least take care so that what we say is not confused with what its adherents say. When, however, we regard a belief to be mummified, it becomes merely an innocuous "manner of speaking." Thus do we calmly speak about the Orient as a region where things are born, precisely because no one still believes in the existence of such a place in cosmic space that specializes in births.

Not only does Parmenides speak about divine maidens, but of a formidable Goddess who will teach him the Truth and of a chariot led by the fleetest, no doubt winged, steeds, driven by the damsels, and who will lead him like an Amadis of Gaul along the "polyphemus road"—the "famous path" that enables "the creature who knows" to travel the entire universe and be left at the gates of heaven. All of this constitutes a solemn theatrical wardrobe extracted by Parmenides from old trunks to serve as a disguise precisely because he used it as a disguise. All that we are obliged to explain is why this man needed a disguise to say what he wished, why he believed it expeditious to feign a religious, mythological tone so that the resounding thunder of his ideas might descend upon us as pathetic outpourings, delivered in a revelatory, apocalyptic tone via a goddess' lips. Had we not foolishly disdained "Rhetorics and Poetics," which studied *genera dicendi*—the manner in which things can be said—we would readily understand the reason why Parmenides, in great seriousness (everything about Parmenides is terribly serious), rejected didactic prose, avoided personal comments, and transferred all of his elocution to vaguely religious characters and figures. *It is a stylistic necessity.* It is not a whim. Style is the distortion of common language to suit the author's special motives. The most frequent motive behind stylization is emotion. It manipulates tepid, ordinary, insipid language, kindling and sharpening it, making it reverberate and quiver.[4] Not only does Parmenides reveal his discoveries but—with a justification soon to be apparent to us—he is dazzled by them, he is so overcome with exalted emotion that they acquire a mystical value for him. If one believes that men are endowed with airtight compartments, nothing human will be understood. It is naïve to believe that because a science may be cold, a frigid truth, that its discovery lacks the mystical element, that it is not fervid, impassioned, and passionate. And yet, it has been, is, and will inevitably and happily be that way always. Every "scientific" *discovery*—that is, every truth—suddenly confronts us with an immediate vision of the world, hitherto unperceived and hence not taken into account. Abruptly, as though a veil were removed, it becomes marvelously evident to us—we become "visionaries"—and in addition feel as though we have been overcome by some strange power and uprooted from our habitual "bourgeois" and totally unmystical world into another one—we fall into ecstasy or "rapture." Irrespective of our prior convictions concerning the real and the divine, the commonplace and the magical, the situation—the manner in which the mystical experience is reproduced—is analogous. Descartes, the innovator of the most radical "pure reason," "pure rationalism"—a rationalism summoned to strangulate religion—discovered suddenly when very young, the *method* (from the "*mathesis universalis*") whereupon he experienced an ecstatic vision that he always regarded as the culminating moment of his life and as something in which he barely had a role, a divine gift, a transcendental revelation. Shaken by that peculiar, unabashed emotion typical of "discoverers," which is infinite humility, he inscribed in his personal notes: "*X novembris 1619, cum plenus forem. Enthousiasmo, et mirabilis scientiae fundamenta reperirem.*" ["10 November 1619, when I was full of enthusiasm, and I discovered the fundamental principles of a wonderful knowledge."]

Parmenides regarded the experience of his discovery as, in a sense, a transcendental phenomenon and hence he was most naturally led to employ a religious vocabulary and imagery in order to express simultaneously his idea and his emotion. And this he did precisely because he was not fearful that his readers would take his mystical utterances literally. Hence not only does Parmenides' style indicate that he did not believe in the gods, but that likewise amongst the social group whom he addressed, religious faith no longer existed. For Parmenides, the ultimate rationalist, to talk in terms of gods and of celestial excursions, and to employ unwieldly images represents something extraordinary and feverish, which serves to satisfy his need to express felt emotion. A genuine believer, however, would find Parmenides' pen palid, tepid, and coldly allegorical. Anaximander, eighty years earlier, had invented prose and composed his exposition of physics in it. This early prose had not yet been consolidated into a "literary genre," for it was still unsure of itself, that is, of being prose and only prose. When least expected, an emotive, almost mythological gale would sweep over Anaximander's "positivist" language, ruffling the prosaic idiom and imbuing it with visionary flashes. Hence Parmenides had no choice. This explains why he resorted to that fusty mechanism, the *deus ex machina*.

Hecataeus, on the other hand, cited names. He did not dodge the issue. He demanded that Homer and Archilochus be reprimanded (frag. 12). He called the master Hesiod ignorant and unaware of the difference between night and day (frag. 57), he accused Pythagoras of being a charlatan (frag. 129, dubious), and charged Hesiod, Xenophanes, and Hecataeus with concealing their ignorance regarding the only thing worth knowing behind a hodgepodge of ideas (frag.

40). The only puppet not beheaded was Thales, and of him he said: "He was the first astronomer." One hair left on the wolf! The absence of any barbed insult indicates a positive attitude on his part toward Thales and what the latter represented. Noteworthy is the fact that all those cited by name were deceased. Names of contemporaries are missing. One must bear in mind that the most important characteristic intellectual output of the sixth century emanated from the region that included Ephesus, the Ionic coast, and adjacent islands.

Unlike Parmenides, Heraclitus speaks from his own untransferable individuality. His pronouncements, which have baffled so many, and seem so utterly "enigmatic," flash forth like lightning from a mighty, highly individualistic I, from this concrete noninterchangeable man Heraclitus, born of the city's founding family, the Codridas, endowed with "royal" status, in the highest sense of the word, that is, his blood contained the inalienable, divine heritage of "charisma." Heraclitus relinquished the exercise of this divine sovereignty to his brother because even it prevented him from being an absolute individual, the highly unique Heraclitus he felt himself to be.

Before stating what this eminent person said, a brief pause is in order to analyze the manner in which he said it, the formal pattern of his language. Here is what one finds: Parmenides, though emanating from a distinguished family and endowed with the monumental self-confidence typical of the early thinkers—inspired both by consciousness of their existence and of their thought, their aristocratic heritage and their original thinking—imposed respect everywhere by his mere presence. The aura of that respectability appears even in Plato. In the final analysis, however, he mingled among men, he argued with them—his school initiated "discussion," dialectics, as a way of life, striving to convince, not only to demonstrate, but attempting to prove. Parmenides was not distant. Hence in his work he had to create distance and to allow his doctrine to pour forth from the veracious lips of a truthful goddess. Heraclitus, on the other hand, the "king," felt a sense of uniqueness and of unmitigated distance. He retired, as I noted before, from public life, renouncing his sacred magistracy. He felt electrifying contempt for the masses of his fellow citizens and considered them incapable of salvation because they did not possess man's fundamental virtue, which consists in the capacity to recognize superiority.[5] Thus Heraclitus returned from the public square to the solitary temple of Artemis. Later he found this to be inadequate and he retired to the innermost depths of a rugged mountain, akin to the merging of iron and diamonds, within the bowels of the earth. Rarely has a man possessed a more unlimited conviction of his superiority over others. *We shall soon see, however, the underlying inverse reason:* We shall see the utter humility from which this absolute arrogance sprang and derived its nourishment. Had Heraclitus still believed in gods, he would have believed himself a God. Hence he did not transpose his opinions, projecting them into some worthier mouth. He did not have to add stylistic distance to his own distance. His doctrine explains why he felt like a God—as, in principle, he believed any man had the right to feel, provided he were not as foolish as men are wont to be.

One must further bear in mind that in Ionia, where new thinking and "modern" life originated, the advance was even greater than that at the other end of Hellas in Magna Graeca and Sicily. The mythological distance was greater and prose—the Roman paladin, simple didactic expression without melodramatism or scenography—had been solidified. Forty years before, not far from Ephesus, Hecataeus had written his books on geography and history in pure didactic prose, prose as prosaic and direct as any to be found in a modern German *Handbuch.*[6] Nevertheless, it was prose that was still inadequate for expounding the strange, transcendental thought that was to be philosophy.[7] Thus Heraclitus *could not* write a continuous text book. He expressed his ideas in spurts, in brief pronouncements, which in their attempt each time to be total statements, were stylistically "compressed" and a sort of doctrinal dynamite. Hence his renowned "obscurity." Heraclitus' style therefore consists in expressing his highly individualistic being in the form of thundering pronouncements of the sort that can spout forth in any biting, "flashing," electric conversation. They are maxims, "slang expressions," and yet they have a certain tone which reveals that Heraclitus was influenced by a *genus dicendi* very much in vogue at the time, one with a religious transcendental overtone. This was none other than the oracular and sibylline formulae. He himself in two preserved "fragments" explained why he chose the literary genre of maxims. Granted his conviction that a thinker should devote his thought to universal reason and not be a recondite wizard dedicated to thought, he found the most suitable vehicle to be *similar* to oracular and sibylline divinations. Frag. 92: "The Sibyl who in a delirium utters things unjokingly, unadorned, and unperfumed, reaches milleniums with her voice, for she is divinely inspired." Frag. 93: "The Lord, to whom the oracle of Delphis belongs, neither affirms nor conceals, but suggests." Clearly—at that venerable, creative threshold of philosophy—"suggestion" was being propounded as philosophy's most suitable *vehicle of expression.* What this entails precisely will occupy us at a later point. These two statements of Heraclitus should, however, be interpreted as emanating from a man radically hostile to traditional religion, to the "mysteries," and the "cults."[8] His discoveries nonetheless were *experienced* along with an aspect of revelation, and the mystical impact of this experience found its natural expression in sentences quivering with quasi-religious emotion.

The foregoing stylistic observations pertaining to Parmenides and to Heraclitus could scarcely have been omitted, for they provide the underlying tone of all their statements, as will soon be concretely illustrated. A keen understanding of style is, in this instance, of prime importance. Since we possess but a few fragments of their work and sparse information regarding the period, we cannot neglect what unwittingly is interwoven in their style. In fact our realization that mythology had degenerated for them into mere vocabulary, a *modus dicendi,* is more conclusive than had they themselves stated that mythology, traditional religion, and everything connected with it represented for them the terminated past, something that had descended beyond their vital horizon. Heraclitus' violent attacks against the cult of the gods—the idols—were directed toward the popular segments of society in which archaic faith still persisted. He and Parmenides, however, were combating newer purely mythological forms of "religion," which were not the traditional ones, and as we shall soon see, *appeared on the scene at the same time as the new mode of thought that engaged Parmenides and Heraclitus:* Orphic theology and the "Dionysian mysteries." Mythology, the traditional religion of the Greek city, by then constituted a subsoil for both thinkers. They were not preoccupied or mentally involved with it; it was simply an old verbal usage, automatic and habitual, such as others comprised by language. Hence it did not matter, if a sentence called for it, to fall back upon the Erinyes, and even less so, to refer to Dike. Nevertheless, Heraclitus made it plainly evident that believers in traditional religion "haven't the slightest notion of what Gods and Heroes really are" (frag. 5).

Heraclitus' *soil* is composed of the intellectual trend that had emerged a century before throughout Greece, particularly in its purest and most pronounced form in Thales of Miletus, in whom it first appeared. In short, what was referred to as Ionian *natural science*. Let us seize the bull by the horns, that is, the one we had in our fingers a moment ago. The only individuals mentioned by Heraclitus without any appended insult are Bias and Thales. And all that he said about the latter was that he was the first astronomer. Heraclitus therefore respected the mode of thinking initiated by Thales, *but* he made it clear that in comparison with his own knowledge, that of Thales and his followers was specialists' knowledge, *nothing more* than astronomy. In order to understand this completely and to diagnose completely, or adequately, the actual *soil* in which both proto-philosophers were implanted, one must recall that Thales flourished around the year 584. It is necessary, therefore, to picture with a certain clarity the profound change that in rapid expansion and accelerated development occurred in Greek life around the year 600 until 500, the date when the work of both proto-philosophers began.

Not only does each of us inhabit a spatial landscape but also a temporal one, with its three dimensions of past, present, and future. Let us for the moment ignore the latter. A certain horizon of the past extends into our own present, it persists, it forms part of the structure of our lives and is an instrument therein. Like every landscape, the past when viewed has perspective, close and distant planes. Each one of these temporal planes acts differently upon our existence. In order to understand a man well one must depict with some precision the chronological topography of his horizon.

The names cited by Heraclitus allow us to reconstruct with considerable clarity the perspective he had of events of Greece's past up to his own day. And with slight modification—due to the fact that the settlements of the west were somewhat less "advanced" than those of the east—the picture serves Parmenides.

In one fragment (42), Heraclitus mentioned Homer and Archilochus together. In another—and in this order—Hesiod, Pythagoras, Xenophanes, and Hecataeus (40). Note that the order in which these names were cited corresponds exactly to historical chronology. Heraclitus' outbursts were written around 475. Hecataeus, the closest to Heraclitus, died when the latter was around twenty years old. Xenophanes, who was a few years older than Hecataeus and Pythagoras, was probably born around 572. These three men therefore "were around" when Heraclitus' life began. Behind them in the intangible distance loomed a character utterly of the past, Hesiod, who composed his *Theogony* around the year 700. Fifty years earlier there was Homer and fifty years later, Archilochus. Thus they were respectively a century and a half, two centuries, and two and a half centuries removed from the youthful Heraclitus—500 B.C. According to Greek temporal optics prior to Aristotle, a century and a half is not a precise time, but rather some hazy, indiscernible, pure "antiquity." Accordingly, Homer and Hesiod are neither more nor less distant than Archilochus. Note that fragment 40 is like a diptych: on the one side Hesiod, and together on the other Pythagoras, Xenophanes, and Hecataeus. In fragment 42 Homer is paired with Archilochus. Hesiod therefore represents the converging point of both groups of names: those completely "ancient" and those completely "modern." They represent for Heraclitus the two great terminal points of the past. . . .

NOTES

[1] As I formerly indicated, a discussion on the chronological relationship between the lives of both is not relevant here. What is crucial for us—and striking—is that the works of both were simultaneous and occurred around 475.

[2] It seems highly improbable to me that the poem had a title, and even more so that it be entitled *On Nature,* as is conventionally held in Sextus Empiricus. A much likelier name, if any, would have been *Aletheia.*

[3] We still name a metal "mercury," Madrilenians go for a stroll to Neptune's fountain, and some hapless souls suffer from venereal diseases, that is, diseases of Venus.

[4] At other times when the emotion is of a different sort, wary and timorous, stylization obtains the opposite effect; it further decapitates normal language, it renders it even more inexpressive—for example, in diplomatic language everything is evasive, the euphemism strongly supplants intuitive expression with fuzzy, watered-down language. Bear in mind that these distortions of normal language, which we call "stylizations," are not, at any given moment, infinite but constitute an available or potential repertory (one already invented or which the individual can invent for the occasion) of limited casuistry. To define the forms of stylization is not, therefore, a pointless task—attempting to fence in the countryside, so to speak. In addition to the grammar of normal speech, there is need to compose an ultra-grammar of stylization.

[5] An absurd defect, since in mankind it transpires amongst those who are simply a wretched flock in need of a shepherd (see frag. 11).

[6] Which does not prevent his prose from occasionally rippling poetically in *Asianic* flourishes.

[7] Perhaps it is further noteworthy that there has never been a *genus dicendi* truly adequate as a vehicle for philosophizing. Aristotle was unable to resolve this problem that fools ignore. His work has been preserved because he held on to his

own lesson notes. I personally have had to contain myself for thirty years while fools accuse me of producing only literature, and the worst part is that even my own students find it necessary to pose the question of whether I have been writing literature or philosophy, along with other ridiculous provincial notions of this order!

[8] See fragments 5, 14, and 15.

17. Paul Friedländer: "Irony"

Born in Berlin, Professor Friedländer (1882–1968) received his Ph.D. from the University of Berlin in 1905. In 1915, he was named Professory Extraordinary of Berlin and subsequently taught at Marburg, Halle, Johns Hopkins University, and the University of California. Well-known for his scholarly contributions on classical philosophy, philology, and archaeology, his books include *Documents of Dying Paganism, Epigrammata: Greek Inscriptions from the Beginnings to the Persian War*, and the three-volume work on *Plato* from which the present selection is taken.

IRONY*

"He who would explain to us when men like Plato spoke in earnest, when in jest or half-jest, what they

* From *Plato* by Paul Friedlander, translated by Hans Meyerhoff, vol. 1, *An Introduction* (copyright © 1958 by

wrote from conviction and what merely for the sake of the argument, would certainly render us an extraordinary service and contribute greatly to our education." These words of Goethe do not seem to have been taken with sufficient seriousness even as an ideal postulate. It is quite certain, however, that one cannot approach Plato without taking into account what irony is and what it means in his work.

If irony were nothing but "a mere swapping of a Yes for a No"—to put it into the jocularly polemical definition of Jean Paul—then we would be at the end of our discussion even before we had started it. It is only recently that we have begun again to learn something about the problem of irony, "incomparably the most profound and alluring problem in the world"—and from whom more than from Thomas Mann, the great ironist. Otherwise our knowledge of the subject has been declining for the last hundred years. The Romanticists, however, especially Friedrich Schlegel and Solger, and later Kierkegaard as their successor, knew about the metaphysical significance of irony and deepened their insight by looking upon Socrates, Plato's Socrates, as their model. "Plato's irony," says Jean Paul, "could, if there is such a thing as world humor, be called world irony, singing and hovering playfully not only over human errors (as humor hovers not only over human folly), but over all human knowledge, free as a flame that devours, delights, moves with ease, yet aspires only toward heaven."

Even though our printers still lack an "irony mark"—which the same Jean Paul, ironically, proposed in addition to the question mark and the exclamation mark—we do not need it in order to know that,

---

besides being a man of sublimity, Plato is a master of irony, and often both at the same moment. But we cannot doubt that the Platonic Socrates did not get his irony from Plato alone, that Socrates was much more exclusively ironical than his more many-sided disciple, and that many people felt or said in conversation with Socrates what Plato puts into the scornful words of the Sophist Thrasymachos: "There we have the usual irony of Socrates" (*Republic* 337A). When a rhetorician talks about the concept of irony and wants to show that it not only has a definite place in the technique of oratory, but that "a whole life may be filled with irony," he calls on the life of Socrates as an example (Quintilian IX 2 46). There is no reason in this case to distinguish sharply between the historical and the Platonic Socrates. We see the former only through the latter, but we cannot doubt that we do see the real Socrates. The question is: What is the place of irony in the Socratic and Platonic way of life?

According to Theophrastus' *Characters,* the ironic man is a person who disparages himself in word and deed, who hides his views and intentions, his actions and energies. The "moral botanist" does not evaluate irony, even though his entire work is based on the ethical system of his master Aristotle, according to whom irony is a deviation from the path of truth. Thus the concept may waver between mean dissimulation, hated or despised, playful hide and seek (a common idiom of the intellectually brilliant and critically suspicious society of democratic Athens), and dangerous concealment, feared or admired. Indeed, friends as well as enemies could talk about Socrates' irony with very different meanings. For in him such a contrast between external conduct and appearance, on the one hand, and inner character, on the other, was particularly striking. Nobody expresses this more pregnantly than Alkibiades in the *Symposium,* who uses as a simile the figures of Silenus that contain images of gods inside. Externally ugly, internally divine; thus Socrates appears more lowly than other beings who are nothing but beautiful, and he *is* so, as long as beauty is taken at its face value. But as soon as we have realized that there is a deeper and more hidden beauty, that "inner beauty" for which Plato makes Socrates pray to Pan and the nymphs at the end of the *Phaedrus* (*δοίητέ μοι καλῷ γενέσθαι τἄνδοθεν*, 279B), then the two levels change place, just as foreground and background may shift in a perspective drawing. He who hitherto seemed more lowly is suddenly seen as superior, and in the end there is the great wonder at the unexpected that has come into sight.

Plato's Alkibiades describes the master primarily in his contact with youth: "Know you that beauty, wealth, and honor, at which the many wonder, are of no account to him, and are utterly despised by him. He regards all this and us as worth nothing. And all his life he spends ironically and playfully mocking people" (*Symposium* 216D *et seq.*). Is even his *Eros* just a mask? To be sure, those who know only Eros Pandemos will see nothing but dissimulation in Socrates' character. In Alkibiades this feeling is very strong; at least he acts as if it were. He hears the flute-playing of Socrates-Marsyas. He sees Socrates following him and in a naïve manner he wants to exploit this, for he feels that Socrates would be his strongest supporter in his desire to excel (*συλλήπτορα οὐδένα κυριώτερον εἶναι σοῦ*, 218D). But he does not see that Socrates could not fulfill this role in a deeper sense if he were possessed by the lower *Eros.* Therefore Socrates, perceptive as he is, says "in the ironical manner so characteristic of him": "If this were so, then indeed my beauty would be much superior to that which I see in you. Then you would really exchange gold for brass. But this is not so." The essential reality becomes manifest in the disguise of this unreal condition. Yes and No are peculiarly intertwined in the words of the ironic man. Repulsion struggles with attraction in the soul of Alkibiades, and attraction finally wins out and retains its opposite only as a goading sting. Socrates, however, shows not by words but by his self-control that he truly possesses the higher beauty.

A great deal in the erotic nature of Socrates is but a mask. He pretends to be subject to the erotic drive, "in thrall to beautiful youths" (ἥττων τῶν καλῶν, *Meno* 76C), and he appears to participate in the erotic play in the same way as the others do; he even seems to surpass them in the degree of erotic, sensuous passion. But Socrates is a magician. Encountering the desired object of his love, he shows immediately that he is the master, not the slave, of his instincts. The conversation with Charmides, as well as that with Alkibiades in the dialogue bearing his name, after the very first words leaves all eroticism behind. And the Alkibiades of the *Symposium* receives a lesson that is more penetrating than the strictest catechism: "I rose from the couch, after I had spent the night with Socrates, as if I had slept with my father or an elder brother" (219D). This, of course, has a tremendous effect: "I wondered at his self-restraint and endurance, as I never imagined I would meet with a man such as he is in wisdom and temperance." Socrates never descends to the level of the others in his dealings with young men, but he sets an example of what they should be like: "Thus, my dear Hippothales, one must converse with a beloved friend in such a way as will bring down his pride and humble him, but not make him more blown up and conceited" (*Lysis* 210E). It is not his *Eros* that is a mask; if anything is a mask, it is the form he adopts, his adaptation to the social forms of his age. The *Eros* of Socrates differs from any other *Eros* just as his notion of ignorance differs. As the latter conceals a profound wisdom, so is his *Eros* an all-encompassing power—equal in weight with the *Logos.* For him who experienced this as something new, a depth opened up, which he had never imagined.

And now irony is carried into the discussion itself, into the pedagogic dialogue. The form this ironic discourse takes is that Socrates places himself side by side and on the same level with the young men, though, according to common opinion and the actual practice of the Sophists, he, as teacher, should hold them at a distance. The *Charmides* begins the inquiry: "Jointly we must inquire and test" (κοινῇ ἂν εἴη σκεπτέον, 158D). The *Alcibiades Major* makes the same point even more strikingly: "Let us jointly consult how we can acquire as much excellence as possible. For I am far from believing that you must be educated while I have no need of education" (124C). Later, when Alkibiades asks what he should do, the reply is: "Answer questions. That is the way which will bring improvement to both of us, to you as well as to me." Or in *Meno:* "We, my dear Menon, seem to be men who are not good for anything; and Gorgias does not seem to have sufficiently educated you, nor Prodikos me. It is, therefore, more important than anything else to be concerned with ourselves and to search for anyone who might improve us in any way" (96D). Or, in *Laches,* Socrates addresses the fathers who want him to be the teacher of their sons: "I maintain, my friends, that every one of us should seek out the best teacher he can find, first for ourselves, who are greatly in need of one, and then for the youths. . . . But I cannot advise that we remain as we are. . . . Let us, then, jointly take care of ourselves and of the youths" (201AB). Again, there is no point in calling this a mask. Socrates can, indeed, seek only in the process of a common conversation; and this search is a perennial task, never completed for anybody, including himself. Yet does not Charmides, still in the process of developing, look to Socrates as to a man who has already attained perfection? Does not Socrates, though never standing still in his quest for knowledge, indeed represent perfection in every moment of his existence? And does not Socrates need Charmides? Indeed, is not even Charmides, as a youth, perfect in his own natural growth? Thus the peculiar seduction lies precisely in this gentle and concealed dialectical tension: irony is the net of the great educator.

Irony is particularly prominent at the conclusion of the aporetic dialogues. To admit ignorance—this experience, this confession, forced upon us by logical reasoning, brings about a humbling of the self. Yet Socrates always includes himself: "I too am ignorant." Thus the partner is received into a human community that almost transforms defeat into its opposite. The participants, in taking leave, realize that they have not discovered what courage is, or temperance. But they also feel that not everything is said with this confession of ignorance. Charmides says (176A): "How can I know whether I have a thing of which even you and Kritias are, as you say, unable to discover the nature—not that I believe you entirely (*ώς φῇς σύ · ἐγὼ μέντοι οὐ πάνυ σοι πείθομαι*). And furthermore I am sure, Socrates, that I do need the charm [the ironic reference to the charm goes through the whole dialogue], and as far as I am concerned I shall be willing to be charmed by you daily until you say that I have had enough." The disciple has observed that Socrates knows more than just nothing, especially that he *is* more than he has expressed, perhaps more than he is able to express. And this superiority, concealed not intentionally but necessarily, and marvelously bound up with love, is the seduction felt by all the disciples. Again, it is Alkibiades who expresses this in almost extreme terms in the *Symposium:* "How badly he deceived me. And he has done this not only to me but also to Charmides and Euthydemos and to many others. He pretends to be their lover and then turns out to be the beloved rather than the lover" (222B). This very transformation takes place in the *Alcibiades.* In the beginning Socrates appears as the pursuer and Alkibiades as reluctant; in the end Alkibiades says: "Our roles will seem to be reversed. . . . From this day, it shall be I who shall wait upon you, and you who will be waited upon by me" (135D). Thus eroticism, not as a mask, but permeated with irony, and the probing dialogue manifest themselves as the highest expression of Socratic nature: he transforms, he educates in the sense of leading upward.

Irony means attraction and repulsion at the same time. In the Alkibiades of the *Symposium,* these two opposing forces struggle with each other most painfully. The more susceptible Alkibiades is to Socrates' education, the more does attraction tend to include its opposite as a sting. The repulsive element in irony becomes dominant at a point where there is no more education because the other has become completely rigid in his ways. This is especially evident in Socrates' contact with professional teachers of wisdom, such as Thrasymachos; with tyrannical natures, such as Kallikles; with bigoted natures, such as Euthyphron. In the *Apology* (21B *et seq.*), Socrates describes how he was summoned by the god to examine the various professions. He goes to the politicians, the poets, the artisans, and examines their "knowledge." It turns out that the higher their claim to knowledge, the less it is confirmed, or can be confirmed, since knowledge is not something that is given to man and since these people even lack insight into their own ignorance. The clash is sharpest with the professional teachers of wisdom who are not mentioned in the *Apology*. For according to the *Meno* (93 A *et seq.*), even politicians may accomplish good results though guided only by instinct. But he who claims to possess wisdom and to act according to its teachings cannot know or accomplish anything.

The conversation about "justice," from which the structure of the *Republic* emerges, has reached a point of admitted ignorance. Here Thrasymachos interrupts as the prototype of the Sophist, the exact counterpart of the genuine philosopher. This, he says, is pure babble. Socrates should not only ask but answer questions. And let him beware of phrasing his answers with reference to this, that, or another thing. This, of course, is an impossible request because it demands one, and only one, already determined answer from a man for whom there is, as an answer, only continuous search. Socrates would be a dogmatist and a Sophist, not a lover of wisdom, if he yielded to this point. Thrasymachos, on the other hand, fails to understand why it is impossible. He regards it as arbitrary dissimulation, as "irony" in the ordinary sense of the word. "I knew you would not answer, but play hide and seek" (*εἰρωνεύσοιο*, 337A). He would have to grow beyond his own nature if he were to understand that this irony is not willful, but necessary.

To be sure, there is play in Socrates' attitude—for example, when he depicts his horror at the interruption by Thrasymachos, or when he asks to be pitied rather than scolded. But precisely that which appears as hypocrisy to Thrasymachos, "we cannot" (336E), is completely genuine, or at least contains an element that is completely genuine. To say "you are the stronger" (*ὑπὸ ὑμῶν τῶν δεινῶν*) is, of course, wrong in Plato's sense. But, from the common point of view, the learned Thrasymachos is superior to the ignorant Socrates. This, however, is only the beginning of the peculiar game that might be called ironic self-entanglement. The learned man "thinks he has a beautiful answer" (*ἡγούμενος ἔχειν ἀπόκρισιν παγκάλην*, 338A), which he wants to display. But this lack of self-knowledge, at the same time a lack of irony, is precisely what fells the "strong" man. For as soon as the answer is out, it is easy for Socrates to show that it is nothing. Just as Socrates' ugliness concealed a beauty of a higher order, the erotic play a more genuine love, so does a profound knowledge become visible behind his ignorance. As soon as this new aspect appears, the knowledge of the Sophist and the ignorance of the philosopher are reversed in rank, and the participants in the discussion experience that strange "reversal" and the inner astonishment awakened by it.

Hegel regarded Socratic irony as one side of the Socratic "method" (maieutics is the other): "What Socrates wanted was to let others express themselves and set forth their principles." This is undoubtedly an essential element. But the phenomenon of irony will always be misunderstood if what can be truly educating only as an inner necessity is held to be an intentional pedagogic rule. Genuine irony contains an element of tension: on the one hand deceptively concealing, on the other uncompromisingly revealing, the truth. Socrates could control the interplay between the outward appearance of a Silenus and his inner beauty as little as he could capriciously conceal knowledge behind ignorance. Both are connected in a continuous circular or pendulous motion. Obviously he did have knowledge. For he led the others; and those who thought they knew were soon exposed in their ignorance. But in particular, as he often said, he knew that he did not know anything. Thus knowledge turns into its opposite. Indeed, he could not express what justice is, and his never-ceasing testing and questioning were determined by this ignorance. But now ignorance turns back to an ultimate stage of wisdom. For the ignorance revealed in the dialectical process was grounded in the living experience of the unknown. And where is a deeper knowledge than that found in a man representing in his life and death what he never ceases to explore in words?

Goethe's aphorism that "Kant limited himself intentionally to a certain field and ironically pointed beyond it" would, if "intentionally" is not pressed too much, apply to Socrates as we have so far seen him in the creative mirror of Plato's art. It applies no less, or even more, to Plato himself, in whose creation Socrates is the central force. Just as, in Emerson's words, "Socrates and Plato are the double star which the most powerful instruments will not entirely separate," so it is impossible to draw a sharp line of demarcation between Socratic and Platonic irony. Even those features of Socrates which we have so far seen—however much they were part of the life of the son of Sophroniskos—required Plato's hand in order to become as visible as they are. But gradually we ascend to forms of irony for which Plato, the artist and thinker, alone is responsible.

How Plato the artist joins and fuses different kinds of irony in a variety of ways—this polyphonic structure of irony—is best illustrated on a narrow scale in the *Euthydemus.* The dialogue consists for the most part of a Punch and Judy show performed by the two Sophistic fencing masters and clowns, with fireworks of amazing eristic acrobatics, fallacies, and equivocations. Here open opposition would be entirely futile and so much below the dignity of Socrates that only the most biting ironic rejection is an appropriate countermeasure. For possessing the true science he deems both of them much happier than the Great King for possessing his power (274A). "You are much better in the art of the philosophical discourse (κάλλιον ἐπίστασαι διαλέγεσθαι, 295E) than I, who have only the art of the common man at my disposal," says the master of the dialogue and dialectics to one of the counterfeiters. Then he encourages them to be serious at the end, since they have only been jesting up to this point (278C). If they should finally turn to a serious discussion, it would undoubtedly result in something very beautiful (288C), in the kind of knowledge that would teach us to spend our future life rightly (293A). Like a cheap comedian, he pretends to be a slave to their wisdom. Interwoven with these Punch and Judy scenes are pieces of a serious educational conversation that Socrates conducts with Kleinias. While he handles the former scenes with a caustic, bitter, or, as it were, repulsive irony, the tone of a gentle, attractive irony may be heard softly and infrequently during the other conversation—for example, when he addresses the disciple as "most beautiful and wisest Kleinias" (290C), or when, in his customary manner, he puts himself on the same level with his pupil: "We have almost made ourselves ridiculous before these strangers, you and I, son of Axiochos" (279C). Both forms of irony give us the "double irony" that Friedrich Schlegel defined as "two lines of irony running parallel, without disturbing one another, one for the pit, the other for the stalls."

These two scenic developments of the dialogues are constantly interacting with each other in ironic tension. To be sure, Socrates shows the two Sophists, with an exemplary conversation, how it should be done. But it is biting irony when he pretends to presuppose that they would follow his example and that the outcome would then be something particularly beautiful (278D, 288C). Seen from the other side, the effect is still more radical. To pretend that both Kleinias and he had made themselves ridiculous, not only in general, but before the strangers (297C), is putting on quite an act. This turns almost into a farce when, reaching a point where he is stuck, he appeals to the Sophists for help: "When I was thrown into this difficulty, I cried out with all my voice, asking the strangers, as one calls upon the Dioscuri, to save us, the boy and myself, from these overwhelming waves of the *Logos*" (ἐκ τῆς τρικυμίας τοῦ λόγου, 293A). He expects them "to reveal the knowledge we must have in order to lead a beautiful life."

But this parallelism of ironies and ironic tensions is not yet the whole story. Now these conversations, full of ironies, are told by Socrates to his disciple Kriton and, of course, told ironically—for how else could Socrates tell a story? Considering the way in which the whole work is once more permeated with irony, we might speak with Schlegel of an "irony of ironies," if at this point we did not reach a still higher dimension. We breathe this air everywhere without always being aware of it. But at a certain place it makes the whole story suddenly transparent. Socrates makes Kleinias say so many intelligent things that Kriton, the listener, becomes suspicious and interrupts (290E). Kriton: "What do you mean, Socrates; did this young fellow say things like that?" Socrates: "Don't you believe me, Kriton?" Kriton: "By Zeus, not at all. For if he said that, he would not need Euthydemos or anybody else for his education." Socrates: "But, my noble Kriton, might it perhaps be that some higher being [i.e., a god] was present and said that?" Kriton: "By Zeus, yes, Socrates, so it seems to me indeed, some higher being, much higher." The conviction that Socrates is giving an accurate account is shaken; the illusion of the inner dialogue is broken through as in a romantic comedy. But we are not in a romantic world; it is inconceivable that this romantic dissolution would also affect the framework of the dialogue. The iridescent motion does not vanish away; and the sharpest ironic rays of light remain fastened upon the figure of Socrates, both knowing and ignorant.

According to Friedrich Schlegel, "Irony contains and excites a feeling of insoluble opposition between the unconditional and the conditional, between the impossibility and the necessity of a complete communication." The words show how irony points straight to a metaphysical dimension, to the ultimate height to which it is raised by Plato, the ironic metaphysician. The Platonic Socrates manifests the Socratic secret and the Socratic irony, which expresses and bridges the tension between the ignorance of his words and the knowledge of his existence; but he also manifests, as he grows in and with Plato, the Platonic secret and the Platonic irony. Is it not astonishing how Plato veils with irony the highest truth he wants to show? When, in the *Phaedo*, he is approaching the archetypes, he says, "If there is such a thing as we constantly babble about, the beautiful, the good, and all the forms of this kind"; and elsewhere he speaks of them as the things "much prated about," as if he intentionally chose derogatory terms. The discussion in the central part of the *Republic* goes still farther. It was shown earlier how long the discussion evaded the last and highest form, and how insistently these deviations are pointed to as the "highest fulfillment" (*τελεωτάτη ἀπεργασία*, 504D) is approached. But despite tense expectations this highest perfection is not reached. Socrates appears as one who does not know. "How would it be right to speak of that about which we have no knowledge as if we did have knowledge?" (506C). When his listeners declare themselves content with this conditional account of the good, he adds ironically: "So am I, more than content. I am afraid it is beyond my power and, with the best will in the world, I should only make myself ridiculous" (506D). This is the ineffability of the highest Platonic vision, symbolized by the irony of Socratic ignorance. At last "the good" appears as something "beyond being and essence, exceeding in dignity and power" (509B). At this point Glaukon interrupts with some amusement: "By Apollo, what a demonic hyperbole" (or: "What an extravagant exaggeration," δαιμονίας ὑπερβολῆς, 509C). And Socrates replies: "It is your fault; you forced me to say what I think." This reveals most clearly, to come back to Schlegel, the impossibility and necessity of a complete communication. The ironic tension is expressed not only through the customary Socratic irony, the Socratic ignorance, but also through the device of putting a coarse jest side by side with the most solemn expression. Thus Socrates is not the only representative of irony; irony is also carried by the interlocutor to the "object" of the discussion; and this shows that we are dealing not only with Socratic irony, but with a matter of a more complex order.

When, in the *Symposium*, after many preliminaries, the speech of Socrates is to open up the road to the realm of eternal forms, a strange thing happens. It is not, strictly speaking, Socrates who leads the way; but he shows how the prophetess Diotima led the way for him. There is little doubt that the essential features of Diotima are a creation of the Platonic Socrates—the highest embodiment, as it were, of the more or less vague "somebody" whom he frequently posits playfully in conversation or debate as another person in order to conceal himself ironically. But there is much disagreement on the meaning or purpose of this creation. Socrates, it is said, is presenting ideas that were not part of the teachings of the historical Socrates. But

Plato has put in the mouth of Socrates an enormous amount of material that the son of Sophroniskos never thought of. Or it is said to be an act of courtesy toward Agathon to show that he is not defeated by Socrates himself. But while the spirit of liberal courtesy characteristic of a secure social order runs through the language and form of the Platonic dialogues, it seems impossible to derive this highest creation of Plato's entirely from the sphere of social conventions. Or it is said that Socrates, as a dialectician, was not permitted to make a long speech, so that Plato, in order to preserve the unity of the Socratic picture, had to break the speech up into the form of a dialogue. But Socrates makes long speeches in the *Phaedrus;* thus this technical consideration is no more satisfactory as a final answer than the social explanation. It is more correct to say that Socrates as the "ignorant" man cannot be the guide to the complete fulfillment of the philosophical quest; but the whole structure of the work requires a deeper analysis.

When Socrates, after his numerous predecessors, begins to speak, it is immediately apparent that a new level of discussion has been reached. "Then I realized how foolish I had been, consenting to take my turn with you in praising *Eros,* and saying that I was a master in this art, when I really have no understanding as to how anything ought to be praised. For in my simplicity I imagined that the truth should be told" (198c). With this last phrase all the former speeches are devaluated; they must be justified before the new, surprisingly simple idea of—truth. "It is the truth, beloved Agathon, that you cannot refute; for Socrates is easily refuted" (201c). This distance of the new level from the old is suggested by the well-known forms of irony. "I did not know the nature of praise and, without knowing it, I consented to take my turn in making a speech of praise. Thus the lips have given a promise, but not the mind. Farewell then to such a promise. For I do not praise in that way; no, indeed, I could not. But if you like to hear the truth, I am ready to speak in my own manner, but not in rivalry with your speeches, lest I make myself ridiculous" (199AB). Thus irony points to (at the same time as it conceals) the road leading from the many to Socrates.

Socrates has hardly begun to speak when he is no longer the highest figure himself. A still higher figure looms above him. Diotima catechizes him as he usually does others. She plays with him ironically and jestingly (202B). The answer to one of his questions, she says, "would be clear even to a child" (204B). But most illuminating are her words pointing out the path of highest fulfillment: "These are the lesser mysteries of love, into which even you, Socrates, may enter; but to the deepest mysteries of the complete vision, to which the former, if you take the right path, will lead, I know not whether you will be able to attain" (209E). The single power by which Socrates opposes the flowery speeches and half-truths of the others thus undergoes an *ironic division*, as it were, into Socrates, representing the principle of truth but otherwise ignorant, and the priestess leading to the highest secrets. The ironic tensions between him and the others are superseded, at the crucial point, by an ironic tension between the seeker for truth and a power that, though shining through him, is also above him. It is uncertain whether Socrates was ever "initiated," and still more so whether we are chosen to be participants of the mystery. Thus the ladder of ironic tensions raises the reader to the divination of a higher being and leaves behind the impulse of unceasing search for what he has divined. It excites, to speak with Friedrich Schlegel, a feeling of the insoluble opposition between the unconditional and the conditional.

Another kind of irony, which serves a similar purpose, is what may be called *ironic shift of balance* in a work of art. The *Symposium* is a dialogue about the nature of *Eros*, and all the speeches aim at this clearly defined goal. The speeches about love in the *Phaedrus* are quite different. This dialogue proceeds from a discussion of the art of rhetoric and the passionate admiration that Phaidros has for it and Socrates pretends to have. Lysias' speech, delivered by Phaidros, is an example of an abstruse rhetorical exercise proving the proposition that it is better to favor the nonlover than the lover. Love for the rhetorician is without any deeper meaning; and Socrates is quite right in saying that, for the lover and nonlover, we might as well substitute the rich man and the poor man, the young man and the old man, or anything else (227C). Socrates' first speech is only supposed to show that something else and something better may be said about the same topic. Only later does Socrates seem to come back to the subject matter itself. Lysias and he have offended *Eros*. He now wants "to wash the brine out of my ears with water from the spring." But apparently we are still on the level of a debating contest; for Socrates now counsels Lysias to write, as soon as possible, another discourse proving the opposite thesis (i.e., that it is better to favor the lover than the nonlover) (243D).

After the third speech about love, Socrates' second, has risen under the impact of mania (madness) into the heaven of forms, the discussion comes abruptly back to earth. It seems as if these sublime topics had not been under discussion at all; what follows deals with the technique of debating, the training of the orator, the relations between the written and the spoken word. If we take the dialogue literally, it is concerned with rhetoric; and the speeches about love are rhetorical illustrations to show the correct or false structure of an oration, or the difference between an improvised and a prepared, written-out speech. But even one's first impression shows that this is not so; and if we were to characterize the content of the dialogue in this way, we would be misled by Plato's ironic art. Just as there are pictures in which the pictorial center remains vacant, and the center of attention is transferred by the arrangement of lines, colors, and light effect to one of the corners, so the dialogue, if seen as a whole, confers essential meaning on that which appeared only as a means; and this meaning, in turn, illuminates and deepens even that which, as long as we did not recognize this ironic shift, appeared to be its primary purpose.

This artistic irony is worked out still more consciously in two late dialogues, the *Sophist* and the *Statesman*. These dialogues show a peculiar mixture: on the one hand, they are long, formal dialectical exercises to reach a definition by the method of division; on the other, they search for those realities designated by the names of Sophist, Statesman, and Philosopher. If we listen to what is said, the inquiry into the subject matter appears only as a formal exercise: "the inquiry about the statesman is only undertaken so that we may become more dialectical in all things" (*Statesman* 285D). "For the immaterial things, the most beautiful and greatest, are shown only through the *Logos*, and in no other way, and all that we are now saying is said for the sake of them" (286A). And yet it is difficult to listen with a straight face to the classification of the Sophist as an angler, and to many other things of this kind. If we really took seriously the grouping of men and birds as bipeds in contrast to the quadrupeds (266E),

Diogenes the Cynic would be quite right with his plucked cock as a satire upon this Platonic classification. But the comic side of these divisions is explicitly touched upon in the dialogue itself (266BC). Ironic tensions are employed between correct and false classifications, on the one hand, in order to arouse critical thinking; between intention and execution, on the other, in order to indicate that these exercises are preparatory—and only preparatory—for the most important task.

While these ironic tensions are concerned with formal elements, another tension permeates the subject matter itself. The nature of the Sophist is the goal of the inquiry; yet, as in a blindfold game, we come up against the Philosopher. And the question arises whether we are not paying too much honor to the Sophist with this definition (231A). But is it not the Philosopher whom we are really looking for, who looms behind the inquiry and whose definition must be given after we have determined the nature of the Sophist and the Statesman? Thus the ironic tension here exists between that which is the immediate subject of definition and that which is ultimately looked for; and this tension is reinforced by coming very close, accidentally as it seems, and for a moment, to the ultimate goal of the inquiry.

The dialectical exercise and the subject matter itself are therefore not combined so arbitrarily as it would at times appear. It is highly unlikely that the definition of the Statesman would seriously serve only the purpose of a dialectical exercise, as the dialogue itself claims it does. In this way the true order of rank and value seems to be rather veiled by irony. For the dialectical exercise is supposed to prepare us ultimately for the goal of the vision of the forms; and this goal is the goal of the Philosopher, whose nature must therefore be distinguished from that of the Sophist and the Statesman.

Thus, ultimately, material and formal elements coincide. Even the ironic tensions of the two lines are not accidentally placed beside each other. In each case they designate the conditional and point suggestively to the depth of the unconditional.

Consequently, both dialogues lead to the last manifestation of ironic play: *wordless irony* consisting in the fact that Socrates, by virtue of his silent presence, represents ironic tensions—unspoken yet felt. Behind the two definitions of the Sophist and the Statesman remains the task of discovering the nature of the Philosopher. This is mentioned frequently and is so much in the center of expectation that it has generally been assumed that there should have been a third dialogue called "Philosophos"; some have either found this dialogue in one of the others which are extant or concluded that the two dialogues are fragments of an uncompleted trilogy. But suppose this only made us victims of Platonic irony? An ironic tension connects Socrates, silently listening, with the Eleatic stranger and his youthful partners in the conversation. The goal is the path to the highest form. Socrates stands by as silent representative of this path. The same ironic dialectic that leads back and forth from the definitions of the two dialogues to the hidden definition of the Philosopher reverberates, in the veiled manner of Plato's late works, between the representatives of the dialectical exercises and the Philosopher, who, like a Homeric god, stands by "hidden in air."

Socratic irony, at its center, expresses the tension between ignorance—that is, the impossibility ultimately to put into words "what justice is"—and the direct experience of the unknown, the existence of the just man, whom justice raises to the level of the divine. For Plato the Socratic question becomes answerable "in words" (ἐν λόγοις). But this answer is only complete in the vision of the eternal forms and in the dawning realization of something that is beyond being. Here once more the same basic relationship, the same opposition between the conditional and the unconditional, is repeated. And thus Platonic irony, incorporating the whole teaching and magic of the figure of Socrates, is revealed as veiling and protecting the Platonic secret. However, as in a Greek statue the garment not only serves as a veil but at the same time reveals that which it veils, so is Plato's irony also a guide on the path to the eternal forms and to that which is beyond being.

18. Robert S. Brumbaugh: "Criticism in Philosophy: Aristotle's Literary Form"

Professor Brumbaugh studied at the University of Chicago, receiving his Ph.D. in 1942. He has taught at Columbia, Bowdoin, and Indiana University. Presently he teaches at Yale, where he is professor of philosophy. His books include *Plato on the One* (1961), *Plato for the Modern Age* (1962), and *The Philosophies of Greece* (1964).

CRITICISM IN PHILOSOPHY: ARISTOTLE'S LITERARY FORM*

The general consensus of philosophers today, with some existentialist dissent, is that literary criticism and the appraisal of argument are distinct enterprises, and that they should be kept so. Even studies of Plato (Murphy's interpretation of the *Republic*, Robinson's of

* Used by permission of the author. This essay is published here for the first time.

the *Parmenides*, Crombie's of all doctrines) separate "literary devices" from "philosophic argument," assuming that it is easy to separate the form of an argument from dramatic development. A more liberal group of philosophers may, if pressed, admit that in some special cases philosophy has overlapped the category of poetry; but they would regard this as accidental and atypical.

My intention here is to show, to the contrary, that the student of philosophy must either be, or consult, the literary critic if he is to understand any piece of philosophical literature. The differences remain crucial, but the relevance of critical considerations—of form, character, unity of plot—can't be ignored if we want to understand philosophy.

All philosophic writing is literature, and as such can be looked at through the lenses Aristotle used in viewing "productive science": the author has ideas which he must communicate through the medium of language and overall ordering form. Aristotle himself, of course, would dissent. He thought he could draw a line half-way, between philosophy that can also be analyzed as poetry (notably the Socratic dialogue, which he admired) and philosophy incurably unaesthetic (notably the verses of Empedocles, which he detested). But this sharp-line project can't be consistently carried out; it turns out, for example, as W. E. Leonard showed, that Empedocles' verses rank very high as cosmologica; epic poetry. And in the very nature of the case, it is clear that every author is also a speaker, every argument a development of an "action" in some probable or necessary sequence, every stylistic device appropriate or inappropriate to the overall "object of imitation."

As critics adapting tools used for poetry to analysis of philosophic literature, there are certain differences that we must take into account. In works of philosophy, thought is the unifying part of the development rather than overt action and change of fortune. The critic is dealing here with literature more like novels of discovery than of adventure. The thought, furthermore, must meet the extra-literary demand that it remains valid outside of the story itself. (In this peculiarity, philosophic literature is like science fiction and the detective story.) This imposes a need for kinds of order and sequence that we might roughly call logical, in addition to sequences that are valid aesthetically. Further, the central character, unless he gives clear warning to the contrary, will be supposed to be the real-life philosopher; we expect a kind of sincerity here that could be quite irrelevant in poetry.

But given these adjustments, the methods of the literary critic apply to philosophic literature, and apply in places that are as unexpected as they are philosophically important. For example, I will show that the perplexing question of the unity of Aristotle's *Metaphysics* cannot be treated properly without establishing the character of the speaker and the specific canons of form of the Aristotelian lecture.

The history of philosophic writing can be written as Aristotle wrote his history of the drama. It opens with a search for forms to fit insights, a period of experiment. We find a range of forms from almanac with Thales to epic with Parmenides, from oracular epigram with Heraclitus to geometrical symbolism with Pythagoras. The search for proper form seems to stabilize in two generic types in the fourth century B.C. On the one hand, philosophers who see philosophy as shared inquiry, a continuing search, follow Plato's example and use dialogue form. On the other hand, philosophers who see their writing as instruction, as an explanation of the *results* of investigation, use various species of the long or short treatise and the Aristotelian lecture. Within each genus, there are species that differ. The dialogue as it is written by Cicero and Hume is a different style from its Platonic original. The autobiography counts as an offshoot of this dialogue tradition, setting up a more direct interpersonal conversation between author and reader, as in St. Augustine's *Confessions* and the *Meditations* of Descartes. There are a few ventures that fall outside of these two main traditions: the epigram returns in Nietzsche's *Zarathustra,* the epic in Camus' *The Stranger.* But on the whole, dialogue and didactic treatise seem to have become stabilized as the best vehicles for the writing of philosophy.

The first tradition, that of dialogue, is clearly attractive to the admirer of literature. It is equally attractive, but sometimes baffling, to the philosopher who wants to extract a body of doctrines and solutions detached from the dramatic dimension. Aristotle's several expressed frustrations with the *Republic* in his *Politics* are a classic example. The reason for this difficulty is that the form and doctrine are not simply separable. The dialogue, well-used, has a kind of self-instantiation and counterpoint: thought motivates characters, and their actions instantiate and reflect on the validity of the thought. In dealing with the tradition of dialogue, I think my main problem is to convince the advocate of philosophy in the didactic mode that the so called "literary devices" are relevant to the logic of the so called "philosophic argument." The literary critic is predisposed to accept this; indeed, to him it seems almost self-evident. (The reverse will be true when we turn to philosophy presented in the finished lecture or critique; the philosopher will see coherent aesthetic form in it, but the literary critic will try to deny that he has any business with, let alone any obligation to read through, this kind of writing at all.)

As samples of criticism applied to the dialogue form, let me show briefly the interaction of drama and argument, and the device of self-instantiation, at work in two of Plato's dialogues, the *Meno* and the *Hippias Minor*.

The *Meno* continues to receive attention today (for example there is Bluck's edition of the text, Klein's commentary, and Malcom Brown's technical study of the mathematical example). The dialogue bears directly on our own contemporary question, "Can values be taught?" It offers a first step toward an answer by suggesting that they cannot; but it does this without doing what the later Platonic dialogues do as they force us into sweeping metaphysical commitments or dissents.

The logical structure of the *Meno* is that of a destructive dilemma. If virtue can be taught, Meno assumes (and Socrates accepts the assumption) that the method of such teaching must either be by precept or by example. Meno has been trained by the master of teaching by precept, Gorgias. By nature and family he was a well-endowed student. We would expect, therefore, if the precept method works, that Meno would know what virtue is; or, at the least, that his excellent education would have made him virtuous, a fact that would count as evidence in the discussion. (Note how argument and drama interpenetrate at this point: Meno's "character" will or will not constitute an implicit existentially quantified proposition that nowhere figures abstractly and explicitly in the "philosophic argument.") But Meno can neither define virtue, nor is he a virtuous person; in fact, Plato presumably chose him as respondent because historically he was so un-virtuous. At the outset of his conversation, he displays ignorance, impatience, unfairness, and petulance.

Well, what about teaching by example: by daily contact with public life, and by taking great men of the past as exemplary? Anytus, willing to defend this method even to Socrates' death, is brought onstage as its spokesman. He, too, fails to embody the ideals he admires; and is forced to admit, angrily, that history does not confirm his passionate belief in the efficacy of example.

Socrates, in summing up, suggests that they test the hypothesis that virtue is knowledge. If it is, then it can be taught; and any possessor of such knowledge, being made virtuous through having it, would want to teach it. Yet in the two test cases presented in the dialogue, Meno and Anytus, the teaching has failed to operate; and Meno has to admit that he can't find a single instance of a teacher of virtue. On the other hand, in the course of discussion, Socrates' experiment with the Slave Boy has shown that Meno's assumption that "teaching" must be didactic transfer of information is false, by actually teaching some elementary geometry by another method. And it becomes pertinent to ask whether the *Meno*, taken as a whole, does not contradict the abstract thesis that concludes its argument. For, if Meno himself improves in virtue through the shared inquiry with Socrates, though the improvement is short-lived, there does exist at least one teacher of virtue, and it is false to say that virtue cannot be taught. It will remain true, though, that the "teaching" was not done either by precept or example, but by "Socratic method."

Now, I hold that in this very dialogue Meno is shown to improve in virtue; and that various literary devices are used to direct our attention to this improvement. He improves because he shares in the discussion; his improvement is an extremely relevant item in relation to the problem being discussed; and I see no way of separating the "dramatic" from the "philosophic" dimension of this imagined encounter.

This device of self-illustration typifies the dialogue form, whether the dialogue is constructive as with Plato or sceptical as it becomes in the works of Hume and Cicero. The wonderfully sardonic opening of the *Lesser Hippias*, when we return to it after surviving the argument's logical involutions, shows the interaction of idea and action in a two-sentence vignette that one can hardly set aside as inadvertent or irrelevant. Hippias' prestige as an intellectual must have annoyed The Academy. The dialogue, aimed at showing Socrates to be a better man than the information-stuffed Hippias, centers at first on a literary question. The question is, which character in fiction is better, Homer's Achilles or his Odysseus? Hippias dislikes Odysseus, because "Odysseus lies deliberately." Socrates now asserts the thesis—which is a deliberate lie on his part—that the voluntary liar must be wiser and better than the involuntary one. The upshot is that, in this case, Socrates' lie seems to be true—at any rate, he comes out ahead of Hippias. The point and standpoint are set up in the very beginning, when Socrates says that Hippias is wise, and Hippias accepts the compliment. For one of them has told a voluntary, the other an involuntary, lie.

Clearly, Plato's dramas are the right form to embody his conviction that you can't teach answers without engaging the student in the questions they answer; that philosophy can't be transmuted into an objective spectator sport to the degree that mathematics or astronomy can. On the other hand, Platonic dialogue has a clear notion of the direction in which answers do lie, and perhaps an even clearer notion of where they do not. They lie in the direction of the theory of forms, forms which are the goals of inquiry. As an objective logical problem, the relevance of these forms to persons and things is probably insoluble. But in the dialogue form, we have it set before us as a fact, as argument shapes action and the ideal attracts the actual.

The second traditional genus of philosophic literature, the didactic form, has been repeatedly commented on and analyzed as though the form contained no varied species, and as though the character speaking could be only an impersonal, didactic voice of thought. But the identification of the specific form, the discovery of its unifying principles, and the motives for its choice suddenly become baffling just where we most want to follow what is going on: and the way in which criticism helps in these extreme cases brings out its general relevance to philosophic literature in the didactic form.

A problem of honorable antiquity is the question of the unity, or lack of it, in Aristotle's *Metaphysics*. Although we are not too eager to tell this to our undergraduates, there is good external reason for an initial doubt as to whether the text we have and the content of the projected science that Aristotle called "first philosophy" are the same. The title is a later editor's label for the treatises that "come after the *Physics*"; the contents show stylistic evidence of very diverse dates of writing; and book Beta, which should be the key to the work since it announces itself as a treatment of the problems of first philosophy, is a maze of questions which don't find subsequent answers. (Ross finds, for Beta, that only 5 out of 12 of the problems as he enumerates them are answered in the subsequent text.) Something must be wrong here, either with the text as a whole, or with our expectations concerning Beta. But on the other hand, the fact that five of Ross's list of problems *are* explicitly solved and are referred back to in later books indicates that there must be *some* relevance between the program and its execution.

Wilamowitz first proposed the thesis that the puzzle results from our loss of a classical literary form, the "School Logos." The purpose of these *logoi* he postulated as an initial pyrotechnical challenge to the student, exhibiting the range and number of problems he must face, and exhibiting them in deliberately disordered patterns. Its literary artistry should then consist in the range of questions posed and in their presentation in a contrived random order. Are there any other instances of works in this unrecognized lost literary form? Yes, Wilamowitz thought, the second part of Plato's *Parmenides* presents itself as a clear case; and the Platonic *Euthydemus* is another example.

I must say that, on its intrinsic merits, the "unrecognized school-logos" hypothesis is very strong. It has not been judged on its merits, because philosophers have hoped for so much more from our *Metaphysics* text that they did not want to believe it, but I think we must either find a better alternative to this thesis, or accept it. What would constitute a better alternative? Either external evidence that in transmission whatever form the original version had has been shattered, or internal evidence that we can find coherence within a perfectly recognizable species of the general didactic form. I will argue for the latter; I believe that there are formal properties specific to Aristotle's lectures, not typical of all species of the lecture form, and that any error we may have made in analysis has only been to place the material in the wrong species within the right genus, not to mislocate it generically.

My first step toward refuting the "School Logos" thesis is an indirect one. In a study in 1961, I proved that while the *Parmenides* hypotheses are in an unfamiliar form, right enough, it is a form of axiomatic-deductive demonstration, not aporematic disorder. The sequence that gives order to this thought progression can in fact be displayed as formally valid by using the rather non-commital "material implication" connective, borrowed from modern logic. (This takes only a sentence to state, but actually took me about six years to establish.) *Why* Plato chose this form here is a different question; *that* he chose it, however, can be so clearly shown that we lose one supposed example of the School Logos. And fairly simple literary analysis also shows that the *Euthydemus* exactly fits standard dialogue form. Thus *Metaphysics* Beta is left as the sole surviving specimen of the postulated lost literary genus.

I would like now to return to this question by way of another book, *Physics II,* which Aristotle evidently was pleased with since he cross refers to it in other works as his definitive treatment of causality. A simple experiment will convince any reader that there is something structurally eccentric about this prize lecture. The experiment is this: to read it once quickly, making an outline of the main topics; then to read it again, line by line, writing down an outline to a proper order of subordination. The first reading is easy, the outline seems clear; but the second time around, the outlining is frustrating. Half a day may still find the deliberate note taker still undecided about where to put into his outline the stone called "lucky" because it was used for an altar. These results reflect two marked traits of the author's character, both of which show in the form. First, he can block out large scale organizations of material clearly. Second, he will not take the time to polish up his notes either by indicating that certain sections can be quickly read because they are subordinate, or by treating such subordinate points in articulated detail. A combination of an ambition to achieve total over-all order, an impatience with polished style, and a reluctance to overlook any minute counter-instances, is projected here. Thus, the detail results from a desire to take account of all the data—whether ordinary language, opinions of experts, or seeming factual anomalies—that might count against the main point. Only, as these considerations become more subordinate, their treatment is more cryptic, until what could be a treatise on geometry compresses to a parenthetical enthymeme. And this is done without stylistic guideposts for the hearer or reader. The overall form is suited to a great project, the details of which may represent loose ends, mentioned in passing, to be tied up later.

In passing, we should note that the text we have is the transcription of what were oral lectures; and the manner of delivery can offer means of indicating outline and emphasis that escape the written record. The most important of such devices include: 1) special diagrams to be shown and pointed to; we find these presupposed particularly in the Ethics lectures; 2) gesture; 3) timing—pauses before returning to a major theme, for example; 4) emphasis and voice volume. In connection with timing, I have just realized in writing this that I myself always tend to go too fast, and slow myself down by puffing a cigarette—quickly at mere sentence ends, slowly and perhaps twice for ends of paragraphs. I could develop this theme of unrecorded elements of lecture style at greater length, if it were helpful for the solution of the present problem. But I'm afraid it is not. For when I tried the idea that oral presentation, with emphasis and gesture, could have made the written text of the third problem in the detailed Beta list lively and clear, the result was an hour of anguished boredom for my captive Aristotle seminar.

This brings us back to *Metaphysics* Beta. I suggested

that the formal structure of *Physics II* might also apply here, and that since the lack of polished indications of coordination in the former was a result of impatience rather than a deliberate deception, the same explanation might hold for Beta. The lack of clarity in many passages results from the fact that Aristotle's Greek offers him far fewer distinct ways of indicating subordination than his topic outlines require. It is not that he fails to indicate the balancing of his major coordinate topics, with a *men-de* or equivalent construction, but that he must repeat the same device to articulate other balanced sections that are subordinate in the total outline. I would describe the result as a style which has weak or partial indications of organization.

Working from this basis, I find that stylistic indications single out an eight problem main outline in Beta. These problems come in three groups: the first treats metaphysics as discursive, the second treats the kind of knowing it involves, the third treats its subject-matter. This exactly matches the scheme that Prof. Richard McKeon proposed as that of the *Metaphysics* as a whole. My list, further, is a set of problems all of which are successively resolved, in order, in the subsequent books of our *Metaphysics* text. This is a much higher level of coherence than Ross's organization, which gives something like 5 out of 12 as the number of key problems actually treated; in fact, my 8 out of 8 is just what we would expect, if Aristotle himself, and not some Roman editor, had organized selected essays to follow out this initial outline.[1]

But what about the unresolved subordinate problems? They vanish without resolution or further mention when the assumptions that generate them are shown to be false. For example, the second problem of Beta, whether there are any substances apart from sensibles, includes some eleven questions one must ask if the objects of mathematics form a group of genuine substances. But once it is shown that the objects of mathematics are not separate substantial entities *at all*, Aristotle obviously does not feel a need to go on and inquire whether they exist *in* sensibles or *apart* from them—and thus there is this set of sub-problems apparently untreated in the subsequent text.

In short, Beta seems to me a typical Aristotelian lecture, with the same properties as *Physics II.* And so far as the match between its initial outline and subsequent discussion is a test, the treatise as a whole seems to be Aristotelian metaphysics after all.[2]

Further, my method of analyzing the character of the lecturer reflected in the text, the development of thought, and the qualities of style, seems to me an application of the art of literary criticism. I sympathize entirely with the critic who finds this prose uncongenial, but not with the attempt to hold that it is critically inaccessible.

The question of locating philosophic works in their proper literary forms is not limited to recognizing the *Parmenides* as deductive dialectic, the *Metaphysics* as didactic lecture-course. One of the most interesting cases of location and mis-location has to do with Rousseau's *Emile*. Given a low grade by critics expecting logical entailment to unify it, as such entailment should unify a treatise on the principles of education, the book continues to influence educators and find admirers. The reason is that it is unified, but by the development of plot, character, and thought proper to a novel.

I have admitted that philosophy differs from poetry. One difference, apparent in the *Parmenides* example, is that the unifying relation of a philosophic work may be different from the "aesthetic compatibility" that underlies probability and necessity in poetic form. Character is different, too. Unless he explicitly claims the contrary, we assume that the philosopher really believes what he says; in other words, that there is agreement between the way he conducts himself in "real life" and the role he plays as onstage or offstage author and manager in his work. This means that we feel entitled, as we do not or should not with the poet, to introduce biographical material to supplement the character who appears within the given work itself. In doing this, we approach the writer of a philosophic work rather as though he were himself a character in a wider Platonic dialogue, asking him, as Socrates did Thrasymachus, "Do you really believe this?" And unless we are strangely incurious about the interaction of life and thought, about sincerity or dissimulation, we refuse to accept the Sophist's answer, "What does it matter? Your job is to refute the argument."

Looked at in this way, the literary critic, who is at home with questions of consistency of character, is the very expert we should consult in trying to understand the philosopher as he appears in his several roles. I am not saying that inconsistency or insincerity are in themselves a philosophical refutation, but that the analysis of character can be relevant to understanding philosophic writing, and that the relation of the author as revealed in a given work to the author in real life is much closer here than it normally is in poetry.

Perhaps the most difficult and crucial case for testing this idea is that of Socrates. What was he really like? Does it matter whether Plato's picture of him is pure idealized drawing, or a study from life with only modest highlighting added? The bibliography of books and articles on this topic is overwhelming proof that the question has mattered to an amazing number of people. In fact, if the literary critic is crucial to the solution of this problem, that alone would justify affiliating him with the department of philosophy.

There is a real enigma in the character of Socrates.

Appearing as hero or villain through a wide range of records, refractions of him abound. But somehow, from his first literary appearance in comedy, riding in his basket like a god, each role he plays finds him wearing another mask. Within the classical period, Aristophanes portrays him as a fake scientist and shyster lawyer; Xenophon as a tough, sensible retired soldier; Plato as an ideal philosopher. But we also get Socrates refracted as the hero who advocates a return to nature, the role he is given by the Cynic school; as advocate of calculated pursuit of maximum pleasure, which is the Cyrenaic view; as abstracted master of formal logic, the Megarian version.

In four cases out of this early six, we can see that Socrates is more a symbol than a character. Aristophanes is clearly determined to attribute to his villain every new tendency that the comedian found subversive and objectionable. The Socratic Schools have a portrait of the philosophic hero who is, in each case, a one-dimensional projection of the doctrine which each school believes a hero should hold. As critics, we can show that none of these is convincing as a characterization from life: real persons, at the very least, have more than one trait of character. Further, the discrepancies among the three School portraits can converge in one person only if each has selected a very thin band from the total spectrum. Xenophon's Socrates looks more credible than Aristophanes', until we realize that he is really a projection of Xenophon. That sensible, soldierly projection could never have been the historical figure accused of impiety and staying to stand trial—as Xenophon admits in the beginning of his *Memories of Socrates*. Plato's characterization, in contrast to these others, is historically believable, three-dimensional rather than one-dimensional. Beyond this, Plato argues an implicit philosophic claim: that the historical existence of Socrates disproves the rather shallow Sophistic thesis that men do not ever act against their material interests. If the claim that Socrates is historical were false, Plato's use of this example to prove the possibility of an ethics of duty of a Kantian kind, as opposed to an ethics of hedonistic utility of the Sophistic sort, would be unjustified.

I would be happy to rest the case there, embroidering it with analyses of Xenophon's interests and attitudes, Euclides' perverse fondness for formal logic, and the like. But a conversation with a colleague who is a dynamic and distinguished literary critic raised another question: how far does one trust Plato, in spite of his claim to historicity? I had been discussing my reasons for rejecting all but two of the *Letters* attributed to Plato. It seemed incredible to me, I said, that so good a stylist would allow himself to appear in the roles of mystagogue, mendicant, rotarian, and plagiarist, which are the roles of the author(s) of *Letters* II, XIII, VI, and IX. Not at all, said my friend; the mark of a literary genius is to throw himself into those many roles; probably he believes that he is each of them when he is writing; but in any case, this variety of personae should count for, rather than against, the authenticity of the collection. And, in that case, of course, we might have to say the same thing about the role of biographer of Socrates as Plato played it; he may just have been acting when he claimed it was true history.

"My friend," I said, "there is a quarrel from of old between philosophy and poetry; and you just renewed it."

NOTES

[1] In an article, "Aristotle's Outline of the Problems of First Philosophy", *Review of Metaphysics* VII (1954), 511–521, I analyzed Beta. I had two theses to offer in that article. The first was that Aristotle in fact did use consistent coordinating devices to mark his main outline, but they were lost in the complex maze of subordinate questions. (For the first listing

in Beta, *men* and *de* mark the main topics; in the more detailed second Beta treatment, *aporia* or *aporeseien* do this; in Kappa, a combination of *men-de* and *poteron* does so.) These indicated topics add up to exactly the set of problems an Aristotelian would expect, and to a set all of which are resolved in the later text. My second thesis was that Jaeger's finding of the great variety of dates of composition indicated by shifts of style probably reflected the practice of a busy lecturer who kept a file of all his back notes and papers. Then, on the occasion of a new lecture series to be designed, Aristotle could, for example, insert his *On the Ideas* notes from his Assos days as part of the history of philosophy he had projected as the first lecture set (*Metaphysics* Alpha). Since then, I have come to appreciate a third literary feature. The picture is not complete until Aristotle has introduced all of his four causes. But in his overall organization, he stops short, in Iota and Kappa, to sum up the interaction of the first three—formal (from Zeta), material (from Eta), and efficient (from Theta). He ends by reviewing the initial problems, and his advances toward their solutions, in Kappa. With Lambda, the introduction of the last, the final, cause snaps the whole picture into focus. Lambda takes care of "problems about entities" from the Beta and Kappa sets, leaving a final rejection of forms and numbers for M and N. This makes the reason for the Beta/Kappa duplication lie in a construction of a climax rather than in an inadvertent repetition. The notes are admittedly rather roughtly joined together, and re-polished to very different degrees.

[2] Organized into problems about metaphysics as discourse, which are treated in Gamma and Delta; metaphysical ways of knowing, taken care of in part in Epsilon, in part in Iota; the subject-matter of metaphysics, changing and eternal substances and their causes. This third set of problems requires a treatment of each cause, and of the causes together. This is developed in the formal: Zeta, material: Eta, efficient: Theta scheme mentioned above in n.l. The unity of these three is treated in Iota; then Lambda: final cause completes the picture. M and N dismiss un-needed Platonic forms and Pythagorean numbers.

19. Ben-Ami Scharfstein: "Descartes' Dreams"

Professor Scharfstein was educated in the United States, and received his Ph.D. from Columbia in 1940. After holding appointments at several American universities, Scharfstein, in 1955, accepted an appointment at the University of Tel-Aviv in the History and Philosophy of Science. He is now Professor of Philosophy there. He served as Rector of the University from 1969–72. Among other works, Professor Scharfstein has written *The Artist in World Art* (1969), *The Mind of China* (1972), and *Mystical Experience* (1972).

DESCARTES' DREAMS*

On March 26, 1619, Descartes wrote to his friend, the young physician-scientist, Isaac Beeckman, that for the past six days he had been cultivating his Muses more

* From *Philosophical Forum* (Spring 1969), vol. I: no. 3, pp. 293–316. Reprinted by permission.

attentively than ever before and had discovered, with the help of his new compasses, "four remarkable and completely new proofs." It was his hope, he wrote, that he would be able to set the entire science of mathematics in order, provided that he could overcome his natural laziness and that Destiny granted him a free life. He hoped to create a new science that would permit the solution of all problems involving quantity. It was an infinite task, an incredibly ambitious project, he exclaimed. But he was confident. "I perceived," he told his friend, "I know not what light in the obscure chaos of this science, and I presume that with the help of this light the thickest shadows may be dissipated."

Descartes went on. He had been travelling. The last voyage had been good. He had been forced back to shore by the wind; but the following day he had sailed into even more violent seas on a very small boat, and this more in pleasure than fear, because he had been testing himself, and now, having crossed the seas, a new experience for him, without suffering any nausea, he felt emboldened to undertake a greater voyage.

Descartes continued travelling on, it seems, a roundabout way to the army of Maximilian of Bavaria, which he joined as a gentleman volunteer. It was at about this time that he made a number of interesting notes that have been preserved. Since we are about to intrude into his dreams, we may as well read the notes over his shoulder. He begins tamely enough, "The fear of God is the beginning of wisdom." Has he had any particular reason to connect any reverence or fear with wisdom? He then writes that he is going on the world's stage masked, like the comedians who wear masks to conceal their flushed faces. The sense of concealment is clear, but not the reason for it. Since he was thinking of himself as destined for fame, perhaps the meaning is that here stands a great mathematician disguised in a uniform, the mask that conceals his nature and his emotion from the public he is beginning to face. He writes, further, that when he was young, he was stimulated by the ingenious discoveries of others to ask himself if he could not have made them himself, without the help of books. Beginning with this question, he reminds himself, he little by little came to see that he could proceed according to fixed rules. He writes that science is like a woman: if modest and always at her husband's side, she is respected; but if she gives herself to everyone, she is vilified. He makes a scornful reference to books with many more pages than ideas. He refers ambitiously to the mathematical treatise he is imagining. The idea of the mask returns to his mind: the sciences are masked; once the masks are removed, they will appear in all their beauty. Whoever sees the entire sequence of the sciences will find them no harder to comprehend than the series of numbers. A sudden modesty or fear then strikes him. He tells himself sternly that fixed limits are set to all our minds, and our minds cannot surpass them.

How many future Cartesian themes have already made their appearance! An all-powerful mathematical science; disinclination to work seriously; Destiny; a voyage whose dangers serve as a test; the fear of God, that is, of punishment for immodesty; a mask for one's emotions and one's unconformity; rivalry with inventors; invention by means of a fixed method—and without the help of any other person; the confinement of the sciences to their rightful spouses; scorn for verbose, empty books; the unmasking of the sciences in their beauty; the ambition to grasp all the sciences together, in their natural sequence; and, finally, some retreat or modesty, the hint of a fear.

Such thoughts must have been occupying Descartes at the time he had his three dreams, which marked a turning point in his life. He dreamed them on the night of November 10, 1619, when he was returning to the army from the Emperor's coronation. The weather had forced him to take refuge, and all day he had remained alone with his thoughts in a well-warmed room. While he thought, he came, it seemed to him, on the foundations of an admirable science, and he went to bed filled with enthusiasm. To make us understand how extraordinary the occurrence was, he insists that he was quite sober, not having had any wine for three months. He adds that the genius responsible for the enthusiasm with which his brain had been inflamed for days had predicted his dreams to him before he had gone to bed, and that the human mind had no part in provoking them.

Since the Muses had visited him in March, Descartes was no stranger to inspiration. Many years later (in October or November of 1646), he wrote to his friend, Elisabeth of Palatine, that he had had "an infinity of experiences" to confirm his opinion that whatever he did out of a feeling of happiness would turn out well. Inward joy, he said to her, has some secret power to influence Fortune. The genius of Socrates must have been just this confidence in acts that flow from inward gaiety. We ought not regard the feeling with superstitious reverence, said Descartes, yet in important matters, when rational guidance is not enough, we should follow the promptings of our genius, that is, act as we feel happy in acting. Descartes' interest in inspiration was strong enough to lead him to write a treatise, now, unfortunately, lost, on the "god" or "familiar spirit" of Socrates.

We return to the night of November 10, 1619. Descartes fell asleep. He than saw some phantoms, which frightened him, so that, imagining himself to be walking along the streets, he turned himself to his left side, to be able to get where he wanted to go, because he felt a great weakness in his right side, on which he could not lean.

This, the beginning of Descartes' first dream, foreshadows a recurrent image in Descartes' as yet unwritten works. He will again and again write of following the right path, of following the path that leads to one's destination, of following the path that leads through difficulty and danger. For example, in the *Discourse*, published some eighteen years after the dreams, Descartes will write, "I spent the rest of my youth travelling . . . proving myself in the encounters that fortune offered me. . . . And I always had an intense desire to learn to distinguish the true from the false, so as to act clear-sightedly and to walk with assurance in this life. . . . After I had spent several years studying the book of life in this way and trying to acquire some experience, I one day took the resolution to study myself as well and to use all the powers of my mind to choose the paths that I should follow."

Descartes' first dream appears to serve the same purpose as the first part of his *Discourse*. The *Discourse*, it is true, is meant for others. "I shall be very pleased," he says in it, "to show the paths that I have followed." In obvious contrast, his dream is meant for himself alone, and while he succeeds in showing himself his path, it is not yet with assurance or pleasure. His right side feels crippled. As he tells us later, he was sleeping on his left side. But there may be another reason for the weakness. Why, after all, should sleeping on one side necessarily make the other feel weak? The additional reason may be hinted at in the first part of the *Discourse*, when Descartes says, "In the judgments I make on myself, I always try to lean to the side of diffidence rather than that of presumption." Because the coincidence of physical with moral leaning may seem to be an artifact of translation, I cite the original French, which reads, "*Je tâche toujours de pencher vers le côté de la défiance, plutôt que vers celui de la présomption.*"

Descartes' stress on walking through life with assurance suggests that he was aware of some weakness in himself. Certainly his childhood could not have promoted much self-assurance. His mother had died, of a lung disease, when he had been an infant of thirteen months. Descartes assumed that he had inherited his own dry cough and pale complexion from her. In a letter of consolation to Elisabeth (a letter of May or June of 1645), he wrote that he had coughed and remained pale till beyond the age of twenty, so that all the doctors who saw him before that age condemned him to an early death. But, he said to console Elisabeth, his sickliness had been overcome by his inclination to see everything in the most agreeable possible light and make his chief satisfaction depend on himself alone.

It is clear that Descartes identifies his ill, youthful self with his mother, as if he had inherited the threat of his own death from hers. He is interested in the paleness that is connected with sadness or anger. In his study of the *Passions* he explains that sadness contracts the orifices of the heart and so causes paleness, "especially when the sadness is great." There are some children, he adds, "who become pale instead of weeping when they are angry, testifying perhaps to an extraordinary judgment and courage in them, when, that is to say, the pallor results from their considering the greatness of the evil and preparing themselves for a strong resistance, in the same way as older people" (*Passions*, pp. 116 and 134). Descartes evidently makes the following equations: coughing, pallor, mother's death; his own coughing, pallor, anticipation of death; pallor, sadness; pallor in place of tears, the judgment and courage to overcome evil; and the ability to react with Stoic cheerfulness, basic self-dependence, and, as the result, good health and contentment.[1]

Descartes connects not only paleness, but also appetite with sadness. In his early notes, he writes that sadness, danger, and preoccupation with serious matters cause him to sleep deeply and eat voraciously. In the *Passions*, he states that the first experience of sadness must be the result of lack of nourishment, and therefore sadness and hunger remain associated throughout life. To Elisabeth's objection that some people lose their appetites when sad, he agrees, but maintains (May 1646) that in his own experience, the opposite is true. He is one of those, he intimates, whose "first cause of sadness at the beginning of their life was that they did not receive enough nourishment." He remains conscious of the survival of an unassuaged infantile appetite.

The absence of Descartes' mother was caused by death; the emotional absence of his father seems to have been caused by circumstance, or unconcern, or both. Business kept the father away from home much of the time. It is also reported that he "was very annoyed to see that his son devoted himself to the study of philosophy, to the point of writing and making books. He no doubt did not foresee the importance that would later be attributed to him when he said . . . 'Of all my children, I have been dissatisfied with only one. Was there any point in giving birth to a son absurd enough to have himself bound in calf!'" (Adam, pp. 433–434, note c). In any case, René was only four years old when his father remarried and left him in the care of his maternal grandmother, whom he learned to call, "mother." It was she who, with the help of his beloved nurse, brought him up. But he was no more than ten when he was sent to the Jesuit school or *collège* at La

Flèche. Father Charlet, a relative, was its Rector, and he took the place, Descartes said, of a father. Charlet's affection for him grew very strong, and the two remained friends. At the age of eighteen, Descartes left the *collège* and went to study law and medicine, after which he joined the army. Neither as a child nor later did he have more than intimations of a stable family life. He walked on by himself, depending, as he had learned, on himself alone. He was neither closely united with others emotionally nor quite separated from them.

We return to the dream. In the dream, Descartes was ashamed of the way he was walking and tried to straighten himself, but he felt a violent wind which swept him round in a kind of swirl and made him revolve three or four times on his left foot. This may remind us of the caution expressed in the third part of the *Discourse*, which compares men who search for knowledge with travellers, who, "finding themselves lost in some forest, ought never to wander, turning now to one side and now to the other." Curiously, Descartes' basic image, of weakness, leaning, straying in circles, and losing his way, finds a contemporary and literal embodiment in the artist, Oskar Kokoschka. Kokoschka had the tendency to lean to one side. When the tendency was aggravated by a wartime injury, he had to learn to walk in partial circles. His biographer tells us that "for a long time after his injury he suffered from persecution mania and agoraphobia. His sense of balance was so deranged that he could only walk in circles and he had to set off in the opposite direction to arrive at his intended goal. He could not stand straight, but always leaned to one side. This tendency already disclosed itself when he walked across the moonlit Stefansplatz in Vienna after the performance of his play *Murder Hope of Women*, but now his wound was the physical reason for its renewal" (Hodin, p. 147).

The motif of turning, circling, or swirling is prominent, we know, in Descartes' physics—the pervasive swirl of his physics is given the same name, *tourbillon*, as his dreamed wind. As the traveller is advised by Descartes to walk as straight as he can in one direction, the unimpeded particle is endowed by him with the inherent power of moving on in a straight line. There is an analogy, one sees, between his social emotions and his physical hypotheses: the ideal traveller moves like an unimpeded particle. Descartes himself was obviously not as unimpeded as he would have liked to be. After his mistress, the mother of his beloved, short-lived daughter, had died, Descartes is reported to have told a friend that the liaison had been "a dangerous commitment" (*un dangereux engagement*) from which God had extricated him and from a renewal of which He was continuing to preserve him (Adam, pp. 576–577). The *Passions* (p. 147) contains a few lines in which Descartes may be recalling his pleasure in escaping the threat of marriage. Speaking of emotions that grow out of their opposites, he says:

> For example, when a husband mourns his dead wife, whom (as sometimes happens) he would be sorry to see revived, his heart may be oppressed by the sadness aroused in it by the funeral array and the absence of a person to whose conversation he was accustomed; and it may happen that some remnants of love or of pity that appear before his imagination draw genuine tears from his eyes, even though he meanwhile feels a secret joy in his inmost soul. . . .

Descartes disliked social commitments and resented social pressure. He corresponded extensively but was afraid that acquaintances present in the flesh might importune him beyond endurance. In his elaborate, conscious way, he decided to conform externally, but no more than necessary. Perhaps because of the unending pressure he felt in his social space, it was more natural for him to conceive of physical space as always full, never truly pressureless, and identical with matter. In this physical space, particles were never in fact unimpeded and were, so to speak, forced to conform and move in approximately circular paths, which expressed, as Descartes did in his everyday life, the exact union of compliance with resistance.[2]

Now, the dream again. What frightened Descartes in the dream was the difficulty he had in dragging himself along, which made him think he was falling at each step. Descartes begins to pay attention to the way he is walking and to each separate step. In the second part of the *Discourse* he writes, as if guarding himself against the memory of the dream, "Like one who walks alone and in the twilight I resolved to go slowly, and to use so much circumspection in all things, that if my advance was but very small, I at least guarded myself well against falling." In the *Meditations* (III) matters appear to be even more difficult:

> All the course of my life may be divided into an infinite number of parts, none of which is in any way dependent on the other; and thus from the fact that I was in existence a short while ago it does not follow that I must be in existence now, unless some cause at this instant, produces me, so to speak, anew, that is to say, conserves me.

Small, cautious, and methodical as the steps may be, they do not cohere by themselves, they form no continuous path, they lead nowhere. Descartes must seek, he says, for the author of his existence, who produces him anew and conserves him. To search for the author of one's existence is not altogether different from searching for one's distant, unfamiliar father, or one's unknown mother. Their emotional support has never become internal and must always be affirmed and reaffirmed. It is not self-evident to Descartes that his life supports itself, and therefore he says, in the same *Meditation*, "I wish to know whether I possess a power which is capable of bringing it to pass that I who now am shall still be in the future." He answers, as his nature prompts him to, that he has no such power. Descartes the methodologist is forced by his childhood's lack to become Descartes the believer and near-Occasionalist.

In the dream, having noticed the open door of a *collège* on his way, he entered it in order to find a refuge and a cure for his trouble. He tried to reach the chapel, to which he had at first wanted to go and pray. This dream-episode seems to refer to Descartes' years at the Jesuit school. He had developed an interest there in Biblical commentaries. Throughout his life, he remained an opponent of the "Libertines," and it was his ambition to bring reason and religious dogma together peacefully. No doubt out of friendship for his old mentors, he was particularly eager that the Jesuits accept his system. Perhaps, then, his dream returns Descartes to the years in which he had lived a sheltered life at La Flèche, among adult admirers. It returns him to the wished-for comfort of prayer. But what can be the attitude of the God to whom he wants to pray. God is a kind of father, and the kind of human father one has influences one's conception of God. Descartes' father had not been ready to disturb himself or his life for his son's benefit. It comes as no surprise, then, that Descartes writes to Elisabeth that it would be useless to inform God of our wants through prayer. God, he says, knows our wants, and it would be sinful to suppose that he would disturb the universal order in our favor. The wind Descartes has blown up for his dream's sake does not allow him to reach the chapel. To be there would not in any case be really helpful.

In the dream, Descartes noticed that he had passed a man of his acquaintance without greeting him, and he tried to retrace his steps in order to pay him his respects, but the wind thrust him back against the chapel. The least that we can say about this contest between wind and politeness is that Descartes is distracted from his goal by a social demand and tries, unsuccessfully, to comply with it. He is dreaming the reality, that he prefers solitude. At the end of the third part of the *Discourse* he writes that "in the crowded throng of a great and active nation (by which he means Holland) I can live as solitary and retired as in the most remote desert." He flees unwanted visitors, he changes residences, he moves to a new address without always telling his nearby friends what it is, he writes to his faraway friend, Balzac, in the same tone in which he addresses posterity in the *Discourse*, that he is happy in Amsterdam, where "each person is so attentive to his profit that I might stay all my life without ever being noticed by anyone" (to Balzac, May 5, 1631). He had his servants and correspondents and scientific contacts, but he needed solitude. Psychically and maybe in fact he passed acquaintances without greeting them, but the lapse made him feel guilty.

Descartes himself tries to interpret the meaning of the wind in his dream. He tells us that the wind which had thrust him against the chapel, to the accompaniment of pain in his right side, was the Evil Genius which had been trying to force him into a place he intended to enter of his own accord. This, he says, God did not allow, though the place was sacred. Descartes' interpretation fits his character. He defies the wind, the spirit of external compulsion, as he had once defied it in his small boat. He as much as says, "I will be good, but in my own way and my own time."

Descartes' determination to make his way without depending seriously on anyone is illustrated by his relations with Beeckman. In the spring of their friendship, in 1619, he wrote to him, "Love me and be sure that I could no more forget you than the Muses themselves. For it is they who have united me to you by the bond of an affection that cannot end." A few months later, on April 23, to be exact, he wrote with equal enthusiasm and greater explicitness,

> You are truly the only one to have shaken me out of my indifference; you alone have recalled the science I had already almost forgotten, and you have led my mind, estranged from every serious occupation, back to better thoughts. If then something not to be scorned accidentally comes from me, you will by rights be able to claim it entirely for yourself.

The spring of friendship lapsed. Eleven years later, in 1630, it had reached its winter. In the winter of friendship, Descartes sets himself immeasurably above Beeckman. Descartes complains that the latter had been heard saying that it was he, Beeckman, who had taught Descartes what Descartes had written in his *Treatise on Music.* This particular treatise may not have been worth fighting over. A modern specialist, Gaston Milhaud, thinks that it does not do much credit to the originality of its author, no matter who he really was. "It is infinitely probable," the specialist says, "that he borrows the basis of his work from Zarlino, whom, to be sure, he cites, but arranges in his own way, and whose reasons he replaces by his own." However this may be, the imputation cast upon his originality angers Descartes. He informs Beeckman that witnesses have again testified to his fault. Descartes' tone rises. Beeckman has perhaps been misled by the French civilities of the letters he, Descartes, has sent him. Yes, the letters may say that he has learned from Beeckman. But everybody knows that he, Descartes, finds even ants and worms instructive.

The following letter to Beeckman, dated October 17, 1630, fills, in print, thirteen abusive pages. When I first read it, I turned to the paragraph in the *Passions* in which Descartes describes anger:

> Anger is a species of hatred or aversion which we have towards those who have done some evil to us or have tried to injure not any chance person but more particularly ourselves. Thus it has the same content as indignation, and all the more so in that it is founded on an action which affects us and for which we desire to avenge ourselves, for this desire almost always accompanies it; and it is directly opposed to gratitude, as indignation is to favor. But it is incomparably more violent than these three other passions, because the desire to repel harmful things and to revenge oneself, is the most persistent of all desires. It is desire, united to self-love, which furnishes anger with the agitation of the blood that courage and bravery can cause; and hatred . . . excites a heat which is more severe and ardent than that which may be excited by love or by joy.

An idea of Descartes' letter to Beeckman may be conveyed by a few excerpts:

> After the silence of a year, you have recently had the fantastic idea of writing to me that if I wish to further the progress of my investigations, I should return to your company, and that I could not profit more than under your direction, and many other remarks of this nature, which you seemed to write to me familiarly and as a friend, as if to one of your disciples. What could I have thought except that you had written this letter so that you could show it to others before sending it to me and could boast that I had often received instruction from you? . . . I could in no way imagine that you had become so stupid and understood yourself so ill that

> you might in effect think that I had ever learned from you, or even that I could ever learn anything from you, if not in the way that I usually learned from everything natural, even the least ants and the smallest worms [Descartes' indignation has contracted the size of the ants and worms of the previous letter]. . . . But I see clearly by your last letters that you have not sinned in this by malice but that it is undoubtedly an illness that holds you in its grip. . . . Consider, I ask you, and see if in all your life you have found or invented anything that is really worth praising? . . . Do you not praise me only in order to gain more glory by the comparison . . . to elevate the throne of your vanity so much the higher? But enough, I want to treat your illness gently now, and not to use harsher remedies, for if I should treat you as you deserve, you would be so laden with shame and infamy that I am afraid I should drive you to despair rather than give you health. . . . I am ashamed to propose myself here as an example, but since you often compare yourself with me, it seems that this is in some way necessary. Have you ever heard me praise myself for having taught anything to anyone? Have I ever, I do not say preferred myself, but even compared myself to anyone?

Descartes ends his letter by hoping that he will not be forced to expose Beeckman in public, but that the sinner's repentance might be followed by a renewed friendship.

Beeckman kept Descartes' two letters of accusation and his two replies to them. He said that if ever he wrote on morality, the four letters would illustrate how ridiculous the fame of a pedant could be. It is hard at this distance to judge the controversy, but the lucky survival of Beeckman's *Journal* shows him to have been an informed and in some ways original scientist. We may also recall that Descartes knew the art of writing of letters. Sometimes, in commenting on Fermat's method, which competed with his own, for establishing maxima and minima, he was conveniently unable to understand. He even asked that Fermat's writings should no longer be sent to him, for he did not care to waste more time on them. Yet Descartes' letters to Beeckman are an uncharacteristically prolonged and violent outburst. Tooth and nail, they defend the independence and originality that evidently constituted Descartes' value in his own eyes. Their anger seems proportional to Descartes former love, or, as he would say, directly opposed to his former gratitude.

Why so angry? I can only speculate on the reason, but it may lie in Beeckman's fatherly relation to Descartes. Descartes was no longer a child who needed the love and teaching of a Father Charlet. Beeckman's desire to continue to be a psychic father to Descartes caused a revival of Descartes' long-concealed anger against his own father, who had scorned and abandoned him. He would not be compared, led, or taught. He would be unique and would teach and lead himself.

It is out of jealousy or, rather, the desire to be original that Descartes refrained from giving even one serious, extended example of the method whose virtues he praised so effectively. At times he claimed that the *Geometry* was such an example. He wrote to Mersenne (at the end of December 1637), "By the *Dioptrics* and the *Meteors* I have tried only to persuade that my method is better than the ordinary, but I assume that I have demonstrated it by my *Geometry*, for at the beginning of it I have solved a problem that by the testimony of Pappus could not be solved by any of the ancients, nor by the moderns."

Descartes assumed, we see, that the solving of a hitherto insoluble problem demonstrated the power of his method. But he did not, all the same, demonstrate the method as he had described it, slow, sure, and complete. He did not want to, for he was intent on making his *Geometry* difficult, in order, he said, that his accomplishment should not be slighted and that his relatives might have the pleasure of rediscovering what he had discovered before them. As he wrote proudly to a correspondent (Plempius, on October 3, 1637):

> I well know that the number of those who will be able to understand my *Geometry* will be very small; for, having omitted all those matters that I judged to be not unknown to others, and having tried to understand or at least touch on many things in few words (even, in truth, all those which might ever be discovered in this science), I have made a book which demands readers not only very learned in all things that have been known up to now in geometry and algebra, but also very industrious, very ingenious, and very attentive persons. I have learned that there are two in your country. . . .

Descartes certainly did not want *his* science to give herself to everyone. He particularly wanted to thwart his scientific enemies. In a letter of April 4, 1648, to Mersenne, he wrote:

> My *Geometry* is as it should be to keep Roberval and his like from vilifying it unless their vilification redound to their own confusion; for they are not able to understand it, and I have composed it so quite on purpose, omitting from it what was easiest, and putting in only the things that were worth the trouble. But I state to you that, if not for these malignant persons, I should have written altogether differently from the way I did, and I should have made it much clearer; and I will perhaps yet do it some day if I see that these monsters are sufficiently vanquished or humbled.

And now, to return to the dream, Descartes, having passed his acquaintance and been thrust against the chapel by the wind, saw someone else in the middle of the courtyard, and this person called him by name in a very polite, obliging way and said to him that if he wished to go and find Monsieur N., he would have something to give him. Descartes imagined this to be a melon brought from some foreign country.

Later in his account, Descartes tells us that "the melon signified the charms of solitude, but presented by purely human solicitations." He gives no further clue. What can make the melon worth dreaming about, and how can it be connected with solitude? Does the answer lie in its qualities of roundness, self-enclosure, and internality of substance? Perhaps so. The book of poetry that appears in Descartes' third dream contains an idyll by Ausonius in praise of the wise, self-sufficient man, who is compared with the round, self-enclosed world. Another possible clue is a later-famous poem, *Le Melon,* which gives decorative, humorously extravagant praise to the "divine" and "Parnassian" fruit, fragrant in smell, eloquent of Nature's love, covered and yet accessible.

Unprinted poems were then often recited to audiences and passed from hand to hand. I do not know when exactly *Le Melon* was written, or if it had been read at Paris in time for Descartes to have incorporated something of it into his dreams. The temptation to believe that Descartes was referring to it arises from the fact that its author, Saint-Amant, had come to Paris the year before the dreams, in 1618, carrying in his pocket a poem, the inspiration of many others, called *l'Ode à la Solitude.* This ode could, therefore, signify just "the charms of solitude" Descartes associated with the melon. It begins, appropriately, with the lines:

O how I love solitude!
How those spots sacred to night
Distant from the world and from turmoil
Are gratifying to my inquietude!

Saint-Amant takes pleasure in successively imagining a rural paradise free of fear and pain, ruined old castles, the skeleton of a man who hanged himself for love, an idyllic shelter for sleep (a fantasy designed to appeal to the poetry-loving, sleep-loving Descartes), a rock-summit, and a seashore. Saint-Amant searches only, he says, for the deserts in which, dreaming alone, he may amuse himself with fluent discourses between his genius and the muse. The words, he says, are born in his soul without restraining the liberty of the demon that has transported him.

This conventional enough presence of genius, muse, and "demon" is reminiscent, of course, of the Muses that Descartes had cultivated, the Genius that had inspired him, the Demon of Socrates he wrote on, the Evil Genius he feared, and the Spirit of Truth he felt, by his dreams' end, to be enlightening him. Descartes has at least an affinity with Saint-Amant and other poets of the time. A poet such as Saint-Amant not only loves solitude and recognizes it as essential to creation, but also despises the derivative and insists on being purely himself. Like the contemporary legislator of poetry, Boileau, he wants every truth to be uttered as if for the first time and yet to be universal, simultaneously his own possession and mankind's.

What else might the melon of the dream recall? Since it is foreign, it suggests something unusual or difficult to get. It is, further, something to be cut open and penetrated. It therefore recalls Decartes' passion for anatomy. We can, for example, sense the passion in a letter he writes to his correspondent, Mersenne (on November 2, 1646). He tells Mersenne that he has investigated the formation of embryos in chicken eggs, but has turned to embryo calves, which are easier to understand because of their size. Since he has learned, he says, that butchers often slaughter pregnant cows, he has been supplied with more than a dozen wombs with little calves, "some as big as mice, others like rats, and others like little dogs." Descartes' interest in embryos must, I think, have been sexual. He must have been, wittingly or, more likely, unwittingly, curious about his own birth, the more so because his mother was a distant mystery to him.

That brings up the subject of Descartes' curiosity in general. Like all philosophers and scientists, he was exceptionally curious. In the *Passions,* he says, "It seems to me that wonder [as the French *admiration* may be translated] is the first of all the passions." The first in time, Descartes means, and here too there may be a hint of the remembered force of curiosity in his own childhood. He defines wonder as "a sudden surprise of the soul which causes it to apply itself with attentive consideration to the objects which seem to it rare and extraordinary" (*Passions*, LXX).

But wonder, though useful, is also dangerous in Descartes' eyes:

> It much more fequently occurs that we wonder too much, and that we are astonished in perceiving things which deserve little or no consideration, than that we wonder too little. And this may entirely prevent or pervert the use of reason. That is why, although it is good to be born with some inclination towards this passion, because that disposes us for the acquisition of the sciences, we must at the same time afterwards try to free ourselves from it as much as possible. For it is easy to supplement its defects by special reflection and attention which our will can always oblige our understanding to give on these occasions when we judge the matter which presents itself is worth the trouble. But there is no other remedy to prevent our wondering to excess than that of acquiring a knowledge of various matters and exercising ourselves in the consideration of all those which may appear the most rare and strange (*Passions*, LXXVI).

Similarly, in Descartes' dialogue, *The Search for Truth*, a participant declares, "The desire for knowledge, which is common to all men, is an evil which cannot be cured." He goes so far as to add, "For curiosity increases with knowledge." The suggested remedy, which seems not to be identical with the previous one, is that one should be satisfied with the general principles of things, with the help of which everything particular can be simply explained, after which "the passion for knowledge . . . will no longer be so violent."

Descartes' exacerbated curiosity seems to have been accompanied by a nagging guilt, which influenced him to try to limit his curiosity and pry more into generalizations than into seductive particulars. The supposition that he felt guilty over his curiosity is confirmed by the careful account his biographer, Baillet, gives of his death. In the course of his loss and recovery of consciousness, Descartes decided, as he told those around him, that God

> had permitted his mind to remain so long perplexed in the shadows, out of fear that his reasoning would not be found to conform closely enough to the will the Creator had to dispose of his life. He concluded that, because God had given him the free use of his reason, He permitted him, consequently, to follow that which it dictated to him, provided that he abstained from desiring to penetrate into His decrees with excessive curiosity, and from causing uneasiness for the event (of death) to appear.

To Descartes, God's mercy was predicated on the restraint of His creature's curiosity.

On the following night, Descartes spoke of his resolve to die in order to obey God, hoping that He agreed to the voluntary sacrifice he offered Him in expiation of all the faults of his life.

We may go back now from death to the dreamer and the dream. Descartes, having been surprised, was still more surprised to see that those who were gathered for conversation around the person he had come on were standing straight and firm, while he, Descartes, was still bent and staggering, and that the wind, which had almost knocked him down a number of times, had grown much weaker.

The theme here is surely Descartes' weakness, in whatever sense, as compared with other people. In a letter (to Chanut, March 6, 1646) he once expressed the half-humorous wish that all the decent men might be assembled in one city and he be allowed to live with them, if, that is, they were willing to receive him in their company. The *if* tells of his sense of inferiority. And so, analogously, others are steady on their feet, not he. Not surprisingly, he came to think of steadiness as a cardinal virtue. In the *Passions* (CLIX) he emphasizes "abjectness" or "vicious humility," which "consists principally in the fact that men are feeble or have a lack of resolution" and cannot therefore "prevent themselves from doing things of which they know they will afterwards repent." He also speaks of irresolution (*Passions*, CLXX) as a fear that is both strong and usual in some people, who show "an excess of irresolution which proceeds from a feebleness of understanding, which, having no clear and distinct conceptions, simply has many confused ones." This fear, irresolution, is the one he is always combatting with his criterion of clarity and distinctness and with his step-by-step method. In the dream, his fear or irresolution are embodied in his bent, staggering self.

The contrast was the end of the dream. Descartes awoke, feeling a sharp pain, which made him fear that "all this" might be the work of some evil genius that wanted to seduce him. I should suppose that it is the evil genius, or evil spirit, as Descartes' Latin makes clear, whose malign influence makes walking and even standing difficult. It is this genius that appears in the second of Descartes' *Meditations*, when Descartes asks, "But what am I, now that I suppose that there is a certain genius which is extremely powerful, and, if I may say so, malicious, who employs all his powers in deceiving me?" We may recall that Descartes identifies Socrates' good genius with optimism and success. The evil genius, then, must be pessimism and failure. Its seductiveness, like its evil, must be excessive curiosity or excessive revelation, like that of the science that prostitutes itself to everyone.

Having awakened, Descartes prayed to God to be guaranteed against the evil effect of his dream and against the misfortunes that might menace him as punishment for his sins, which he recognized as possibly serious enough to call down heaven's thunderbolts on his head, even though he had led an irreproachable life in the eyes of men.

Descartes' sense of guilt grows more acute. It does not stem, as far as he knows, from anything his neighbors might say against him: he has preserved appearances. He prays to the Being he has offended and asks, typically, for a guarantee.

In this situation, after an interval of nearly two hours spent in various thoughts on the good and evil of this world, Descartes fell asleep again. Immediately he dreamed a new dream, in which he believed he heard a piercing sound, which he took for a clap of thunder. The fright it gave him woke him up immediately and, opening his eyes, he saw many fiery sparks spread about in the room. This had happened to him often in the past, for it was nothing very extraordinary for him to wake in the middle of the night and find his eyes emitting sparks bright enough to give him a glimpse of the objects nearest him. This time he took to philosophical reasoning and, having observed the quality of the objects thus brought before him by alternately opening and closing his eyes, he came to conclusions favorable to his intellect. His fear was dispelled and he fell asleep again, sufficiently calm.

The thunderbolt Descartes, as the author of his own dream, had called down on himself did not strike him directly, but he was frightened awake by what might have been its sound. The sparks he saw on awakening were as if a residue of the bolt. It has been supposed that they were symptoms of an attack related to migraine or some convulsive condition. It is easy to associate Descartes' premonition of the dream with the premonitory aura of an attack, and his spinning and one-sided pain and frightening phantoms fit the hypothesis of a brain disturbance.

The possible physiological causes of Descartes' experiences do not rule out psychological causes or associations. Like many of the scientists of his time, he was interested in optics, though, unlike many of them, he considered light to be a phenomenon of pressure. He used his knowledge of optics to create playful illusions. For example, with a moving mirror he enlarged toy soldiers and made them seem to march, larger than life, across the wall of his room. He enjoyed deceiving his assistant with these images. Is it too much to say that, in doing this, he was acting the role of the deceiving genius he had created and feared in his dream?

In the process of grasping his dream philosophically, Descartes opened and closed his eyes. He was testing the reality of the objects—*espèces*, the French text calls them—that the light revealed. The test made sense to him in terms of his optical theories. When Mersenne, his scientific friend, wrote to him that he had often seen a halo around a candle, Descartes wrote back (on December 8, 1629) that he preferred to believe that the cause lay in the humors of the eye, especially if it could be shown that not everyone saw such a halo at the same time. If, he wrote, Mersenne would specify whether he had seen the halos at night, when the eyes are heavy with the vapors of sleep, or after heavy reading or a fast, or in clear or rainy weather, he would explain the phenomenon to him. On another occasion, he wrote to Golius (on May 19, 1635) that after he had leaned his head on his right hand for a while one night, he had opened his right eye, which had been closed, and had seen two halos around the candle that was brought into the room. "They did not form in the air at all," he wrote, "but only in the humors of one of my eyes. This is a matter I think I can explain well enough."

Descartes, it may be concluded, experimented a good deal with his eyes. The sparks he often saw might have caused him to do so.[3] Besides, his lifelong habit of remaining in bed during the morning to think and dream made it both hard and interesting to notice when, exactly, he had awakened. In a letter he sent from Amsterdam (to Balzac, April 15, 1631) he wrote:

> I sleep here ten hours every night, and no care awakens me; after sleep has promenaded my mind for a long time in woods, gardens, and enchanted palaces, where I experience all the pleasures that are imagined in fables, I mingle my reveries of the day insensibly with those of the night; and when I notice that I am awake, it is only in order that my contentment should be more perfect and my senses participate, for I am not so severe as to refuse them anything that a philosopher might permit them without offending his conscience.

The attention Descartes paid to his dreams and to their insensible transition to waking life recalls one of Lichtenberg's aphorisms, in which he said:

> Once again, I recommend dreams. We live and experience sensations as much in dream as in the waking

> state. The one constitutes a part of our existence no less than the other. It is one of the privileges of the human being to dream and to be conscious of doing so . . . . Dreaming is a life which, with the other part of our existence, forms what we call human life. Dreams disappear in our waking state little by little, and it is impossible to say where the one state begins or the other ends (*Aphorisms*, III).

Descartes fell asleep again. He had a third dream, which had none of the terrifying quality of the first two. This time he found a book on his table but did not know who had put it there. He opened it and, seeing that it was a dictionary, was delighted, for he hoped that it might be very useful to him. At that very moment, he found he had another book, no less new to him than the first. It was the collection of poems by different authors, entitled *Corpus poetarum*. Out of curiosity, he wanted to read something in it, and on opening it came on the words, with which a poem by Ausonius begins, "What path will I follow in life?" At the same moment he saw a man he did not know, but who presented him with some verses, by the same poet, beginning with *Est et Non*, which he recommended as an excellent poem. Descartes told him that he knew what it was and that this poem was among those in the big collection on the table. He wanted to show it himself to the man and began to leaf through the book, the order and arrangement of which he prided himself on knowing perfectly. While he was looking for the place, the man asked him where he had got this book, and Descartes answered that he could not tell him how he had got it, but that a moment ago he had been handling another, which had just disappeared, and he did not know who had brought it to him or who had taken it back. He had not finished saying this, when he saw the book reappear at the other end of the table. But he found that this *Dictionary* was no longer quite as he had seen it the first time. There was some further conversation, and Descartes found several small portrait engravings, which made him remark that the volume was beautiful, and then book and man disappeared.

Descartes claims to have begun interpreting the dream while still asleep. He decided that the *Dictionary* represented all the sciences together, while the collection of poems marked the union of Philosophy with Wisdom. The poets, he thought to himself, often wrote with more meaning and better expression than the philosophers. This marvel he ascribed to the divine nature of inspiration and the force of imagination, which reveal the seeds of wisdom, existing in all men's minds like sparks of fire in flints, far more easily and brilliantly than reason reveals them in philosophers. Continuing his interpretation while asleep, Descartes found that the poem beginning, "What path will I follow in life?" marked the good advice of a wise person or even of Moral Theology itself.

Thereupon, doubting whether he was dreaming or meditating, he awoke without emotion and continued, eyes open, to interpret his dream along the same lines. By the poets assembled in the collection he understood the revelation and enthusiasm with which he hoped to be favored. By the piece of verse *Yes and No* he understood truth and falsehood in human knowledge and the profane sciences. Seeing that all these meanings were much to his liking, he grew confident enough to persuade himself that it was the Spirit of Truth that had used this dream to open the treasures of all the sciences before him.

This last dream, Descartes says, was extremely sweet and extremely agreeable, and marked the future, that which should happen to him during the rest of his life. But he took the two earlier dreams to be severe warnings over his past life, which might not have been as innocent in the eyes of God as those of men. That, he thought, was the reason for the great fear that had accompanied the two dreams. The dread by which he had been struck in the second marked his remorse for all the sins he had committed up till then. The lightning, the sound of which he had heard, was the signal of the Spirit of Truth descending upon him to possess him.

The interpretation finished, Descartes again prayed to God and vowed to make a pilgrimage to the shrine of the Virgin Mary in Loretto. He slowly returned to his ordinary frame of mind, but the enthusiasm in which the dreams had ended changed his life.

According to Freud, Descartes' dream is "from above," that is, of the kind the dreamer himself is able to interpret with substantial accuracy. We may, however, add to Descartes' interpretation of the third dream. He was always in search of a systematic, infallible guide to thought and life, an omnicompetent dictionary. His father, we remember, had said that Descartes was absurd enough to have himself bound in calfskin covers; now Descartes was binding the world in them, for to him a book was the sort of thing that could both be mastered and promise mastery. Even when he ventured away from books, it was to seek the truth either in himself or in "the great book of the world." Now he finds something like this great book on the table. This book, the dictionary, foreshadows his later ideal of a universal language, the order of whose words would be as clear as that of numbers. Descartes also finds a book that, like himself, weighs pros and cons. But in spite of the dictionary and the inspired book of advice, the shifts of his dreams express his feeling that his life shifts and is discontinuous. Nature is performing some sleight-of-hand. The dictionary disappears and reappears, subtly changed. All his life, Descartes was afraid of losing things. He was afraid of losing himself, that is, of being or appearing derivative; he was afraid of losing his ideas to others; he was even afraid, he later complained, that his letters would be stolen. And in physics, he was convinced that there was no single point in the whole universe that was truly immobile (*Principles*, II, p. 13). No place of anything in the world is firm and arrested, he said, except as we arrest it in our minds.

Before we assess Descartes' dreams, there is at least one general comment that should be made on them. In the context of his life and philosophy, they suggest some ego-splitting and depersonalization. As the psychoanalyst, Bertram Lewin, has pointed out, there is a great deal of body-feeling in the first two dreams. In these dreams, Descartes was painfully aware of his body's materiality, its effort to move, and he awoke in pain. His body or body-feeling did not allow him to continue to dream. But by the third dream, Descartes was able to become the ordinary dream-spectator, unaware of his body as such. His observing and thinking self took over the dream completely. He had, so to speak, separated his bodily from his conscious self, the observer-as-such from the world, including his body, that he perceived outside of him.

In depersonalization, the sense of the estrangement of some part of oneself, one's body, often, may become strong, and the problem of the dreamlikeness of reality genuinely troublesome. Descartes' relative parentlessness, his relative detachment from people, his hatred of hesitation, his desire to test for the sake of certainty, his themes of dream and deceiver, and his doubt and "*cogito*," all argue a tendency towards depersonalization. His habit of mingling dream-fantasies and waking fantasies and his testing of reality by the shutting and opening of his eyes argue the same conclusion.

Another psychoanalyst, Paul Federn, has drawn attention to a defence against depersonalization that resembles Descartes' method—defence and method both protect the sense of reality by fixing the attention on continuous, unbroken perception. Men who suffer from depersonalization may try to coerce themselves into perceptual continuity, in order to save ordinary reality from fading or dissolving. Sometimes, for example, they "must follow the curves of the train or car in which they ride with great attention. In severe cases they cannot do so any more; they ride with closed eyes and immobilized body. Even so they sense the changes of direction of the vehicle and react to every single one with a depersonalized feeling" (Federn, p. 252).

I do not wish to imply that Descartes was in such straits; yet he was, we know, the father of the Occasionalists, who seem, if we allow ourselves an unverified guess, to transpose the illness of psychic discontinuity and of estrangement from one's body, into philosophical terms.

The immediate interpretation of the dreams has been finished, and we can, in imitation of Descartes, review the whole and try to grasp our conjectural restoration as a unity. Descartes' dreams, his life, and his philosophy, reflect a number of characteristic fears and hopes. We remember a mother vanished, almost at once, and then, at four, his father married to a stranger; but also two compensatory mothers, Descartes' grandmother and his nurse. We remember his partially and then almost wholly absent father, scornful, too, it appears, of his son's lack of clear aims; but we can also remember a loving, fatherly teacher, a friend who inspired Descartes for a brief but critical time, closeness to a woman (followed by relief at her death), and a beloved but distant and short-lived child. The result, in Descartes, is loneliness—he never learned how not to be lonely—and the fear of being lost; but also the courage and intelligence, those of the pale child who refused to cry, to find a methodical way of going on and of discovering, a method he could not really allow himself to follow in his thought, which gave it an idealized form, but which he followed in his life.

All his life, Descartes seems to have been searching for something unknown, immensely attractive, perfectly healing, a mother-knowledge to take the place of the mother he could not clearly remember. Searching, he observed the still-beating hearts of calves and the different-sized fetuses in the wombs of slaughtered cows. He cut veins open. He imagined the mechanisms of blood-circulation and perception and the workings of the minute pipes that, he thought, made up the nervous system. He watched so much, made these so external, that he often found it hard to believe that these could also be himself, that he was his own body too and not some half-witness, half-director lodged in his body with a Kafkesque incomprehension of his status there.

The notion of the incomprehensible, Kafkesque trial may be exaggerated, yet it is not inapt for Descartes. He longed to know, and at optimistic moments knew that he could know, and exactly; but knowing too much made him feel remorse. Then he would say to himself that he wanted to know things only in general. Finally, the only truth comprehensible to him was that truth or reality was incomprehensible. Its name, of course, was God.

All his life, Descartes was also defying what he

thought was demanded of him. The defiance of others' demands is equivalent to his guilt and to the company in him of himself and his father. He would not, as his father had wished, become conventionally social. He would not become a lawyer, like his father, or a doctor, like his grandfather. He would, it is true, live in or near cities, but in the select company of himself, his thoughts, his optical experiments, his anatomized animals, his correspondents, his assistants, his scientific acquaintances. Alone in this way, he became his own kind of doctor. He looked, quite consciously, for the causes and cures of diseases and for a saving understanding of physiology. And he indirectly became a lawyer as well, for he set up a method to discover the truth infallibly. He wanted to give the universe its law, or, if not to give the law, to interpret it rightly to men. But then he drew back. His will and knowledge were not those of God. Long ago he had known his father as a distant, incomprehensible will, and so, he discovered in time, was the world's will. And so he too would be. Into his most rational accomplishment, his geometry, the best instance he thought of his method, he introduced deliberate difficulty and unintelligibility, in order to thwart the wicked Robervals and reward only a tiny group of trustworthy savants, who would not try to rob him of his glory. He would, that is, be like God in creating his geometry and like Him in admitting no one to his full logic and intimacy. A friend should be only close enough to stimulate and admire, but not to rival him.

Like dream, like thought, the structure grew, with its maze of clarity and unclarity, confidence and doubt, independence and dependence, pride and abasement. This most passionate philosopher had to give part of his day to serious thought, but could not bear to give more than a little. This most logic-loving of philosophers reasoned with transparent circularity, for he gave one *possibly* clear and distinct idea, that there must be at least as much reality in the cause as in its effect, priority over the *surely* clear and distinct idea that two and two make four; then, from the equal or superior reality of causes, established the existence of the superlative cause, the truthful God; and then, by means of this truthful God, established the truth of all clear and distinct ideas, including that of the sum of two and two. This lover of the mathematiform truth and its clarity and distinctness drove himself to believe that the truth was created as it was because God wanted it so, and no human being could hope to understand why God had so wanted it. And having decided, by clear, indubitable thought, that thought and extension could not come into contact with one another, he decided that they were nevertheless united, as we knew by the unimpeachable testimony of our senses. He pushed and pulled, advanced and retreated, dissociated body and thought and reassociated them.

Descartes is a great philosopher for more than one reason. He is great historically because his physics was comprehensive, audacious, and simple enough to be put, if only by other scientists, into mathematical form, and because his physiology was entirely mechanical and easy to grasp and investigate. He was in part the scientist himself and in part the inspirer of scientists, even of the great Newton, who made good use of the principle of inertia, which Descartes, it seems, was the first to state in unambiguously universal form, but who hated him and scribbled "error, error" on his copy of Descartes' geometry. But Descartes the scientific philosopher belongs to his own time, for his science, though not the ideal he held of it, is primitive and outmoded. His attractiveness has come to be centered in the way in which he dramatizes his predicament of doubt and certainty and, forgetting precedent, begins from himself. As a beginning, this is permanent, and it remains in the endless present of a lyric or autobiography. It is his need to be original and find his way, for himself, not in the company of parents or traditions, that we feel most keenly. He begins from a beginning that each of us can reenact, for it corresponds to feelings shared by everyone to whom philosophy is natural. His science is crystallized in the history of science, but his self as such is alive, renewed in each of his readers. It is his dreaming that lives, or, rather, his dreaming concealed behind his mask of reason, or, perhaps, his dreaming mingled insensibly with his open-eyed reason. He stands at the point where the difference cannot easily be made out.

References

The text of the dreams and of Descartes' other early writings is taken from the convenient, well-annotated edition by Alquié. The *Passions* is cited from Rodis-Lewis, and the description of Descartes' death from the Pléiade edition. The dreams are fully translated in Kemp Smith. Most of the translations are my own, but I have consulted those of Kemp Smith and of Haldane and Ross, the latter of which I have sometimes quoted. Gouhier's book is a meticulous discussion of Descartes' early writings, including the record, in indirect speech, of his dreams.

The books cited in the following bibliography appear in the order of their relevance.

Descartes, *Œuvres philosophiques,* Vols. I (1618–1637), II (1638–1642), ed. by F. Alquié (Paris, 1963, 1967).

—*Œuvres et lettres,* ed. by A. Bridoux (Paris, 1953).

—*Les passions de l'âme,* ed. by G. Rodis-Lewis (Paris, 1955).

—*Philosophical Works of Descartes,* trans. by E. S. Haldane and G. R. T. Ross, 2 vols. (Cambridge, 1931).

C. Adam, *Vie et Œuvres de Descartes* (Paris, 1910), reprinted in 1957.

N. K. Smith, *New Studies in the Philosophy of Descartes* (London, 1953).

H. Gouhier, *Les premières pensées de Descartes* (Paris, 1958).
P. Hodin, *Oskar Kokoschka* (London, 1966).
G. Milhaud, *Descartes savant* (Paris, 1921).
M. Allem, *Anthologie poétique française, XVII siècle*, Vol. I (Paris, 1965).
F. S. Klaf, *Strindberg* (New York, 1963).
S. Freud, *Gesammelte Werke*, Vol. XIV (London, 1948), pp. 558–560 ("Brief an Maxim Leroy uber einen Traum des Cartesius").
B. D. Lewin, *Dreams and the Uses of Regression* (New York, 1958).
P. Federn, *Ego Psychology and the Psychoses* (London, 1953).
J. Herivel, *The Background to Newton's* Principia (Oxford, 1965).
A. Koyré, *Newtonian Studies* (Cambridge, Mass., 1965), cf. esp. p. 79, n. 2.

NOTES

[1] Descartes' personal associations seem, at this point, to join the analysis made in a book he had read. His attention had been drawn to the phenomena of blushing and pallor by the *De Anima* of J. L. Vives, the seventeenth-century humanist. Like Descartes, Vives referred openly to his own experiences. See the introduction to Rodis-Lewis's edition of *Les passions de l'âme*.

[2] The analogy is of course only a guess. Even if justified, it does not exclude other reasons for the tourbillion theory. To Descartes, fine matter is a fluid, and he thinks in terms of hydraulic models, somewhat as do Freud and the ethologists, Lorenz and Tinbergen. He sees the body as a circulatory system in which more or less rarefied fluid flows through pipes of varying degrees of fineness. The image and the theory of circulation dominate much of his thought. The analogy, like a crime, might be pursued and compounded. Since Descartes' particles rub shoulders densely everywhere while Newton's are separate, relatively sparse inhabitants of a vacuum, their difference might be related to Descartes' feeling of inescapable social pressure as against Newton's social isolation—mitigated by the pulls of gravity. (I thank Prof. Joseph Agassi for leading me on to this last comparison.)

[3] Reality-testing may be a response to nascent schizophrenia. August Strindberg, whose psychological problems were more severe than Descartes', felt the need, not unlike Descartes, to test. One night in 1896, when tormented by "electricity" passing through his body, he found that the apparent inrush of electric fluid had no effect on the compass. This test seems to have helped him decide that he was mentally ill. Strindberg gave much time and effort to alchemical and other "scientific" studies. Once, having renewed the studies and sensing a return of the strange noises and chest compression he had experienced before, he said, "I understand the hint. It is forbidden to penetrate into the secrets of the powers" (Klaf, pp. 114–116, 132).

20. Gary Shapiro: "The Rhetoric of Nietzsche's *Zarathustra*"

Professor Shapiro received his Ph.D. from Columbia University. He is currently Associate Professor of Philosophy at the University of Kansas.

THE RHETORIC OF NIETZSCHE'S *ZARATHUSTRA* *

Thus Spoke Zarathustra: A Book for Everyone and No One. The duplicity of Nietzsche's whole title is obvious, but its sense is uncertain. It manages to cast into doubt both the substance of the book and the manner of its reception. The speech promised by the title is contrasted with the self-conscious bookishness invoked in the subtitle. Will the text be dominated by a single prophetic voice with a coherent message or will it take its place among the many literary patterns (the

* Used by permission of the author. This essay is published here for the first time.

narrative, the romance, the philosophical tale) which already exist? And who, if anyone, is its proper reader? Just as the thought of eternal recurrence collapses the distinction between the one and the many (for there is no way of individuating a plurality of absolutely exact repetitions), so as a book *Zarathustra* challenges us to think through the conceptions of the unity or plurality of a text which we tend to presuppose in our reading. The unity of philosophical thought and understanding is classically opposed to the plurality of poetry which is always contradicting itself. We need to know the rhetoric of *Zarathustra,* the manner in which it demands to be read.

I

In the very beginning of the *Vorrede,* the discourse preceding discourse, Zarathustra announces both a concern with wisdom and a novel approach to its dissemination. "I am weary of my wisdom" (*Ich bin meiner Weisheit uberdrussig*) he says.[1] Zarathustra, it seems, wants to impart his wisdom to men and so must descend to them. Such imparting is usually a matter of sharing and communicating in which ownership is extended without any loss or dilution. Spinoza sums up the philosophical tradition with his claim that knowledge is a unique good in that it can be commonly owned and need not give rise to any competition. Yet Zarathustra speaks not of extending possession of a good thing, but of emptying himself of something which has filled him to the point of satiation. Not only does *uberdrussig* convey a sense of being sated, but wisdom is metaphorically linked to a bee's uncomfortable superfluity of honey. Wisdom is to be given away, that is dispersed or possibly exchanged for folly, rather than socialized. Zarathustra does not speak of attaining completion through a community of intelligence as do philosophers from Plato to Hegel, but of a cleansing through surrender, an *askesis* not for the sake of wisdom but *of* wisdom:

> Behold! This cup wants to be empty again, and Zarathustra wants to be man again.

Yet such *askesis* does not signal a capitulation of philosophy to poetry. In the chapter "Of Poets" in part II, there is a somewhat parallel disavowal of poetry: "I have grown weary of the poets, the old and the new: they all seem to be superficial and shallow seas." This suggests that in the ancient quarrel between philosophy and poetry *Zarathustra* is not simply an object to be classified, captured, or given over to the enemy but that it is to be read as being one of the more self-conscious reconsiderations of the struggle itself.

To see how *Zarathustra* situates itself in relation to this struggle I propose to take one large step outside the text and then to undertake several tentative incursions back into it. Finally I want to indicate some ways in which the problematic of this text suggest a way of reading a large and puzzling part of European philosophy of the last hundred and fifty years. In the chapter "Of Poets," to which I will return, Zarathustra criticizes poetry in terms of two fundamental rhetorical dimensions. The poets are said to fail in the realm of thought and feeling by their penchant for vague and indefinite metaphorical constructions—that is, they are deficient in their use of and self-consciousness regarding the tropes or figures of speech. They are also criticized for their excessive vanity which leads them to strut like peacocks for an audience of buffaloes. Whether this extravagant comparison violates Zarathustra's first stricture is an intriguing question which must be postponed. What the two criteria taken together suggest is that a successful text, such as *Zarathustra* is presumed to be, will exhibit a careful handling of tropes and an attention to the nature of its audience, the latter being sufficiently cultured and aristocratic so that the writer need not humble himself to be understood. One consequence is that we ought to be cautious in assuming that the peacock's tail of *Zarathustra's* metaphorical texture is simply identical with the poetic or literary aspect of the text. In Nietzsche's early but posthumously published essays on rhetoric there is a discussion of the tropological and audience-directed dimensions of discourse which helps to explain how *Zarathustra* can contain criticisms of both philosophy and poetry while not disintegrating into fragments.

In these two essays "History of Greek Eloquence" and "Rhetoric," Nietzsche attempts to overturn his contemporaries' low evaluation of rhetoric by representing it as one of the highest achievements of ancient culture.[2] He argues that moderns cannot maintain a knowledgeable critique of rhetoric while preserving their own textual values, because through the influence of Cicero ancient rhetoric is the foundation of all modern prose style. Given Nietzsche's use of the ancients as a criterion for judging modern culture, his claims that the Greeks devoted more continual energy to this pursuit than to any other, and that the Hellenic world concentrated all of its power into rhetoric are striking. They also indicate that tragedy is not the only model for the rejuvenation of modern culture which Nietzsche found among the Greeks. If around this time (1872–4) Nietzsche saw Wagnerian opera as the modern repetition of classical tragedy, he may also have projected his own literary career, already underway, as the contemporary counterpart of ancient rhetoric. (At one point he calls Leopardi the greatest prose writer of the century and notes favorably that Leopardi translated and modeled himself on Isocrates). Nietzsche makes several points which are suggestive for the interpretation of *Zarathustra*. Ancient rhetoric was formed on the basis of the spoken word, while print is normative for the discourse of the modern world. Because we require the mediation of a book, Nietzsche says, "We are paler and more abstract."[3] *Zarathustra*, of course, has the form of speech mediated by a book. To whom such mediation is directed in the modern world is a question; for the Greeks the rhetorical audience was immediately present in the citizenry. Eloquence had its basis in the speeches of the Homeric heroes; if we think of Homer as *the* book, the Bible of the Greeks, we may get a preliminary sense of what a sacred book without an authoritative base could be for the author of *Zarathustra*. Rhetoric was institutionalized for those already educated by Homer in the discourse of deliberative assemblies dealing with judicial and legislative matters. Rhetoric is thus a republican art supposing a rhetorically educated citizenry, a tolerance for a plurality of viewpoints—in brief, a polity of aristocratic equals. When rhetorical speeches eventually come to be written in order to be read, weakening their connection with the spoken word, the auditor becomes a reader. Nietzsche describes him:

> one can imagine the image of the Greek reader at the time of Isocrates: he is a slow reader who sips sentence by sentence, with lingering eye and ear, and takes in a text like a costly wine, empathizing with all the art of the author; it is a delight to write for one who doesn't have to be intoxicated, or carried along but has the natural mood (*Stimmung*) of a *reader:* the acting or passionate or suffering man is not a reader.[4]

Nietzsche imagines his own ideal reader along similar lines in a variety of texts distributed through his whole authorship. That the modern reader does not live up to his ideal is clear to him. What is interesting about this particular image of the reader is his connection with the point at which spoken rhetoric is crystallizing in writing. Might he not be the ideal reader of *Zarathustra?*

Nietzsche characterizes the rhetorical text as ineluctably figurative or tropological—just what we would expect his ideal reader to enjoy. However, rhetoric cannot be contrasted with ordinary language as decoration or ornament is contrasted with a plain or natural style, because "there is no such thing as an unrhetorical 'naturalness' of language to which one could appeal: language itself is the result of spoken rhetorical arts." Here we are deep into Nietzsche's epistemology: language is inevitably figurative, unable to grasp or portray things as they are. "*Language is rhetoric,* for it can only convey a *doxa* and never *episteme.*"[5] Therefore all words are tropes and there is no standard language from which they can turn. When we say "the stone is hard" or "the leaf is green" we are uttering metonymies which confuse the cause (the external object) with the effect (our sensation). In the last section of this essay Nietzsche proceeds to characterize the various tropes, but the text breaks off after a brief discussion of metaphor, synecdoche, and metonymy. What is significant here is that Nietzsche does not appear to privilege metaphor as the basic trope but recognizes a variety of forms; he notes that at least thirty-eight have been distinguished but is reluctant to say anything about the "logical justification" of this great number!

Although there may be no transcendental deduction of the nature and number of the tropes, Nietzsche does offer a concept of rhetoric which would, at least in principle, allow him to explain the tropological and readerly aspects of rhetoric as dimensions of a unitary phenomenon. He begins his second essay on "Rhetoric" by citing the definitions of Kant and Schopenhauer. Kant had defined rhetoric as the art of carrying on an activity of the understanding as a free play (*Spiel*) of the imagination. Schopenhauer, on the other hand, emphasized the persuasive and empathetic elements of rhetoric by characterizing its aim as the coincidence of thought in speaker and hearer. Nietzsche says that Kant's definition is true of Greek rhetoric and Schopenhauer's of Roman. Nietzsche sees Greek rhetoric as not only artistically superior but paradigmatic for a whole culture: "Thus the specific nature of Hellenic life is characterized: all the business of the understanding, of the serious affairs of life, of need, even of danger are made into play."[6] A rhetoric of *Spiel* rather than persuasion aims at an audience of all who can enjoy the *Spiel* but at none who read in order to agree or disagree.

Nietzsche's preference for Greek rhetoric conceived as play has moral as well as epistemological implications. Aristotle conceived of rhetoric within the framework of both an epistemological and a moral realism. It is because knowledge of the world is possible that the probabilistic arguments of rhetoric can be given some scientific respectability; starting as they do with what is ordinarily said or believed rather than with the first principles of science, they are nevertheless necessary when addressing those who cannot follow a scientific demonstration and when dealing with a subject matter—politics and human life—in which general principles are subject to an indefinite number of contingencies. Because there is some general correspondence between common valuations and the true good for men and communities, and especially because there are such true goods, rhetoric is a form of practical science. Although Nietzsche has little to say explicitly about Aristotle's *Rhetoric* it is clear that his rejection of morality (and therefore of any moral realism) entails that the art of rhetoric cannot be anchored by what is said or believed about morality, much less by any moral truth. If, as Paul Ricoeur suggests, it was Aristotle's task to mark out a territory for rhetoric between philosophy's scientific contemplation and the violence of and poetry of the *agora*, it is Nietzsche (himself torn between the classical world and philosophy) who returns to the artful practice of Greek rhetoric rather than its philosophical theory. The choice persistently faced by modern European philosophers with a classical background (i.e., virtually all of them) was Demosthenes or Cicero, Greek artistry (and its possible obscurity) or Roman persuasion oriented to a vision of the community's good. When such a choice was confronted by those with a commitment to morality (such as Hume) the answer was given with the question; but when play is substituted for morality (as in Zarathustra's parable of the camel, lion, and child) the understanding of the alternatives is transformed.

Spiel carries with it a cluster of associations in German aesthetics, notably through Kant and Schiller.[7] The notion occurs in Nietzsche with cosmological overtones, as when he frequently cites Heraclitus' saying that the world is *pais paizon*—a child playing. In the three stages of the spirit which Zarathustra announces just after the *Vorrede* the child at play is the richest or ripest phase. Nietzsche's rhetorical *Spiel* leads us back to his metaphysical *Spiel;* but the latter concept is itself artistic, art always serving as ontological paradigm for Nietzsche. So the *Spiel* of *Spiele* in Nietzsche's whole work is like the constant interplay of the discourses and meta-discourses in *Zarathustra*. (Surely there is something significant in the anglicized use of "spiel" to designate a rhetorical discourse.) This already allows us to see some of the characteristics of *Spiel*. *Spiel* is ceaseless activity which always involves a plurality of poles, or aspects, or dimensions—it is decentered. *Spiel* is not simply a subjective mood or disposition but has a standing of its own: we can enter into play or leave it, we may say that somebody is in play or at play, but not that play is in him.

Zarathustra is a rhetorical *Spiel*. It plays with serious affairs of the understanding but does not aim at persuasion. It speaks without authority, and so we will be hopelessly confused if we see it as a new gospel and not as an anti-gospel. (Nietzsche said once that the gospels should be called dysangles or bringers of bad news.) A few of the poles of this rhetorical play can be specified. We have already encountered the play between philosophy and poetry in which there is a ceaseless alternation. Another is the play between poetry and prose. This may at first appear anomalous, for rhetoric is thought to be concerned with prose rather than poetry, and Nietzsche sometimes describes it so in his writings on rhetoric. Yet even there he notes how *Kunstprosa* can take on an indefinite number of poetic features. More to the point is that there is a larger rhetorical organization which governs the varying textures of the work—which can be designated (in part) as parable, poetry, song, teaching, and silence. The distinction between immediate texture and larger structure appears, for example, when we try to ascertain the role of metaphor in *Zarathustra*. The book's immediate texture is no doubt highly metaphorical. Many of the recent studies of Nietzsche by the followers of Jacques Derrida tend to see all of Nietzsche's works, including *Zarathustra*, as a *Spiel der Metaphern*.[8] Yet Nietzsche distinguished other tropes, Zarathustra criticizes metaphor at one point, and there is in fact a tropological ordering principle in *Zarathustra* in which metaphor is only one of the tropes employed. The structure in question is a rather traditional rhetorical *Spiel* in which the main divisions of the work are, successively, metaphorical, metonymical, synecdochic, and ironic.[9] There is a predominant tone to each of the parts which allows the play to continue by providing variant contexts for the treatment of themes, situations, and teachings. Soon this will be illustrated for the intriguing *topos* of discourse itself, but for now it will be useful to sketch the sequence of the book's main parts. (As the third part of this paper should make clear, I do not see this tropological method of analysis as necessarily appropriate to all texts; in Nietzsche's case it is justified by his own rhetorical education and his need to make a new start in a philosophical tradition—that is, by what may be described as intentional criteria.)

The *Vorrede* of Zarathustra precedes the main text in a logical as well as a chronological sense. In it Zarathustra attempts to teach the superman to those in the marketplace, but can represent him only as a distant goal. For his audience of contented townspeople he can produce only vague intimations of what lies totally beyond. This is symbolic or prophetic poetry (in Hegel's sense): the vague adumbration of a transcendent or distant object which can be suggested at best indirectly by a negation of the actual and the present. Symbolic discourse, because of its inadequacy to its subject, is in a sense prediscursive; accordingly the action of the *Vorrede* revolves around Zarathustra's failures to communicate to the crowd and their ridicule of him.

Part One of Zarathustra consists of a series of metaphorical discourses. The *Vorrede* spoke of man as a bridge, as something to be overcome for the sake of the superman. This talk was starkly abstract, full of plays on *ubergehen* and *untergehen*, suggesting a sheer up or down movement with little sense of a concrete goal. In Part One Zarathustra begins by giving some metaphorical content to the projected notion by teaching the three metamorphoses of the spirit—camel, lion, and child. Childhood is of course an almost unavoidable romantic metaphor for regained innocence and spontaneity but other parts of the metaphorical complex are more novel. Traditional virtue is sleep, longing after heaven is burying one's head in the sand, and reading and writing are matters of blood and violence. Zarathustra, aware of his own poetic energy, urges his listeners to join him in making new metaphorical identifications: body will be spirit, peace should be victory, the state is a cold monster. The creation of new metaphors and the destruction of old ones is the activity of transvaluation itself, for "all names of good and evil are images" (*Gleichnisse*) and "he who has to be a creator always has to destroy." The richness of metaphor in Part One could be detailed indefinitely; Zarathustra's remarks (often confused with Nietzsche's views) about war and woman can be seen as metaphorical identifications of freedom and dependence. Yet as Paul de Man suggests, such a rich cluster of imagery "is itself a sign of divine absence, and the conscious use of poetic imagery an admission of this absence."[10] God is absent from the very beginning in *Zarathustra;* but by the time of the extended series of metaphorical discourses in Part One, the superman is also absent and there is a frenzied effort to fill his place with poetry. In terms of "The Three Metamorphoses of the Spirit," Part One consists of a heavy burden of metaphorical baggage which the camel must bear to prepare it for higher things.

The tone of Part Two is reductive. The idea of will

and will to power are prominent and are employed to set up a series of dualities which present clear choices to the will. The will is said to be the cause of all things and in a stronger sense things are said to be nothing but will. This reduction of effects to causes is metonymical as is the sharp series of contrasts which the will must confront. Paradigmatic for this series is Zarathustra's teaching "On the Blissful Islands":

> But to reveal my heart entirely to you, friends: *if* there were gods, how could I endure not to be a god! *Therefore* there are no gods.

The inference is not logical but tropological. When all is reduced to the will, experience becomes a series of oppositions and dichotomies between the will and all of its possible impediments. Some of the polarities are philosophically familiar—god and man, self-denial and self-affirmation, permanence and becoming—but they are given a new twist by the will's repudiation of the traditionally privileged members of these pairs. Other dichotomies are peculiar to the focus on the will. For example, one must choose between revenge (rationalized as justice) and life as continual self-overcoming. Revenge may at first appear to be a strong exercise of the will but in its dependence on the object exciting the revenge it reveals a weakness. Moreover, one of the dichotomies facing the will is apparently ineluctable and seems to condemn the will to a cycle of revenge:

> The will itself is still a prisoner Willing liberates: but what is it that fastens in fetters even the liberator?
>
> "It was": that is what the will's teeth-gnashing and most lonely affliction is called. Powerless against that which has been done, the will is an angry spectator of all things past.
>
> The will cannot will backwards; that it cannot break time and time's desire—that is the will's most lonely affliction. ("Of Redemption")

It is appropriate to the trope of Part Two that the dichotomy is not resolved. There are similar dichotomies which appear in the treatment of poetry and interpretation (even the interpretation of dreams) in this part. The dichotomic structure is even carried into the relation between Zarathustra and his auditors: here there are more questions and problems posed by the listeners and Zarathustra often abruptly shifts from external address to inner soliloquy.

Part Three has often been taken to be the philosophical heart of *Zarathustra* because it contains the idea of the eternal recurrence. This philosophical valuation of Part Three is a consequence of the governing trope, which is synecdoche, understood as thorough parallelism of microcosm and macrocosm. Synecdoche has normally been the privileged philosophical trope because it produces a sense of totality and comprehensibility—it is not subject to perpetual shifting, as is metaphorical identification, or to the overly simple reductions and frustrating dichotomies of metonymy. Plato's *Republic* enjoys most of its pedagogical prestige just because of its synecdochic series of concentric circles linking political and individual justice, social and personal psychology, and, of course, the true, the beautiful, and the good. That the concept of the eternal return can be seen as a this-worldly version of Platonic longings for eternity has been perspicuously shown by Heidegger, among others. Yet it is perhaps the synecdochic suggestion of totality which, in general, produces the sense of eternity. In the notion of eternal recurrence, each moment is "baptized in eternity," it brings with it the whole train of past and previous moments. The eternal thing in this perspective is just the eternal ring of becoming itself, so to talk or think about eternity is to be brought back to the cycle of particular moments. Nietzsche himself, in *Ecce Homo*, calls the eternal recurrence the fundamental conception of *Zarathustra*. This may well be, but to read the book in a search for its basic conceptions is already to have privileged the synecdochic and philosophical troping of Part Three. In the same *Ecce Homo* sections Nietzsche also makes some extravagant claims about the significance of the poetry of Zarathustra, but philosophers have seen little reason to privilege those. If *Zarathustra* is a more or less straightforward philosophical book, then an emphasis on Part Three is in order; but the status of philosophical doctrines and arguments is constantly at stake in the book; as a text, *Zarathustra* simply does not privilege the philosophical trope. An emphasis on the trope of Part Three, however, does bring to light other synecdochic motifs which surround the famous idea. Zarathustra's homecoming is a return to origins in which language becomes totally adequate, leaving no residues or accidents. The weighing of the world and the handing down of a new set of law tables amount to a totalistic revaluation in line with the concept of the eternal recurrence.

Part Four has been something of a puzzle for Nietzsche's interpreters because of its apparently radical change of tone. Some have suspected, on the basis of its private publication subsequent to the bulk of the book, that it is not a real part of the whole; others have thought, despite Nietzsche's subtitle—"Fourth and Last Part"—and conclusion—"The end of *Thus Spoke Zarathustra*"—that the Part must be transitional to others which were never written. Yet tropologically, this part is completely in order by contributing to the planned disorder of rhetorical play. The governing trope is irony here, as Zarathustra struggles with his pity for higher men. His answer to a cry of distress leads to the assemblage of a motley collection of guests and petitioners; when the whole gathering (including the last Pope) is about to engage in an ass festival which parodies the last supper, Zarathustra parodies the community of god and man by his refrain "Truly, you may all be Higher Men but for me—you are not high and strong enough." Each higher man embodies a misunderstanding or oversimplification of Zarathustra and his teachings from which Zarathustra distances himself by ridicule. Zarathustra finds all of the praise directed at him by his would-be disciples misplaced and misdirected. When he finally expresses some pleasure in his visitors it is to instruct them regarding their asinine festival:

> "And if you celebrate it again, this ass festival, do it for love of yourselves, do it for love of me! And in remembrance of *me*!

Surely the ass suggests the absence of God or of anything which could properly take his place. Zarathustra does not want to be worshipped himself, and he will be remembered only by continual dance and play which by its very nature must avoid any centering of a privileged object or person. Even the notion of eternal recurrence is treated playfully in a number of ambiguous references to the confusion of times. That a play upon the tropes should end with irony makes the fact of play itself unavoidable but it does not leave much standing in the way of straightforward doctrines or teachings—just as the higher men must surrender their desperately gleaned fragments of doctrine for Zarathustra's dances.

This sketch of the structure of *Zarathustra* may seem opposed to the still common view of the book as formless, bombastic and enthusiastic but it does agree with Nietzsche's own standards of literary integrity. Clarity, order, coherence and *esprit* are the criteria of excellent writing which Nietzsche constantly employs. Two remarks from the *Gay Science* are appropriate here, although they are ostensibly contradictory:

> Those who know that they are profound strive for clarity. Those who would like to seem profound to the crowd strive for obscurity. (par. 173) One does not only wish to be understood when one writes; one wishes just as surely *not* to be understood. It is not by any means necessarily an objection to a book when anyone finds it impossible to understand: perhaps that was part of the author's intention—he did not want to be understood by just "anybody." All the nobler spirits and tastes select their audience when they wish to communicate; and choosing that, one at the same time erects barriers against "the others." All the more subtle laws of any style have their origin at this point. . . (par. 381).[11]

Philosophers too often operate with a presupposed and therefore unclarified notion of clarity. Yet as Nietzsche recognizes, the nature of clarity is itself a philosophical problem which in the case of a written text involves rhetorical and generic considerations. A genre is rhetorically determined by its inclusions and exclusions; it does not only generate an audience but functions as a conspiracy of "the happy few" to keep the deeper nature of the text unprofaned by outsiders. A work may be intrinsically clear but initially puzzling to its proper audience and a perpetual possibility of misunderstanding to any others. This describes the form of Nietzsche's writing, expecially that of his works from the time of the *Gay Science* on. The rhetorical *Spiel* of *Zarathustra*, with its reverberations of the aristocratic Greek audience willing to savor the troping of topics is just such a Janus-faced genre. To stop at the level of an aphoristic and epigrammatic reading of Nietzsche is to see the decentered nature of his discourse but to ignore the playing field within which makes such decentering possible and delightful.

II

Zarathustra, like that wisest and most playful of the Greeks, is *polytropos.* Almost every topic that emerges in the book becomes the occasion for ringing the changes through the succession of parts. This is especially interesting in the case of discourse itself. The nature of writing, the quarrel between philosophy and poetry, the value of the poetic tradition, the referentiality of language are constant preoccupations in *Zarathustra.* To see what the text does with these themes and to determine in what sense Nietzsche has any final views or positions about them, it is necessary to see how they are handled in a variety of places. I wish to examine several of these places, keeping in mind their situation within the rhetorical structure of *Zarathustra.*

"Of Reading and Writing," in Part One, is the first chapter of *Zarathustra* primarily devoted to discourse. It captures the predominant metaphorical tone of that part by a rapid series of images connecting reading and writing with violence, sexuality, and a dancing god. But its rhetorical stance is also metaphorical. It is presumably addressed, like many of Zarathustra's talks in Part One, to a vaguely defined group of listeners in the town called The Motley Cow. As a figure of the narrative, Zarathustra is concerned only with the variations of oral discourse—speech, song, and silence. By his *speaking* of reading and writing, especially aphoristic writing which is done in blood, the chapter refers us back to the text itself. It need not be addressed to anyone in particular because metaphorical and symbolic discourse operates on the assumption that its images are concrete universals which are universally accessible. When the *topos* reappears under the other tropes, the nature of the speaker's relation to his audience is much more determinate. Just as metaphorical theories of poetry dispense with rhetorical considerations, the metaphorical presentation here achieves an image of universality by being indeterminately addressed to all and none. The metaphorical chains of the chapter trace the decline of reading and writing while projecting their rejuvenation. Zarathustra's play on the incarnation gives a capsule history of literary decay: "Once spirit was God, then it became man, and now it is even becoming mob." Augustine, the first great Christian literary theorist, abjured his own rhetorical training in the high and noble style in order to espouse the "holy humility" of the gospels. The incarnation is a figure for the possibility of spirit entering into the everyday. Hegel and his follower, Erich Auerbach, have written progressive histories of romantic or realistic literature in which the incarnation is the watershed after which literature can portray ever larger areas of human experience and can aim, like the Bible, at speaking to all. For Zarathustra this is a degeneration to the reader as the "last man": "He who knows the reader, does nothing further for the reader. Another century of readers—and spirit itself will stink."

We who are reading these texts are invited to step outside the modern rabble to become part of a drastically narrowed circle of readers and writers. This leap from indeterminate universality to conspiratorial isolation is made possible by the elastic nature of the metaphorical discourse which we are reading. The reader, left on his own, will either meet the challenge or fall back into the mass of "reading idlers." Zarathustra himself makes this connection between the difficult form of the writing and the strength of its readers: "aphorisms should be peaks, and those to whom they are spoken should be big and tall of stature." What this height consists in is spelled out by a series of images which may seem to shift radically away from the *topos* of discourse, but which should be read as expansions of it. The successful reader will understand what's written in blood and rejoice in the danger and thin air which accompanies it. Danger calls up the image of the warrior:

> Untroubled, scornful, outrageous—that is how wisdom wants us to be: she is a woman and never loves anyone but a warrior.

When we read this reflexively it is reading and writing which are violent assaults. The warrior Nietzsche has in mind is at the opposite pole from Sartre's engaged writer: "You say it is the good cause that hallows even war? I tell you: it is the good war that hallows every cause." To explore this chain of metaphors further we would need to look at the other discourses in this part on woman and the warrior: to see that these are already metaphorized in the discourse on reading and writing immediately helps to dissociate them from the crude readings of the idling reader who sees Zarathustra or Nietzsche as a simple misogynist and warmonger.

Although God had been sublimated in the descent of writing, he now reappears as *a* dancing god. The indefinite article and the play of the dance suggest an answer to Nietzsche's problematic: how can one write a sacred book when God is dead? The problem of authority in a book that has surrendered both theological guarantees and their realistic substitutes cannot be solved, but only dissolved within play itself. When Zarathustra invites us to "kill the Spirit of Gravity" by laughter he traces an ascent to the dance which is the reversal of the descent to the mob of readers:

> I have learned to walk: since then I have run. I have learned to fly: since then I do not have to be pushed in order to move.

> Now I am nimble, now I fly, now I see myself under myself, now a god dances within me.

Surely the repeated *now* (*jetzt*) secures the metaphorical identification of Zarathustra's discourse and our reading with the dance.

Heidegger suggests that the metaphor exists only within metaphysics. I take this to mean that the notion of a transference or assimilation of meanings (as in the classical treatments of metaphor which proceed from Aristotle) is possible only within a way of thinking which has a sense of clearly delineated ontological categories. Paradigmatically the metaphor is understood as a transference of sensible or bodily qualities to spiritual things or the reverse. Yet Heidegger has proposed that the rigid understanding of identity and difference which characterizes the philosophical tradition and allows the construction of such categorical schemes is part of a misguided attempt to articulate Being as present, mastered, and understood. The alternative would be a discourse which frankly accepted the indefiniteness and absence which is the ground of all presence. In Part One Nietzsche's use of what would traditionally be called metaphorical language explores the limits of such a mode of discourse; in particular it offers a challenge to the philosophical ideals of clarity and distinctness which are so often invoked without any awareness that they derive (perhaps indirectly through traditional rhetoric) from a philosophical view whose clarity may be questioned. Yet even this mode (so characteristic of Heidegger's later writings) is a limited one, if the aim is a radical play and plurality of discourse. For it does not allow the possibility of criticism, serious or playful (again abundantly illustrated in the writings of the later Heidegger).

Yet Nietzsche does allow such continuous criticism and creation. The whole tone of the treatment of discourse has changed by the time Zarathustra comes to speak "Of Poets" in Part Two. Among other things the chapter is an elaborate play upon the poetic version of the liar's paradox: the poet, Zarathustra, says that poets lie, proceeding to parody the famous final chorus of *Faust* and to attack the metaphorical principle itself. This reductive treatment of poetry is startling when juxtaposed with Zarathustra's earlier metaphorical attempts to empty himself of his wisdom, but it is thoroughly in keeping with the reductive metonymies in this section. Just as the will founders on the ineluctability of the "it was" so the poetic principle collapses when it is interrogated through dialogue; its attempts to bridge the gap between earth and heaven are exposed as fabrications. This is Nietzsche's version of the Platonic critique of poetry in the *Republic*; but Zarathustra, unlike Socrates, acknowledges that he himself is a poet. The structure of the chapter is itself dyadic: in the first part Zarathustra converses with a disciple and then, in the second, abruptly turns to the soul's converse with itself. And the tone of both conversations is set by the larger *Auseinandersetzung* between Zarathustra's discourse and Goethe's poetry, which is taken to be representative of the whole poetic tradition.

Zarathustra's initial remark seems to regard poetry as simply a collection of doctrines one of which happens to clash with his own reduction of spirit to the body:

> "Since I have known the body better," said Zarathustra to one of his disciples, "the spirit has been only figuratively (*gleichsam*) spirit to me; and all that is "intransitory"—that too has been only an "image" ("*und alles das 'unvergängliche'–das ist auch nur ein Gleichnis*")

The parody of the *Faust* chorus is continued through the chapter, and it parallels a more serious critique of poetry's metaphorical longings for the eternal ("we desire even those things the old women tell one another in the evening. We call that the eternal-womanly in us") and its vain desire for an audience. That *Faust* should be the basis of the critique shows that Zarathustra is ready to take on the big guns of poetry, as Socrates declared battle against "Homer and all his tribe." Goethe is usually taken to be the supreme German poet and *Faust* to be his masterpiece; the final scene in heaven, ending with the mystic chorus can be regarded as his last poetic testament. It records Faust's salvation by stressing the priority of the eternal. Zarathustra aims at reducing such poetic metamorphoses to the pathetic fallacy and the surreptitious introduction of the eternal into poetry. Poets, says Zarathustra, imagine that their impressions when lying in the grass are nature's speech to them; emboldened by these imaginary secrets they project their fantasies into the heavens: "we set our motley puppets on the clouds and then call them gods and supermen." Apparent metaphorical unities can be reduced to the metonymic opposition of poet and nature, or poet's fantasies and imaginary eternity. Metaphor (*Gleichniss*) is here connected with metamorphosis—but such metamorphoses must be *only* imaginary. If we first missed the point that the critique applies to Zarathustra's own metaphorical chains, the self-critique is underscored by the lumping together of "gods and supermen" as "motley puppets."

Zarathustra's critique of unitary metaphor occurs in a dialogue with his disciple; in a play upon binary structures, his analysis of the poet's vain need of an audience comes when he turns away from the disciple to talk to himself. *Faust* is still the appropriate example because of Goethe's dramatic inclinations (even if *Faust* II is unactable). Wagner's universalistic aspirations are undoubtedly in the background as may be the Hegelian dialectic which sees drama's universalism and its community of author, actors, and audience as the high point of all art and poetry. Zarathustra's deflation of such community takes place by means of images, mirroring his deconstruction of metaphor through dialogue with another. The false unity of the poetic peacock with his audience of buffaloes (rhetorical fiction) is just the other side of those illegitimate metamorphoses (metaphorical tropes) which attempt to bridge the gap between heaven and earth. Zarathustra's repeated exclamation of his weariness of the poets who can carry on such subterfuges continues the pastiche of Goethe by transforming his "*Ach, ich bin des Treibens müde!*" into "*Ach, wie bin ich der Dichter müde!*" If there is any hope for the poets it lies in their own weariness of themselves. Zarathustra prophesies the appearance of such self-conscious figures who will have grown out of the poets and calls them "penitents of the spirit" ("*Büsser des Geistes*"). This prophecy of poetry's self-overcoming is still parody for it refers back to the penitents at the end of *Faust*. What the poets of the future are to give up are not earthly things but fictions of metamorphosis and common understanding with their audience. They are to turn inward, as Zarathustra has turned away from his disciple and as he will turn further inward in the next part of the book. Yet Zarathustra's discourse here is not the self-consciously hermetic and difficult modernism which he sees coming; it is itself a play upon the opposition of prose and poetry which heightens their tensions. Much of Nietzsche's *Gay Science* revolves around this same tension and helps to clarify "Of Poets." The book's very title is duplicitious, referring both to the Provencal term for the art of poetry and to the more prosaic idea of science only to set up another incongruity by the addition of gaity or joy. The text itself alternates between poetic and prosaic passages. In one section Nietzsche suggests the fruitfulness of the tension:

> Good prose is written only face to face with poetry. For it is an uninterrupted, well-mannered war with poetry: all of its attractions depend on the way in which poetry is continually avoided and contradicted. Everything abstract wants to be read as a prank against poetry and as with a mocking voice; everything dry and cool is meant to drive the lovely goddess into lovely despair. . . *War is the father of all good things;* war is also the father of good prose. (par. 92).

This explicit statement of the metonymical principle suggests its own alternative. If war is the "father" of all good things the healthy child may nevertheless be seen in its spontaneity independent of the father. This is the suggestion of Zarathustra's three metamorphoses in which the child is born from the willful wars of the lion but overcomes them. It is just this surmounting of sheer otherness which is crucial to understanding the treatment of discourse in Part Three. As Heidegger has pointed out, we must comprehend the eternal recurrence, which is the central conception of this part (if not the basic theme of the whole text) through the image of its teacher, Zarathustra, and Zarathustra through his teaching. But in Part Three Zarathustra's presentation of his *Spruch* or *Wort* (suggesting the "saying" of the sage more than the "doctrine" of the philosopher) is elaborately indirect. It takes place by means of a visionary dialogue with a dwarf, a hermeneutic puzzle concerning an imaged riddle, and finally through Zarathustra's animals telling him that he is the teacher of the eternal recurrence. Yet what is indirect on the dramatic level is intelligible in terms of the synecdochic trope to which discourse is subject in this part. This may emerge more clearly if we look at a chapter which handles the *topos* of discourse head on rather than at those philosophically crucial chapters like "The Convalescent"; for in order to interpret the latter we must know what kind of discourse they are. "The Home-Coming" plays on a rich theme in German poetry: being alone when one is at home. Here Zarathustra's soul converses with itself joyfully and from the beginning. The true homecoming is not simply to return to one's geographical origins but to enjoy solitude (*Einsamkeit*). The speech of this chapter is a dialogue between Zarathustra and his home—and his home *is* solitude—which revolves around the meaning of language in solitude and its distinction from the discourse of a false community. This internal colloquy is sufficient unto itself; it is a microcosmic version of a poetic cosmos. It is a distinct alternative to the indefinite metaphorical union with an audience of all or none projected in "Of Reading and Writing" or the metonymical opposition of teacher and disciple or inner and outer discourse found in "Of Poets." *Einsamkeit* is not *Verlassenheit* (loneliness) which one can very well experience in company. Zarathustra's solitude would reassure him that:

> "Here all things come caressingly to your discourse and flatter you: for they want to ride upon your back. Upon every image (*Gleichniss*) you here ride to every truth."

Talk in solitude is wholly adequate to things—Zarathustra can speak to them now and they will speak to him. He has overcome the detours of loneliness which forced him to speak to another. His speech will now be a *Dinggedicht*, a poetry of things, unlike the speech "down there" where speech is not heard in a deep sense, but simply cheapens and betrays. The inauthentic speech "down there" is constitutive for ordinary morality and knowledge. Those who *call* themselves "the good" are actually poisonous flies. Life among those who conceal their weakness with such words leads to pity—and pity leads to the confusion of names, as when gravediggers are called investigators and scholars. In Part One Zarathustra would have metaphorically identified scholars as gravediggers; now that he has his *own* language of solitude he can say that gravediggers are by confusion called scholars among them. Given the adequate circle of one's own language there is no need to produce a metaphorical chain to move from older meanings to new.

Zarathustra's solitude is the conscious recognition that his quest is an internal one. There is a subtle distinction between the gaps and obstacles of mundane, external speech and the differences within identity of solitary discourse. The crudity of referential speech among the many involves a play on the German philosophical tradition:

> He who wants to understand (*begreifen*) all things among men has to touch (*angreifen*) all things. But my hands are too clean for that.

As in Kant and Hegel one understands things by means of concepts (*Begriffe*). Nietzsche's punning brings out the overtones of grasping with the hands which still cling to this understanding of understanding. Speaking and thinking which are assaults on things necessarily encounter unpleasant objects which one would rather not touch and leaves open only two unsatisfactory possibilities: by greedily grasping everything to oneself all room for the play of thought and discourse is destroyed (Hegel), or else speech must always run up against an impenetrable other (Kant). Here, however, Zarathustra and his solitude, Zarathustra and his animals, Zarathustra and things belong to one another without collapsing into an unqualified identity.[12] It is in terms of this self-contained play of a language adequate to one's whole world that we can understand the emphasis on the eternal recurrence as Zarathustra's *own* teaching. It is not an abstract doctrine which can be passed from mouth to mouth or hand to hand; its home is in Zarathustra's solitary silence or song, not in being handled or conceptually understood (*ergriffen* or *begriffen*).

It is the transvaluation of language from metaphorical and metonymical models to synecdochic adequacy which gives Zarathustra strength for a rapid series of transvaluations of values. These occur at first in a dream "Of the Three Evil Things" in which sensual pleasure, lust for power, and selfishness are weighed by a new measure. Zarathustra then sings himself a song to lift himself beyond the spirit of gravity and talks to himself in order to promulgate new law-tables to replace the old. In each instance the emphasis on the interiority of the speech is what assures the adequacy of the new valuations. There is a deceptive plausibility in reading *Zarathustra* as the work of a desperately lonely man. This synecdochic section of the book makes a crucial distinction between solitude and loneliness which involves a transvaluation of the former. If we want to make an intentional connection between Nietzsche and his text here, it cannot be that of pathology and symptom; instead there is a repetition of isolation and its macrocosmic projection which involve an acutely conscious deepening of the problematic, not its evasion. The primal naming in *Zarathustra* cannot depend on divine authority but must proceed from a linguistic center which is willed to serve as a model of the whole. One way in which Nietzsche's book is an anti-Bible is its alteration of the trope of Eden, shifting if from metaphorical origin to synecdochic enclosure.

In the Biblical Eden, as Hegel has incisively shown, there is a latent otherness disguised by the metaphorical blurring of subject-object distinctions.[13] In Zarathustra's solitude, called his "garden" by his animals, otherness is known as excluded and overcome; it cannot be a threat because its elimination depends on Zarathustra's own willful troping, not on an external authority who preserves the metaphorical connections of the garden.

In the fourth part of *Zarathustra* the synecdochic unity which might be the conclusion of a more conventional philsophical work is deliberately unraveled. This is signalled in a striking way in the very first episode, which involves Zarathustra's deception of his animals. Although he announces to them that he is leaving his cave in order to make the honey-offering, as soon as he is out of range he declares that this is

> a ruse and, truly, a useful piece of folly! Up here I can speak more freely than before hermits' caves and hermits' pets.

Zarathustra's animals, his snake and his eagle, are aspects of himself, his cleverness and pride. When Zarathustra discourses with his animals, especially in Part Three, he is moving within the circuit of self-contained language. To leave part of himself through deception is part of an ironic movement which continues throughout Part Four. Every expectation that Zarathustra has reached a final, determinate conclusion of some sort is attacked in the text. Zarathustra's own approach to the honey-sacrifice recalls his need, announced in the *Vorrede*, to pour out his wisdom (which is likened to honey there):

> Offer—what? I squander what is given me, I, a squanderer with a thousand hands: how could I call that—an offering!

Zarathustra lacks the stability required for the almost contractual arrangements implicit in sacrifice. His honey (wisdom) cannot be parcelled out to preserve such stability. Instead it will be "bait" to catch "the strangest human fish." Zarathustra's ironic movement in this part is already present in outline: it involves a distancing from the self, a mocking attitude toward his own wisdom, and the idea of snaring others in order to force them to come up to his own level. The last process will, of course, never be completed because Zarathustra is always climbing higher in a game of catch-me-if-you-can.

Because of this constant movement, there is no single chapter or episode in this part which offers a sustained treatment of the *topos* of discourse. The point of the ironic trope is, in a way, just to explode any appearance of centrality. In his long episodic series of meetings with the higher men Zarathustra sees nothing but parodies, misunderstandings and fragments of himself. His conversation with each emphasizes his distance from all of them, so that the only community and solidarity attainable is the comic and parodic ass-festival in which the higher men begin to see that wisdom is also folly. Zarathustra's great struggle in this part is with his own pity for the higher men. As Aristotle points out, pity presupposes community and identification; we can only feel sorry for those who are somewhat like ourselves. Zarathustra does not begin from such community but he is concerned not to be seduced to it. His defense is not the fear which, as Aristotle says, drives out pity, but a laughter which celebrates distances.

In a series of conversations with the higher men Zarathustra exhibits his own self-overcoming by making it clear that he cannot be identified with any of these versions or parts of himself. He does this not to suggest some substantial self or ego which underlies these partial selves, but in order to exhibit the need to revise and dissolve our desire to find substance in the self. Perhaps the most suggestive of these encounters is the one with the magician (*Zauberer*). The magician, like Zarathustra and like some of the other partial selves of Part Four, is an author of sorts. As several attentive readers of Nietzsche have recently suggested, the magician can be seen as Nietzsche's own incursion into the text of *Zarathustra*.[14] Like Nietzsche perhaps, the magician claims an indifference to any audience in his first song, where he pretends to be alone; yet this charade is enacted for the sake of Zarathustra. Later the magician entertains the group of higher men (in Zarathustra's absence) with a long song of melancholy in which he professes to be "only a fool, only a poet." He thus parodies the author who writes for all and none; in seeking to manipulate Zarathustra and the higher men he embodies a traditional conception of the author as one who achieves mastery of men's consciousness through the mastery of his text.

Zarathustra rejects such claims to authorship in his response to the magician's first song. That song purports to be a lament addressed to the unknown god whom the magician has somehow disposed of or dispensed with. He would rather have his god back, with all his torments, than the pain of solitude. Zarathustra, stronger than this author who could regret his own banishment of God, responds not to *what* is said—he has no use for gods or their lamenters—but to the manner of the saying (or singing). He strikes the wailing man with a stick "with all his force" and "with furious laughter." The magician is forced to confess his imposture, admitting finally that he was playing the "penitent of the spirit" whom Zarathustra had described earlier. But Zarathustra replies that this confession is "not nearly true enough and not nearly false enough for me!" because it masks a sense in which the magician is charged with unsufficient irony; for the true ironist's sayings are both true and false, not simply the false disguises of a true reality. The unmasking theme in which we find out the truth behind the poetry's song means one thing in the first reductive appearance of the *topos* and something quite different in this ironic conclusion. In attacking the magician Zarathustra is attacking the illusion of authorship. Those who have thought of the magician as an analogue of Wagner are right to the extent that for Nietzsche Wagner does represent an artist with the highest pretensions to mastery. But Nietzsche has these pretensions himself; unlike Wagner he at least occasionally allows his creations to rebuke him for such megalomania.

II

Let us recall Kant's definition of rhetoric as "carrying on a serious business of the understanding as if it were a free play of the imagination." Nietzsche does not explicitly adopt the definition in a programmatic sense, but he does use it to characterize the playful aspects of Greek rhetoric, contrasting them with the Roman commitment to persuasion. It is inconceivable that Nietzsche could have taken the formula entirely in Kant's sense, for that would have entailed his adopting a distinction between the imagination and the understanding which he seems to repudiate at every turn of thought and speech. It may be worth returning to Nietzsche's citation of Kant, however, because the definition (taken independently of Kant's systematic context) suggests several possible interpretations. These, in turn, govern a whole set of concrete elucidations of those puzzling works, like *Zarathustra*, which seem to carry on philosophy's serious business within the playful mode of poetry or rhetoric. Since such works include (in part) Nietzsche's other texts, Kierkegaard's pseudonymous writings, much of Sartre's voluminous work, and the essays of the later Heidegger, the hermeneutical stakes are large. A reductionistic account of the Kantian definition (no doubt the one which Kant himself would have favored) would see the serious business of the understanding as something to be abstracted from a text; this is the familiar view that scientific or philosophical ideas are largely independent of their particular mode of expression and statement. A second direction to be taken from the same definition lays the greatest stress on the play of the imagination; this is the position of the deconstructionists, who read texts so as to dissolve the work of the understanding in a play of self-referential negations. These may seem to be exhaustive alternatives and much of the power of each depends upon its polemics against the apparent over-simplifications or over-sophistications of the other side. In this way they carry on the ancient quarrel between philosophy and poetry on the modern battlefield of textual interpretation. At least in Nietzsche's case, a third reading of the definition may be possible, however. Rhetorical play need not be conceived as dispensable sugarcoating for ideas nor as a deconstructive vanishing act; it may take the form of a play of ideas in which neither play nor ideas cancel each other (or themselves) out. Ideas are there but they are there in a playful way; in *Zarathustra*, for example, the picture of the superman, the notion of the will to power, the teaching of the eternal recurrence and the necessity of ironic transcendence are presented not as subordinated one to the other but as the variant tropological expressions of a single complex. This play can also have an agonistic form; the text embodies a playful war between philosophy and poetry which is like the productive tensions between poetry and prose described in *The Gay Science.* No mode of discourse is master, but there is a tropological variation of the *topos* of discourse which rings the changes on their possible relationships.

How one reads *Zarathustra* may determine not only how one reads Nietzsche generally, but may also have consequences for an interpretation of the history of philosophy. Heidegger's reading of Nietzsche is a case in point and so should sharpen the significance of the hermeneutic alternatives. Heidegger sees Nietzsche as the last great metaphysician whose doctrine of the will to power brings Western metaphysics to a close. The ingenuity of Heidegger's reading of the history of philosophy—in which the presence of the Platonic ideas begets the Cartesian *cogito* which in turn begets Hegelian *Geist* and Nietzschean will to power—is often breathtaking as well as subtle. In addition, his own conception of interpretation offers a defense of the violence of his readings; this seems to make a holistic confrontation with his entire system mandatory if one questions his reading of a single text. What I want to suggest here is that Heidegger's reading of the literary structure of *Zarathustra* ignores the playful side of its rhetoric; by seeing the consequences of this oversight (which may seem hopelessly trivial in the light of the history of Being) we can sketch an alternative outline for reading philosophy in the poetic mode.

Heidegger's analysis of *Zarathustra* occurs in the context of an explanation of the thought of the eternal recurrence. He correctly points out that to regard the book as a poetic presentation of philosophical thoughts would be to leave the question of the nature of philosophy and poetry completely indeterminate.[15] From our perspective, what he omits to point out is that this question is itself raised in the text in various ways and on various levels. Heidegger's own interpretation of the book revolves around the notion that Nietzsche is offering us a poetic portrait of the teacher of the eternal recurrence in which the difficulties of communicating such a heavy thought are made evident in the narrative of Zarathustra's speech and actions. Such a reading implicitly privileges the synecdochic tropes of Part Three while apparently opting for a narrative model for the entire text. For Heidegger, *Zarathustra* is a book for everyone and no one just because it deals with a thought which is so heavy that we cannot grasp it without transforming ourselves;[16] he does not see the possibility that the text itself involves a complex way of adjusting itself to its ideal readers and excluding others. Given Heidegger's reduction of *Zarathustra* to the single thought of eternal recurrence he is able to insert it into his own study of Nietzsche which revolves around *The Will to Power.* Since the latter book is nothing but a set of notes, posthumously organized and published, what Heidegger does is to reverse Nietzsche's own priorities. These are fairly clear from his own frequent, if sometimes wildly extravagant, praise for *Zarathustra* and from his repeated insistence on form, style and completion as normative textual standards. Where Heidegger suggests that the eternal recurrence, and *a fortioni,* the presentation of it in *Zarathustra,* must be understood on the basis of "Nietzsche's whole metaphysics,"[17] we may suspect that Nietzsche's rhetorical strategy should make us cautious about reading his metaphysics as a set of doctrines or *Lehren*—especially when this metaphysics is constructed from notes and fragments. One of Nietzsche's own fragmentary plans for *The Will to Power* expresses regret that the book cannot appear in French rather than German;[18] what Nietzsche consistently admires in the French is their playful *esprit*, which embodies an aversion to being boringly correct, and their sense for literary form. It is just this reduction to *Lehre* without regard to the writer's strategy which is the key to Heidegger's interpretation.

The larger question to which Heidegger's reading of Nietzsche leads is that of the proper narrative context (if any) within which to place works such as Nietzsche's and Heidegger's own which stand on the precarious boundary of poetry and philosophy. In a very general way, Heidegger follows the Hegelian narrative scheme which reads the history of philosophy as coming to an end or conclusion already immanent in its origins. Heidegger's most important variations on Hegel depend upon his view that Nietzschean will to power is a fuller realization of the destiny of metaphysics than Hegelian *Geist* and in his transvaluation of Hegel's history in which the veiling over of the philosophical tradition rather than its progressive illumination is stressed.[19]

The implication of my rhetorical reading of *Zarathustra* is that Nietzsche is already moving beyond the boundaries of the philosophical tradition in so far as he signals a new combination of philosophy with imaginative literature. The old Hegelian story may have to be partially rehabilitated in order to serve as the basis for a new narrative in which Hegelian absolute knowledge is not an absolute conclusion but the mark of a shift into other modes. After this point, the directions taken by philosophers, and especially the move toward poetry made by Kierkegaard, Nietzsche, Heidegger and others are determined by their rejection of some part of the Hegelian synthesis. In such a history Zarathustra's "*Ich bin meiner Weisheit überdrüssig*" is to be taken not only as Nietzsche's own statement but as the expression of an anxiety of influence which is determinative for other philosopher-poets. Two sides of the Hegelian synthesis which may provoke such anxieties and therefore form the basis of revolts in what Harold Bloom would call a "strong" writer like Nietzsche may be distinguished. They lie in the content or matter of thought on one hand and in its expression on the other; although in good Hegelian fashion we will not treat aspects distinguished as capable of existing outside a totality. In regard to content, Kant seemed to have left philosophers with the choice of thinking only within the bounds of sense and understanding or of attempting to think the whole of things and therefore falling into contradiction by a surreptitious extension of the imagination to the supersensible realm. Hegel's claim is to have escaped the necessity of limitation by showing that the thought of the whole is possible by means of a rationality which thinks the contradictoriness of things. Since this thought of the whole abolishes the distinctions between appearance and reality and thought and being it claims to have surpassed the imaginative speculations of art and religion. This leaves several alternatives open. It is possible to go back to Kant's position, in which the limits of philosophical thought are accepted. The Hegelian attempt to think totality by means of a dialectical logic can be continued, as by the Marxists and the British neo-Hegelians. The Nietzschean move is to think the contradictory totality by means of a mode of discourse which is better suited to it than Hegelian rationality. Here language itself becomes a play which is suggestive of cosmic play.

A similar set of alternatives issues from Hegel's claim to have established philosophy as a universal form of discourse, free of all the particularities of temperament, nationality, and imagination which color the languages of art and religion. While philosophers from Descartes on have assumed that their readers were in principle capable of working through the philosophers' own thoughts and arriving at a community of understanding, Hegel set out to show that this assumption could be validated by the history of philosophy itself. To work through the *Phenomenology of Mind* is to cooperate in that "effort of the notion" in which the history of thought traverses a series of misunderstandings to a state of absolute self-certainty and to fuse with the "we," the omniscient narrator of the spirit's development. When the separations between what a consciousness is for-itself and what it is in-itself have been transcended, one just is in fact part of that absolute spirit, both subject and object of history. Yet the identity-in-difference of spirit and finite individuals, or of Hegel and his readers, is subject to the same tensions as is the attempt to think contradiction. The potential contradiction between the writer and his readers breaks out again when the claims of the former appear overwhelmingly presumptuous or when the latter finds some ineluctable characteristics of his own which resist assimilation to a single master-text. Kierkegaard, Marx, Sartre, and Heidegger all reflect these problems in a variety of ways. Nietzsche's turn to rhetorical models embodies his own complex solution to the contradictions of thought and of the relation of author and reader. If the play of the imagination takes the place of the conceptual thought of contradiction, the appeal to the elite rhetorical audience of "all and none" breaks away from the burden of universal communicability which Hegel laid upon those who undertook to philosophize after him. If the history of philosophy after Hegel appears to be a capitulation to poetry which would end their ancient quarrel, perhaps the history of philosophy did come to the end which Hegel proclaimed; those who came later, if they were to do something novel, were forced into radical deviations from the tradition which seemed to be completed. In the large story of philosophy's devolution into poetry, which has yet to find its philosophical or literary historian, Nietzsche's rhetorical maneuvers form a significant episode.[20]

NOTES

[1] Quotations from *Thus Spoke Zarathustra* are all from the translation by R. J. Hollingdale in the Penguin Classics edition (Baltimore, 1965).

[2] The essays appear in the Kroner edition of Nietzsche's *Werke* (1912), Bd. XVIII, pp. 199–268. The only discussion of them I have found in English is Paul de Man's "Nietzsche's Theory of Rhetoric," in *Symposium*, Spring 1974.

[3] *Werke*, XVIII, p. 214. The translation is mine.

[4] XVIII, p. 248.

[5] XVIII, p. 249.

[6] XVIII, p. 240.

[7] The main texts are Kant's *Critique of Judgment* and Schiller's *Letters on Aesthetic Education*. Hans-Georg Gadamer has a valuable discussion of *Spiel* in *Truth and Method* (New York: Seabury Press, 1975), pp. 91–119.

[8] Two such works are Sarah Kofman, *Nietzsche et la metaphore* (Paris, 1972) and Bernard Pautrat, *Versions du soleil* (Paris, 1971). Derrida's *Spurs: Nietzsche's Styles* is available in a multilingual edition (Venezia: Corbo e Fiore Editori, 1976). There are a number of important essays in *The New Nietzsche*, ed. by David Allison (New York: Dell, 1977). There is a useful review of recent French studies of Nietzsche by Rudolf Kunzli, "Nietzsche und die Semiologie" in *Nietzsche-Studien*, 1976.

[9] I'm grateful to Hayden White for showing me the surprisingly frequent applicability of analyzing texts in these terms. See his *Metahistory* (Baltimore: Johns Hopkins Press, 1973), esp. pp. 31–39 and Kenneth Burke, "Four Master Tropes" in *A Grammar of Motives* (Berkeley: University of California Press, 1969), pp. 503–517.

[10] "The Intentional Structure of the Romantic Image" in

Romanticism and Consciousness, ed. Harold Bloom (New York: W. W. Norton, 1970), p. 69.

[11] *The Gay Science*, translated by Walter Kaufmann. (New York: Random House, 1974).

[12] For suggestive accounts of a distinction between identity and being own or belonging, see Heidegger's *Identity and Difference* and Albert Hofstadter's essay "Being: the Act of Belonging," in *Agony and Epitaph*.

[13] *Hegel's Logic*, trans, William Wallace (Oxford: Oxford University Press, 1975), pp. 42ff.

[14] Interesting accounts of Zarathustra's meeting with the magician are to be found in Leonard Robbins "Zarathustra and the Magician Or, Nietzsche Contra Nietzsche: Some Difficulties in the Conception of the Overman" *Man and World*, June 1976 and in James Ogilvy, *Many Dimensional Man* (New York: Oxford, 1977), pp. 176ff.

[15] Martin Heidegger, *Nietzsche* vol. I, p. 288. See Harold Alderman *Nietzsche's Gift* (Athens: Ohio University Press, 1977) for a serious confrontation with Heidegger's interpretation of Nietzsche in terms of *Seinsgeschichte*. Alderman's book offers a dramatic reading of Zarathustra which places the greatest emphasis on the modalities of the human voice. See my review in *Philosophy and Literature* (forthcoming).

[16] *Nietzsche* I, pp. 288–289.

[17] *Nietzsche*, I, p. 287.

[18] *The Will to Power*, trans. by Walter Kaufmann and R. J. Hollingdale (New York: Random House, 1968), pp. xxii–xxiii.

[19] See *Nietzsche* vol. II, and the selections translated by Joan Stambaugh as *The End of Philosophy* (New York: Harper and Row, 1973).

[20] I want to acknowledge the support of The School of Criticism and Theory at the University of California, Irvine, which allowed me to begin work on this paper and research grant 3121-0038 from the University of Kansas which aided me in completing it.

21. Alan Donagan: "Victorian Philosophical Prose: J. S. Mill and F. H. Bradley"

Professor Donagan received his B.A. from the University at Melbourne, Melbourne, Australia, and his Ph.D. from Oxford in 1953. From 1957–61, he was chairman of the Department of Philosophy at Indiana University, and since 1970, he has taught at the University of Chicago. His publications include *The Later Philosophy of R. G. Collingwood* (1962) and *Philosophy and History*, which he coauthored in 1965.

VICTORIAN PHILOSOPHICAL PROSE: J. S. MILL AND F. H. BRADLEY*

Philosophy is a more ancient form of prose literature than fiction. The classics of ancient Greek and Latin prose are works of history, of philosophy, of oratory.

* From *The Art of Victorian Prose*, edited by George Levine and William Madden. Copyright © 1968 by Oxford University Press, Inc. Reprinted by permission.

Even of prose written in English, Yvor Winters has contended that, when compared with writers of fiction, "the superiority in achievement to date lies with the historiographers."[1] Probably no literary critic would make such a claim on behalf of philosophy. Yet T. S. Eliot has described the prose style of F. H. Bradley as "for his purposes—and his purposes are more varied than is usually supposed—a perfect style."[2] Whatever its comparative rank among the varieties of prose literature, Victorian philosophical prose deserves more study than it has received.

No serious challenge has been offered to the conventional judgment that English prose was perfected in the classical age begun by Dryden, Temple, and Halifax, and continued by Swift, Addison, and Steele. Yet the chief philosopher contemporary with Dryden and Halifax was Locke, whose style Saintsbury justly deplored as "a disgusting style, bald, dull, plebian, giving indeed the author's meaning, but giving it ungraced with any due apparatus or ministry."[3] True, the way to the literary achievement of Dryden and his followers had been pioneered by the philosopher Hobbes; and in the fullness of the classical age, Berkeley wrote three philosophical masterpieces which as prose bear comparison with Addison's essays. Berkeley, indeed, was singled out by Saintsbury, who said of him that "he, again with Hume as a second, is as unlikely to be surpassed in philosophical style as Hume and Gibbon are unlikely to be surpassed in the style of history." [4] But Berkeley's prose, admirable as it is, breaks no new ground. From a literary point of view, he is less interesting than Swift; for nothing he had to say as a philosopher called for a prose different from that of his nonphilosophical contemporaries.

By the nineteenth century, philosophy could no longer be written in the prose of Berkeley. There were new things to say, and they could not be said in old ways. Why then did a critic as intelligent as Saintsbury, in 1876—the year in which Bradley published *Ethical Studies*—denounce the "antinomian" decadence of philosophical writing? "Philosophy," he scolded, ". . . has now turned stepmother, and turns out her nurselings to wander in 'thorniest queaches' of terminology and jargon, instead of the ordered gardens wherein Plato and Berkeley walked."[5] Nor did the decade that followed change his opinion: "take almost any living philosopher," he complained in 1885, "and compare him with Berkeley, with Hume, or even with Mill, and the difference is obvious at once."[6]

Saintsbury's strength as a critic is technical. Nobody has better analyzed how Dryden and his successors, paying heed to the genius of colloquial English, reformed the long sentence by expelling imitations of Latin syntax for which an uninflected language is unfit; how they learned to balance and proportion their sentences, and to dispense with rhetorical ornament.[7] His weakness is that his theory is only technical. His literary criticism is criticism of style, and he was capable of defining style as "the choice and arrangement of language with only a subordinate regard to the meaning to be conveyed."[8] Hence he considered "the art of rhythmical arrangement" to be "undoubtedly the principal thing in prose," with "simplicity of language, and directness of expression in the shorter clause and phrase" as the two most important of its "subsidiary arts."[9]

Saintsbury's practice was better than his theory. Many of his critical perceptions were sound. The classical prose he admired was indeed good, and the sins he denounced in Victorian prose—the ugly rhythms of Herbert Spencer, the gaudy epithets of J. R. Green, and the tub-thumping of the journalists—were indeed sins.

But it does not follow that the principles he extracted from his perceptions were true. A theory is established by seeking and failing to find unfavorable evidence, not by accumulating evidence that is favorable. Saintsbury's theory was destroyed by the deluge of *belles lettres* at the close of the century, which demonstrated that all his criteria for rhythm and diction could be satisfied by work that was inane, pretentious, and corrupt.

Literary criticism cannot have "only a subordinate regard" to the meaning conveyed. Saintsbury's dictum might even be reversed, and style defined as the choice and arrangement of words having regard *solely* to the meaning to be conveyed. His own examples may be turned against him. Thus, his specimens of bungled rhythm and badly articulated syntax turn out to convey thoughts unformed or ill-formed, and emotions only partly clear.[10] Style, in a word, is expression. Every act of literary composition has its aesthetic side, the writer's effort to grasp something clearly, which is inseparable from his effort to make clear his emotions about it.

The inseparability of the expression of thought from the expression of emotion, which is presupposed by all serious criticism, is seldom fully recognized or clearly understood. Failing to discern the crucial difference between formulating a thought and repeating, perhaps in other words, a thought already formulated, some critics have written as though, even to the man who first arrives at it, a thought can exist before its expression. On the contrary, the stages through which the expression of a thought passes, from clumsy imitation to exact statement, are stages through which the thought itself passes. Finding better words is the same thing as refining a thought. Still other critics have written as though, having arrived at a thought about a certain subject, there is a further process of having emotions about it. They have failed to perceive that a man's emotions about a thing depend on his awareness of it, and of how it is related to other things, himself among them. The way to change his emotions about it is to bring him to think differently of it.

Hence the theory of art as the expression of emotion does not imply that critics can attend to the emotion expressed by a work of art to the neglect of its thought: emotion and thought can only be studied together. Rather, it defines the special nature of a critic's interest in the *thought* a work embodies. He is interested in that thought only as it has to do with the expression of emotion. Genuine art is exploratory. In it, the artist simultaneously becomes aware of something he was unclear about before, and aware of his emotions about it. Bad art is the counterfeit, often not wholly conscious, of genuine art. In it, the artist only pretends to explore; and what he offers is a faked report, designed to present himself as thinking and feeling in some approved way. Its betraying symptom is *cliché*.[11]

This aesthetic theory, or something like it, I take to be embodied in the best work of critics both in the Romantic tradition (like Coleridge and Matthew Arnold) and in the partial post-Romantic reaction from it (like T. S. Eliot and F. R. Leavis). If it should be true, then it is possible to separate what is true from what is false in a deeply interesting antithesis once proposed by T. S. Eliot.

> I should say [Eliot wrote] that in one's prose reflections one may be legitimately occupied with ideals, whereas in the writing of verse one can only deal with actuality. Why, I would ask, is most religious verse so bad; and why does so little religious verse reach the highest levels of poetry? Largely, I think, because of a pious insincerity.[12]

Eliot's diagnosis of what ails most religious verse was definitive, but he mistook the nature of pious insincerity. It does not consist in being occupied with ideals, but in pretending to ideals you do not really have, or in pretending that your ideals are realities although you do not believe they are. Pious insincerity of these kinds is as fatal in prose as in verse. It is as common in religious prose as in religious verse, and it is far from uncommon in philosophy.

Consider the following passage, fortunately uncharacteristic, from Bertrand Russell, one of the first philosophers of our time.

> Brief and powerless is Man's life; on him and all his race the slow, sure doom falls pitiless and dark. Blind to good and evil, reckless of destruction, omnipotent matter rolls on its relentless way; for Man, condemned today to lose his dearest, tomorrow himself to pass through the gate of darkness, it remains only to cherish, ere yet the blow falls, the lofty thoughts that ennoble his little day; disdaining the coward terrors of the slave of Fate, to worship at the shrine his own hands have built; undismayed by the empire of chance, to preserve a mind free from the wanton tyranny that rules his outward life; proudly defiant of the irresistible forces that tolerate, for a moment, his knowledge and his condemnation, to sustain alone, a weary but unyielding Atlas, the world that his own ideals have fashioned despite the trampling march of unconscious power.[13]

This declamation is philosophically puzzling, because Russell appears in it to embrace an epiphenomenalism that is neither novel nor plausible. How, in his postulated "empire of chance," of "omnipotent matter," could the free minds, whose "ideals" and "lofty thoughts" he celebrates, exist at all? From a literary point of view, it is worse than puzzling. It is piously insincere: "an indulgence," as F. R. Leavis described it, "in the dramatization of one's nobly suffering self."[14]

Nor is it characteristic of Russell. The following passage, which expresses his usual attitude, is also better prose:

> In religion, and in every deeply serious view of the world and of human destiny, there is an element of submission, a realization of the limits of human power, which is somewhat lacking in the modern world, with its quick material successes and its insolent belief in the boundless possibilities of progress. "He that loveth his life shall lose it"; and there is danger lest, through a too confident love of life, life itself should lose much of what gives it its highest worth. The submission which religion inculcates in action is essentially the same as that which science teaches in thought; and the ethical neutrality by which its victories have been achieved is the outcome of that submission.[15]

There is not a particle of defiance here; yet here Russell's thought is genuinely courageous.

Suppose an objector were to make the following retort. "Your criticism is as arbitrary as it is unmethodical. Of the two passages you quote from Russell you praise the latter as expressive, and decry the former as insincere, faked, and attitudinizing. But your saying these things does not make them so. How could you show me to be wrong if I were to declare that the former is deeply moving, hard-headed, and nobly written, and the latter timid, commonplace, and flat?"

It would be an easy matter to change ground, and appeal to Saintsbury's technical criteria. The passage from "A Free Man's Worship" might be condemned, as Saintsbury condemned certain passages in Ruskin, for too closely approaching the rhythm of verse.[16] It contains no fewer than five complete heroic verses:

> "The slow sure doom falls pitiless and dark"
> "For Man, condemned today to lose his dearest"
> "The coward terrors of the slave of Fate"
> "Free from the wanton tyranny that rules
> His outward life; proudly defiant of . . ."

Yet this but illustrates an observation already made, that the technical faults analyzed by Saintsbury derive from a deeper nontechnical disorder. They are symptoms, not the disease.

If literary criticism is at bottom about success or failure in expression, then no serious critical dispute can be settled by formal demonstration from agreed premises. This fact is sometimes advanced to show that critical differences are matters of taste, concerning which reason can pronounce no verdict. But that does not follow. Not all rational disputes are about what can be formally demonstrated. Literary criticism does not presuppose that all competent judges share the same ultimate premises, but only that they have had the universal experience of trying to express what they feel, and have been aware sometimes that they succeeded and sometimes that they failed. Critical judgments are the fruit neither of demonstration nor logical intuition. They are fallible, but we are reasonably confident that many of them are trustworthy. They can be refined by analysis, and corrected or confirmed by comparing them with judgments of similar successes and failures.

Just as a man learns to understand what others say in the course of learning to speak, so he learns to judge others' successes or failures of expression in the course of learning to judge his own attempts at it. It is impossible to separate either process from the other. Both rest, at bottom, on the same foundation: the comparison of cases that are doubtful with others that are less doubtful. Although questions about the relevance and adequacy of such comparisons can sometimes be settled by analyzing the passages compared, analysis in itself cannot settle critical questions. It clarifies what is to be judged; but it would be pointless if the critic had not the power to judge what his analysis has clarified. T. S. Eliot was, I think, right when he declared that "comparison and analysis . . . are the chief tools of the critic"; and right too, when he added: "They are not used with conspicuous success by many contemporary writers. You must know what to compare and what to analyse."[17]

In reply to the imaginary objector to my harsh judgment of Russell's "A Free Man's Worship," I can say no more than this. That there are those whom its rhetoric may move need not be questioned; whether they are deeply moved by it depends in part on how serious its philosophy is (I do not think it is serious), and in greater part, on what, if anything, it expresses. That the passage is "nobly written," all too nobly written, was part of my reason for saying that it is not expression, but counterfeit. Further comparisons are unnecessary, because every reader can provide them for himself.

II

The work of John Stuart Mill (1806–1873) must occupy a central place in any study of Victorian philosophical prose. From the publication of *A System of Logic* (1843) until that of his posthumous *Three Essays on Religion* (1874), his philosophical writings were generally received as the most important appearing in England. And although in the sixty years after his death it was the academic fashion to scorn him, even in writings of that period by philosophers hostile to him, it is common "to find in the Index the acknowledgement which the Preface withholds."[18] At no time did Mill lose his hold on the educated middle class; and he was studied by the academic philosophers he would most have desired as readers: by William James at Harvard (who dedicated *Pragmatism* to his memory); by Henry Sidgwick, Venn and W. E. Johnson at Cambridge; and, on the Continent, by Brentano and his school. As an academic classic in philosophy his position is now unassailable.

As we have seen, Saintsbury contrasted Mill's prose with that of the late Victorian philosophers he denounced, recognizing it as belonging to the classical tradition of Berkeley and Hume: and indeed it has many of the classical virtues. However, I suspect that the passages in Mill's philosophical writings that are remembered most vividly are polemical; and, for all their formal propriety, Mill's polemics betray an influence that is not at all classical. Here he is on Professor Adam Sedgwick's argument that utilitarianism is impossible as an ethical theory, because, in most situations, an agent has no time to make utilitarian calculations as he acts.

> Mr. Sedgwick is a master of the stock phrases of those who know nothing of the principle of utility but the name. To act upon rules of conduct, of which utility is recognized as the basis, he calls "waiting for the calculations of utility"—a thing, according to him, in itself immoral, since "to hesitate is to rebel." On the same principle, navigating by rule instead of by instinct, might be called waiting for the calculations of astronomy. There seems no absolute necessity for putting off the calculations until the ship is in the middle of the South Sea. Because a sailor has not verified all the computations in the Nautical Almanac, does he therefore "hesitate" to use it?[19]

It is evident from this that Mill had studied Macaulay's polemical use of concrete examples, although he avoids Macaulay's "hard, metallic movement" of which Matthew Arnold complained.[20] Here is Macaulay, in controversy with Bentham,

> Mr. Bentham seems to imagine that we have said something implying an opinion favourable to despotism. . . . Despotism is bad; but it is scarcely anywhere as bad as Mr. Mill says that it is everywhere. This we are sure Mr. Bentham will allow. If a man were to say that five hundred thousand people die every year in London of dram-drinking, he would not assert a propo-

> sition more monstrously false than Mr. Mill's. Would it be just to charge us with defending intoxication because we might say that such a man was grossly in the wrong?[21]

Yet despite the similarity of these passages in structure and polemical method, the difference they exhibit between Macaulay's and Mill's style of thought is striking. It is not merely in the contrast between "he would not assert a proposition more monstrously false than . . ." and "there seems no absolute necessity for putting off the calculations until . . ."; for Macaulay can be sarcastic, and Mill positive. It is that Mill, whose opinion of Sedgewick's *Discourse* was no higher than Macaulay's of Mill's father's *Essay on Government*, entered into Sedgwick's thought in order to expose it; and so presented the considerations that demolish it, that the reader has the sense of producing them himself. Macaulay overwhelms, but Mill converts.

In polemical writing the object primarily contemplated is what your adversary has said, and the emotions expressed are such as go with exposing it as error. Even when done as well as Macaulay and Mill did it, sheerly polemical writing can no more be the highest kind of political or philosophical writing than can sheer satire be the highest kind of poetry. Philosophers ought certainly to express the emotions with which they remove the rubbish that lies in the road to knowledge; but we look to philosophy for more than that.

Mill's philosophical work was essentially critical. He constructed a system of logic, but not of metaphysics. In philosophical theology, his results have been fairly described by Fr. F. C. Copleston as "a rational scepticism, which is more than sheer agnosticism, but less than firm assent."[22] Even his theory of the external world as consisting of "permanent possibilities of sensation" was developed in the course of an "examination" of the philosophy of Sir William Hamilton. Yet Mill's best critical writing is beyond polemics. In his essays on Bentham and Coleridge, in his *Autobiography*, and in less sustained passages in almost all his later philosophical writings, his purpose in criticizing other philosophers was less to disprove them, than by determining their shortcomings to define an approach by which philosophy may hope to discover truth. In fulfilling that purpose, as he largely did, he opened new possibilities for English prose.

The following well-known passage from the essay on Bentham points directly to the nature of Mill's achievement.

> Bentham failed in deriving light from other minds. His writings contain few traces of the accurate knowledge of any schools of thinking but his own; and many proofs of his entire conviction that they could teach him nothing worth knowing. For some of the most illustrious of previous thinkers, his contempt was unmeasured. In almost the only passage of the "Deontology" which . . . may be known to be Bentham's, Socrates, and Plato are spoken of in terms distressing to his greatest admirers; and the incapacity to appreciate such men, is a fact perfectly in unison with the general habits of Bentham's mind. He has a phrase, expressive of the view he took of all moral speculations to which his method has not been applied, or (which he considered the same thing) not founded on a recognition of utility as the moral standard; this phrase was "vague generalities." Whatever presented itself to him in such a shape, he dismissed as unworthy of notice, or dwelt upon only to denounce as absurd. He did not heed, or rather the nature of his mind prevented it from occurring to him, that these generalities contained the whole unanalysed experience of the human race.[23]

Although external marks betraying the nineteenth century can be removed, like the use of the word "thinkers" for what Berkeley would have called "philosophers," this passage cannot be rewritten in Berkeley's style. To Berkeley, as to all the classical English prose-writers, the fundamental philosophical question to be asked of any opinion is: what reasons are there for accepting or rejecting it? His style is lucid and pure because it has but one function: to convey to the reader's intellect an intelligible object. W. B. Yeats once observed of Berkeley, that "though he could not describe mystery—his age had no fitting language—his suave glittering sentences suggest it."[24] In that respect Berkeley outdid not only Addison, but Mill as well. What Mill was aware of was not a mystery, but an intelligibility in things that is not directly intelligible to every mind.

If you concede that much of the experience of the human race is unanalyzed, and that no human mind is well-fitted to analyze all of it, when a pronouncement by a thinker of alien approach or tradition seems absurd to you, you cannot escape asking whether it seems absurd because it is so, or because it treats of something not directly intelligible to you. It may, indeed, be mere confusion or insolent bluff. But if it is not? Mill suggested—he was not, of course, the first to do so—that by carefully considering such apparent absurdities, you may come indirectly to recognize and understand things in human experience that are not directly intelligible to you. A philosophical method that in part studies its objects by studying what others have made of them calls for a style more complex than the classical: one that is less direct, and, in its treatment of others' thoughts, more sensitive.

Mill's most extended study of a thinker in an alien tradition is his essay on Coleridge. Unfortunately, specimens of philosophical analysis from it that would not be too short to exhibit Mill's style are too long to quote. Its spirit, however, is shown in the following appraisal of the "Germano-Coleridgean" school.

> Every reaction in opinion, of course, brings into view that portion of the truth which was overlooked before. . . . This is the easy merit of all Tory and Royalist writers. But the peculiarity of the Germano-Coleridgean school is, that they saw beyond the immediate controversy, to the fundamental principles involved in all such controversies. They were the first (except a solitary thinker here and there) who inquired with any comprehensiveness or depth, into the inductive laws of the existence and growth of human society. They were the first to bring prominently forward the three requisites which we have enumerated, as essential principles of all permanent forms of social existence; as principles, we say, and not as mere accidental advantages inherent in the particular policy or religion which the writer happened to patronize. . . . They thus produced, not a piece of party advocacy, but a philosophy of society, in the only form in which it is yet possible, that of a philosophy of history. . . .[25]

Unfortunately, Mill did not perceive how much of his Benthamite inheritance his enlarged philosophical vision required him to renounce; and the greatest of his nineteenth-century adversaries, F. H. Bradley (1846–1924), gained his most enduring victories over him by pointing out what he had overlooked.

III

Not a little misunderstanding of what were the Benthamite errors that Mill failed to jettison can be laid at the door of T. S. Eliot's brilliant essay on Bradley.

> Bradley did not [Eliot wrote] attempt to destroy Mill's logic. Anyone who reads his own *Principles* will see that his force is directed not against Mill's logic as a whole but only against certain limitations, imperfections and abuses. He left the structure of Mill's logic standing, and never meant to do anything else. On the

> other hand, the *Ethical Studies* are not merely a demolition of the Utilitarian theory of conduct but an attack upon the whole Utilitarian mind. For Utilitarianism was, as every reader of Arnold knows, a great temple in Philistia. . . . And this is the social basis of Bradley's distinction . . . : he replaced a philosophy which was crude and raw and provincial by one which was, in comparison, catholic, civilized, and universal.[26]

That the founder of Utilitarianism was a Philistine, and that Utilitarianism has numbered many a Philistine among its adherents, may be granted; but it does not follow that "the whole Utilitarian mind" was Philistine. Mill and Henry Sidgwick were Utilitarians, as well as Bentham and Frederic Harrison. If Utilitarians provided themselves with a temple in Philistia, so also did Roman Catholics and members of the Church Established.

Neither Mill, nor Henry Sidgwick, his most distinguished successor, was able to make Utilitarianism either theoretically satisfactory, or inoffensive to the "vulgar moral consciousness," which they respected at least as much as Bradley did. That Bradley, writing fifteen years later, should have made telling objections to Mill's *Utilitarianism* (1861) should therefore surprise nobody. Bradley's criticism of Sidgwick,[27] which exposes the inadequacy of Sidgwick's "suppression" of egoism, throws a harsh light on Bradley's own discussion of selfishness and self-sacrifice. Few idealists today would confidently maintain that as an ethical theorist Bradley bettered Sidgwick. In his recent Gifford Lectures, the most distinguished of contemporary American idealists endorsed C. D. Broad's judgement that Sidgwick's *Methods of Ethics* is "on the whole the best treatise on moral theory that has ever been written," and, in an extended discussion of it, found no occasion even to mention Bradley's criticism.[28]

Bradley advanced as "in the main . . . satisfactory," and as decidedly improving on the views of Mill and Kant, the moral theory of "my station and its duties." He never wearied in proclaiming the consonance of that theory with the ordinary moral consciousness: sometimes, as in the following passage, in a style he acknowledged to be "heated."[29]

> If the popularizing of superficial views inclines [the nontheoretical person] to bitterness, he comforts himself when he sees that they live in the head, and but little, if at all, in the heart and life; that still at the push the doctrinaire and the quacksalver go to the wall, and that even that too is as it ought to be. He sees the true account of the state (which holds it to be neither mere force nor convention, but the moral organism, the real identity of might and right) unknown or "refuted," laughed at and despised, but he sees the state every day in its practice refute every other doctrine, and do with the moral approval of all what the explicit theory of scarcely one will justify. He sees instincts are better and stronger than so-called "principles." He sees in the hour of need what are called "rights" laughed at, "freedom," the liberty to do what one pleases, trampled on, the claims of the individual trodden under foot, and theories burst like cobwebs. And he sees, as of old, the heart of a nation rise high and beat in the breast of each one of her citizens, till her safety and honour are dearer to each than life, till to those who live her shame and sorrow, if such is allotted, outweigh their loss, and death seems a little thing to those who go for her to their common and nameless grave.[30]

These sentiments were common enough in the German Empire after the Franco-Prussian War of 1870; and later in the century were to become still commoner. Unquestionably, states in time of war do, with the approval of large majorities, what the explicit theory of scarcely one will justify; but nobody in England before Bradley thought to make a moral theory out of it.

By Saintsbury's formal standards, the passage is magnificent as literature, except perhaps for its last sentence, the iambic-anapaestic rhythm of which is dangerously close to verse. Here again, a formal fault may be traced to a corruption of expression. I believe I will not be alone in finding a difference between the staccato—

> He sees in the hour of need what are called "rights" laughed at, "freedom," the liberty to do what one pleases, trampled on, the claims of the individual trodden under foot, and theories burst like cobwebs—

and the final incantation, moving from ". . . he sees, as of old, the heart of a nation rise high," to its affecting climax. That the former is genuinely felt it is impossible to doubt, however little one may applaud it; but the latter is unashamed, and probably unconscious, pulpit oratory. To try, and fail, to express what few artists have ever expressed is no disgrace. But Bradley allowed his failure to stand, and it infects the whole passage. He offered to express the thought of intellectual scruples being overcome by a higher devotion. In failing imaginatively to realize that devotion, he betrayed his hatred of the scruples themselves: hatred in search of a justification.

How could Eliot have failed to discover the significance of such passages? They are not rare in *Ethical Studies*, although, writing in 1927, Eliot may not have known of things in Bradley's occasional papers even more disturbing: his crude pseudo-Darwinism in "Some Remarks on Punishment,"[31] or his defense of "violence, and even extermination" now and then—for the "good of mankind," of course—in "Individualism and National Self-Sacrifice."[32] Eliot's moral obtuseness in matters political goes some way to explain it: as an admirer of Charles Maurras he may even have found

Bradley tame. But there is another reason. Eliot correctly perceived in *Ethical Studies* the influence of the urbane and ironical style of Matthew Arnold's *Culture and Anarchy* and *Friendship's Garland*. The supreme specimen, quoted at length by Eliot, is the criticism of *Literature and Dogma* in the Concluding Remarks. Eliot's contrast between the "crude and raw and provincial" Utilitarians and the "in comparison, catholic, civilized, and universal" Bradley, rests on a delusion to which critics with a horror of provinciality are subject: the delusion that to be nonprovincial is to be civilized. Mill and Sidgwick were, in their writings, stiff, earnest, and upright. They could be witty, although in a manner intellectual rather than urbane. These characteristics, no doubt, are limitations; but they are compatible with being catholic and civilized. To be willing to write as Bradley sometimes wrote is not.

IV

It is not impossible that Bradley himself became aware of the flaws, both philosophical and literary, in *Ethical Studies*. Desiring to rewrite it, he withheld his consent to its reprinting; and in the preface to the posthumous second edition there is said to be "reason to believe that, had he been able to carry out his intention of re-writing the book, much would have been softened or omitted."[33] Bradley's acknowledged preeminence as a philosophical stylist, however, does not rest on his ethical writings. Nor, admirable though it is, does it lie in his mastery of Arnoldian irony.

The ordinary reader of Bradley's major works, *The Principles of Logic* (1882) and *Appearance and Reality* (1893) probably carries away an impression recorded by his best recent critic, Professor Richard Wollheim, of a "heavy, luxuriant growth of rhetoric and dialectic that is usually allowed to swell and sprawl across the pages often enough obscuring the true lines of the discussion."[34] But Bradley's "rhetoric and dialectic" are vigorously alive, and in *Appearance and Reality* their luxuriance is pruned. The following brief specimen, on the error of Cartesian dualism, gives their flavor:

> The soul and its organism are each a phenomenal series. Each, to speak in general, is implicated in the changes of the other. Their supposed independence is therefore imaginary, and to overcome it by invoking a faculty such as Will—is the effort to heal a delusion by means of a fiction.[35]

This is a little baroque for today's *Baubaus* taste; but it perfectly expresses Bradley's passionate absorption in his thought. Thinking ought to be a passion in philosophers; and for those in whom it is, Bradley's mature prose will always be worth studying.

It must not be forgotten that, in Berkeley, the eighteenth century produced an unsurpassed rhetorician and dialectician; or that, unlike Mill at his best, Bradley in his treatment of his adversaries reverted to the methods of the eighteenth century. Yet as a writer, Bradley is more than a Victorian Berkeley. To identify his peculiar genius, we must examine another aspect of his relation to Mill.

In his *System of Logic*, Mill contrived to analyze the methodology of nineteenth-century science in terms of traditional British empiricism. Nothing so comprehensive has been done since; and his methodological analyses are still of value. Perhaps that is what Eliot meant when he said that "Bradley left the structure of Mill's logic standing, and never meant to do anything else." Yet it is absurd to say that Bradley's attack on Mill's logic is directed only against "certain limitations, imperfections, and abuses." Adopting Eliot's metaphor, it would be more accurate to say that Bradley left the wings and extensive outbuildings of Mill's logic standing, but destroyed its central block: its theory of terms and propositions.

Traditional empiricism had great difficulty in acknowledging the existence of anything except what Hume called "perceptions" and Mill "feelings" or "phenomena" or "states of consciousness." In his *System of Logic,* Mill recognized only two kinds of nameable thing besides states of consciousness: substances and attributes. Following the Cartesian tradition, he acknowledged two kinds of substances—minds, which experience states of consciousness; and bodies, the unsentient causes that excite certain of those states. "But," he added, "of the nature of either body or mind, further than the feelings which the former excites, which the latter experiences, we do not, according to the best existing doctrine, know anything."[36] As for attributes, he declared that "if we . . . cannot know, anything of bodies but the sensations which they excite in us or in others, those sensations must be all that we can, at bottom, mean by their attributes."[37] In sum, except for something we know not what that causes states of consciousness, and something we know not what that experiences them, we cannot even think of anything but states of consciousness. A corollary of this doctrine is that philosophical studies like logic and epistemology are fundamentally branches of traditional psychology.

In *The Principles of Logic* (1883), a year before Frege in his *Grundlagen der Arithmetik* attached psychologism in mathematical theory, Bradley demolished this impossible but tenacious theory.

> In England [he declared] . . . we have lived too long in the psychological attitude. We take it for granted and as a matter of course that, like sensations and emotions, ideas are phenomena. And, considering these phe-

> nomena as psychical facts, we have tried (with what success I will not ask) to distinguish between ideas and sensations. But, intent on this, we have as good as forgotten the way in which logic uses ideas. We have not seen that in judgment no fact ever *is* just that which it *means*, or can mean what it is; and we have not learnt that, whenever we have truth or falsehood, it is the signification we use, and not the existence. We never assert the fact in our heads, but something else which that fact stands for.[38]

This is less an argument than a reminder; and it is conclusive. The essential thing in any mental act is what Brentano called its "intentionality": its reference to an object, not necessarily a real one.[39] No feeling, taken in itself, has intentionality, or means anything. Its meaning, if it has one, is conferred on it. A philosophical theory of mind is therefore a theory, not of psychical facts like Mill's "states of consciousness," but of the meanings conferred on them.

In the empiricist tradition, the fundamental relation that is believed to hold between a word and what it refers to is like that of a label to what it labels. This is not an implausible view of the relation between a proper name, like "John Stuart Mill" or "London," and whatever it names. But, as the empiricists themselves recognized, most words are not proper names. The word "man" does not stand for some individual man, or for anything individual at all, but rather for certain attributes or properties (being a rational animal, perhaps) that all men by nature exemplify. In philosophical jargon, such attributes or properties are *universal:* they can be exemplified by many individuals, but are not themselves individuals.

The precise status of universals is still a matter of contention. One thing, however, it cannot be. Universals cannot be individuals. Yet Mill's doctrine that certain sensations "must be all that we can, at bottom, mean" when we refer to the attributes of bodies, implies that attributes, which are universals, are individuals; for sensations are individual occurrences. It is remarkable that Mill did not see this, because in his theory of denotation and connotation he clearly distinguished proper names from "connotative" or attributive terms.

His failure to see it was disastrous. It led him to hold that all attributes are "grounded" in individual states of consciousness, and that what any proposition ultimately means is that certain individual states of consciousness are "associated" with certain others. This result, as Bradley pointed out, is bankruptcy.

> The ideas which are recalled according to [the] laws [of association] are particular existences. Individual atoms are the units of association. And I should maintain, on the contrary, that in all reproduction what operates everywhere is a common identity. No particular ideas are ever associated or ever could be. What is associated is and must be always universal.[40]

When I say that all men are mortal, I do not mean that the "individual atoms," Socrates, Plato, and the rest are mortal, but that individual *men* are mortal. Individual atoms are here of interest only as having a "common identity" as men; and that common identity Mill's individual states of consciousness cannot provide.

Bradley did not always write with the classical purity of his criticism of associationism. The variety of his prose is unequalled in English philosophical literature. Henry Sidgwick considered the style of *Ethical Studies* to be in bad taste. Bradley, however, refused to tidy up his thoughts to meet Victorian standards of decorum.

> I maintain that all association is between universals, and that no other association exists . . . "And do you really," there may here come a protest, "do you really believe this holds good with emotions? If castor-oil has

> made me sick once, so that I can not see it or even think of it without uneasiness, is this too a connection between universals?" I reply without hesitation that I believe it is so; and that I must believe this or else accept a miracle, a miracle moreover which is not in harmony with the facts it is invoked to explain. You believe then, I feel inclined to reply, that the actual feelings, which accompanied your vomiting, have risen from the dead in a paler form to trouble you. I could not credit that even if it answered to the facts.[41]

His contemporaries, and most of ours, would have censored this example, and curbed the inclinations to which Bradley gave free rein. But Bradley did not stop at outright black humor:

> What is recalled has not only got different relations; itself is different. . . . If then there is a resurrection, assuredly what rises must be the ghost and not the individual. And if the ghost is not content with his spiritual body, it must come with some members which are not its own. In the hurry of the moment, we have reason to suspect, that the bodies of the dead may be used as common stock.[42]

Bradley's twofold perception that what is essential to mind is not the psychical states that compose it, as they are in themselves, but rather their meanings, and that the meanings it is most important to study are universal, was a turning point in British philosophy. Those who would not, or could not, learn from him forfeited all claim to be considered seriously as philosophers. The opening sentences of an early paper by G. E. Moore, already a formidable adversary, bear ample witness to the importance of his influence:

> Now to Mr. Bradley's argument that "the idea in judgment is the universal meaning" I have nothing to add. It appears to me conclusive, as against those, of whom there have been too many, who have treated this idea as

> a mental state. But he seems to me to be infected by the same error as theirs. . . .[43]

Not even Moore would criticize Bradley except on Bradley's own terms.

Just as Mill could not carry out his indirect investigation into "the unanalysed experience of the human race" in the direct style of the eighteenth-century classics, so Bradley could not write about mind in the style of Mill. Yet it is extremely difficult to state precisely what Bradley's stylistic problem was. If the fundamental problem about mind is the nature of intentionality, philosophers must find a way of speaking about how signs, mental images, and the like can be made to be *about* things other than themselves. Ordinary language, with its devices of quotation and *oratio obliqua*, enables us to talk about what we say, and so, indirectly, about what we think; but it does not enable us to talk about the intentionality in virtue of which something said expresses a thought. The familiar logico-philosophical notion that concepts, propositions, and the like must be postulated as intermediate between words and sentences on the one hand, and things and facts on the other, merely deepens the mystery. The natures of concepts and propositions turn out to be elusive. Frege's discovery that in order to talk about a concept we seem to be obliged to treat it as an object, which it demonstrably cannot be, is only one of the problems raised.

These problems are not merely philosophical; or, if they are philosophical, then solving them will solve a stylistic problem as well. To the present, formalized semantics offers little hope that salvation may be found in some artificial formalism; for the same problem arises about such formalisms as about the natural languages. The passages I have quoted from Bradley's

Principles of Logic illustrate one of the earliest and most serious attempts to treat of the philosophy of mind, as it is now understood, in natural English prose. Bradley did not succeed, as his successors Bertrand Russell, G. E. Moore, and C. I. Lewis have not succeeded; but he did make progress, and his work continues to reward careful study.

It may be objected that prose that is concerned with the theory of meaning must be too abstract, too remote from any human emotion to engage the attention of students of literature. Even though argument is unlikely to persuade those who have remained unpersuaded by the above quotations from Bradley, I nevertheless recommend to their attention an observation of R. G. Collingwood. "The progressive intellectualization of language, its progressive conversion by the work of grammar and logic into a scientific symbolism, . . . represents not a progressive drying-up of emotion, but its progressive articulation and specialization. We are not getting away from an emotional atmosphere into a dry, rational atmosphere. We are acquiring new emotions and new means of expressing them."[44]

NOTES

[1] Yvor Winters, *The Functions of Criticism*, Denver, 1957, p. 50.

[2] T. S. Eliot, *Selected Essays*, 3d ed., London, 1951, p. 445.

[3] George Saintsbury, "English Prose Style," in *Miscellaneous Essays*, London, 1892, p. 13.

[4] Ibid., p. 15.

[5] "Modern English Prose" [1876], in *Miscellaneous Essays*, p. 94.

[6] "English Prose Style," *Miscellaneous Essays*, p. 24.

[7] *Miscellaneous Essays*, pp. 10–18, 27–29.

[8] Ibid., p. 84.

[9] Ibid., p. 38.

[10] Cf. *Miscellaneous Essays*, pp. 17–18, 36–37.

[11] My debt here to Benedetto Croce, *Aesthetic,* trans. Douglas Ainslie, 2d ed., London, 1922, and to R. G. Collingwood, *The Principles of Art,* Oxford, 1938, will be evident.

[12] *After Strange Gods,* New York, 1933, p. 27.

[13] The concluding paragraph of Bertrand Russell's "A Free Man's Worship," in *Mysticism and Logic,* London, 1917, pp. 46–57. Russell records that it was "written in 1902," and that it "appeared originally . . . in the *New Quarterly,* November 1907" (ibid., p. v).

[14] F. R. Leavis, "Tragedy and the 'Medium': A Note on Mr. Santayana's 'Tragic Philosophy,' " *Scrutiny* 12 (1943–44); reprinted in F. R. Leavis, *The Common Pursuit,* London, 1952.

[15] *Mysticism and Logic,* p. 31. The quotation is from the essay "Mysticism and Logic," which, Russell records, "appeared in the *Hibbert Journal* for July 1914" (ibid., p. v).

[16] *Miscellaneous Essays,* p. 36.

[17] "The Function of Criticism" (1923) in *Selected Essays,* pp. 32–33. I have examined the philosophical questions to which this conception of criticism gives rise in my *The Later Philosophy of R. G. Collingwood,* Oxford, 1962, ch. 5.

[18] Reginald Jackson, *An Examination of the Deductive Logic of John Stuart Mill,* Oxford, 1941, p. v.

[19] "Professor Sedgwick's Discourse on the Studies of the University of Cambridge," in *Dissertations and Discussions,* 2 vols., London, 1859, 1: 146–47.

[20] Matthew Arnold, *Friendship's Garland,* 2d ed., London, 1897, p. 71.

[21] "Westminster Reviewer's Defense of Mill" (June 1829), from *The Works of Lord Macaulay.* Albany ed., London, 1897, p. 71.

J. S. Mill, *Autobiography,* World's Classics ed., London, 1924, pp. 133–36.

[22] F. C. Copleston, *A History of Philosophy,* London, 1966, 8: 90.

[23] *Dissertations and Discussions,* 1: 350–51.

[24] W. B. Yeats's introduction to *Bishop Berkeley,* by T. M. Hone and M. M. Rossi. I owe both quotation and reference to Bonamy Dobrée, "Berkeley as a Man of Letters" in *Hermathena* 82 (1953): 59.

[25] *Dissertations and Discussions,* 1: 425.

[26] "Francis Herbert Bradley," in *Selected Essays,* p. 448.

[27] F. H. Bradley, *Ethical Studies*, 2d ed., Oxford, 1927, pp. 126–28; *Collected Essays*, Oxford, 1935, 1: 71–132.

[28] Brand Blanshard, *Reason and Goodness*, London, 1961, p. 90.

[29] *Ethical Studies*, p. 202.

[30] *Ethical Studies*, p. 184.

[31] Reprinted in *Collected Essays*, Oxford, 1935, 1: 149–64.

[32] Reprinted in *Collected Essays*, 1: 165–76. The passage in which the quoted phrases occur is on p. 175.

[33] *Ethical Studies*, 2d ed., Oxford, 1927, p. vi.

[34] Richard Wollheim, *F. H. Bradley*, Penguin Books, Harmondsworth, 1959, p. 110.

[35] F. H. Bradley, *Appearance and Reality*, 2d ed. corr., Oxford, 1946, p. 296.

[36] J. S. Mill, *A System of Logic*, 5th ed., London, 1862, 1: 69.

[37] Ibid.

[38] F. H. Bradley, *The Principles of Logic*, 2d ed. corr., Oxford, 1928, 1: 2.

[39] Franz Brentano, *Psychologie vom empirischen Standpankt*, Leipzig, 1874, 1: Book 2, Ch. 1.

[40] *The Principles of Logic*, 1: 304.

[41] Ibid., pp. 307–8.

[42] *The Principles of Logic*, 2: 306.

[43] G. E. Moore, "The Nature of Judgment," *Mind*, n.s., 8 (1899) 177.

[44] R. G. Collingwood, *The Principles of Art*, Oxford, 1938, p. 269.

22. Ernest Gellner: "Sociology"

Born in Paris, Professor Gellner studied at Oxford and the University of London (Ph.D., 1961). He taught at the University of Edinburgh (1947–49) and since then has been on the faculty of the London School of Economics. He is the author of *Words and Things* (1959) and *Thought and Change* (1964).

SOCIOLOGY*

1. PHILOSOPHY AND SOCIOLOGY

It is unfortunately not customary to include sketches of the social background and consequences of philosophies in expositions of them. This is deplorable, because their social role is frequently an essential clue to understanding them. People do not think in a

* From *Words and Things* by Ernest Gellner. Copyright © 1959 by Victor Gollancz Ltd. Reprinted by permission.

vacuum, and even if the content and direction of their thought is in part determined by rational considerations, by where the wind of argument and the force of reasons and evidence drive them, these factors never uniquely determine what people think. By this I mean not that people are incapable of overcoming their emotional, non-rational inclinations (this may or may not be true as well), but that it is in the very nature of thought that its course is not rigidly dictated by some inherent rules. Some evidence may be incontrovertible and inescapable, some inferences cannot be resisted, and in those cases "we can no other." But the choice of problems, the choice of criteria of solutions, of rigour, of permissible evidence, the selection of hunches to be followed up and of those to be ignored, the choice of the "language game" or of the "form of life," if you like—all these matters which make up a *style* of thought or the spirit of the times, are not dictated by an immovable reason, and they are at the very least influenced by the social and institutional milieu of the thinker.

Any sociologist of knowledge, wishing to trace the mechanism of the institutional and social influence on thought, could hardly do better than choose modern philosophy as his field of enquiry. It provides him with an area of thought where the social factors—the tacit choice of criteria of acceptability, for instance—operate, if not in an experimentally ideal state of isolation, at least in greater purity than they generally do in other fields. Philosophy, quite patently and also self-confessedly, is not a kind of thought which stands or falls with factual evidence; nor is it a matter of operating (or ingeniously constructing *within*) a formal calculus with clear and agreed criteria of validity. (I am *not* saying that philosophy is arbitrary.) Philosophy is in large part a matter of explicating—and *choosing*—

our concepts, and, incidentally, *of choosing what kinds of explications we find acceptable* (which amounts to: how in general we view the world and ideas, and what kind of role, say passive or active, we are willing to see them play in our life and society. The curious, and logically quite indefensible, insistence on the neutrality of concepts and on the passivity of accounts of concepts, which is such a striking and self-advertised feature of Linguistic Philosophy, is also profoundly revealing.)

The kind of concepts we choose (and the *kind of explication* of concepts) is perhaps more intimately and more directly connected with what we are, and what our institutions and values are, than, say, current chemical theory. Given this, the sociology of philosophy may be a more revealing, as well as a more manageable, field.

For some curious reason, itself not clearly connected with the logic of its ideas, but closely tied to its social background, the syndrome of attitudes describable as Linguistic Philosophy also frequently includes a hostility—verging on contempt—to sociology. This widespread and marked attitude is not based—to put it mildly—on any accurate, close or up-to-date acquaintance with the actual working of social studies.[1] There are exceptions to this, but they certainly are exceptions.[2]

It is ironical that this should be so, for a number of reasons. Linguistic Philosophy is itself a pseudo-sociology, just as it is a pseudo-metaphysics. Secondly, some of its insights logically call for sociological enquiry, if indeed they do not imply that sociology should replace philosophy. Thirdly, social factors which affected the nature of Linguistic Philosophy are themselves rather conspicuous.

Just as Linguistic Philosophy contains a metaphysic

incapsulated in its rules of procedure—in insisting on minute investigations of the behavioural context of speech—so it also implicitly insinuates a sociology.

Professor Austin and Mr. Warnock have resuscitated the Survival of the Fittest—or, at any rate, of the pretty fit—in conjunction with the theory of the functional adjustment of institutions, both of which ideas they apply to language.[3] (Why only to language?) Must one really go through all this again?[4]

Or consider Austin's suggestion, in the same Address, to the effect that it should not be difficult to notice superstitions that are built into the use of words. Professor Austin must have a very strange vision of human history and society. Not only is it rather difficult, but the kind of method he favours—very minute, detailed investigations of the nuances of usage—could never lead to such a discovery. A "superstition" is such in virtue of violating some *standard* of rationality, and of course the minuteness of the enquiry would preclude the formulation of standards.

This kind of sociology, even though overtly formulated, is particularly harmful, like the insinuated kind, because it is only stated *en passant*, taken for granted, presupposed, treated as more or less uncontroversial in the course of seriously discussing only minor points about usage. . . .

In fact, Linguistic Philosophy calls for sociology. If the meaning of terms is their use and context, then those contexts and the activities therein should be investigated seriously—and *without* making the mistaken assumption that we already know enough about the world and about society to identify the actual functioning of our use of words.

2. *An Ideology*

Linguistic Philosophy is an ideology. I use the term "ideology" in a non-pejorative and very general sense.

Linguistic Philosophy happens to be *bad* ideology, but that is not a pleonasm.

An ideology manifests itself simultaneously as a set of ideas or doctrines, a set of practices, and a more or less closely organised, more or less institutionalised social group. The ideas form a reasonably connected system, related in part by mutual entailment such that if key ideas are understood, the others follow, and in part by weaker relationships of similarity and mutual suggestiveness.

There can be no doubt that ideologies in this sense exist "in the air," as general ways of going about things, suggesting approaches, facilitating interpretation and communication, whilst blocking alternative approaches or interpretations.

So far, in talking of "ideology," I have in effect been defining my use of the term. I now wish to specify some important characteristics which are, I think, often displayed by successful ideologies:

(1) A great plausibility, a powerful *click* at some one or more points which gives it a compulsiveness of a kind.

(2) A great absurdity, a violent intellectual resistance-generating offensiveness at some one or more other points.

The first of these is a kind of bait. An appealing outlook must somehow account for some striking features of our experience which otherwise remain unaccounted for, or are otherwise less well explained. The second feature, though initially repellent, is what binds the group, what singles out the cluster of ideas from the general realm of true ideas. The swallowing of an absurdity is, in the acceptance of an ideology, what a painful *rite de passage* is in joining a tribal group—the act of commitment, the investment of emotional capital which ensures that one does not leave it too easily. The intellectually offensive characteristics may even be objectively valid: it is only essential that, at the beginning, and perhaps in some measure always, they should be difficult to accept.

The plausibilities of Linguistic Philosophy are numerous and striking. It seems to account for the sterility of past philosophy, for how philosophy is possible despite the lack of experimentation, etc., on the part of philosophers. It appears to follow from the obvious, but nevertheless striking and often neglected, insight that there is such a thing as language, that it has rules like any other non-random activity, that words have meanings which must not be violated if one is to talk sense; it explains why common sense is so often right and justifies our daily reliance on it: it unmasks pretentiousness and vacuity, and diagnoses it. It fits in with the general naturalistic, antidoctrinaire temper of the time.

Its intellectual offensiveness on the other hand resides in its claim that it denies legitimacy to certain questions, doubts, and a certain kind of ignorance, which in our hearts we know full well to be legitimate: we do *not* know whether others see the same colours as we do, whether other people have feelings, whether we are free to choose our aims, whether induction is legitimate, whether morality is truly binding or merely an illusion, etc. Many or all of these doubts and questions, which Linguistic Philosophy characteristically "cures" as misunderstandings of language, are in fact genuine. Their suppression without real conviction is an acceptance of an absurdity which binds the adherent to the movement. (This is also what is liable to produce such anger in him when he encounters a doubter of the movement.)

Of its plausibilities, the most important perhaps is that it is positivist—in the sense of allocating the exploration and understanding of nature and things in general to experimental science (whilst nevertheless reserving other functions for itself). It is doubtful whether ideologies which are not positivist in some sense have much chance of success in the modern world. This is due not so much to the existence of plausible epistemological models showing that only experimental science *can* explore the world—such models have always been available, almost since the beginning of thought, and they have not always been felt to be cogent—as to the conjunction of these models with the overwhelming, manifest success of natural science, contrasted with the unprogressive and woolly squabbling in non-scientific fields such as philosophy or theology. This makes some recognition of the place of science essential to an ideology if it is to appeal to modern man. Pure positivism, in the traditional sense, consists *au fond* of recommending that all thinking should emulate the ways of science, whatever they be, or pack up. This particular way out has certain disadvantages, notably that the ways of science (whatever they be) do not provide answers to some pressing questions, or fail to provide definite or intelligible answers, or provide uncomfortable ones. This being so, modern ideologies must, on the one hand, supplement science, and, on the other, make sure that they do not conflict with it and do not appear to trespass on its domain.

Contemporary theological doctrines, for instance, tend to take care to convey by their very tone and style that they are somehow at an altogether different level from scientific or ordinary thinking: gone are the days when the existence of God, the creation of the world and so on were debated between pro-religious and pro-scientific parties on the assumption that the meaning of the issue was clear but its truth was in dispute. In its own domain, the greater reliability of science is no longer seriously in doubt: the question is now how to delimit what its domain is and discover or establish whether other domains exist; and, if so, to indicate their features and the truths to be found in them. (Modern theologians no longer explain strange Revelations about the ordinary world, but tend to seek strange realms in which those Revelations will be ordinary truths.)

But what is true of the adjustment of theology to the hegemony of science is doubly true of those ideologies which actually emerged in the modern world.

3. *Some Comparisons*

The striking examples, with which it is illuminating to compare the linguistic tradition in philosophy, are Marxism, psychoanalysis and Existentialism. Of these, the first two claim to be parts of science, but, unlike the big bulk of science, they provide suggestive, all-embracing and immediately striking systems of concepts, implicit guidance and so forth, which fit them, if true, to be orientations for life. The last does not claim to be part of science, but abstains from trespassing on it and contains an implicit explanation of why there is room for Existentialism in a region not open to science. Marxism resembles Linguistic Philosophy in possessing a monolithic theory of error: intellectual delusion will wither away with the State when the class struggle, which is responsible for their emergence, ceases. There are positive affinities in doctrine—the naturalistic view of man, the Third Person view of knowledge[5]—and in type of ideological device, notably the Two-Tier trick (see above), the custom of explaining away opposition and the associated Revelation complex. There are, of course, far more important and profound differences between the two outlooks, and it is in a way offensive to Marxism to compare the two. Marxism is about more serious matters and has an incomparably wider appeal, Linguistic Philosophy being of its essence an ivory tower pursuit, which can only make sense in an extremely limited environment.

Psycho-analysis, again, is profoundly possessed by a Revelation complex and the custom of explaining away disagreement in terms of the characteristics of the objector. It, too, has its values camouflaged under the notion of health. It, too, makes a specious claim to neutrality, and pliably insinuates the values of the practitioner. It, too, considers itself primarily a study of pathology, though the insights gained are generalised, and it, too, fails to recognise with sufficient clarity that doctrines and values are presupposed by the very drawing of the line between health and disease. As with Marxism and Linguistic Philosophy, the committing of the Naturalist Fallacy is inherent in it when it is treated as a world-outlook.

The similarities and divergences with Existentialism are of a different kind. Despite the profound divergence in the style and tone of the two movements, there is even a positive similarity in their starting points: both started from the realisation that certain questions are very strange and cannot be answered in ordinary ways. There is even a resemblance in the diagnosis of *why* these questions are strange: because we are inescapably involved in the asking and the matter questioned. To ask a conceptual question is, generally, not to ask something that "the world" can answer, at any rate directly, but is rather to ask something about the manner in which *we* handle things. To ask fundamental religious questions—including sceptical queries *about* religion—is to query the manner in which we look at the world. This is one of the key ideas of Wittgenstein's, just as it is of Kierkegaard's account of the religious quest. There is, of course, a difference: for Wittgenstein it was the man the knower, the conceptualiser, the language-user who was inherently too involved in saying things to be able to say what saying things about the world amounted to; whereas, for Kierkegaard, it was man the agent or the chooser who *was* the act or the choice and could not therefore guarantee it by some ratiocination. But this is a difference in the *application* of a similar idea.

There is a further interesting analogy: both sprang from a reaction to pan-logism. Both were born from a rejection of a view that the appearances of this world are a cloak thrown over an underlying structure, which in turn was conceived as a kind of reified version of a current logical theory. It is true that the logical theory in question was quite different in the two cases: in one case, Hegel's dialectic, in the other, modern mathematical logic. A kind of visual concretisation of the former makes some sense with regard to history and society, whilst an interpretation of the latter makes sense for parts of higher mathematics. Neither lends itself to a generalised application as a model outside its home subject, so to speak—if indeed either should be reified at all. But both have been so applied, and in both cases the *reaction* was a doctrine stressing involvement (as opposed to reliance on the alleged underlying structure) and the essential-ness of idiosyncrasy (as opposed to placing stress on the alleged underlying homogeneity). In this way, Kierkegaard and Wittgenstein resemble each other both in the form of their views and in their manner of reaching them.

But from this point onward the two movements cease to be parallel and become almost diametrically opposed mirror-images of each other. Some later Existentialism, just because the question is so strange, makes a positive cult of the act of answering it, and places no taboo on necessarily strange talk about the nature and conditions of such *engagé* and unbacked "answering," or rather, deciding. Linguistic Philosophy, on the other hand, either rules out the odd questions and their answers, or (and here it gets closest to Existentialism) makes a mystique of their ineffability, or (and here it comes to differ from it and becomes most characteristic of itself) comes to claim that answers are not merely impermissible but actually redundant.

It is almost tempting to explain the difference in terms of temperament: on the one side, because there can never be a validated or objective answer, a great fuss is made of this and the matter treated with the greatest of reverence as central to life; on the other, for the same reason, the matter is discounted as pathological and as doomed to wither away when the nature of its oddity is fully understood.

On the side of Continental philosophy, a greater and greater cult of paradox and obscurity, an appetite which feeds on what it consumes and, as with a galloping illness, hardly allows the imagination to conceive its end: who can outdo Heidegger? On the other side, a patient diagnosis of paradox, and an equation of philosophy with the recovery of platitude, and the realisation that an unsatisfiable lament *is* pointless . . . a trend to an era of increasing platitude, dullness and vacuity. On the fundamental issue of values, the two doctrines, disregarding idiosyncrasies of expression and the associated meta-philosophy, are identical: both, in effect, maintain the subjectivity of value as an inescapable feature of the human situation. But one side maintains that, just because it is a necessary fact, it is most deeply tragic or glorious; the other, for the very same reason, maintains that it must therefore be trivial, no cause for worry, or indeed that it cannot be asserted at all. . . .

Thus Existentialism gives odd answers, or quasi-answers of an odd kind, to odd questions: the linguistic philosopher declines to answer the question because it is odd and because the answer would be odd. Both, as it were, find man in the condemned cell, as imagined by Pascal to convey the human situation: one makes a great fuss because the situation is inescapable, the other, because it is inescapable, tries to convince himself that there is no fuss to be made. (He might say: "There is no contrast to this situation, the possibility of death, so how can a contrast-less characteristic be usefully asserted, let alone be a matter for sorrow?") On the one side, a little too much fuss is being made, perhaps; but the nonchalance on the other side is, indisputably, somewhat affected. . . .

The diagnoses of the oddity of the fundamental question remain similar: the involvement, the impossibility of transcendence, the cult of the irreducible idiosyncrasy of the concrete situation in which the question arises.

Both styles of thought make use of these features to account for the fact that they deal with something not covered by science. In both cases, the essential, inescapable idiosyncrasy of the object investigated accounts for how science and its systematic and generalising procedure are avoided; the involvement accounts for the difficulty of any but oblique expression; whilst the impulse to transcendence and its necessary frustration provide the problem.

4. *The Narodniks of North Oxford*

Linguistic Philosophy differs from the other ideologies mentioned by sometimes affecting a certain modesty. It *can* be preached in a dramatic or messianic style, and it is very easy to interpret it as being of the utmost importance (if all past philosophies are wrong, this is no small matter, especially if one understands *why*, and how to avoid mistakes in the future); and although its protagonists are messianic in the sense of being deeply imbued with the conviction of their own rightness, nevertheless it is extremely modest in one important way—it claims not to interfere with anything. It not merely does not teach anyone how to make shoes, but it also claims to abstain from telling anyone how to live, how to find his soul, how to choose his pictures, how to vote, how or where or whether to worship, whether or which authority to obey, and even how to think or talk! Not only does it claim not to do these things, or very seldom (its prescriptions and prohibitions are only directed at other philosophers, and are meant to interfere only with philosophising, and with nothing else), it is extremely proud of this fact, and its practitioners are liable to begin their works with such emphatic disclaimers of evaluative or prescriptive intent that one feels they protest too much.

Linguistic Philosophy, at long last, provided a philosophic form eminently suitable for gentlemen. Nothing is justified. It is merely explained that justification is redundant, that the need for it is pathological. The philosophy is simultaneously esoteric—it is so refined and subtle in its effects that a prolonged habituation to its practices, and hence leisure, is necessary before one sees the point—and yet its message is that everything remains as it is, and no technicality is required. No vulgar new revelation about the world, no guttersnipe demands for reform, no technical specialisms are encouraged.

It is, at the same time, a kind of vindication of the extravert against the introvert. Those who see the world through the haze of their thoughts or their feelings are shown up as somehow philosophically mistaken: those who concentrate on inner feelings, or on the other hand see things as instances of abstract characteristics, are shown up as people who are under the sway of a misunderstanding of language which leads them to overrate and over-value what is in fact trivial.

Those who see things bluntly and straightforwardly—in effect, conventionally—with no room for strange or unusual doubts, are vindicated. "Nothing is hidden."

The arguments of Linguistic Philosophy are really a kind of inverted mystical exercise—they quite avowedly bring no new truth and change nothing, they simply confirm us in our faith in what we knew anyway: it is, indeed, a mysticism of philistinism, but a mysticism none the less, for it does not argue, it initiates. It seeks devices for making fully acceptable truths which it really holds not merely beyond doubt, but beyond argument. It concentrates on bringing out why argument is unnecessary and irrelevant. Now there may be truths which deserve such reverent treatment: but Linguistic Philosophy equates philosophy with this kind of reverent illumination of the allegedly indubitable, and suggests that common sense or the rules of current use have such a status.

In its preference for and vindication of the simple unspoilt popular view against the reasoned subtleties of the ratiocinator, Linguistic Philosophy is a kind of Populism. The folk whose simple but sound folk-culture is being defended and preserved against corruption by specious, theoretical philosophy is the folk of North Oxford, roughly.

5. *Science, Power, Ideas*

There are certain features of Linguistic Philosophy which throw a special light on why it was so very acceptable at the very time and place when and where it became fashionable. It provides a powerful rationale for anyone wishing to have nothing or as little as possible to do with any one or more of the following three things:

(1) Science and technicality.
(2) Power and responsibility.
(3) Ideas.

Linguistic Philosophy showed that all these have nothing to do with philosophy (and when it could not show it, it proved it by convenient re-definition); that philosophy has little connection with the deeper intellectual, emotional or moral preoccupations of men. It implicitly and indeed explicitly ridiculed moral and intellectual inquisitiveness. The world is what it is, our duties are what they are, everything is just what it is. To puzzle about it is a sign of confusion, and the unravelling of these confusions is the task of an entertaining specialised discipline whose only final result, however, is to show that the confusions and the utterances made in the course of grappling with them make no difference to anything whatever. Of course, there are people who explore the universe in the factual sense, and indeed there are moral innovators, but the activities of either of these have nothing to do with philosophy.

It is not difficult to understand why the exclusion of science and technicality, of power and responsibility, and of all ideas should be attractive.

Technicality is naturally repulsive to a professional intelligentsia, trained in an untechnical, literary manner. To switch over late in life is painful, and liable to be embarrassingly humiliating. It is seldom, if ever, fertile.

In addition to this powerful motive, the untechnical manner with which Linguistic Philosophy carries on its business fits in well with a certain tradition which abhors "shop" and despises the specialist. For although Linguistic Philosophy is profoundly esoteric in its ideas, tricks, techniques, at the same time its style of discussion is, in a way, non-technical. Anyone accustomed to a certain conversational tradition, one which avoids both ideas and technicality, but indulges in a kind of conspicuous, light-hearted triviality, can take part in a linguo-philosophical discussion without much training: he will easily recognise its rules. He may not know the history or the hidden currents of the activity, but the rules of the game are very much like those of this conversational tradition. Indeed, it hardly matters if he does not know the rationale of Linguistic Philosophy, for, after all, those who practise it try to disdain and forget it. (By the time the stage of pure research has arrived the doctrines about therapy and so on are almost forgotten.)

The abhorrence of responsibility and power—which makes a philosophy proving that the philosopher cannot have them so attractive—is more intriguing.

In the past, philosophers, particularly those employed by educational systems, were often justifiers, rationalisers of contemporary values. Their job was to encourage the young by giving them the conviction that their aspirations, or the best amongst them, were philosophically or cosmically underwritten. The arguments they employed to give this impression may or may not have been good ones.

Now the situation is, at any rate superficially, reversed. There is a set of philosophers who positively glory in proving by arguments (whose logic is not in general so superior to that employed earlier for the opposite purpose) that philosophy has no guidance whatever to offer (although, inconsistently, they also show, or think they do, that there can be no philosophic reasons for revising our concepts, and hence, incidentally, our values). A future social historian may well speculate whether we have here a class of people already convinced of the unimportance of their thought and endeavour, embracing a philosophy which provides them with a seeming justification of their feeling. Their hostility to ideas—which presumes new and general ideas to be "paradoxes," and all "paradoxes" to be confusions—is perhaps intelligible on similar lines, and also in terms of the particular educational institutions in which Linguistic Philosophy flourishes.

The emphasis and manifest enthusiasm with which philosophers of this school stress the impotence, the formality, the general irrelevance of their own work, is something which one must perhaps leave to the social historian to explain. Perhaps the finding of a philosophical theme rationalising the decline in power of an old ruling class may have something to do with it.

A contemporary novelist who does help me to empathise the linguo-philosophic vision of the world is Angus Wilson. The conspicuous thing about Mr. Wilson's novels is that they *are* about intellectuals and yet are *not* about ideas. Ideas are not much present either in direct or in indirect speech. Compare this with the works of Aldous Huxley which, one should have thought, are about the same world at a different point of time: or, further back, with Bernard Shaw. Of course, the idea-saturated conversations in either Huxley or Shaw are in the first instance expressions of the habitual and possibly idiosyncratic ratiocinations of their authors: nevertheless, they must have some resemblance to what did or could take place, and at least the kind of fittingness which could make them into models.

Any similar preoccupation with ideas and argument is largely lacking amongst Mr. Wilson's characters—

and that is *not*, I think, an idiosyncrasy of their author's, but, on the contrary, a valid perception on his part. The sociology of this species of intelligentsia-without-ideas is obscure to me, but as far as I can make out, the explanation must be something like this: we have here a sub-group consisting of people who belong to, or emulate, the upper class in manner; who differentiate themselves from the heartier rest of the upper class by a kind of heightened sensibility and preciousness, *and*, at the same time, from the non-U kind of intelligentsia by a lack of interest in ideas, argument, fundamentals or reform. *Both* of these *differentiae* are essential to such a group, and both are conspicuously present. If this diagnosis is correct, it would explain those striking features of the linguo-philosophic fad—the cult of meticulousness, the dislike of ideas, the preciousness, the insistence on practical irrelevance and so on, the conversion of understatement into a philosophy. Linguistic Philosophy is, quite plainly, the suitable academic expression of such an attitude.

6. *Internal Organisation*

Many of the sociological reflections so far have concerned themselves with what may be called the external sociology of the movement—the reasons for its acceptability and appeal, and so on. One should also deal with its internal sociology, i.e. the customs and relationships which hold between believers and partial adherents of the movement. Two institutions are of great importance for the understanding of the movement:

(1) The esoteric discussion group, and
(2) The tutorial.

The movement has been characterised by being centred on esoteric discussion groups from its very inception. The world has always been given to understand that the truths and mysteries in possession of the movement are too difficult, too oblique, too volatile in their essence to be communicable in ordinary ways. Their communication on the contrary requires a special atmosphere, a special willingness and a special preparation. It is true that the members of the movement have published, but not soon and not much and not willingly;[6] and it has always been made clear that a perusal of such publications is wholly insufficient for an understanding of a true significance of the ideas contained in them. More is required and that *more* found its home in small circles of the faithful. The authoritarian, capricious, messianic and exclusive characteristics of Wittgenstein's practice are well known.[7] The features of the circles which have succeeded it and which mutually dispute the succession to leadership are less well known.

The psychological effects of belief reinforced by participation in a group, each member of which sees all others as fully convinced, are fairly obvious, especially when combined with a disregard for and disinterest in the outside world.[8] The reflection which this inspires is how like the behaviour of groups of believers may be to what is observed in group therapy. The conclaves of linguistic philosophers have much in common with therapeutic groups and with some religious groups, in that the activity consists largely of confession: not indeed of confession of one's sins, memories or emotions, but the confession of one's *concepts*. But this difference may not be psychologically significant: linguistic philosophers would be the first to point out that the sharp line normally drawn between concepts and emotions is invalid. A further possibly important parallel with the therapeutic groups of psychoanalytic inspiration is that there is an assumption that the leader has access to a theory or insights which have healing powers, without, however, this saving truth being directly or succinctly communicable. It must emerge, intangibly, in the course of the confessions. One imagines that the confusion and complexity of one's concepts is as guilt-inspiring, transference-producing and loyalty-safeguarding as the confession of one's misbehaviours and secret desires. Once indulged over a period of time it probably becomes similarly habit-forming: indeed, there is evidence that it does, and that it constitutes the investment of a kind of emotional capital which makes it difficult to break away. There is evidence that powerful transference on leaders of these groups occurs (the inability to suppose him mistaken, etc.).

Some linguistic philosophers believe that the milieu in which Linguistic Philosophy flourishes constitutes a guarantee against dogmatism and uncritical acceptance; and, conversely, they believe that the practices of Linguistic Philosophy are merely an accentuated form of tradition in education, which constitutes a kind of severe and fair natural selection of ideas and is ruled by repeated criticisms. The argument runs something as follows: the very institutions and their ethos ensure maximum criticism. For one thing, the cornerstone of the educational process is the tutorial, which consists of a critical activity of the tutor, helping the student to examine carefully his own reasonings and presuppositions by cross-examining him on his work, without explicitly teaching him any doctrine of his own. This teaches the pupil to be severely self-critical, without actually prejudging any substantive issues, and leaves him to decide for himself in due course. This theory is extremely naïve. There are many ways of conveying doctrines apart from explicitly stating them: above all, the doctrine may be built into the criteria which determine what the tutor lets pass and what he questions. When the pupil starts the game of "learning philosophy," he does not know the rules of the new game which he is to be taught. It is not very difficult for the tutor to convey by his practice that the game that is now being played, and which is infinitely superior to previous games, is one called common sense. It would of course have been no harder to insinuate the rules of the game which consisted of speculating about the private habits of the Absolute. The very ease with which either game can be taught, and the fact that in either case it seems proper and obvious once learnt, should make one beware.

The existence and stress on tutorial teaching, whilst thus providing no barrier against tacit indoctrination, may moreover help explain why the views, or alleged lack of views, of Linguistic Philosophy are so acceptable. The tutorial system places the teacher in the embarrassing position of having to tell the student something, and a lack of anything to say is more painfully evident than it is in the more distant relationship of the lecture-room. A doctrine which insists that it is not the teacher's job to impart information, but only to aid in the midwifery of ideas already incapsulated in the pupil (in this case, in his knowledge of how to use language), is plainly a doctrine to be welcomed in such circumstances.

The role of ineffability, oblique communication, dark insights, etc., as a camouflage has already been explored. This cluster of ideas is of course tied up with the notion of *therapy* (cure from confusion, not the provision of statable doctrine). The therapy-cum-ineffability view of philosophy is but a new, and negative, version of the Incapsulation theory of knowledge. Unlike the Socratic technique version of it, this one does not elicit buried truths: *its* midwifery elicits buried confusions, simple compulsive models, etc. On the positive side, it only uncovers platitudes, as indeed it itself insists. The usefulness of an incapsulation doctrine for tutorial teaching is obvious, and this is an additional factor in its appeal.

In general, one can say about incapsulation doctrines (cf. the Socratic or psycho-analytic versions) that they are—and cannot but be—selective in what their midwifery elicits[9] and that this selectiveness is systematic, and that the theories or practices are in effect insinuations of the criteria—and implicit doctrines thereof—which they use. Incapsulators are insinuators.

Another institutional factor which is naïvely supposed to be a guarantee of the critical spirit is the large number of philosophers who happen to be congregated in Oxford, plus the fact that on the whole they are not ambitious for extra-Oxonian recognition; they content themselves with criticising each other, and in general it is the limit of their mission to do something acceptable to their colleagues. But in fact this absence of an external court of appeal[10] may make the strength of local pressures almost irresistible.

7. Conspicuous Triviality

It is a remarkable characteristic of typical discussions carried on by linguistic philosophers that they combine a firm rejection of technicality with an extreme esotericism. The world is what it seems, and it is to be seen in ordinary concepts—and yet to *see* this requires a philosophic illumination! The exclusiveness which after all is acquired by an esotericism is assured not on the whole by a specialised vocabulary, but by a kind of oddity of approach or manner. This type of attitude is characteristic of the dilettante, the unspecialised man of culture, who wishes to distinguish himself both from the uncultured on the one hand and from the despised "professional" specialist on the other. Linguistic Philosophy as a style of thought and speech is reinforced by this tradition and in turn reinforces it. The motives underlying adherence to that tradition and those responsible for the success of Linguistic Philosophy are similar, and indeed the two flourish in the same places.

The minuteness, pedantry, lack of obvious purpose, in brief, the notorious triviality of those discussions, or many of them, can only be explained in Veblenesque terms. Conspicuous Triviality is a kind of Conspicuous Waste (of time, talent and so forth). Not everyone can afford it; in fact the whole existence and survival of Linguistic Philosophy in terms of its own account of its nature and purposes is unintelligible to anyone of a practical orientation.[11] If indeed this kind of examination of usage makes an end of traditional philosophic problems, if there are good reasons for supposing this to be so, be those reasons formal or pragmatic, ineffable or articulable, why then let us, on seeing those good reasons, give it up and do something more important. There is no need to protract euthanasia quite so long, still less to turn it into an art for art's sake. This objection, or an attitude based on a semi-explicit awareness of it, is the main problem facing those unfortunate linguistic philosophers condemned to teach their creed in Redbrick universities. Pleasing and natural though its practices may be in Oxford, students reaching a university not without sacrifices in some industrial town do not wish to spend their studies acquiring techniques which only cure a conceptual illness from which they barely suffer, with which they have to be artificially infected so as to give the techniques something to work on; still less if they are told that the techniques may be therapeutically ineffective, and must therefore be adopted for their own sake as a kind of pleasurable exercise. There is indeed something particularly comic about those unfortunate linguistic philosophers who are condemned to spreading the illumination in Redbrick universities. In one such place, a philosopher always spent the first term deliberately teaching old-fashioned, "pathological" philosophy, in order to give his colleague the opportunity of then curing the recently infected students in the approved way. One feels that much time could have been saved all around.

8. *Philosophy as an Institution*

It is illuminating to think of Linguistic Philosophy in the context of the problem of the institutionalisation of philosophy. Philosophy, roughly speaking, is the discussion of fundamentals, of the central features and problems of the universe, of life, of man, of thought, of society, of the sciences.

Given such a definition of philosophy, it easily becomes manifest why there are difficulties about institutionalising the subject: difficulties which do not arise institutionalising other kinds of activity. To institutionalise a subject means having a steady stream of teachers and doctrine. The regularity of this supply of philosophy is after all required by the high degree of organisation and stability of advanced educational systems. But the kind of talent or vision required for having something of interest to say about fundamental issues, where no recognised techniques are available, is not something that can be regulated: indeed, it cannot be regulated by definition, for if it could we should have a technique. Nor can the occurrence of fundamental conceptual crises, calling for philosophical reorientation, be predicted or regulated.

Strictly speaking, this problem only arises for societies that do not have an established official creed, or which do not take their nominally established creed seriously. Where there is an officially and/or generally recognised body of truth, the problem does not arise; philosophers in such a society have their job clearly defined. It is the exegesis of the known and recognised truth. This was more or less the situation in the universities when most of the teachers of philosophy were ordained.

But a variety of factors made the continuation of this state of affairs impossible: the widening of the functions and recruitment of the universities, the growing importance of science and technology, the decline both of religion and the importance of classical education (themes from which were incorporated in the established creed).

In this situation Linguistic Philosophy was a godsend. The ideas of Wittgenstein—or most of them—though surely evolved by him with no such motives in mind, could hardly have been better designed to suit the needs of those who have to teach philosophy and yet wish neither to make fools of themselves by mystically communing with the Absolute, nor to be firebrands undermining all bases of morality and society (still less firebrands condemned to combine their arson with a belated mugging up of mathematics).

The professional teacher of philosophy must be engaged in the exegesis of *something*. Linguistic Philosophy provided him with that something on which he could employ his time and talents: common sense and ordinary language. This was neither disagreeably transcendental or archaic, nor on the other hand embarrassingly revolutionary and destructive. It was tangible, and yet pliable and adaptable to personal taste, and it was at the same time eminently accessible without undue and painful mental strain. It enabled him to perform the exegesis—or midwifery—of a kind of secularised established religion, or rather of a secularised established something-or-other conveniently ambiguous between religion and its absence. But then, compromise is the characteristic of successful established doctrine.

9. *A Secularised Established Religion*

As indicated, the convolutions of modern philosophy can be explained in part as the consequences of attempting to institutionalise fundamental thought in a society which has no official creed. Of course, Linguistic Philosophy has flourished most in places which until comparatively recently *did* have an official creed, and whose organisation and ethos still reflects this fact.

As Professor G. Ryle remarks,[12] "In Bradley's youth most Fellows of colleges were in orders, and a big proportion of the undergraduates came from, and were destined to go to, the vicarage or the manse." In such circumstances, the finding of the doctrine whose exegesis should be the heart of philosophic teaching did not constitute a great difficulty. In fact, it was a suitable mixture of religion and classics.

This mixture became gradually more and more unusable with the various changes, social and intellectual, internal and external to the University, which made their impact towards the end of the last and throughout the present century. The admission of Nonconformists and unbelievers, scientists and, finally, members of the lower classes; the admission of students doubtful of religion and ignorant of classics, made the old ingredients inadequate.

The first reaction to the situation included the manufacture of philosophies which were secular surrogates for religion, and were sometimes frankly seen to be such. They were not tied to any historical dogma and were thus not vulnerable to the scientific and historical criticisms to which the religions proper were vulnerable. At the same time, they provided some of what religion was meant to provide—a sense of Unity, a foundation for morals, a solace, and so on. Of these surrogates, Absolute Idealism was the most famous and striking. In substance, it maintained that everything was part of one all-embracing, meaningful unity, and it derived many consoling and inspiring particular truths from this view.

Mr. G. J. Warnock, in many ways a typical linguistic philosopher, has suggested[13] that this type of doctrine declined because people no longer require religion-surrogates.

But this is absurd. The religion—in a literal sense—which preceded Absolute Idealism was an *Established* Religion. In other words, it was an old, living tradition built into the life of a nation, and particularly connected with the ethos of its ruling class. Its age and involvement had mellowed it: it was held without fanaticism, it was not exclusive and jealous, it was not obsessed with doctrine or consistency, it was used to compromise and to being but one amongst many of the beliefs and preoccupations of its adherents.

Absolute Idealism, on the other hand, was a total and all-embracing vision. It failed, not because people do not require a surrogate for religion (which may or may not be the case), but because it was a surrogate for a kind of total, demanding, radical religion which was not locally known, desired or valued.

Linguistic Philosophy, on the other hand, is an excellent secular substitute for an Established Religion. It has its vision—in the background. Its practical implications are a careful but pliable conceptual conservatism, a strong distrust of intellectual innovation, a disregard of general consistency (Polymorphism!). It provides something, the exegesis of which can become the content of teaching: the exegesis of common sense or of the contents of the Oxford English Dictionary, which replaces exegesis of a Creed or of the classics; a respect for a linguistic tradition which replaces respect for a Revealed one.

Its deep and effectively armed predisposition against conceptual innovation is invaluable. Let us consider the characteristics of an Establishment Religion:

It is not conspicuously given to criticism or conceptual revision.

It is not conspicuously given to insisting on coherent views of things. It is much given to compromises. Too great an inheritance, too many hostages to fortune, make intellectual rigour impossible.

It is quietly confident—it feels in its bones that it is right, that *right-thinking* is defined in terms of agreement with its ideas. It hence conceives its own intellectual task as the "removal of objections,"[14] not as the attainment of new truths. It conceives of itself as ferreting out the mistakes of reformist innovations (and not of errors well embedded in the tradition). It should do this in a generally intelligible, non-technical way.

Its strength lies in doing this in a supple, non-fanatical way: not *all* traditions need be right, not *all* innovations wrong.

These features are found reproduced in Linguistic Philosophy.

It is also interesting to note how very similar the exegesis of common sense or usage is to the traditional deference of reason to Faith in scholasticism (only the object of reverence has changed): reason explains and defends common sense or usage, and only very seldom, or never, corrects it. . . .

Philosophy was once inherently ungentlemanly. (Aristocrats such as Descartes or Russell who took to philosophy were an embarrassment for their families.) Philosophy consisted of arguing, of justifying and defending, and moreover defending points and issues intimately connected with a man's vision of himself and the world.

To *justify*, to put in doubt, to make dependent a basic position on cleverness—that is, plainly, *un*gentlemanly. Goethe, a not unsympathetic expert on snobbery as on so many other matters, remarked somewhere that the nobility lies in *being*, not knowing or doing. ("Never explain!") Philosophy has always been the ignoble attempt to root or justify or confirm *being* in *knowing*.

Linguistic Philosophy has put an end to all that. It has shown, or so it believes, that no proofs or justifications are required for those fundamental and intimate convictions and ideas that are central to our vision of ourselves and the world. Bradley defined metaphysics as the finding of bad reasons for what we believe by instinct. Linguistic Philosophy has shown that no reasons are required for what we believe through linguistic habit.

By a stroke of genius, it has invented a philosophy fit for gentlemen and, *at the same time*, found a home for professional philosophy, sore pressed for a field by the recession of faith in the transcendent realm and the conquest by science of the immanent world. Professional philosophy was like a tribe on the march in search of new pastures, having lost the old. It has found, or invented, a realm eminently suited to gentlemanly pursuits and to the provision of a home for an untechnical, yet ethereal and esoteric, profession. And this realm is at the same time inaccessible to science because it is idiosyncratic; it is neither committed to transcendentalism nor yet necessarily hostile to established customary forms of it: it is the realm of the diversified, essentially *sui generis* habits of words—too human to admit of any technique, too formal and (allegedly) neutral to be of vulgar practical relevance or to be classed as subversive, too diversified to allow general ideas. The consequence of ordinary language analysis is to give people who lack or dislike ideas and technical tools or an awareness of real problems something else to do. Who can wonder at the success of so attractive a philosophy? It is well deserved.

10. *Rival Styles*

As yet, there is not a great deal that can be said with accuracy about the internal segmentation of this secularised Established Religion: partly because the situation has not crystallised adequately, partly for lack of documentary evidence. It was a matter of decades before some of the most obvious facts about Wittgenstein, his practices and entourage could be reported and substantiated from printed evidence; and prior to 1953, every exegesis of his ideas was challenged as a misunderstanding, but, although this is still done, the existence of copies of his works and documentation by his devotees now makes it possible to substantiate one's views; moreover, the aura of infallibility and holiness has begun to fade. Concerning the present situation, however, quotable evidence is still scarce.

Nevertheless, certain trends and polarities are discernible. Of these, the most important is the division between what I shall call the Low Church and the High Church. The former venerate the ideas and distrust the ritual. The latter venerate the ritual and distrust the ideas.

The Low Church venerates primarily Wittgenstein's *doctrines* (generally called "insights," in view of their elusiveness), and treat the rituals which he has introduced (study of usage, etc.) as secondary and as something not to be pursued for its own sake.

The High Church is devoted to the ritual, the idolatry

of usage, and indeed claims to have pushed further in the direction of details than he has.[15] On the other hand it views his ideas with distrust or embarrassment, especially the eschatological promises of a *cure*. Though it invokes the doctrines on occasion, on the whole it treats them as an encumbrance—they are a hostage to fortune, they may be implicitly radical, etc. It clearly prefers the ritual as a case of *l'art pour l'art*, and sometimes does not hesitate to say so. ("Pure research": this is a very U activity for obvious Veblenesque reasons.)

The Low Churchmen are earnest and dedicated, and although one or two of them are found in Oxford, most of them teach in provincial Universities. The High Churchmen tend to be concentrated in Oxford. Some of them display a measure of blandness, preciousness and smoothness which would be a credit to the therapeutic power of Wittgensteinian practices, but for the fact that one feels that the dissolution of intellectual cramps could not in their case have been unduly difficult.

There is evidence of hostility between the two camps.[16] Thus Mr. R. F. Holland, for instance, writes with contempt of the school of pure research, describing it as ". . . lexicographical diligence, a collector's interest (methodical or not) in words, an eye for the nattiest line in usages."[17] The Low Churchmen are liable to see the High as trivialisers and corrupters of the doctrines.

The High Churchmen, however, are liable to see the Low, elusive though Wittgenstein's doctrinal commitment is, as excessively and perilously committed to general ideas. They see themselves as having progressed beyond Wittgenstein in their *caution*.

This progress consists of the following things: stressing the ritual at the expense of the ideas; shedding the ideas as much as possible, especially checkable ones, such as the promise of therapy;[18] and a systematic indulgence in the device I have called the Whole Circle, and of watering down generally, minimising the possible area open to criticism. Many of the paradoxical denials by Linguistic Philosophy of views which no one had doubted prior to its emergence, are themselves denied in turn, and all this with an air of discovery.

This style tends to avoid any rash claims of Linguistic Philosophy such as the denial of the possibility of improvements to ordinary language: but it tacitly assumes that the discussion will be carried on in the context of taking the ordinary world for granted. This style is parasitic on more full-blooded Linguistic Philosophy, in a manner resembling the way *it* was on Logical Positivism: it both denies it and presupposes its results. It takes the promise (the cure of the temptation to adopt un-ordinary views) for the deed, *and* disowns the arguments which inspired that promise and the promise itself.

Over and above these general stylistic trends, some particular ones are worthy of note. There is Professor John Wisdom's linguistic Hegelianism and pan-relativism, ready to see some illumination and role in anything whatever and ready to play the game at any level of abstraction or repetition. There is the magnificent practice by Professor G. Ryle of the style that may be called the Aphoristic Extravert, or the O. Henry of philosophy: a skilful build-up of puzzlement, resolved with a sudden *volte-face* by a neat phrase which shows that, after all, the plain view was right.[19] There is, again, the tradition of inspired pedantry, of usage-collecting so careful, so resistant to general ideas (and not unenlivened with wit), so consistently common-sensical that it almost has a kind of perverse poetry of its own, and of which one can say that, like logic, it is never wrong, for it says nothing. The idea that there are no ideas is itself a mildly interesting one.

11. Existence Precedes Essence

The completely irrefutable—in a sense—sub-school which bases its position on the rituals and not on the ideas, calls for some further comment.

Its behaviour is on the whole predictable and can be defined as obedience to the following law: If an idea can be found which will justify the perpetuation of verbal ritualism, and that idea is weaker, less exposed to fortune or argument, than the original ideas which led to interest in words, then that new and weaker idea will be adopted.[20]

This spirit can be found expressed and epitomised in Professor Austin's *A Plea for Excuses*[21] and in Mr. G. J. Warnock's *English Philosophy since 1900*, both of which contain attempts at justification of the linguistic procedures. Both are minor masterpieces in the art of Hedging One's Bets, although of course in each case it is quite easy to distinguish the statements which express ideas that are in fact cordially believed, practised and followed up, from qualifications which are introduced primarily in order to protect a flank. Without, however, appealing to this distinction (essential though it is to the understanding of their works), the positions outlined call forth some reflections.

The watering-down of the Wittgenstein rationale of the practice of looking at how we use words proceeds in various directions: for instance, there is the matter of *why* ordinary language is supposed to be so inspired, or, again, of *what* is to be expected from an understanding of it.

With regard to the first issue, there is a shift from the Wittgensteinian idea that ordinary language is always and perfectly in order—because to suppose otherwise would be to adhere to the myth of some absolute language which can sit in judgment on the actual employment of words—to the *apparently* weaker and less exposed idea that ordinary language is only very, very likely to be right in the distinctions it draws, given that it has been tested by time and is presumably adapted to the purposes it serves.

This *seems* weaker and less exposed, but in fact is not. Wittgenstein's idea—though, I think, mistaken—was based on the immensely powerful insight that we cannot say how language fits the world, nor improve its *fit*, because to do so would involve our looking at things as they are prior to being described or specified in language. Once this insight is abandoned, once it is conceded that we *can* look at things and decide whether language fits or does not, the whole position crumbles. Its sole persuasive prop has collapsed. Of course, it is still possible to argue in favour of the validity of usage from its *age*. . . . Yes, it *has* survived. But this, by itself, is neither new nor persuasive nor interesting. Moreover, as shown, this argument does not logically *mix* with the Wittgensteinian one.

Consider the matter of what is *expected* from the thorough observation, description of usage. In Wittgenstein, there was the powerful argument that such an observation *must* "dissolve" any philosophic problem, for what else could? And how could it fail?

The latter-day, watered-down version abandons the claims that observing language *must* have therapeutic effects, that there can be no other kind of philosophic problem. At least nominally, it concedes other possibilities. Again, this seems a less exposed, less vulnerable position. In fact, it is much sillier.

The Wittgensteinian argument was powerful, even if mistaken. It was so powerful that it sustained faith in the imminence, or at least in the coming in the distant future, of the "cures" of philosophic problems which were not conspicuous by their immediate arrival (for the tacitly employed model showed that they *had* to be available).

Once, however, the "*must*" of Wittgenstein's (more or less) tacit argument is abandoned, *nothing* remains. We then need specific reasons why detailed examination of the nuances, vagaries and accidents of daily usage are relevant philosophically, or at all. And what specific evidence have we? Actual cures?

The argument is often put in the form that, when we have cleared up the verbal misunderstandings, we shall be better equipped to proceed with the real problems (if any). This assumes, absurdly, that we can tell, without knowing what the real solutions of the real problems will be, what are the preconditions of their solution. . . . Note, incidentally, that the value of clarity is not at issue: people have always realised that they must be as clear and consistent as they can be (with some exceptions—but those exceptions are more numerous among linguistic philosophers, where, as an obverse and reaction to the cult of clarity, one finds a strand of high valuation of mystical aphorism, etc.). What *is* at issue is the very protracted, very meticulous burrowing in the nuances of usage, to the detriment of interest in argument and ideas. And it is absurd to claim, in advance of knowing what the solution of a problem will look like, that it is necessary to begin with *that*.

It should be added that these protestations of modesty, the proclamations of a less ambitious form of Linguistic Philosophy, should not be taken at their face value. For one thing, the insistence on the thoroughness and minuteness of the preliminary study of usage makes it very, very unlikely that the subsequent stage of doing something else will ever be reached. It is possible that those who so assiduously observe usage will one day declare the pre-history of philosophy to be at an end, and inaugurate a new era. This picture, though indisputably entertaining (especially if one imagines some of the particular linguistic philosophers in the role of such a herald), is not convincing. In franker moments, they confess anyway that they still see the alleged propædeutic to be, really, an exorcism. We have, moreoever, Professor Austin's programmatic vision of a new science[22]—there is not much modesty about that. We also have his contemptuous description of the *alternative* to investigating usage: ". . . our common stock of words embodies all the distinctions men have found worth drawing . . . they surely are likely to be . . . more sound . . . than any you or I are likely to think up in our armchairs of an afternoon—the most favoured alternative method." What we "think up in an armchair of an afternoon"—so much for the history of human ideas!

One of the characteristic defences of Linguistic Philosophy very recently has been that it, or some of it, is really no different from past philosophy—and hence should not be attacked. This is a strange defence for a movement which began by claiming to be a *revolution*, the discovery—at long last—of the right way to philosophise, and the herald of the euthanasia of old philosophy. . . .

This initial promise of the withering away of philosophy, of the "dissolution" of philosophic puzzlement, was of course an odd and a rash one. It was a promise which would mean, if fulfilled, that the linguistic philosopher had worked himself out of a job, and, if not fulfilled, that he was wrong. . . . So, although one still hears views with which linguistic philosophers disagree treated as pathological, as requiring a cure, one tends to hear little about the euthanasia of philosophy. Of course, this promise is too well on record to be simply forgotten, but one is somehow given to understand that they were just kidding. . . .

Mr. Warnock has one or two additional entertaining ideas in defence of Professor Austin's method. In defence of the practice of minute and protracted investigations into the use of words irrespective of whether either the words or the analyses are relevant to some problem, he points out, rightly in a sense, that individual therapy needs to be backed by research if it is not to be "jumbled, improvised, and *ad hoc.*"[23] Indeed! This discovery was long overdue: the very notion of therapy presupposes some tacit ideas both of how things are and how they should be, and this is precisely why the purely therapeutic, neutral, doctrineless and un-general conception of philosophy is absurd.

But the matter is in no way remedied by having *more* of the same kind of minute investigations also undertaken in regions where there is no problem, and hence no call for "therapy." Therapeutic procedure is not made less "jumbled, improvised and *ad hoc*" by the fact that further jumbled, improvised and *ad hoc* enquiries are made in non-problematic regions. It is ingenious, in a way, of Warnock to invoke one defect—pointless investigations—in aid of another, namely criterion-less therapy. . . . Unfortunately, *this* kind of aid is of no use.[24]

One should add that it is curious that, with all their stress on the fact that language is not used out of concrete contexts and that the purposes which are served by ways of speaking must be considered, linguistic philosophers of this brand appear to suppose that one can *give an account* of a use of language quite irrespective of any purposes. . . .

Warnock's re-admission of New Visions into philosophy, a fine example of the Full Circle ploy, has been noted. One would have thought that this view would not co-exist easily with the insistence on the minute studies—which by their very nature preclude the possibility of vision, and indeed were initially justified as *cures* of vision—but in fact the two views appear to co-habit happily in the book, a case of betting both ways. Their symbiosis is facilitated by the Interregnum theory, the view that it is apposite to be a minute thinker in the periods between great ideas. That may be so in a general sense—if one has no important ideas, there is little that one can do about it—but the kind of filling-in described and favoured by Warnock is not a neutral and universal stand-by for uninspired thought waiting for the inspiration: it is, on the contrary, with all its stress on minuteness, etc., as positive and liberating virtues, itself the feeble fag-end of one particular vision, Wittgenstein's.

There is one point at which Warnock is right—though his insight, alas, requires a kind of 180 degrees correction—and that is when he connects the features (virtues, as he thinks) of the philosophy he favours with the recent *professionalisation* of philosophy.[25] The activities and fruits of this profession are indeed such that mostly "the general public neither finds nor could well be expected to find any sort of interest" (Warnock). Quite so. Warnock proceeds to say that "it is only quite recently that the subject-matter, or rather the tasks, of philosophy have come to be clearly distinguished from those of other disciplines." (This, no doubt, is the great *Revolution in Philosophy*.) Given that this field is alleged to cover the general concepts, modes of reasoning, the formal aspects of our way of life, one is rather surprised to hear that philosophy is of no public interest. As now practised, it certainly isn't—but the explanation is slightly different from what Warnock supposes.[26]

The real situation is not that advances in technique and a revelational revolution have at last turned philosophers into a profession, but that a *pre-existing* profession, lacking something to do, has found a revelation to justify what it wanted to do. The approximate number, distribution, social role, origin and previous training, etc., of academic philosophers would obviously be much the same whether Wittgensteinian ideas had conquered the philosophic world or not. The situation can best be understood in terms of Parkinson's Law, which operates at the level of whole professions as well as individual institutions: *subjects* are found, and expand to occupy the personnel available for teaching them.

Or alternatively, one can understand the situation in terms of Jean-Paul Sartre's principle, *Existence precedes essence.* Irrespective of whether this is true of things in general, it is clearly true of the philosophic profession, which *exists* well before it defines its own essence. In fact, it frequently *re*-defines its own essence without changing its institutional or personal identity. (A cleric who loses his faith abandons his calling, a philosopher who loses *his* re-defines his subject.)

The emergence of Linguistic Philosophy, this strange love-child of Wittgenstein's messianism and Oxonian complacency, is best understood in the light of this. Transcendental surrogates were unsatisfactory, going counter to the empiricist spirit of the age. Logical Positivism was unsatisfactory for a number of reasons: the logical activities it programmatically implies are disagreeable; the nihilistic implications which in fact it has, if taken seriously, are embarrassing (the world seen, in effect, as a reiteration or conglomeration of sensation and feeling).

In this situation, the practices and ideas of Wittgenstein were a godsend. He provided interesting, though mistaken, ideas why philosophers should indulge in the exegesis of the Oxford English Dictionary—why they should say nothing philosophical, but merely describe what we normally say.

His reasons for saying nothing were not themselves empty, though they were elusive, cryptic and "ineffable." The second generation of the movement, "Oxford philosphy" proper, consists essentially in saying nothing at *two* levels instead of one, shedding the ideas which Wittgenstein had—though did not clearly avow—which entailed that one could have nothing to say.

My contention that the linguo-philosophic syndrome of views, definitions, practices and values is so to speak independent[27] of its rationalisations (though of course supported by them) can be supported by noting the divergence and fluctuation in those rationalisations. The therapeutic doctrine or the euthanasia theory, or the view of (good) philosophy as a kind of permanent night-watchman, on guard against false and confused doctrines without producing any of its own, are not in harmony with the "propædeutic" theory, nor with the midwifery (of a new science of Higher Lexicography) idea. A multiplicity of incompatible justifications, eschatologies,[28] inaugurations,[29] or regencies[30] are invoked, whilst the thing justified remains, without corresponding differences.

One should add some comments on the harmfulness of the substance. When philosophers simply carried out exegesis of (literally) Established doctrine, this was right and proper. I have neither the competence nor the impertinence to discuss the merits of Established theology, but the important thing is that the whole matter was entirely above board. It is wholly legitimate for a religion to have training seminaries, and it is wholly reasonable for those seminaries to engage in training and exegesis rather than in the subversion of the views they teach. Those who wish to doubt or argue about fundamentals can do it elsewhere: they are not obliged to come to the seminary and argue according to its rules.

The matter is quite different when a secularised version of that Established doctrine is taught under the pretence that it is wholly neutral, and the very paradigm of clear and uncommitted thought. The democratisation of the country, the Scholarship system, have as their consequence that Oxford is the main centre for training, and so to speak socialising, talent drawn from all classes and types of opinion, and especially, of course, non-technical talent.

Through the dominance of Oxford Linguistic Philosophy, such men are tacitly indoctrinated by a general atmosphere, which takes it for granted that the best kind of thought, the best kind of intellectual procedure, is minute, pedantic, dull, allows its conclusions to be dictated by "common sense," and so forth, and, conversely, that ideas are generally products of carelessness and confusion.

This insinuated and presupposed view does most harm, I suspect, to the non-specialist majority who merely imbibe it *en passant*, rather than to the "philosophy specialist" who knows how to discount it. It is the non-specialist who may half-unconsciously accept the linguo-philosophic view of thought and its role in life. And, given the present recruitment of undergraduates, the harm done may be on a national scale.

A curious kind of dialectic can be discerned as the underlying pattern of thought of the last hundred years. The first stage, when the centre of gravity of thought still lies outside the universities, is characterised by preoccupation with objective issues, stimulated by new vistas such as those opened up by Darwinism. The next stage, coinciding with a "professionalisation" of philosophic thought, is marked by an emergence of formal and epistemological themes: by concentrating on the Absolute, or on the sense-datum, social and scientific reality is somehow relegated to the status of mere "content," whose specific features do not really matter for the most ultimate and important kind of truth. This is the first stage of the emasculation of thought.

But the formal and epistemological tradition is not, alas, without its dangers: it cannot be relied upon to be innocuous. For epistemology can be radical. The clarification of the criteria of knowledge soon leads to positions such as Logical Positivism. These are radical not because they include radical substantive material, but because their formal, epistemological criteria are so severe as to undermine much of what orthodoxy requires.

This provokes a further movement of the dialectic: the whole epistemological, formal, critical orientation is rejected, in the name of the priority, inescapable reality of the objective world. ("There is no private language etc., etc. . . ." Wittgenstein "proved" what the more comfortable dons had always been inclined to believe—and, in Moore's case, assert—though they hardly dared hope that it could ever be *demonstrated*, namely, that the world was much as it seemed to them, and that to suppose anything else, or to indulge in deep or general doubts, was but a sign of confusion and of deviation from the healthy state. . . .)

But—this return to objectivity does not mean a return to those interesting substantive issues within it which originally stimulated thought—the discoveries and insights of natural and social science. *Those* are still kept out of bounds, away from philosophy, in virtue of philosophy's formal, linguistic status. . . . Whilst any critical visions which are suggested by reflections on knowledge and meaning are *also* ruled out in virtue of the priority of the objective world. . . .

So we are left with an effectively censored and trivialised objective world, and a necessarily innocuous philosophy. . . . The two successive shifts, skilfully superimposed and blended, now *guarantee* triviality.

NOTES

[1] See for example Mr. Isaiah Berlin's *Historical Inevitability*, London 1954.

[2] I have in mind Mr. P. Gardiner or Mr. P. Winch, or indeed Mr. A. Quinton's programmatic remarks in *The Nature of Metaphysics*, p. 161.

[3] Presidential Address to the Aristotelian Society, *Proceedings*, 1956, and *English Philosophy since 1900*.

[4] The argument fails through the inapplicability of the selection argument to small populations and short runs in unstable environments—languages have short lives compared with species—and the illegitimacy of the transitions from survival to fit or from fit to good. A linguistic philosopher once defined Existentialism as systematic misuse of the verb "to be." Linguistic Philosophy is the systematic misuse of the verb "to use"—and this argument hinges on that. Note that linguistic philosophers are perfectly familiar with the defects of natural selection and functional adjustment arguments in their habitual contexts—but when they are formulated in terms of or about *language*, they apparently fail to see their defectiveness.

[5] Cf. A. MacIntyre, *Universities and Left Review*, Summer 1958.

[6] Cf. Mr. R. Hare's article in *Ratio*, 1959.

[7] Cf. N. Malcolm, *Ludwig Wittgenstein*, London 1958.

[8] Cf. R. Hare in *Ratio*, 1959.

[9] There are, of course, great differences in the rationale of how things come to be incapsulated—be it in a metaphysical memory, or an Unconscious, or one's speech dispositions.

[10] This situation is very well described—and claimed to be a salutary one—by Mr. R. Hare, cf. *Ratio* 1959.

[11] Cf. Professor C. Broad's comments on it in *Inquiry* (Oslo University Press), Summer 1958, p. 102: "An influential

contemporary school, with many very able adherents in England and the U.S.A., would reduce philosophy to the modest task of attempting to cure the occupational diseases of philosophers. In their writings the word 'Philosopher' is commonly used to denote the holder of some opinion . . . which the writer regards as characteristically fatuous. . . . (I will not speculate) how long an impoverished community, such as contemporary England, will continue to pay the salaries of individuals whose only function, on their own showing, is to treat a disease which they catch from each other and impart to their pupils."

[12] *The Revolution in Philosophy*, 1956, p. 2.

[13] *English Philosophy since 1900*, p. 145.

[14] David Hume comments somewhere on the dogmatics of another age, who treat arguments and refutations as *difficulties*, on the assumption, as the term implies, of the rightness of their own views.

[15] Cf. J. O. Urmson's paper at the Royaumont Conference, 1958, to be published. I am greatly indebted to Professor Urmson for letting me have a copy.

[16] The present writer, having previously published in article form some criticisms of Linguistic Philosophy, has had the entertaining experience of having members of *each* of these two groupings assure him, on separate occasions, that his strictures might have been justified had he restricted them to the *other* camp.

[17] *The Universities Quarterly*, Nov. 1957, p. 81.

[18] Though Professor Austin, much though he may disavow any general claims, still uses the language of "tertiary stage," etc., to characterise philosophic theses proper as pathological.

[19] His British Academy lecture, 1958, is a masterpiece of this *genre*.

[20] The transformation of the ideologies of sects under the impact of external pressures, not least amongst these being the fruits of success and social acceptance, is excellently explored by Dr. B. Wilson in his study of sects in a small English town; the phenomenon discussed appears to be similar in kind. Cf. B. Wilson's doctoral thesis, available in London University and LSE libraries.

[21] Presidential Address to the Aristotelian Society, 1956.

[22] *Ifs and Cans*, London 1956.

[23] *English Philosophy since 1900*, p. 159.

[24] In Wittgensteinianism proper, there is an amusing symbiosis, a logical circularity, between the therapeutic view of philosophy and the polymorphic view of language: *if* philosophy is essentially therapeutic, then indeed attention to the individual cases is essential, and generalities are irrelevant (for therapy is always of the individual) even if true, and hence one must see language polymorphically. In the reverse direction: *if* the correct view of language is polymorphic, then indeed philosophy must be therapeutic, for in an inherently diversified field, where nothing general can be said, we can cure but we cannot build theories.

This circle is complete, and one can amuse oneself by demonstrations of either of the two conclusions—from the other. . . .

Latter-day Wittgensteinians use the conclusions and steps in this circular argument without even sticking consistently to the circle—they keep a doctrine-less and non-general philosophy, without either guaranteeing therapy or maintaining the "countless kinds" view of language. . . . Cf. *English Philosophy since 1900*, p. 152.

[25] *English Philosophy since 1900*, p. 171. See also G. Ryle in *The Revolution in Philosophy*, p. 4.

[26] Warnock quite rightly notes a parallel between the situation in philosophy and in literary criticism, where something similar has occurred. Cf. *English Philosophy since 1900*, p. 172.

[27] On the subject of the continuity of certain attitudes and ideas I am greatly indebted to a brilliant unpublished essay by Professor W. B. Gallie, though of course he cannot be held responsible for any of my assertions.

[28] Cf. John Wisdom, *Philosophy and Psycho-Analysis*, Oxford 1953, p. 197.

[29] Cf. J. L. Austin, *Ifs and Cans*, London 1956, p. 131.

[30] Cf. G. Ryle, *The Nature of Metaphysics* (ed. Pears), London 1957, p. 156.

23. Carlotta Smith: "Sentences in Discourse: An Analysis of a Discourse by Bertrand Russell"

Professor Smith received her Ph.D. from the University of Pennsylvania in 1967. She has taught at the University of Pennsylvania and M.I.T., and is presently an associate professor of linguistics at the University of Texas at Austin.

SENTENCES IN DISCOURSE: AN ANALYSIS OF A DISCOURSE BY BERTRAND RUSSELL*

In this paper I present a stylistic analysis of a short discourse by Bertrand Russell. My purpose is twofold: first, to suggest an approach to syntactically based stylistic analysis that goes beyond mere frequency counts, and, second, to draw out some linguistic ramifications of the approach.

* Reprinted from *Journal of Linguistics*, VII(1971): 213–235, by permission of Cambridge University Press.

The aim of the stylistic analysis is to find the structures that are characteristic of Russell's discourse, and to give an explanation of why these structures were chosen. This is, of course, a traditional goal of stylistic analysis. Frequently such analysis is based mainly on syntactic information. I suggest that one can arrive at interesting results by considering, in addition, certain aspects of sentences that are not strictly syntactic: the structures that occur in key locations, and their importance in the discourse.

In analysing the sentences of Russell's discourse, I shall look for the structure and location of the most important information unit, in sentences where such a unit can be identified. I shall also be interested in the structures that occur at the beginnings and ends of long sentences; these locations are, I argue, naturally prominent. Finally, a syntactic analysis of each sentence will be used. I will show that Russell presents important material in a distinct and patterned way; the force of this pattern explains, to a certain extent, the occurrence of particular constructions in the text.

The surface structure of sentences plays a crucial rôle in the pattern of presentation and emphasis, as I show below. The rôle of surface structure is particularly striking when one examines a succession of sentences, that is, a discourse. At the end of this paper I turn to a linguistic discussion of *subject* and *topic*. The notion of subject is usually taken to pertain to both deep and surface structures, while topic is a surface structure notion. I shall try to clarify differences between the two, drawing on syntactic evidence as well as the analysis of this paper.

In the first section I discuss the types of information on which the stylistic analysis is based; section 2 presents the analysis itself; section 3 is devoted to the linguistic discussion mentioned above.

SECTION 1

In this section I attempt to justify my approach: I discuss the notion of locations of natural prominence, important information unit in a sentence, and the type of syntactic analysis used in the study that follows.

1.1 Locations of Natural Prominence

One feature of Russell's sentences that immediately strikes the reader is that many of them are quite long. In long sentences there are certain locations, I think, that readers tend to notice more than others: I call these locations of natural prominence. The way these locations are used can be an important feature of style. I will show that Russell uses these locations consistently and to advantage.

People tend to notice the beginning and end of anything that is too long for them to attend to or remember *en toto.* This is not a particularly new or startling observation, of course. In speeches, poems, plays, movies, books, processions, etc., the first and last moments tend to be of particular significance. One reason for this is simply that the initial and final moments are most likely to receive the attention of an audience. Apparently the human faculties of memory and attention are such that, in a work of some length, the middle tends to recede.

Experimental evidence from the field of psychology can be presented in support of the comments above. When they hear a series of digits, syllables, words, a long sentence or a series of sentences, subjects tend to remember the material that begins and ends the series (Neisser, 1967: 222).

In a sentence or discourse there are many ways, of course, to emphasize material, wherever it occurs. Special type faces, spacing, violations of standard punctuation, and many other things can be used to draw the reader's attention. Note that they involve the use of some device that is special and unusual, in the context of conventions, for the written language. The initial and final positions of long sentences, however, tend to be noticed without the use of special devices.

Thus, a natural way of emphasizing one part of a long sentence is to locate it at the beginning or the end of the sentence. Grammatical transformations allow one to accomplish this in various ways: the topicalization transformation in English, for instance, moves material to the beginning of a sentence; extraposition moves material to the end.

Location is a feature of the surface of a sentence, but perhaps not precisely of surface structure. Location does not involve hierarchical relationships, but only successiveness.[1] Presumably when one understands a sentence there is some interaction between location and other features. To appreciate the force, for instance, of a final deeply embedded relative clause, or a preposed adverbial, one must know its grammatical relation to the rest of the sentence as well as its location in the sentence.

The initial or final unit of a sentence need not be related to the surface structure in a particular way: e.g. a final verb phrase adjunction may be relatively high on the surface structure tree, while a final relative clause may be relatively low on the surface structure tree. Thus the part of a sentence that tends to receive attention is not necessarily dominant in surface (or in deep) structure.

If a series of sentences comprise a discourse, the naturally prominent locations can be used to establish patterns of emphasis and expectation. For instance, if time or place adverbials consistently begin the sentences of a particular discourse, time or place will probably be important in some way in that particular discourse, and will be noticed as such by the reader. If the name of a particular person occurs frequently in initial location, emphasis will gradually accrue to that name, partly because it is placed consistently and partly because the reader will come to expect and recognize it.

I shall examine the way Russell uses the naturally emphatic locations in long sentences. To find whether there is a consistent pattern of use, it is necessary to find whether the same structures occur frequently in these locations. Therefore I shall count the frequency with which different structures occur in initial final locations in long sentences.

1.2 Important Information Unit

In many sentences one part is taken to be the most important.[2] The most important part may contain the answer to a question, introduce new material in a text, carry an argument one step farther, make a dramatic point of comment, etc. (Chomsky, 1969) discusses the FOCUS of a sentence; the notion appears to be similar to that of important information unit, except that Chomsky deals only with short units. What constitutes the most important unit of a sentence depends on the linguistic and extralinguistic context: it is not intrinsic to the semantic or syntactic structure.

In speaking, one indicates the most important unit, or focus, of a sentence by suprasegmental cues. In the written language a variety of attention-getting devices are available, as noted above. One way to indicate importance is to exploit the naturally emphatic locations: to place the important unit at the beginning or the end of a sentence.

The study of an author's placements of the most important units in sentences can lead to interesting discoveries. For instance, Henry James tends to use the naturally emphatic locations by ignoring them; he often places important information units in the middle of long sentences, where their natural emphasis is minimal. (This has the effect of indicating something about the judgement of the narrator of the story.) A discourse may be patterned by the consistent occurrence of important units in particular locations. For Russell's discourse, I shall identify and locate the most important units, in sentences where one unit can be said to be most important, and look for consistency of placement.

What one takes to be a unit in a long sentence cannot be neatly defined: it may be a simple noun phrase, a relative clause, an adverbial, etc. Probably there is an upper bound on how long one unit can be, but such a bound is difficult to state.[3] A sentence may be optionally organized into units of different length, depending on the intention of the speaker or writer.[4] In talking, a speaker indicates with phonological cues how his utterance is organized. In writing, punctuation can often give this information, although there are many cases where it does not do so. I shall not discuss here the cues that enable one to arrive at units where there is no punctuation or other visual cue.

To decide on the units of Russell's sentences, I used his punctuation whenever possible (Russell uses punctuation frequently). In cases where the punctuation was not sufficiently informative, I take one unit to be no greater, and sometimes less, than an embedded full sentence.

1.3 Syntactic Considerations

The stylistic analysis of Russell's discourse is based on syntactic information. For each sentence a derivation was constructed, roughly according to the model of generative grammar in *Aspects of the theory of syn-*

tax (Chomsky, 1965). I consulted the derivations to find structures that occurred in particular locations in sentences, and structures that were particularly frequent in the discourse as a whole. Structures were noted for the analysis by the transformations that form them.

The derivations do not follow *Aspects* very closely: many transformations that are required to generate a sentence are not included. The omissions are due to the fact that there is a problematic relation between a linguistic grammar and the way people understand sentences. It is clear that the relationship is not of a simple one-to-one nature, and that not all the transformations involved in a linguistic derivation are important in the understanding of a sentence (Fodor & Garrett, 1966; Smith, 1970; Watt, 1970). Style has to do with the deployment of language with a certain force or effect, and a psycholinguistic rather than a strictly linguistic approach might be preferable for an analysis of style. Yet little is known about how people understand sentences: there is no grammar that is psycholinguistically sophisticated.

I have chosen, therefore, to use a linguistic grammar, but to limit the derivations to certain transformations. The transformations were selected according to this principle: they were included if they directly affect the surface presentation of underlying grammatical relations. Thus for instance subject-raising and pronominalization were excluded, but transformations that affect the form in which a sentence is embedded, such as relative clause or factive nominal, were included.[5] My intention was to restrict the transformations considered to those likely to be important in a linguistic grammar and also in a grammar that directly reflects the way people understand sentences. Probably these are the transformations that affect style.

It is generally agreed that to understand a sentence one must be aware of the underlying grammatical relations among its parts. It seems likely, then, that at least those transformations that affect the presentation of grammatical relations play some role in the understanding of a sentence. I thus suppose the minimal awareness of linguistic derivations in understanding: knowledge of surface form, and of underlying grammatical relations.

SECTION 2: STYLISTIC ANALYSIS

2.1 Preview

A stylistic analysis attempts to characterize a given style or discourse so that the properties that make it unique are apparent.[6] The analyst looks for the constructions that are most frequent, and, therefore, characteristic (although of course it may be characteristic of a discourse that certain structures are employed rarely but tellingly). One may pose and attempt to answer the question, why were these constructions used? Some interesting interpretive work has focused on a writer's stylistic choices as keys to his literary work and personality (Milic, 1967; Ohmann, 1964). Here too I shall ask about the choice of particular constructions. I discuss their selection in terms of the way they function in the sentences of Russell's essay, "The Elements of Ethics, Part I" (Russell, 1967).

There are no one or two constructions that contribute to the unique style of the discourse: no construction is most frequent. However, one can identify a general principle that explains the choice of constructions in many of Russell's sentences. I state this principle now; the detailed analysis that follows explicates it more fully.

With great regularity, Russell constructs sentences so that the material that is new and/or emphatic—the most important information unit—occurs in final location. The underlying relations among the units of his rather complex sentences do not follow a regular pattern. Thus, in different cases different combinations of transformations are required to locate the desired unit at the end of the sentence, and no transformation is most frequent.

The function of the transformations that Russell uses is to organize his sentences so that the important material comes last. The result is a strongly yet subtly patterned discourse.

2.2 Procedure

The data for this conclusion come from study of the key aspects of Russell's sentences discussed in section 1. For each sentence, I noted what structures occurred in the naturally prominent locations, and where the most important information unit (if any) occurred. I also noted the location of sentence connexion, if any, the type of main surface verb, and the transformations that appeared in its derivation.

The next step was to look for patterns of usage among the sentences. From the material on individual sentences I compiled lists that showed the frequency with which certain structures occurred in certain locations. (I did not deal with structures that might be called characteristic, although infrequent.)

Interpreting the frequency counts was the final step. In the presentation below I show that Russell's patterns of usage are complementary, all supporting the rhetorical principle that important materials be located at the end of long sentences.

2.3 Analysis

First the results of the counts are given, with discussion of each; following, the analysis of four representative sentences is presented, so that the reader can have a clear idea of how the analysis was conducted; finally, some details of the syntactic analysis are mentioned. Russell's discourse is reprinted at the end of the paper, with numbered sentences for easy reference.

The counts are as follows: (1) Transformations most frequently used, (2) Structures occurring in sentence-initial location, (3) Structures occurring in sentence-final location, (4) Location of sentence-connecting material, (5) Type of main verb in surface structure, (6) Location of most important information unit, (7) Sentence length.

I have chosen a short discourse so that it can be discussed in some detail and reprinted along with the discussion. Inevitably, the numbers that result from counting frequencies are not very impressive. However, I am interested in demonstrating a general tendency or pattern only, and the small numbers are sufficient, I think, for that purpose.

According to Russell's punctuation there are 31 sentences in the discourse. Seven of these are counted as 2 sentences (they contain separate sentences, requiring separate derivations), so that the total number is 38.

(1) *Transformations frequently used*

By simply counting the occurrence of transformations in the derivation of each sentence, and listing those that occur nine times or more, I obtain the following list (in order of frequency):

SubS[7]	30	Conjunction	17
Prenom Adj.	22	Factive nom.	16
Preposing	21	Genitive nom.	16
Zeroing	19	Question nom.	14
Passive	18	Rel. reduction	10
Rel. Embedding	17		

No particular pattern is discernible here: in fact, except for the largest category, SubS, most of the numbers are quite close together. One can arrive at slightly more illuminating figures by grouping certain transformations together. I group below transformations that produce similar effects in surface structure. By this criterion I form three groups: transformations that embed or adjoin full sentences, with verbals; transformations that result in complex NPs without verbals; transformations that change the order of elements.

The frequencies for the groups of transformations are these (certain transformations appear only in the second list because they occur less than nine times):

Ts that embed or adjoin full sentences

Adjunction	30
Relative	17
Factive	16
Conjunction	17
Question nom.	14
Action nom.	8
Comparative	6
Apposition	4
As-embedding[8]	2
	121

Ts that form complex NPs without verbals

Prenominal adj.	22
Genitive nom.	16
Rel. reduction	10
N of N	6
Conjunction of simple NPs	3
	57

Ts that change order

Passive	18
Preposing	21
Extraposition	3
There-insertion	1
	44

By far the most frequent type of transformation is that which embeds a sentence in more or less full form. The fact that such embeddings occur often in the essay is perhaps one formal correlate for the impression of energy and activity that Russell's style conveys.

(2) *Structures in sentence-initial position*

It might seem appropriate to compare the beginnings and endings of sentences, following the procedure used to make the counts above. Thus one could compare the frequency with which transformations underlie the structures that occur in initial and final position. However, such a proposal is not well conceived, for not all constructions can begin and end a sentence. For instance, relative clauses and adjective phrases cannot begin a sentence, nor can the reduced part of a conjunction; dummy subjects cannot end a sentence. There are some constructions that can occur in both initial and final position, e.g. sentence nominals, but they usually play different grammatical rôles.

Moreover, the grammatical rôle of a structure is signalled differently to the reader in different positions. If a sentence adjoined with *because*, for instance, is preposed, then its subordinate or adverbial function is immediately evident because of the constant. Even if the adjunction is itself a complex sentence, the comma (in most written discourse) between the adjoined and main sentence keeps the relation between them clear. However, if a complex adjunction follows the main sentence, the relation of e.g. a deeply embedded relative clause to the material that precedes it may be less clear to the reader: he has more to keep track of.

Three kinds of information about initial and final structures may be noted: (1) type of structure (relative, SubS, etc.); (2) what structure dominates it (main S, SubS, relative, etc.); (3) its internal structure (simple

NP, nominal, etc.). In the case of initial structures, preposed SubS can be dominated only by the main sentence. It is sometimes ungrammatical to prepose material that is dominated by a lower sentence; if the result is not ungrammatical, the preposed material is taken to pertain to the main sentence. These examples illustrate:

I asked Mary to come late because she arrived early last week.

? Last week I asked Mary to come late because she arrived early.

I asked Mary to come home after John called me because he was worried.

? Because he was worried I asked Mary to come home after John called me.

The second kind of information is important only for final structures, then. The lists below are limited to information of the first kind, type of structure.

Since the positions of initial and final are not comparable, I have looked at each separately. The degree of overlap is obvious on inspection.

The frequency of structures in initial position are these:

Preposed adverbial (no S)	10
Preposed SubS	8
Reordered main S	7
Subject NP, main S	7
Nominal subj, main S	6

The most frequent structures are preposed adverbials (*in ordinary life, in the first place*) and preposed SubS; these two, for syntactic and semantic reasons, should perhaps be in one category. Sentences also begin with derived subjects (the result of reorderings), nominalized sentences as subjects, or simple subjects.

All but one of the reordering transformations have the effect of placing important material at the end of the sentence: three are Extraposition and *There*-insertion, and three are passives in which the derived subject is essentially introductory (sentences 1, 2, and 11). Contrast these with sentence 29, where preposing directs one's attention to the beginning of the sentence.

In roughly two-thirds of the sentences, then, Russell has taken one of several options of rearrangement for a beginning. These different transformations have the same function, in the sentences under examination: to position important material elsewhere. In six of the seven sentences with simple NP subjects, the same arrangement of information occurs. A definite pattern is thus established, a pattern in which the sentence tends to begin with introductory or subordinate material, and the reader finds the most significant point in the middle or at the end.

(3) *Structures in sentence-final position*

These structures occur in sentence-final position:

Relative	9
SubS	7
Compar or *As*-embedding	7
Factive, main S obj including conjoined factive	5
Simple main S predicate	7
Conjoined nominal other than factive	2
Apposition	1

Of the relative clauses, four occur on NPs in the predicate of a main sentence, and the others in more embedded positions (on other relative clauses, on a comparative in a SubS, etc.).

Two points are striking about this list: first, most of the structures are embedded full sentences, and second, there is great variety among them.

Only with the other information assembled here do these facts have any significance for an analysis of Russell's essay. Sheer frequency or the lack of it, *in vacuo,* can tell us little. But information about structure and information about position and importance together indicate the organizing principle of Russell's essay. The varied structures that occur at the end of Russell's sentences have different grammatical functions, but the same function of presenting important material in final position. The variety keeps the pattern from being too obtrusive, and at the same time allows Russell great flexibility.

(4) *Location of sentence connexions*

I now look briefly at the explicit connexions between sentences in Russell's essay. The connexions are made in a consistent manner, one that reinforces the pattern of information placement noted above.

There are many ways in which sentence connexion can be indicated in English. One of the most common is simple anaphora, e.g. *I saw a dog, The dog was spotted.* Anaphora can relate nouns even if they do not immediately follow each other, as the direct object and subject of the preceding simple sentence do, thus, *I saw a dog, I called the dog.* These well-known facts are repeated here simply to emphasize the point that anaphora can be used in different grammatical and surface positions. (There are several recent discussions of sentence connexion: Halliday, 1967; Hiz, 1968; Keenan, 1969.)

Parallelism and repetition can also be used to indicate connexions between sentences. These devices have long been recognized: see Jakobson's insightful comments (Jakobson, 1966, and Levin, 1962). They are, of course, enormously flexible.

Russell uses all three of these types of sentence connexion, and they usually occur at the beginning of a sentence. Rather than linking sentences consecutively, so that a word or phrase at the end of one sentence is picked up at the beginning of the next, Russell places the linking material at the beginning of each sentence. This pattern of connexion is another aspect of the fact that the essay is organized so as to present new and important material towards the ends of sentences. I give several examples of Russell's sentence beginnings: in the first paragraph of the essay Russell uses these devices, viz. the first four sentence beginnings:

1. The study of Ethics is perhaps most commonly conceived as . . .
2. It is conceived, that is to say, as . . .
3. Owing to this view of the province of ethics . . .
4. This view, however . . .

The ends of the sentences do not have other explicit connectives. Consider also the beginnings of sentences 10–14:

10. When we are told . . .
11. We shall be told . . .
12. If we ask why . . .
13. If we still ask why . . . feel irritation . . .
14. His irritation . . .

Sentence 14 contrasts with the others, since it picks up the predicate of the previous sentence. Connexions such as this are unusual in Russell's essay.

In some cases Russell uses inversion to place the explicit connectives in initial position, as in sentences 15 and 19:

15. In the second of these feelings . . . ; in the first . . .
19. But in this he is mistaken . . .

Not all of Russell's sentences have explicit linkings with each other. In 28 of the 38 sentences, the link is made from the beginning of one sentence to the beginning of the next.

(5) *Type of main verb in surface structure*

The main surface verb has little semantic import in most of the sentences of the essay. Sixteen sentences have *is* as the main verb, and fifteen have a verb that is almost empty semantically (such as *concern*). Such main verbs allow great variety in the placement of sentence embeddings.

(6) *Location of most important information unit*

The judgements as to the position of the most important unit are my own, as are the other judgements given here. With this particular category I was especially careful: several counts were made on different occasions and the results compared, in order to check the stability of the judgements. They appeared to be quite stable.

In categorizing the position of the main information unit I used three categories: Final, Non-Final, and ?. The third category was for sentences in which no single information unit seemed to be most important. The numbers of sentences in each category were:

Final	*Non-final*	?
22	5	II

In 60 per cent of the sentences, the most important unit appears in final position. Even more striking, of the sentences where I could identify one unit as most important, that unit occurred finally 86 per cent of the time.

The sentences in the third category are those in which Russell develops the philosophical foundations of his argument. One expects in close reasoning and scientific discourse to find that the steps are as important as the conclusion.

(7) *Sentence length*

Number of words	*Number of sentences*
up to 10	4
10–19	9
20–29	13
30–39	7
40–49	5
over 50	1

Over two-thirds of the sentences have 20 words or more. Because of this the short sentences are highly foregrounded.[9]

2.4 Analyses of Representative Sentences

In order to make clear the type of analysis on which the counts are based, I present here the details of the treatment of four sentences. After each sentence, the transformations that occur in its derivation are listed, with whatever comments seem appropriate. Similar analyses were made for each sentence of the essay.

(23) Thus in the case of ethics, we must ask why such and such actions ought to be performed, and continue our backward inquiry until we reach the kind of proposition of which proof is impossible, because it is so simple or so obvious that nothing more fundamental can be found from which to deduce it.

Transformations:

N of N (Adv)	Passive (Qnom) (Compar (Sub_1Sub_2))	SubS (mainS) (SubS)
Qnom	Preposed Adv	Conjunction

Prenom Adj	Zeroing	Rel (SubS) (Compar)
Genitive		Compar (SubS)

In the overall count, all of these transformations are listed for sentence 23. The notations in parentheses indicate what dominates the material introduced by the transformation, e.g., the relative clauses occur on a NP in SubS and in a comparative. The structures in initial and final position were also noted:

Initial structure:	Final structure:
Preposed Adv N of N	Compar (SubS(Rel(SubS)))

(10) When we are told that actions of certain kinds ought to be performed or avoided, as, for example, that we ought not to steal, or that we ought to speak the truth, we may always legitimately ask for a reason.

Transformations:

N of N (SubS)	Passive (SubS)	Apposition (Fac) SubS
Factive (Ap) 2 (SubS) 2	Preposed SubS	
	Conjunction (Fac) (Ap)	

Initial structure:	Final structure:
Preposed SubS with factive conjunct	Object main S

This sentence is typical of the essay. The adverbial adjunction is preposed, placing the main information unit in final position (the material preposed is repetitive of previous sentences). Note that the passive in the preposed sentence positions the words *ought to be performed* or *avoided* at the end of the sentence, giving them more emphasis than the less specific *actions of certain kinds.*

(3) Owing to this view of the province of ethics, it is sometimes regarded as *the* practical study, to which all others may be opposed as theoretical.

Transformations:

Prenom Adj	Passive (main S) (Rel)	Relative
Genitive (SubS) Zeroing	Preposed SubS	SubS Equative *as*

Here a SubS is preposed and a relative clause takes prominence as the final and most important unit of the sentence. Note that the relative clause is several transformational steps away from its deep structure. The deep structure of the relative may be roughly represented in this way:

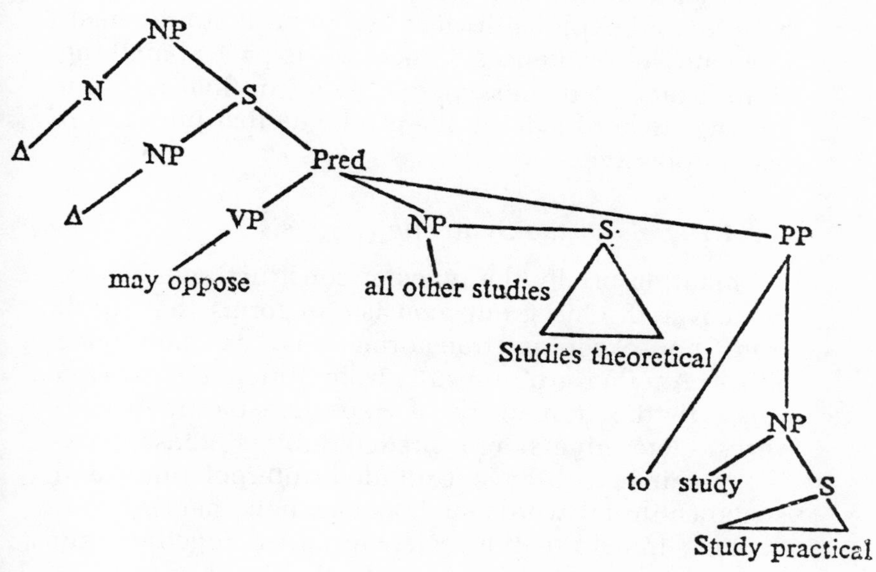

In surface structure the relative is almost parallel to the main sentence, although the first *as* has a different derivation than the second.

(11) We shall be told that truth-speaking generates mutual confidence, cements friendship, facilitates the dispatch of business, and hence increases the wealth of the society which practises it, and so on.

Transformations:

Genitive (Fac) 2	Passive	Relative (Fac)
Prenom Adj (Fac)	Zeroing 4	Conjunction 4
Factive 4		

Initial structure:	Final structure:
Main S	Object
passive	4th factive conjunct

In this sentence the final unit is simply a pro-form that refers back to the four other conjuncts. I suggest that here Russell exploits the fact that important units usually end his sentences. Since we expect something significant, the dismissive *and so on* in final position has the effect of making the catalogue that precedes it less impressive.

2.5 Details of the Syntactic Analysis

I mention briefly the types of constructions that are not covered. One group consists of forms that result from housekeeping transformations, as mentioned above. Another group results from optional expansion rules, in the framework of *Aspects:* quantifiers, adverbs, determiners and predeterminers, tense, auxiliary. Finally, I have excluded interpolations and sentence-initial words such as *but, now, hence.*

Some transformations were grouped together into portmanteau categories, to make the lists as perspicuous as possible. The largest portmanteau category is *SubS*. This category includes a number of transformations that adjoin a sentence, in full or nominalized form, to the predicate of another sentence. The adjoined sentence is usually preceded by a constant that indicates the semantics of the adjunction—whether it relates to time, causation, etc., e.g. *John left to meet Mary, John left because of Mary's singing, John left because he had a dentist appointment*. These constructions are usually taken to be adverbial, in a very general sense.

Another portmanteau category is that of *Comparative*. This includes comparatives with *er . . . than, as . . . as*, superlatives, and sentences embedded with *so . . . that*.

Conjunctions include sentences conjoined with *and, or, but,* and the forms (*not*) *only . . . but* (*also*). Conjunctions of simple noun phrases are kept separate from sentence conjunction, since the former may not be transformationally derived (Lakoff & Peters, 1969; Smith, 1969).

Zeroing is a fourth portmanteau category, perhaps the least satisfactory since I am interested in identifying transformations that affect presentation. This category covers all cases where material has been optionally deleted, and gives equal value to the deletion of many words and the deletion of one or a few.

Nominals are listed separately according to their surface form, as mentioned in footnote 5. Genitives are distinguished from nominals such as *propositions about practice, the wealth of society;* the latter are listed separately as N of N forms.

2.6 Summary

The facts adduced here allow an explanation of Russell's stylistic choices, and enable one to find a pattern in the very diversity of structures that he uses. The sentences tend to be long, with relatively many empty main surface verbs and many embedded sentences. The sentences tend to be explicitly connected at the beginnings, frequently the result of a transformation that reorders. The endings of Russell's sentences vary in structure, although most of them have an embedded sentence of some kind. And finally, the most important material tends to occur at the end of the sentence. This pattern of presentation is taken to be the organizing principle which explains, to a certain extent, Russell's choices of particular constructions.

This study shows the importance of surface features of sentences, and of judgements of importance, in the analysis of a discourse. By combining answers to questions about these matters with a syntactic analysis, we have been able to arrive at an interesting account of the organization of Russell's sentences.

SECTION 3: LINGUISTIC COMMENTS AND RAMIFICATIONS

I have said that the function of the transformations in Russell's essay is to make possible the pattern of information position that characterizes the essay. In fact, this sort of explanation constitutes a general raison d'être for transformations. Transformations allow the presentation of linguistic material in a variety of positions and surface structure relations without affecting the underlying grammatical relations, that is, the way a sentence is understood. This formulation is slightly different from, but not in conflict with, some other recent explanations of transformations. It has been noted with good reason, I think, that underlying structures are frequently complex and involuted, and that transformations, by stringing out and rearranging the material, make it easier to grasp (Langendoen, 1970). This explanation is particularly attractive, of course, if one posits underlying structures that are more abstract than those of *Aspects*, e.g. those of Lakoff and Ross.

Transformations affect only surface phenomena. I have stressed in this paper that surface phenomena are important, and that their importance is more apparent in discourse than in single sentences. In discourse, as I have tried to show, significant patterns of emphasis and expectation can be established. Such patterns are due to similarities in the surfaces of successive sentences; and the flexibility of surface structures, the possibility of consistency and variety, is due to the fact that transformations are available to the user of the language.

If the function of transformations is to allow positioning of linguistic elements, the function of surface structure is twofold: to organize, and make retrievable the underlying grammatical relations; and to display emphasis, topic, and comment. It might be useful to designate these last as 'discourse features'.

I should like here to make a few remarks about deep and surface structures, and the notion of topic and subject. These remarks will, hopefully, support the suggestion that discourse features be regarded as separate from, and simultaneous with, the underlying structure of a sentence. It seems to me that some of the confusion surrounding the notion of 'subject' can be dispelled if deep and surface subjects are taken to have separate functions that coincide when the deep and surface subjects are the same.

I shall argue that derived subjects do not behave as do underlying subjects with respect to several kinds of adverbial modification. Since they also differ from underlying subjects with respect to notional or basic grammatical relations, they are derived 'subject' in only a very weak sense. None of the attributes of underlying subjects devolve on them. In fact, it would be clarifying to reserve the term 'subject' for underlying structures, and to refer to surface subjects (derived or not) as 'topics'.

3.1 Subjects and Adverbial Modification

Consider first the behaviour of subjects with manner adverbials. Certain adverbials are taken to pertain to the underlying subject of a sentence (in these first examples, also the surface subject):

John followed Bill reluctantly.
John watched Mary delightedly.
John fought Michael happily.

If the sentences are made passive, the relation of the adverb to the underlying subject is unchanged:

Bill was followed by John reluctantly.
Mary was watched by John delightedly.
Michael was fought by John happily.

Other relevant data on transformations and underlying subjects emerge when one considers the interaction of transformations that affect or pertain to the underlying subject of a sentence. I deal here with reordering transformations that result in derived subjects, and a certain group of adjunctions. There are several transformations in English that adjoin the predicate of one sentence to another, in cases where the two sentences have identical subjects (henceforth =subj adjunctions). Examples of sentences with =subj adjunctions:

He won the race by tripping his opponent.
He mumbled to infuriate the teacher.
He opened the door with a smile.

How are the adjunctions taken when such sentences are made passive? Do they then pertain to underlying or surface subject? Consistently, the adjunction pertains to the underlying subject (with varying degrees of acceptability), as the following examples show:

John teased Mary to infuriate the teacher.
? Mary was teased by John to infuriate the teacher.

John chased the robber with a yell.
?The robber was chased by John with a yell.
John terrified Bill by brandishing a knife.
*Bill was terrified by John by brandishing a knife.[10]

One can also ask, what happens when =subj adjunctions are made to sentences that have derived subjects? Consider first adjunctions with *(in order) to:*

*Mary was followed by John to fool her pursuers.
*Mary was beaten by Bill at chess to cheer him up.

The semantics of the purported adjunctions are fairly clear; it is also clear that, in English, a different construction is required to express them. In both sentences above, a plausible adjunction involves the derived subject's allowing something to take place, letting or arranging for something to happen. Thus, in the first sentence, Mary arranged for John to follow her; in the second, she allowed Bill to win the chess game.

The fit between syntax and semantics is no better when an instrumental adjunction is involved:

*Mary was heard by John by forgetting to tiptoe.
*Mary was caught by John by letting him find her.

In the other type of =subj adjunction presented here, the adjunction is simply taken to pertain to the underlying subject, even if semantically it is more plausible as pertaining to the derived subject, e.g.

Mary was hit by John with a groan.
Janet was seduced by Tim with a smile.[11]

Time adverbials seem to constitute a class of counter-examples to the claim that =subj adjunctions pertain only to underlying subjects. Time adverbials can occur, with deleted subject, pertaining to the surface subject of a sentence rather than the underlying subject (when the two do not coincide):

Mary was scolded by John after spilling the milk.

The criminal was seen by a passer-by while burying the body.

John was questioned before leaving the country.

While walking in the park, Mary was seen by Fred.

However, time adverbials need not pertain to the surface subject. With appropriate intonation and choice of words, they are taken as pertaining to the deep structure subject, or ambiguously to either deep or surface subject:

The roses were pruned by Daniel after putting on gloves.

Tony was invited by Jim before consulting the committee.

Mary was seen by John while walking in the park.

The thief was found by Gideon after leaving the station.

There is a good deal of variation among speakers on the acceptability of these sentences; for discussion see Fodor (1970) and Elliot, Legum & Thompson (1969).

Time adverbials can occur, without deletion, pertaining either to the surface or underlying subject of a sentence (they can also occur pertaining to neither). In this full form they seem to be acceptable to speakers without variation:

John surprised Susan when she was reading the comics.

John startled Mary when he opened the door.

Thus time adverbials are different from the =subj adjunctions mentioned above: the latter cannot occur as full sentences, and must pertain to the underlying subject. It seems that time adverbials are not a type of

=subj adjunction, and do not relate in a particular way to the subject of a sentence.

3.2 Subjects and Topics

Derived subjects, then, do not supersede underlying subjects. This is true with respect to transformations that pertain to the subject of a sentence, and of course to grammatical relations. In view of these facts, it is appropriate to ask, what is the function of the derived or surface subject?

I suggest that one function of surface subjects is to signal what a sentence is 'about': in other words, surface subjects signal the 'topic' of a sentence. Fillmore points out (Fillmore, 1970) that this is the traditional meaning of 'subject'; his own work (Fillmore, 1968) shows that there is no such unity to the notion of underlying subject. In many instances the underlying subject coincides with the surface subject: that is, the topic of the sentence is also its (underlying) subject.

In a simplex sentence, the subject NP is taken to be the topic: *Sam chased Willie* is about what Sam did. In sentences with derived subjects, the derived subject is taken to be the topic: *Willie was chased by Sam* is about what happened to Willie. Depending on the context, it might be appropriate to begin a sentence with a certain topic, irrespective of its underlying grammatical rôle in the sentence. (By context I mean, for example, what question preceded, what is the topic of the conversation or discourse, what presuppositions are involved.) Note that topic is quite different from emphatic. The passive transformation is sometimes said to emphasize the underlying object of a sentence, presumably because it is placed in initial position by the transformation. However one can easily imagine a context in which just the opposite were the case: the agent phrase might receive greater stress and attention.

The initial NP functions as topic, then, in simplex sentences and passives. Consider now sentences with derived dummy subjects, and sentences with preposed material:

1. Bill is (the one) who(m) John watched.
2. It was Bill that John watched.
3. There is a unicorn in the garden.
4. It surprised me that the bell rang.
5. In the evening John played tennis.
6. To please his father, John mowed the lawn.
7. In his profession Robert was unfortunate.
8. Chicken salad Tom likes.
9. John Mary was beaten by.
10. Lucille Harry reminded of a gorilla (*pace* Postal).

I suggest here only a general statement about distinguishing the topic NP which seems to cover the facts of sentences in isolation. In sentences 1–4, all of which have derived subjects, the first NP in the sentence is the topic; when the derived subject is also a dummy subject, the NP that followed is the topic. Indirectly the dummy subject emphasizes the topic NP, by postponing yet anticipating it. In the sentences with preposing, the main sentence subject—whether the same or different from the underlying subject—is the topic. Examples 8–10 show that preposed material is emphasized but does not become the topic.

Tentatively, then, I will say that the topic of a sentence is the first NP of the main sentence, provided it has not been preposed. There is thus an important difference between reordering transformations that replace underlying subjects with derived subjects, and reorderings that do not. A derived subject is the topic of a sentence; a dummy subject focusses on the next NP as topic; an underlying subject, if not replaced, functions as the topic of a sentence. I assume then that a NP can simultaneously play two or three different types of rôles in a sentence, e.g. underlying object, topic, and perhaps emphatic.

The preceding discussion has been limited to sentences in isolation. One might say in summary that the natural position for a topic is at the beginning of a sentence, just as, earlier in this paper, the beginning and ending of a sentence were said to be naturally emphatic positions. In an actual discourse or context, however, the topic of a sentence might occur in some position other than the first NP. For instance, if in a story or conversation about Harry, the sentence *Jane likes Harry* occurs, *Harry* will probably be taken as the topic although it is the object NP, and at the end of the sentence. Similarly, in written discourse if a series of six sentences deal with *Harry*, or *the notion*, these NPs will probably be taken as the topic of the seventh sentence, wherever it occurs in that sentence.

But, if in discourse the position of the topic is so free, it seems that the function of derived subjects is extremely limited. However, this is not the case: transformations resulting in derived subjects allow the presentation of the units of a sentence in various positions. I hope that the foregoing analysis of Russell's essay demonstrates the great importance of this function in discourse.

"THE ELEMENTS OF ETHICS," BY BERTRAND RUSSELL

The Subject-Matter of Ethics

(1) The study of Ethics is perhaps most commonly conceived as being concerned with the questions, "What sort of actions ought men to perform?" and "What sort of actions ought men to avoid?" (2) It is conceived, that

is to say, as dealing with human conduct, and as deciding what is virtuous and what vicious among the kinds of conduct between which, in practice, people are called upon to choose. (3) Owing to this view of the province of ethics, it is sometimes regarded as *the* practical study to which all others may be opposed as theoretical; the good and the true are sometimes spoken of as independent kingdoms, the former belonging to ethics, while the latter belongs to the sciences.

(4) This view, however, is doubly defective. (5) In the first place, it overlooks the fact that the object of ethics, by its own account, is to discover true propositions about virtuous and vicious conduct, and that these are just as much a part of truth as true propositions about oxygen or the multiplication table. (6) The aim is, not practice, but propositions about practice; and propositions about practice are not themselves practical, any more than propositions about gas are gaseous. (7) One might as well maintain that botany is vegetable or zoology animal. (8) Thus the study of ethics is not something outside science and coordinate with it: it is merely one among sciences.

(9) In the second place, the view in question unduly limits the province of ethics. (10) When we are told that actions of certain kinds ought to be performed or avoided, as, for example, that we ought to speak the truth, or that we ought not to steal, we may always legitimately ask for a reason, and this reason will always be concerned, not only with the actions themselves, but also with the goodness or badness of the consequences likely to follow from such actions. (11) We shall be told that truth-speaking generates mutual confidence, cements friendship, facilitates the dispatch of business, and hence increases the wealth of the society which practices it, and so on. (12) If we ask why we should aim at increasing mutual confidence, or cementing friendship, we may be told that obviously these things are good, or that they lead to happiness, and happiness is good. (13) If we still ask why, the plain man will probably feel irritation, and will reply that he does not know. (14) His irritation is due to the conflict

of two feelings—the one, that whatever is true must have a reason; the other, that the reason he has already given is so obvious that it is merely contentious to demand a reason for the reason. (15) In the second of these feelings he may be right; in the first, he is certainly wrong. (16) In ordinary life, people only ask *why* when they are unconvinced. (17) If a reason is given which they do not doubt, they are satisfied. (18) Hence, when they do ask *why*, they usually have a logical right to expect an answer, and they come to think that a belief for which no reason can be given is an unreasonable belief. (19) But in this they are mistaken, as they would soon discover if their habit of asking *why* were more persistent.

(20) It is the business of the philosopher to ask for reasons as long as reasons can legitimately be demanded, and to register the propositions which give the most ultimate reasons that are obtainable. (21) Since a proposition can only be proved by means of other propositions, it is obvious that not all propositions can be proved, for proofs can only begin by assuming something. (22) And since the consequences have no more certainty than their premisses, the things that are proved are no more certain than the things that are accepted merely because they are obvious, and are then made the basis of our proofs. (23) Thus in the case of ethics, we must ask why such and such actions ought to be performed, and continue our backward inquiry for reasons until we reach the kind of proposition of which proof is impossible, because it is so simple or so obvious that nothing more fundamental can be found from which to deduce it.

(24) Now when we ask for the reasons in favour of the actions which moralists recommend, these reasons are, usually, that the consequences of the actions are likely to be *good*, or, if not wholly good, at least the best possible under the circumstances. (25) Hence all questions of conduct presuppose the decision as to what things other than conduct are *good* and what *bad*. (26) What is called good conduct is conduct which is a means to other things which are good on their own

account; and hence the study of what is good on its own account is necessary before we can decide on rules of conduct. (27) And the study of what is good or bad on its own account must be included in ethics, which thus ceases to be concerned only with human conduct.

(28) The first step in ethics, therefore, is to be quite clear as to what we mean by good and bad. (29) Only then can we return to conduct, and ask how right conduct is related to the production of goods and the avoidance of evils. (30) In this, as in all philosophical inquiries, after a preliminary analysis of complex data we proceed again to build up complex things from their simpler constituents, starting from ideas which we understand though we cannot define them, and from premisses which we know though we cannot prove them. (31) The appearance of dogmatism in this procedure is deceptive, for the premisses are such as ordinary reasoning unconsciously assumes, and there is less real dogmatism in believing them after a critical scrutiny than in employing them implicitly without examination.

References

Chomsky, N. (1965). *Aspects of the theory of syntax*. Cambridge, Mass.: MIT Press.

Chomsky, N. (1969). Deep structure, surface structure, and semantic interpretation. In R. Jakobson & S. Kawamoto (eds.), *Studies in General and Oriental Linguistics*. Tokyo.

Elliot, D., Legum, S. & Thompson, S. A. (1969). Syntactic variation as linguistic data. *Papers from the 5th Regional Meeting of the Chicago Linguistic Society*. Chicago: University of Chicago Press.

Fillmore, C. J. (1968). The case for case. In E. Bach & R. Harms (eds.), *Universals in linguistic theory*. New York: Holt, Rinehart & Winston.

Fillmore, C. J. (1970). Subjects, speakers, and roles, *Working papers in linguistics No. 4*. Columbus: The Ohio State University.

Fodor, J. (1970). Three reasons for not deriving "kill" from "cause to die." *Linguistic Inquiry* **1. 4.**

Fodor, H. & Garrett, M. (1966). Some reflections on competence and performance. In J. Lyons & R. Wales (eds.),

Psycholinguistics papers. Edinburgh: Edinburgh University Press.

Gopnik, I. (forthcoming). *The style of Richardson's Clarissa.* The Hague: Mouton.

Halliday, M. A. K. (1967). Notes on transitivity and theme in English, Part 2, *JL* **3**, 199–244.

Halliday, M. A. K. (1967). The linguistic study of literary texts. In S. Chatman & S. R. Levin (eds.), *Essays on the language of literature.* Boston: Houghton Mifflin.

Hiz, H. (1968). Referentials. *Transformations and discourse analysis papers,* **76.** Philadelphia: The University of Pennsylvania.

Jakobson, R. (1960). The language of poetry. In T. R. Sebeok (ed.), *Style and language.* Cambridge, Mass.: MIT Press.

Jakobson, R. (1966). Grammatical parallelism and its Russian facet, *Lg.* **42.** 2, 399–429.

Keenan, E. (1969). A theory of extended discourse. Unpublished paper, University of Pennsylvania.

Lakoff, G. & Peters, S. (1969). Phrasal conjunction and symmetric predicates. In D. Reibel and S. Schane (eds.), *Modern studies in English.* Englewood: Prentice Hall.

Langedoen, D. (1970). The accessibility of deep structures. In R. A. Jacobs & P. S. Rosenbaum (eds.), *Readings in English transformational grammar.* Waltham: Ginn & Co.

Levin, S. (1962). *Linguistic structures in poetry.* The Hague: Mouton.

Milic, L. (1967). *A quantitative approach to the style of Jonathan Swift.* The Hague: Mouton.

Mukarovsky, J. (1967). Standard language and poetic language. In S. Chatman & S. R. Levin (eds.), *Essays in the language of literature.* Boston: Houghton Mifflin.

Neisser, U. (1967). *Cognitive psychology.* New York: Appleton Century Crofts.

Ohmann, R. (1964). Generative grammars and the concept of literary style. *Word* **20,** 423–39.

Ross, J. (1967). *Constraints on variables in syntax.* (MIT dissertation.)

Russell, B. (1967). *Philosophical essays.* Simon & Schuster.

Smith, C. S. (1969). Ambiguous sentences with And. In D. Reibel & S. Schane (eds.), *Modern studies in English,* Englewood Cliffs: Prentice Hall.

Smith, C. S. (1970). An experimental approach to children's

linguistic competence. In J. R. Hayes (ed.), *Cognition and the development of language*. New York: John Wiley Press.

Watt, W. (1970). Two issues concerning psycholinguistics. In J. R. Hayes (ed.), *Cognition and the study of language*. New York: John Wiley Press.

NOTES

[1] For a stimulating discussion of successiveness and simultaneity in language, see Jakobson (1960).

[2] Except various technical sentences, as of mathematics or chemistry, for instance; or on the other hand, sentences of poetry.

[3] See Ross (1967) for a discussion of the problem of pinning down the characteristics of linguistic units of a certain length.

[4] An interesting discussion of how such units are signalled is given in Halliday (1967).

[5] Different types of nominals are listed separately: there are listings for factive, genitive, action, question, infinitive, and N of N nominals. Whether these nominals should be considered separately is debatable. I consider them separately here since the underlying elements are presented in different surface forms, depending on the type of nominal. However, this difference may turn out to be unimportant in understanding.

[6] A discourse is unique with respect to a particular period and a particular genre, among other things; Thomas Pynchon would be more unique had he written during the eighteenth century than he is today, and Samuel Johnson would be more unique today than in his own time.

[7] For an explanation of what is covered by this category, and by others in the lists, see the section on details of the syntactic analysis, 2.4

[8] I refer here to constructions like that in the relative clause of sentence 3. Such constructions are to be distinguished from *as* that can be replaced by *about* (as in the main clause of the same sentence) and from cases with a PP with *as* as an obligatory verb complement, e.g. with the words *speak of, conceive, regard,* in Russell's discourse.

[9] In the sense of the Russian formalists, cf. Mukarovsky

(1967). The approach of the formalists is introduced with notable clarity in the first chapter of Gopnik, forthcoming.

[10] It is not clear why such sentences are ungrammatical. Fodor (1970) suggests that a surface constraint blocks two *by*-phrases, but note that not all successions of *by*-phrases are ungrammatical: *Mary was seen by John by the river bank.* A possible explanation, offered only tentatively, is that in the offending sentence both *by*-phrases come from the same sentence, and that it is this that must be blocked.

[11] This sentence was suggested by Senta Plotz.

24. O. K. Bouwsma: "Naturalism"

Receiving his Ph.D. from the University of Michigan in 1928, Bouwsma (1898–1978) was first an instructor of English at the University of Michigan, and then professor of philosophy, first at the University of Nebraska from 1928–65, then at the University of Texas at Austin since 1965. He was named John Locke Lecturer at Oxford in 1951. He was the author of *Philosophical Essays*.

NATURALISM*

I should like first of all to state as precisely as I can that proposition or those propositions with which in part, at least, naturalism is to be identified. For this purpose, I should like to take sentences straight out of the test tube—a much more authentic source even than the horse's mouth. Once having identified these sentences, I intend to examine them in order to discover further how to deal with them. Are the sentences in question exclamatory, or empirical, or are they tautologies?

The sentences which I am to quote are sentences in which their authors, respectively, aim to define naturalism. These sentences fall into two groups, and the distinction between them will immediately be evident. Here now are three in the first group. The first is from Edel. Here it is: "Reliance on scientific method together with an appreciation of the primacy of matter, and the pervasiveness of change, I take to be the central points of naturalism as a philosophic outlook."[1] The second is from Hook: "What unites them all is the whole-hearted acceptance of scientific method as the only reliable way of reaching truth about the world, nature, society, and man. The least common denominator of all historic naturalisms, therefore, is not so much a set of specific doctrines as the method of scientific or rational empiricism."[2] The third is from Dewey; it runs: "It suffices here to note that the naturalist is one who has respect for the conclusions of natural science."[3]

Now these three sentences agree in identifying naturalism with a certain attitude toward scientific method, variously described as "reliance upon," "whole-hearted acceptance of," and "respect for." Every naturalist is one who maintains an attitude similar to the attitude here described. He is excited about something. The excitement may vary in intensity, but in some degree naturalists all share it. This is not difficult to understand. In many cases, no doubt such excitement is the spontaneous overflow of new curiosities looking forward to tomorrow. There are secrets in 10,000 boxes, and you have opened forty, and know now how to go on opening a box a day for the rest of your life. What a feast for eager eyes! Who has not shaken a box and wondered, keyless, what was inside it—and later, furnished with a key, found out? Precious key! Well, a naturalist is a man with 10,000 unopened boxes, newly furnished with a key. No wonder he dances, key in hand up-raised, among the boxes.

But this is idle curiosity, idle secrets for idle eyes, and is only half the motive of the naturalists' dance. For in those boxes snuggled away out of men's sight is the furniture of the land of hearts' desire. Here is a box of the beauty that will not fade in the rain. Here is a heart that will not fail, a pump with scrutable controls. Here are pellets for stretching the hours, and wobbling all dimensions. Here are new snuffers for old pains and here are new pleasures for old duffers. Besides, there are new and quick get-aways, new smashers, new glue better than love, daisies that will tell even what the old ones wouldn't, rapid transit swifter than *gloria mundi,* lightning to keep your orange-juice cold, falling water to dry your feet, shocks to give you peace, a drop or two to make you jump, babies delivered in cellophane, bloodless wars, holocaust by button, one big rumble for all last "whimpers," a piece of powder for a gland, teeth from Dupont's, everlasting shoes, a feather to lighten your load, suspenders to keep up your courage, a new Joseph for all your dreams, cant about what man can, the last straw, and so on from 9,000 and more other boxes. So the naturalist does his dazzle dance. Who then would not accept scientific method, and prefer to go to Babylon by candle-light? Scientific method is successful.

So far then there is no issue, no controversy, and by that token we may be sure that we have not yet ventured to be philosophical. Be reminded, then, of what so far we missed and be prepared to resist. Mr. Hook speaks of "the whole-hearted acceptance of scientific method as the only reliable way of reaching truth." And now we are prepared to introduce that second group of sentences. In this group are these sentences: The first from Dennes, which is this: "There is for naturalism no knowledge except of the type ordinarily called scientific,"[4] and this one from Krikorian: "For naturalism as a philosophy, the universal applicability of the experimental method is a basic belief."[5] By the pricking of the hair on your chinny chin chin I realize that these are philosophic statements.

Let us now consider these sentences, with special attention to the phrases: "the only reliable way," "no knowledge except," "the universal applicability of." Obviously the point of such sentences is that other men have spoken of "other reliable ways," of "knowledge other than," of "a certain inapplicability." Notice first the form of Dennes's sentence. Mr. Ringling might say: "There is for Ringling Brothers no elephant except of the type ordinarily called big." Does Mr. Ringling intend to deny there are any little elephants? Does he mean that besides Jumbo and Mumbo there is no little Nimblo? I think he means no more than that there is a difference between big elephants and little elephants, and that Mr. Ringling has no use for little elephants. If you tried to sell him one, he wouldn't buy. He can't use any. Or try this sentence: "For all the boys in our alley, there's no girl but pretty Sally." What, have the boys in our alley seen no girl but pretty Sally? Don't be silly. Of course, they know Helen and Ruth and Betty. It's just a way of saying that above all the girls they know, they prefer Sally.

And this is now the way in which we are to understand Mr. Dennes? Does he mean to be stating a preference? Mr. Ringling says: "There are really no elephants but big ones," and the boys in our alley say: "'There's really no girl but Sally." So Mr. Dennes: "There's really no knowledge but. . . ." In this case, of course, Mr. Dennes might have admitted other types of knowledge too, but would in this instance merely have intended to say: "Well, so long as I have my choice, let mine be scientific." In this case, once more there would be no issue. If Mr. Dennes prefers blondes or gas-heat or lemonade, or a hard mattress or scientific knowledge, well, that's all there is to it. I think that this is certainly something like what Dennes is saying, but not quite.

Before we settle these matters, let us inspect Krikorian's sentence. It is: "For naturalism as a philosophy, the universal applicability of the experimental method is a basic belief." Consider the parallel sentence of the vacuum cleaner salesman: "For vacuumism as a philosophy, the universal applicability of the suction nozzle is a basic belief." He may argue to himself: "If I ever give this up, I'll never sell another vacuum cleaner. It is basic." To the house-wife who asks: "And can you use it to dust books?" he replies: "Of course." And when he shows her and finds that it does not do so well, does he deny the universal applicability of the nozzle? No such thing. He may complain that he himself is not skillful, or that what seems like dust to the house-wife is not dust. The universal applicability of the nozzle is now the touchstone of dust. If the nozzle is applicable, it's dust. If it is not applicable, it is not dust. Is Krikorian's statement now like the statement of the vacuum-cleaner salesman? Well, for the moment, I should like to say that it is, and then to add, before I breathe, that it isn't. And for the next moment I should like to postpone my decision.

It will be remembered that at the outset I proposed to determine whether the sentences defining naturalism were exclamatory, or empirical, or tautologies. I think, though I have made no point of it, that naturalists are very fervent. But I also think now that without further trial of these sentences it will be misleading to classify them in either way. I propose accordingly to dandle them some more before deciding. Let us, then, just playfully bounce them.

There are, in any case, at least three ways of frisking a philosophical theory. You may try to misunderstand it which in philosophy requires almost no effort at all. Almost anyone can at once misunderstand a philosophical statement. This method is very popular, very chuckling, but also very exasperating. In any case I have already forsworn the obvious advantages of this and must resort to something else. Fortunately there are other ways. You may then in the second place try to refute the theory in question. In this case you settle upon some clear and plausible import of the theory, and then you discover some contradiction. The contradiction must be hidden, subtle, and for the best results should pop out like a jack-in-the-box. You show that the theory conceals a jack-in-the-theory, which the theory on its face denied. The theory said: "No, no, there's no little jack," and then you pressed a little word, and out popped jack. This method is ideal, absolutely ruinous, guaranteed to fluster. Every philosopher submits to it with modesty, and, after three minutes, with cheers, whenever, that is, he also recognizes the little jack. The most authentic and last case of this sort is, as you will remember, recorded with a new-fangled pen in the reminiscences of a certain Thales whose comment on this has amused many scholars since. His comment is, "Of this too it may be said that all is wet." There is a third method which is this. You may try to understand the theory in question. This is, of course, a very dangerous expedient. It is clear that having understood the theory you may be taken in by it, and so suffer the corruption which you certainly intended at the outset to avoid. On the other hand you may discover that what you have come to understand turns out now to be so trivial that all your effort can scarcely be dignified by the admission. It's quite all right to leap bravely from one's horse to let the blood of a wind-mill, so long as you can keep on calling the wind-mill Beelzebub. But who would fence with a piece of wood? So the risk is great. There are, however, rewards. A little corruption will no doubt improve everyone.

And now I should like to try the second of these methods, refutation. And let us settle without very nice circumspection upon this sentence: "Only scientific method is successful." Can this sentence be refuted?

Now there certainly are people who think that it can be refuted. These refutations take at least two forms. There are first of all people who argue in this way. They say: "The application of scientific method, whatever it is, does involve thinking. Now thinking itself pre-supposes certain facts, namely, the laws of thought. For the truth of these laws there can be no evidence, for any evidence at all would once again pre-suppose them. Hence, since we obviously do know these laws, there obviously is knowledge, other than knowledge arrived at by scientific method." Nor is this all. It is clear that without the application of mathematics, scientific method would have been almost impotent. Now then, mathematics is also knowledge, and it is not commonly maintained even by those who are so excited by scientific method that there is anything experimental about mathematics. Once more, then, there is a type of knowledge, namely, mathematics—ask any mathematician whether he knows mathematics. And this is not knowledge which in any way depends upon scientific method. Both of these considerations seem so obvious that it is very curious there should be naturalists at all. Doesn't the naturalist then know, has he never heard, about the laws of thought and about numbers?

Of course he does and has, and yet he does not admit the refutation. What, then, does he say? Well, bluntly, that what in the proposed refutation is cited as knowledge, is not knowledge at all. There are logicians and there are mathematicians, but in these capacities they are not Knowers. The question here is as to what leads naturalists to speak so curiously, and then, once we have understood this, the further question is whether or not there still remains some intelligible issue as between the naturalist and his refuter. I am not at all certain now that I can represent this matter correctly, but I will do my best. Suppose we admit that knowledge is always about something or other. So if we know that thunder follows lightning, then what we know is something described by that sentence, and not at all to be identified with that sentence. We all know what this means. Now suppose we ask: "Do the laws of thought describe anything? Is that they do not, what you mean by their being laws? Further does 2 + 2 = 4 describe something?" If you hesitate over these questions, then I think that you have some inkling as to what the naturalist here has in mind. That thunder follows lightning may be knowledge, since you can very well imagine what it would be like for it to be false. But that the laws of thought should be false, or that 2 + 2 should not equal 4, both of these are inconceivable. This, so far as I can see, is the main motive underlying the statement that logic and mathematics are not knowledge. And so far at any rate there is no issue. Both the naturalist and the refuter are agreed. Scientific method does not pre-suppose any other type of knowledge. For logic and mathematics are not knowledge.

The issue which we have just now discussed has turned out to be a verbal one. There are, however, related issues which are interesting. We all remember that when Socrates questioned the boy in the *Meno* he showed that the boy knew things which he had never been taught, that these things were true, and that he must have come to know them by recollection. When Kant questioned the same boy he too showed that the boy knew *a priori* things which he had never been taught, that these things were true, and that he came to know them because all little boys are like that. When today the naturalist questions that boy he discovers that boy still answering as he answered Socrates and Kant. He knows his grammar. Where did he get it? Well, grammar and the laws of thought are historical accidents. Who could have predicted that the squirrel would have such a bushy tail? Who could have predicted that a creature without any tail at all should have written the *Iliad*? You never can tell. Now Socrates was amazed at the bright boy, and describes him as a reminiscing soul on tour. He learns his mathematics in one world and is furnished with it, ready for Euclid in the next, a romance of two worlds! Kant too is puzzled by the boy, but not by the origins of his prodigy. Marvelous boy! anticipating the whole structure of the world by being the creator of it. Both Socrates and Kant did not know what we now know. The little boy is an organism, part of a long line of adaptation, missing poisons, dodging rocks, escaping tigers, milking cows, sowing seed, fetching fish, but, most important of all, saying the word. To milk a cow one must have a hand to fit and flush an udder. To say the word one must have an order to fit and flash one's prescience. What is the history of the hand, from hoof to dainty pats upon your cheek? Ask Darwin. What is the history of the laws of thought and 2 + 2 = 4? Ask

Darwin's brother. No one could have predicted what the laws of thought would be, had prediction been possible without the laws of thought.

I have no intention, however, of considering this matter further. The issue appears to be empirical. It is interesting, however, as an illustration of how the naturalist's view of scientific method, and of distinctions involved in it, is intertwined with certain results of the application of scientific method. This is the biologist's view of the origin of the *a priori*. And part of the point here is to insist that the presence of logic and mathematics are as irrelevant to the existence of anything else as is the presence of the monkey's tail. The tail like the appendix may be positively misleading. There may be a tail and no trees, and no flies. So what about the laws of thought. They too may turn out to be useless. Am I talking nonsense? I'm sorry.

And now there is a second type of refutation. The refuter goes on: "You may be quite right when you say that scientific method is successful. The libraries and the stores are full of its success. But we also know that scientific method has never been justified from a purely intellectual point of view. Now I do not necessarily mean that we know what that justification is, so that once more we have knowledge which is not arrived at by pursuing scientific method. I mean rather that this request for a justification involves a question which can not possibly be answered by any such method. If you tried to answer it in this way, your method would, of course, give rise to the same request. Hence, unless we admit that there are altogether reasonable questions, but no method at all for answering them, there must be at least one method other than scientific method for answering questions. And so it is not true that scientific method alone is successful."

And is the naturalist now quite perturbed by this? He

is not. His reply might be as follows: "I think I understand you. You are assuming that a good argument must be tight like a syllogism or like a proof in geometry. That's what you mean by the phrase 'from a purely intellectual point of view.' So you are worried about the uniformity of nature, that every event in nature has a cause, that tomorrow the sun will rise, and tomorrow and tomorrow and petty-paced tomorrow. If you only knew things like this, then you would consider conclusions about fruit flies, about hydrogen, about vitamins, etc., as justified. But actually the conclusions of science are not presumed to be tight in any such sense. Now listen. It's all very simple. Yesterday and today we find uranium, under certain circumstances, behaving as though it were very angry. Tomorrow it is angry again. Next week it still behaves angrily. So we go on expecting that it will continue to do so and it does. If, however, in four weeks it should quite suddenly be mild and bleat like a little lamb, this would certainly surprise us. Who knows, however, a little angry uranium may be enough to put all the remainder fast asleep, so that even bombardment could scarcely make it yawn. Scientists after all are only human. They do no more than record the genesis of their expectations. So what we mean, in any case, by the success of scientific method is something so modest that it requires no such justification. It is justified, if you like, in the same way that your expectations generally are. If you expect to eat at six, and do eat at six, what more do you want?"

This reply is, I take it, sufficient. Refutation has failed. If you claim for science that its arguments require some necessary propositions about the order of nature, then obviously the justification of these arguments will require them. But the naturalist's account of scientific method need not involve any such necessary propositions. So once again, that scientific method is successful does not pre-suppose that there is besides this some other method.

The statement of naturalism, then, involves no contradiction. Can we not, however, move him by confronting him with a discrepant instance? No. But let's see.

Mr. Dennes says that there are no other proofs. X, which vaunteth itself a proof, comes up and says: "Am I a proof? They call me a proof." So the doctor touches a nerve, the nerve of the argument, and says: "No, you're not a proof." X replies: "But I wear a 'since' and a 'therefore.' " The doctor says: "And that's all. You've no nerve, so you're not a proof." He knows what he means by a "proof." Other candidates come up, each asking: "Am I a proof?" And the doctor separates them. Now up comes a philosophical proof. "Am I a proof?" The answer is: "No." But the proof now argues: "That's what you say, and I see what you mean, I am not the kind of proof you are talking about. My friends do not use the word 'proof' at all in the way in which you do. I'm a proof all right, but you just don't like me. So you won't call me proof. It's as though I asked you 'Am I a darling?' and you had another sweetheart, and so, of course, you said: 'No.' All the same I am a darling."

This, now, is a very difficult situation. Nobody is lying. Nobody is insincere. Does the doctor see something which the philosophical argument does not see? Maybe. He sees both types of argument, and sees that the one is good and the other is not. And what does the philosophical argument see? It sees both arguments and says that both are good. So once more if the argument asks: "And why do you say I am not a proof?" the doctor must say: "Because you are not like this." And that is all there is to it. And if this is all, then, clearly, the philosophical argument may feel thoroughly vindicated. If all the doctor means is that a philosophical argument is different from an empirical argument, the argument may respond: "Of course, that's true, but it has no bearing upon my status. After all I am another man's darling."

Suppose that he goes on to say: "No, I don't mean simply that you are not like this argument. What I mean is this: 'This type of argument is successful, and you are not.' " The response is: "And what is the criterion of success? If you mean that by means of me you can never predict the weather, well, of course, that's true. But if you ask those who love me whether I am successful, you'll get a different answer. I determine in some much subtler way the spiritual weather, and that not by prediction but by seasoning all time and eternity. Success! How would you like to be a thinking substance?"

So far as I can see there is nothing further for the doctor to do. He has judged the proof, but he can not now justify that judgment to the argument. There is no agreed-upon principle of adjudication. Further argument is futile. To each other they must continue to be queer and incomprehensible. It's as though the boys in our alley all sang out: "There's no girl but pretty Sally," and someone objected: "Oh, but that can't be!" This didn't quiet the boys. They said: "Oh, you forget that once Eve was the only girl. So it can be." And then along came Helen. "Tut! Tut!" said she, "Look at me. I'm a girl," to which the boys responded, "No, you're not." And when she said "Prove it," they laughed, told her to go home and be quiet. "You're just a girl out of a store window, that's what you are."

So far I have shown that you can not refute this apparent main thesis of naturalism. You can not do it by detecting any contradiction, nor by adducing any evidence. And you can not do this because there is no thesis. When Mr. Krikorian speaks of this sentence as a basic belief, this is strictly a mistake. There is no belief at all. There is no belief because nothing has been said which could be false.

How, then, are these several sentences to be interpreted? I think that something like this may do. These sentences are strictly an enunciation of policy. In effect they say: "Let us be scientific." And negatively: "No more metaphysics." In a sober and quiet way a naturalist might say: "I've tried to do metaphysics. I can't grasp it. So I've turned to matters within my reach and grasp. I can do botany so much better. Or I can cut hair or polish teeth." If this were now what naturalists did, there would, I think, be no mystery at all. What causes the difficulty is that having said: "We are going to do science," they do not do science. If a man who sold groceries suddenly tired of selling groceries, exclaimed: "Enough! I am going to wash automobiles," and went out and washed automobiles, there would be no puzzle about this. But if he repeated his resolution frequently, put on his hat and coat and walked to the door, and then started for the other side of the store to sort potatoes, what then? Well, so it is.

Is, then, naturalism, in any case, a good policy? I think that the naturalists' defense is this. Metaphysics and science aim at the same thing. Metaphysics fails. Science succeeds. Accordingly, naturalism is nothing but adoption of the successful policy. Who, to get home, would deliberately take the way that won't get him there? And the naturalist might go on. Even though it were true that metaphysics and science do not aim at the same thing, it is clear that metaphysics fails in whatever it aims at, whereas science succeeds. How foolish, then, to engage in failure. So in either case naturalism is the best policy.

Once more, then, the dispute breaks out. Do

metaphysics and science aim at the same thing? Is metaphysics a failure? Disregarding, for the moment, the obscurity of both these questions, I should, throwing my words about wildly, make this noise. Metaphysics and science do not aim at the same thing. And now I should first like to explain this. Metaphysics arises out of the fact that men come to have a variety of beliefs, beliefs about God, about how they should live, about the material world, about their own otherworldly destiny, etc. Some expurgated people escape nearly all such beliefs, but most people either believe or are uneasy. In any case, with respect to such beliefs, men have tried to do two things. They have first tried to prove that what they believe is true. In this respect there certainly is an analogy between science and metaphysics, and this may be what justifies the naturalist thesis. For if he now also holds that it is precisely in this respect that metaphysics has failed, namely, in its attempt to prove, then I, at least, am inclined to agree that he is right. For there is in metaphysics no criterion of proof. It take it that there is among metaphysicians no agreement upon even one purported proof. If, then, the purpose of metaphysics is to prove, metaphysics provides no intelligible account of what this could be.

This is not, however, the whole story. Men have also tried in their metaphysical adventures to weave together the contents of their beliefs into some coherent pattern, to keep more steadfastly before their minds the scene of their hopes, their aspirations, and their fears. In the past the aim to prove has clouded and vexed this endeavor by an ungainly and tortured vocabulary, but, even so, the present ruins in some way, no doubt, served. I expect that varieties of belief will continue, and that this motive to elaborate and to fashion a crazy or a sane quilt in which to wrap oneself against all temporary weathers will continue. And I do not mind. I shall continue to be entertained by it, and will in one instance even love it. Nevertheless, I think that metaphysics with this single aim will, when successful, be much more like poetry or a novel than like the metaphysics which, with divided and obscure aims, has puzzled and pleased men in the past.

Naturalism, as a policy, is then no mystery. It has seized upon a certain clear notion of proof, and in the light of this clear notion of proof it is easy to see from what defect metaphysics has come to be so sick. Metaphysics will walk again only when it surrenders pretension to proof, and, as humbly as the Apostles' Creed, begins its words with: I believe!

NOTES

[1] *Naturalism and the Human Spirit*, ed. Y. H. Krikorian (New York: Columbia University Press, 1944), p. 63.

[2] *Ibid.*, p. 45.

[3] *Ibid.*, p. 2.

[4] *Ibid.*, p. 289.

[5] *Ibid.*, p. 242.

25. D. T. Suzuki: "The Ten Cow-Herding Pictures"

D. T. Suzuki (1870–1966) was substantially responsible for the introduction of Zen Buddhism to the Western mind. Simplicity in approach and mastery of clarity and scholarship combined to make his works, which include *Studies in Zen* and *Mysticism, Christian and Buddhist,* among the most accessible studies in comparative religion. At the time of his death, he was Professor Emeritus of Buddhist Philosophy from Otani University, and had been active as a teacher of Buddhism in California.

THE TEN COW-HERDING PICTURES*

The attainment of Buddhahood or the realization of Enlightenment is what is aimed at by all pious Buddhists, though not necessarily during this one earthly

* From *Essays in Zen Buddhism,* Series 1, 1949. Used by permission of Hutchinson Publishing Group, Ltd.

life; and Zen, as one of the Mahāyāna schools, also teaches that all our efforts must be directed towards this supreme end. While most of the other schools distinguish so many steps of spiritual development and insist on one's going through all the grades successively in order to reach the consummation of the Buddhist discipline, Zen ignores all these, and boldly declares that when one sees into the inmost nature of one's own being, one instantly becomes a Buddha, and that there is no necessity of climbing up each rung of perfection through eternal cycles of transmigration. This has been one of the most characteristic tenets of Zen ever since the coming east of Bodhidharma in the sixth century. "See into thy own nature and be a Buddha" has thus grown the watchword of the Sect. And this "seeing" was not the outcome of much learning or speculation, nor was it due to the grace of the supreme Buddha conferred upon his ascetic followers; but it grew out of the special training of the mind prescribed by the Zen masters. This being so, Zen could not very well recognize any form of gradation in the attainment of Buddhahood. The "seeing into one's nature" was an instant act. There could not be any process in it which would permit scales or steps of development.

But in point of fact, where the time-element rules supreme, this was not necessarily the case. So long as our relative minds are made to comprehend one thing after another by degrees and in succession and not all at once and simultaneously, it is impossible not to speak of some kind of progress. Even Zen as something possible of demonstration in one way or another must be subjected to the limitations of time. That is to say, there are, after all, grades of development in its study; and some must be said to have more deeply, more penetratingly realized the truth of Zen. In itself the truth may transcend all form of limitation, but when it is to be realized in the human mind, its psychological laws are to be observed. The "seeing into thy nature" must admit degrees of clearness. Transcendentally we are all Buddhas just as we are, ignorant and sinful if you like; but when we come down to this practical life, pure idealism has to give way to a more particular and palpable form of activity. This side of Zen is known as its "constructive" aspect, in contradistinction to its "all-sweeping" aspect. And here Zen fully recognizes degrees of spiritual development among its followers, as the truth reveals itself gradually in their minds until the "seeing into one's nature" is perfected.

Technically speaking, Zen belongs to the group of Buddhist doctrines known as "discrete" or "discontinuous" or "abrupt" (*tun* in Chinese), in opposition to "continuous" or "gradual" (*chien*)[1]; and naturally the opening of the mind, according to Zen, comes upon one as a matter of discrete or sudden happening and not as the result of a gradual, continuous development whose every step can be traced and analysed. The coming of satori is not like the rising of the sun gradually bringing things to light, but it is like the freezing of water, which takes place abruptly. There is no middle or twilight condition before the mind is opened to the truth, in which there prevails a sort of neutral zone, or a state of intellectual indifference. As we have already observed in several instances of satori, the transition from ignorance to enlightenment is so abrupt, the common cur, as it were, suddenly turns into a golden-haired lion. Zen is an ultra-discrete wing of Buddhism. But this holds true only when the truth of Zen itself is considered, apart from its relation to the human mind in which it is disclosed. Inasmuch as the truth is true only when it is considered in the light it gives to the mind and cannot be thought of at all independent of the latter, we may speak of its gradual and progressive realization in us. The psychological laws exist here as elsewhere. Therefore when Bodhidharma was ready to leave China he said that Dōfuku got the skin, the nun Sōji got the flesh, and Dōiku the bone, while Yeka had the marrow (or essence) of Zen.

Nangaku, who succeeded the sixth patriarch, had six accomplished disciples, but their attainments differed in depth. He compared them with various parts of the body, and said: "You all have testified to my body, but each has grasped a part of it. The one who has my eyebrows is the master of manners; the second, who has my eyes, knows how to look around; the third, who has my ears, understands how to listen to reasoning; the fourth, who has my nose, is well versed in the act of breathing; the fifth, who has my tongue, is a great arguer; and finally, the one who has my mind knows the past and the present." This gradation was impossible if "seeing into one's nature" alone was considered; for the seeing is one indivisible act, allowing no stages of transition. It is, however, no contradiction of the principle of satori, as we have repeatedly asserted, to say that in fact there is a progressive realization in the seeing, leading one deeper and deeper into the truth of Zen, finally culminating in one's complete identification with it.

Lieh-tzŭ, the Chinese philosopher of Taoism, describes in the following passage certain marked stages of development in the practice of Tao:

> The teacher of Lieh-tzŭ was Lao-shang-shih, and his friend Pai-kao-tzŭ. When Lieh-tzŭ was well advanced in the teachings of these two philosophers, he came home riding on the wind. Yin-shêng heard of this and came to Lieh-tzŭ to be instructed. Yin-shêng neglected his own household for several months. He never lost opportunities to ask the master to instruct him in the arts [of

riding on the wind]; he asked ten times, and was refused each time. Yin-shêng grew impatient and wanted to depart. Lieh-tzŭ did not urge him to stay. For several months Yin-shêng kept himself away from the master, but did not feel any easier in his mind. He came over to Lieh-tzŭ again. Asked the master, "Why this constant coming back and forth?" Yin-shêng replied, "The other day, I, Chang Tai, wished to be instructed by you, but you refused to teach me, which naturally I did not like. I feel, however, no grudge against you now, hence my presence here again."

"I thought the other time," said the master, "you understood it all. But seeing now what a commonplace mortal you are, I will tell you what I have learned under the master. Sit down and listen! It was three years after I went to my master Lao-shang and my friend Pai-kao that my mind began to cease thinking of right and wrong, and my tongue talking of gain and loss, whereby he favoured me with just a glance. At the end of five years my mind again began to think of right and wrong, and my tongue to talk about gain and loss. Then for the first time the master relaxed his expression and gave me a smile. At the end of seven years I just let my mind think of whatever it pleased, and there was no more question of right and wrong, I just let my tongue talk of whatever it pleased, and there was no more question of gain and loss. Then for the first time the master beckoned me to sit beside him. At the end of nine years, just letting my mind think of whatever it pleased and letting my tongue talk of whatever it pleased, I was not conscious whether I or anybody else was in the right or wrong, whether I or anybody else gained or lost; nor was I aware of the old master's being my teacher or the young Pai-kao's being my friend. Both inwardly and outwardly I was advanced. It was then that the eye was like the ear, and the ear like the nose, and the nose like the mouth; for they were all one and the same. The mind was in rapture, the form dissolved, and the bones and flesh all thawed away; and I did not know how the frame supported itself and what the feet were treading upon. I gave myself away to the wind, eastward or westward, like leaves of a tree or like a dry chaff. Was the wind riding on me? or was I riding on the wind? I did not know either way.

"Your stay with the master has not covered much space of time, and you are already feeling grudge against him. The air will not hold even a fragment of your body, nor will the earth support one member of yours. How then could you ever think of treading on empty space and riding the wind?"

Yin-shêng was much ashamed and kept quiet for some time, not uttering even a word.

The Christian and Mahommedan mystics also mark the stages of spiritual development. Some Sufis describe the "seven valleys"[2] to traverse in order to reach the court of Simburgh, where the mystic "birds" find themselves gloriously effaced and yet fully reflected in the Awful Presence of themselves. The "seven valleys" are: 1. The Valley of Search; 2. The Valley of Love, which has no limits; 3. The Valley of Knowledge; 4. The Valley of Independence; 5. The Valley of Unity, pure and simple; 6. The Valley of Amazement; and 7. The Valley of Poverty and Annihilation, beyond which there is no advance. According to St. Teresa, there are four degrees of mystic life: Meditation, Quiet, a numberless intermediate degree, and the Orison of Unity; while Hugo of St. Victor has also his own four degrees: Meditation, Soliloquy, Consideration, and Rapture. There are other Christian mystics having their own three or four steps of "ardent love" or of "contemplation."[3]

Professor R. A. Nicholson gives in his *Studies in Islamic Mysticism* a translation of Ibnu 'I-Fárid's "The Poem of the Mystic's Progress" (*Tá'iyya*), parts of which at least are such exact counterparts of Buddhist mysticism as to make us think that the Persian poet is simply echoing the Zen sentiment. Whenever we come across such a piece of mystic literature, we cannot help being struck with the inmost harmony of thought and feeling resonant in the depths of human soul, regardless of its outward accidental differences. The verses 326 and 327 of the *Tá'iyya* read:

> From "I am She" I mounted to where is no "to," and I perfumed [phenomenal] existence by my returning:
> And [I returned] from "I am I" for the sake of an esoteric wisdom and external laws which were instituted that I might call [the people to God].

The passage as it stands here is not very intelligible, but read the translator's comments which throw so much light on the way the Persian thought flows:

> Three stages of Oneness (*ittihád*) are distinguished here: 1. "I am She," i.e. union (*jam'*) without real separation (*tafriqa*), although the appearance of separation is maintained. This was the stage in which al-Halláj said "*Ana 'l-Haqq*," "I am God." 2. "I am I," i.e. pure union without any trace of separation (individuality). This stage is technically known as the "intoxication of union" (*sukru 'l-jam'*). 3. The "sobriety of union" (*sahwu 'l-jam'*), i.e. the stage in which the mystic returns from the pure oneness of the second stage to plurality in oneness and to separation in union and to the Law in the Truth, so that while continuing to be united with God he serves Him as a slave serves his lord and manifests the Divine Life in its perfection to mankind.
>
> "Where is no 'to,' " i.e. the stage of "I am I," beyond which no advance is possible except by means of retrogression. In this stage the mystic is entirely absorbed in the undifferentiated oneness of God. Only after he had "returned," i.e. entered upon the third stage (plurality in oneness), can he communicate to his fellows some perfume (hint) of the experience through which he has passed. "An esoteric wisdom," i.e. the Divine providence manifested by means of the religious law. By

returning to consciousness, the "united" mystic is enabled to fulfill the law and to act as a spiritual director.

When this is compared with the progress of the Zen mystic, as is pictorially illustrated and poetically commented in the following pages, we feel that the comments were written expressly for Zen Buddhism.

During the Sung dynasty a Zen teacher called Seikyo illustrated stages of spiritual progress by a gradual purification or whitening of the cow until she herself disappears. But the pictures, six in number, are lost now.[4] Those that are still in existence, illustrating the end of Zen discipline in a more thorough and consistent manner, come from the ingenious brush of Kakuan, a monk belonging to the Rinzai school. His are, in fact, a revision and perfection of those of his predecessor. The pictures are ten in number, and each has a short introduction in prose, followed by a commentary verse, both of which are translated below. There were some other masters who composed stanzas on the same subjects using the rhymes of the first commentator, and some of them are found in the popular edition of "The Ten Cow-herding Pictures."

The cow has been worshipped by the Indians from very early periods of their history. The allusions are found in various connections in the Buddhist scriptures. In a Hinayana Sutra entitled "On the Herding of Cattle,"[5] eleven ways of properly attending them are described. In a similar manner a monk ought to observe eleven things properly in order to become a good Buddhist; and if he fails to do so, just like the cow-herd who neglects his duties, he will be condemned. The eleven ways of properly attending cattle are: 1. To know the colours; 2. To know the signs; 3. Brushing; 4.

Dressing the wounds; 5. Making smoke; 6. Walking the right path; 7. Tenderly feeling for them; 8. Fording the streams; 9. Pasturing; 10. Milking; 11. Selecting. Some of the items cited here are not quite intelligible.

In the *Saddharma-pundaríka Sūtra,* chapter iii, "A Parable," the Buddha gives the famous parable of three carts—bullock-carts, goat-carts, and deer-carts—which a man promises to give to his children if they come out of a house on fire. The finest of the carts is the one drawn by bullocks or cows (*goratha*), which represents the vehicle for the Bodhisattvas, the greatest and most magnificent of all vehicles, leading them directly to the attainment of supreme enlightenment. The cart is described thus in the Sūtra: "Made of seven precious substances, provided with benches, hung with a multitude of small bells, lofty, adorned with rare and wonderful jewels, embellished with jewel wreaths, decorated with garlands of flowers, carpeted with cotton mattresses and woollen coverlets, covered with white cloth and silk, having on both sides rosy cushions, yoked with white, very fair and fleet bullocks, led by a multitude of men."

Thus reference came to be made quite frequently in Zen literature to the "white cow on the open-air square of the village," or to the cow in general. For instance, Tai-an of Fu-chou asked Pai-chang, "I wish to know about the Buddha; what is he?" Answered Pai-chang, "It is like seeking for an ox while you are yourself on it." "What shall I do after I know?" "It is like going home riding on it." "How do I look after it all the time in order to be in accordance with [the Dharma]?" The master then told him, "You should behave like a cowherd, who, carrying a staff, sees to it that his cattle won't wander away into somebody else's rice-fields."

"The Ten Cow-herding Pictures" showing the upward steps of spiritual training is doubtless another such instance, more elaborate and systematized than the one just cited.

THE TEN STAGES OF SPIRITUAL COW-HERDING

I

Looking for the Cow. She has never gone astray, so what is the use of searching for her? We are not on intimate terms with her, because we have contrived against our inmost nature. She is lost, for we have ourselves been led out of the way through the deluding senses. The home is growing farther away, and byways and crossways are ever confusing. Desire for gain and fear of loss burn like fire, ideas of right and wrong shoot up like a phalanx.

Alone in the wilderness, lost in the jungle, he is searching, searching!
The swelling waters, far-away mountains, and unending path;
Exhausted and in despair, he knows not where to go,
He only hears the evening cicadas singing in the maple-woods.

II

Seeing the Traces of the Cow. By the aid of the Sūtras and by inquiring into the doctrines he has come to understand something; he has found the traces. He now knows that things, however multitudinous, are of one substance, and that the objective world is a reflection of the self. Yet he is unable to distinguish what is good from what is not; his mind is still confused as to truth and falsehood. As he has not yet entered the gate, he is provisionally said to have noticed the traces.

By the water, under the trees, scattered are the traces of the lost:

Fragrant woods are growing thick—did he find the way?
However remote, over the hills and far away, the cow may wander,
Her nose reaches the heavens and none can conceal it.

III

Seeing the Cow. He finds the way through the sound; he sees into the origin of things, and all his senses are in harmonious order. In all his activities it is manifestly present. It is like the salt in water and the glue in colour. [It is there, though not separably distinguishable.] When the eye is properly directed, he will find that it is no other thing than himself.

Yonder perching on a branch a nightingale sings cheerfully;
The sun is warm, the soothing breeze blows through the willows green on the bank;
The cow is there all by herself; nowhere is there room to hide herself;
The splendid head decorated with stately horns, what painter can reproduce her?

IV

Catching the Cow. After getting lost long in the wilderness, he has at last found the cow and laid hand on her. But owing to the overwhelming pressure of the objective world, the cow is found hard to keep under control. She constantly longs for sweet grasses. The wild nature is still unruly, and altogether refuses to be broken in. If he wishes to have her completely in subjection, he ought to use the whip freely.

With the energy of his whole soul, he has at last taken hold of the cow:

But how wild her will, ungovernable her power!
At times she struts up a plateau,
When lo! she is lost in a misty, impenetrable mountain-pass.

V

Herding the Cow. When a thought moves, another follows, and then another—there is thus awakened an endless train of thoughts. Through enlightenment all this turns into truth; but falsehood asserts itself when confusion prevails. Things oppress us not because of an objective world, but because of a self-deceiving mind. Do not get the nose-string loose; hold it tight, and allow yourself no indulgence.

Never let yourself be separated from the whip and the tether,
Lest she should wander away into a world of defilement:
When she is properly tended, she will grow pure and docile,
Even without chain, nothing binding, she will by herself follow you.

VI

Coming Home on the Cow's Back. The struggle is over; he is no more concerned with gain and loss. He hums a rustic tune of the woodman, he sings simple songs of the village-boy. Saddling himself on the cow's back, his eyes are fixed on things not of the earth, earthy. Even if he is called to, he will not turn his head; however enticed, he will no more be kept back.

Riding the cow he leisurely wends his way home:
Enveloped in the evening mist, how tunefully the flute vanishes away!

Singing a ditty, beating time, his heart is filled with a
joy indescribable!
That he is now one of those who know, need it be told?

VII

The Cow Forgotten, Leaving the Man Alone. Things are one and the cow is symbolic. When you know that what you need is not the snare or set-net but the hare or fish, it is like gold separated from the dross, it is like the moon rising out of the clouds. The one ray of light serene and penetrating shines even before days of creation.

Riding on the cow he is at last back in his home,
Where lo! there is no more the cow, and how serenely
he sits all alone!
Though the red sun is held up in the sky, he seems to
be still quietly asleep;
Under a straw-thatched roof are his whip and rope idly
lying beside him.

VIII

The Cow and the Man Both Gone out of Sight. All confusion is set aside, and serenity alone prevails; even the idea of holiness does not obtain. He does not linger about where the Buddha is, and as to where there is no Buddha he speedily passes on. When there exists no form of dualism, even a thousand-eyed one fails to detect a loophole. A holiness before which birds offer flowers is but a farce.[6]

All is empty, the whip, the rope, the man, and the cow:
Who has ever surveyed the vastness of heaven?
Over the furnace burning ablaze, not a flake of snow
can fall:
When this state of things obtains, manifest is the spirit
of the ancient master.

IX

Returning to the Origin, Back to the Source. From the very beginning, pure and immaculate, he has never been affected by defilement. He calmly watches the growth and decay of things with form, while himself abiding in the immovable serenity of non-assertion. When he does not identify himself with magic-like transformations, what has he to do with artificialities of self-discipline? The water flows blue, the mountain towers green. Sitting alone, he observes things undergoing changes.

To return to the Origin, to be back at the Source—already a false step this!
Far better it is to stay home, blind and deaf, straightway and without much ado.
Sitting within the hut he takes no cognizance of things outside,
Behold the water flowing on—whither nobody knows; and those flowers red and fresh—for whom are they?

X

Entering the City with Bliss-bestowing Hands. His humble cottage door is closed, and the wisest know him not. No glimpses of his inner life are to be caught; for he goes on his own way without following the steps of the ancient sages. Carrying a gourd he goes out into the market; leaning against a stick he comes home. He is found in company with wine-bibbers and butchers; he and they are all converted into Buddhas.

Barechested and barefooted, he comes out into the marketplace;
Daubed with mud and ashes, how broadly he smiles!
There is no need for the miraculous power of the gods,

For he touches, and lo! the dead trees come into full bloom.

[1] Cf. also "History of Zen Buddhism," where reference is made to the Northern and Southern school of Zen under the fifth patriarch in China.

[2] According to Fariduddin Attar, A.D. 1119–1229, of Khorassan, Persia. Cf. Claud Field's *Mystics and Saints of Islam*, p. 123 et seq.

[3] Underhill—*Mysticism*, p. 369.

[4] Since this book went to press I have come across an old edition of the spiritual cow-herding pictures, which end with an empty circle corresponding to the eighth of the present series. Is this the work of Seikyo as referred to in Kakuan's Preface? The cow is shown to be whitening here gradually with the progress of discipline.

[5] See also a Sūtra in the Anguttara Āgama bearing the same title which is evidently another translation of the same text. Also compare "The Herdsman, I," in *The First Fifty Discourses of Gotama the Buddha*, Vol. II, by Bhikkhu Śīlācāra. (Leipzig, 1913.) This is a partial translation of the Majjhima Nikāya of the Pāli Tripitaka. The eleven items as enumerated in the Chinese version are just a little differently given. Essentially, of course, they are the same in both texts. A Buddhist dictionary called *Daizo Hossu* gives reference on the subject to the great Mahāyāna work of Nāgārjuan, the Mahāprajñāpāramitā-Sūtra, but so far I have not been able to identify the passage.

[6] It will be interesting to note what a mystic philosopher would say about this: "A man shall become truly poor and as free from his creature will as he was when he was born. And I say to you, by the eternal truth, that as long as ye desire to fulfil the will of God, and have any desire after eternity and God; so long are ye not truly poor. He alone hath true spiritual poverty who wills nothing, knows nothing, desires nothing."—From Eckhart as quoted by Inge in *Light, Life, and Love.*

Selected Bibliography

Adorno, T. *The Jargon of Authenticity,* tr. by K. Ternowski and F. Will. Evanston: Northwestern Univ. Press, 1973.

Aldrich, Virgil C. "John Dewey's Use of Language." *Journal of Philosophy,* 41 (1944), pp. 261–270.

Barthes, R. *Essais critiques.* Paris: Editions du Seuil, 1964.

Brown, N. O. *Life Against Death.* Middletown, Conn.: Wesleyan Univ. Press, 1959.

Brown, R. H. *A Poetic for Sociology.* New York: Cambridge Univ. Press, 1977.

Charlton, W. "Is Philosophy a Form of Literature?" *British Journal of Aesthetics,* 14 (1974), pp. 3–16.

Colie, R. "The Essayist in the Essay." *John Locke: Problems and Perspectives,* ed. by J. W. Yolton. Cambridge: Cambridge Univ. Press, 1969.

Curtius, E. R. *European Literature and the Latin Middle Ages,* tr. by W. R. Trask. Princeton: Princeton Univ. Press, 1953.

De Man, P. "Political Allegory in Rousseau." *Critical Inquiry,* 2 (1976), pp. 649–75.

Derrida, J. "White Mythology." *New Literary History*, 6 (1974), pp. 5–74.

Derrida, J. *Writing and Difference*, tr. by A. Bass. Chicago: Univ. of Chicago Press, 1978.

Donato, E. "Idioms of the Text: Notes on the Language of Philosophy and the Fictions of Literature." *Glyph*, 2 (1977), pp. 1–13.

Foucault, M. "What Is an Author?" *Partisan Review*, 42 (1975), pp. 603–14.

Gadamer, H. G. *Philosophical Hermeneutics*, tr. by D. E. Linge. Berkeley: Univ. of California Press, 1976.

Gray, J. G. "Poets and Thinkers: Their Kindred Role in the Philosophy of Martin Heidegger." *Phenomenology and Existentialism*, ed. by E. N. Lee and M. Mandelbaum. Baltimore: Johns Hopkins Univ. Press, 1967.

Habermas, J. *Knowledge and Human Interest*, tr. by J. J. Shapiro. Boston: Beacon Press, 1971.

Hippolyte, J. "The Structure of Philosophical Language according to the 'Preface' to Hegel's *Phenomenology of the Mind*." *The Languages of Criticism and the Sciences of Man*, ed. by R. Macksey and E. Donato. Baltimore: Johns Hopkins Univ. Press, 1970.

Jameson, F. *Sartre: The Origins of a Style*. New Haven: Yale Univ. Press, 1961.

Johnstone, J. W. *Philosophy and Argument*. University Park, Pa.: Pennsylvania State Univ. Press, 1959.

Kenney, A. "The Stylometric Study of the Aristotelian Writings." *Cirpho*, 3 (1975), pp. 5–32.

Lang, B. "Presentation and Representation in Plato's Dialogues." *Philosophical Forum*, 4 (1974), pp. 224–40.

Levi, A. W. *Philosophy as Social Expression*. Chicago: Univ. of Chicago Press, 1974.

Mackey, L. *Kierkegaard: A Kind of Poet*. Philadelphia: Univ. of Pennsylvania Press, 1971.

Marcuse, H. *One-Dimensional Man*. Boston: Beacon Press, 1964.

Marias, J. *Philosophy as Dramatic Theory*, tr. by J. Parsons. University Park, Pa.: Pennsylvania State Univ. Press, 1971.

McKeon, R. "Philosophy and Method." *Journal of Philosophy*, 48 (1951), pp. 653–82.

McLuhan, M. *The Gutenberg Galaxy*. Toronto: Univ. of Toronto Press, 1962.

Mink, L. *Mind, History, and Dialectic.* Bloomington: Indiana Univ. Press, 1969.

Ong, W. J. *The Presence of the Word.* New Haven: Yale Univ. Press, 1967.

Passmore, J. A. *Philosophical Reasoning.* New York: Scribner's, 1961.

Perelman, C. and L. Olbrechts-Tyteca. *Rhetorique et philosophie: pour une theorie de l'argumentation en philosophie.* Paris: Press Universitaire de France, 1952.

Pines, S. "The Philosophic Sources of *The Guide of the Perplexed.*" Introduction to M. Maimonides, *The Guide of the Perplexed.* Chicago: Univ. of Chicago Press, 1963.

Ricoeur, P. *The Conflict of Interpretations,* ed. by D. Ihde. Evanston: Northwestern Univ. Press, 1974.

Rotenstreich, N. "On the Justification of Philosophical Systems." *Entretieus de L'Institut International de Philosophie* (September, 1967), pp. 305–10.

Simpson, D. "Putting One's House in Order: The Career of the Self in Descartes' Method." *New Literary History,* 9 (1977), pp. 83–102.

Stallknecht, N. P. and R. S. Brumbaugh. *The Compass of Philosophy.* New York: Longmans, Green, 1954.

Vickers, B. *Francis Bacon and Renaissance Prose.* Cambridge: Harvard Univ. Press, 1968.

White, H. *Metahistory.* Baltimore: Johns Hopkins Univ. Press, 1973.

Wolfson, H. *Philo.* Cambridge: Harvard Univ. Press, 1947.

Yates, F. *The Art of Memory.* Chicago: Univ. of Chicago Press, 1966.

Zaner, R. "Philosophy and Rhetoric: A Critical Discussion." *Philosophy and Rhetoric,* 1 (1968), pp. 61–78.

Sources

Selections are taken from the following sources with permission of the publishers:

Plato. VIIth Letter, 341b–345b; *Phaedrus*, 274b–278b; *Phaedo*, 89d–91c. From *Plato: Collected Dialogues*, ed. by E. Hamilton and H. Cairns. New York: Bollingen Series, Pantheon, 1964.

Aristotle. *Physics*, Bk I, Ch 1, 184a9–184b13; *Posterior Analytics*, Bk II, Ch 19, 89b20–100a12; *Nicomachean Ethics*, Bk I, Ch 3, 1094b12–1095a13; *Rhetoric*, Bk III, Ch 1, 1403b15–20, Bk III, Ch 27, 1418a37–1418b1; *On the Heavens*, 294b6–13, 299l5–6, 306a6–16; *Poetics*, 1447a2b–1447b16 (Loeb Library Editions).

Augustine. *De Magistro*, trans. and ed. by J. H. S. Burleigh, in *Augustine: Earlier Writings*. Philadelphia: The Westminster Press, 1953, pp. 94–101.

D. Hume. *A Treatise on Human Nature*, Bk I, Part IV, Section VII; *Essays: Moral, Political, and Literary*. Oxford: Oxford Univ. Press, 1963, pp. 196–202, 568–572.

I. Kant. *Critique of Pure Reason*, tr. by N. K. Smith. New

York: St. Martin's Press, 1961, pp. 10–14, 654–658; letter to M. Mendelssohn, 16 August 1783. Reprinted and tr. by A. Zweig, *Kant: Philosophical Correspondence (1759–99)*. Chicago: Univ. of Chicago Press, 1967, pp. 105–107.

S. Kierkegaard. *Either/Or*, Vol. I, tr. by D. F. Swenson. New York: Doubleday Anchor Books, 1959, pp. 20, 31; *The Point of View for My Work as an Author*, tr. by W. Lowrie. New York: Harper & Row, 1962, pp. 22–41; *The Concept of Dread*, tr. by W. Lowrie. Princeton: Princeton Univ. Press, 1946, pp. 9–13.

C. S. Peirce. "Philosophical Nomenclature," in *Collected Papers*, Vol. V, ed. by C. Hartshorne and P. Weiss. Cambridge: Harvard Univ. Press, 1934, pp. 274–276.

M. Merleau-Ponty. *Sense and Non-Sense*, tr. by H. L. Dreyfus and P. A. Dreyfus. Evanston: Northwestern Univ. Press, 1964, pp. 26–28; *Signs*, tr. by R. C. McCleary. Evanston: Northwestern Univ. Press, 1964, pp. 159–160.

B. Blanshard. "On Philosophical Style," from *On Philosophical Style* (Manchester: Manchester Univ. Press, 1954), pp. 1–37.

L. Strauss. "Persecution and the Art of Writing," from *Persecution and the Art of Writing* (Glencoe, Ill.: Free Press, 1952), pp. 22–37.

S. Pepper. "Root Metaphors," from *World Hypotheses* (Berkeley: Univ. of California Press, 1942), pp. 84–114.

Jose Ortega y Gasset. "The Attitude of Parmenides and Heraclitus," from *The Origin of Philosophy* (New York: W. W. Norton and Co., 1967).

M. Natanson, "Rhetoric and Philosophical Argument," from *Quarterly Journal of Speech* 48 (1962), pp. 24–30.

P. Friedlander. "Irony," from *Plato*, Volume I, tr. by H. Meyerhoff. (Princeton: Princeton Univ. Press, 1968), pp. 137–153.

B. A. Scharfstein. "Descartes' Dreams," from *Philosophical Forum*, I (1969), pp. 293–316.

A. Donagan. "Victorian Philosophical Prose: J. S. Mill and F. H. Bradley," from G. Levine and W. Madden, eds., *The Art of Victorian Prose* (New York: Oxford Univ. Press, 1968), pp. 208–228.

E. Gellner. "Sociology," from *Words and Things* (Boston: Beacon Press, 1959), pp. 229–262.

C. Smith, "An Analysis of a Discourse by Bertrand Russell," from *Journal of Linguistics* 7 (1971), pp. 213–235.

O. K. Bouwsma. "Naturalism," from *Philosophical Essays* (Lincoln: Univ. of Nebraska Press, 1965), pp. 71–83.

D. T. Suzuki. "The Ten Cow-Herding Pictures," from *Essays in Zen Buddhism,* First Series (London: Rider and Co., 1949), pp. 363–367.

Index